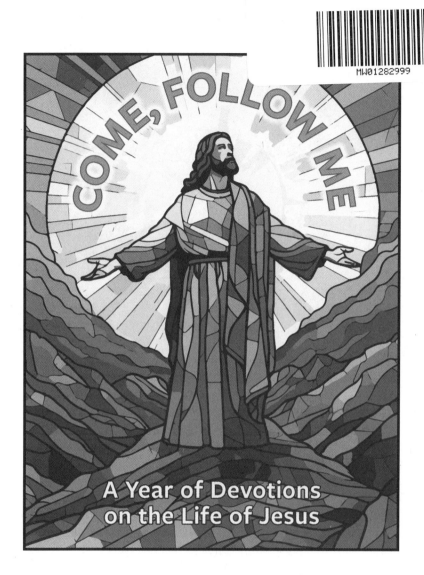

COME, FOLLOW ME

A Year of Devotions on the Life of Jesus

Amy Bird
Ted Doering
Alfonso Espinosa
Noemí E. Guerra
Hannah Hansen
Chad Janetzke
Andrew R. Jones

Gabe Kasper
Rehema Kavugha
Christopher M. Kennedy
Ethan Luhman
Daniel E. Paavola
Wayne Palmer

CONCORDIA PUBLISHING HOUSE · SAINT LOUIS

1 2 3 4 5 6 7 8 9 10   33 32 31 30 29 28 27 26 25 24

Contents

INTRODUCTION

Come, Follow Me: A Year of Devotions on the Life of Jesus is a 52-week devotional that works through the life and work of God's Son, our Savior, Jesus Christ, as presented in the New Testament writings of Matthew, Mark, Luke, and John. In these devotions, you will see the grace and love of God's dear Son, who became human

· to live among us;

· to teach us of God's unsurpassable love;

· to suffer and die to take away our sin and guilt; and

· to give us eternal life with Him in heaven.

Each week will focus on one event in Jesus' life. Each day will look at a slightly different angle of that event. We have devoted six days to each week, which enables you to worship at church one day, then spend a few minutes with Jesus on the other days of the week. Here is the basic outline:

MONDAY provides the historical context in which the event takes place. From the beginning of the Bible in Genesis to its close in Revelation, the Bible traces the story of God creating the world, the fall of Adam and Eve shattering that creation, God sending His dear Son, Jesus, to save us fallen creatures, ending with Jesus' return on the Last Day to restore His broken creation and all believers. Monday's study will orient you to where this event falls in that epic plan of God.

TUESDAY zooms into the week's passage to focus on its message. We look at questions such as who, what, when, where, how, and why to understand what is happening in the text.

WEDNESDAY steps back to look at how the event of each week fits into Jesus' earthly ministry so we can understand how it relates to Jesus' saving mission.

THURSDAY brings together related Bible passages from the other Gospels and from various places in the Old and New Testaments. The whole Bible is God's revelation of His rescue mission through Jesus Christ. These other passages help us better understand how the week's event fits into the whole Bible.

FRIDAY looks closely at difficult ideas or challenging questions that arise because of something Jesus says or does—or the things that happen to Him. It will help us understand the difficulties that sometimes arise in the Bible.

SATURDAY brings the week's themes to our own lives to see how Jesus' words and actions relate to us today. Each week, we will look specifically at how the week's event impacts us as we look forward to gathering with our Christian brothers and sisters in church to hear God's Word and receive His gifts.

May God bless you richly as you spend this year with Jesus.

IN THE BEGINNING

Week 1—John 1:1–18

In the beginning was the Word, and the Word was with God, and the Word was God. He was in the beginning with God. All things were made through Him, and without Him was not any thing made that was made. In Him was life, and the life was the light of men. The light shines in the darkness, and the darkness has not overcome it.

There was a man sent from God, whose name was John. He came as a witness, to bear witness about the light, that all might believe through him. He was not the light, but came to bear witness about the light.

The true light, which gives light to everyone, was coming into the world. He was in the world, and the world was made through Him, yet the world did not know Him. He came to His own, and His own people did not receive Him. But to all who did receive Him, who believed in His name, He gave the right to become children of God, who were born, not of blood nor of the will of the flesh nor of the will of man, but of God.

And the Word became flesh and dwelt among us, and we have seen His glory, glory as of the only Son from the Father, full of grace and truth. (John bore witness about Him, and cried out, "This was He of whom I said, 'He who comes after me ranks before me, because He was before me.'") For from His fullness we have all received, grace upon grace. For the law was given through Moses; grace and truth came through Jesus Christ. No one has ever seen God; the only God, who is at the Father's side, He has made Him known.

BACK TO THE VERY BEGINNING

*In the beginning was the Word,
and the Word was with God, and
the Word was God. He was in the
beginning with God.* (JOHN 1:1–2)

I n the beginning. Here we are at the beginning of a year with Jesus. No one enters into a journey through the Scriptures without some preconceived notions. We are all coming with thoughts, hopes, fears, anxieties, and anticipation. In these first words of His Gospel account, the apostle John sets the tone we need as we enter into our encounter with the light of the world. The first readers and hearers of John's Gospel would have been very acquainted with who Jesus is, the birth narratives, and all that historically took place in Jesus' life. But John encourages us to go earlier, to look deeper, and to see anew how high and far and deep and wide is the love of God.

John 1:1–18 is to the New Testament as Genesis 1 is to the Old Testament. Foundational. Fundamental. Community existed before creation; the Father exists alongside the Word from the very beginning. Heaven and earth are bridged with the Word from the very beginning. These verses set the tone for our walk with the Word—the Word of life and light and truth. *The Word made flesh.* Although it doesn't make sense to our minds, Jesus existed before He was born. The Son of God is the Word that has made His dwelling among us, that has given us the right to become children of God. The Word came forth from the Father: "Be Light!" (Genesis 1:3). As we marvel at the sunrise, so we approach this Light breaking into the world with awe and reverence. Our journey with Jesus must go back to the very beginning too.

Not only must we look earlier than Jesus' birth but those walking with Jesus must also dig deeper than current theology or philosophy allows. All in the ancient world would have found familiarity in this text, but they would have been taken aback at the same time. The Jews would have recognized the parallels with Genesis 1, yet they would have been challenged by "the only God, who is at the Father's side, He has made Him known" (John 1:18). The Greek Platonists would have been comfortable with this "Word from the beginning" but shocked that it would become flesh. As we begin a year with Jesus, we must allow ourselves to be taken aback too. Whether this is your first year with Jesus or your forty-first, are you ready to behold His glory anew? Are you ready for a face-to-face encounter with truth and grace?

Jesus, Word made flesh, reveal to us Your character and Your love. Enable us to see You clearly on every page of Scripture and in every moment of our days. Amen.

THE WORD BECAME FLESH AND BROUGHT GRACE UPON GRACE

No one has ever seen God; the only God, who is at the Father's side, He has made Him known. (JOHN 1:18)

Jesus has made it possible for God to be known, seen, and experienced. Jesus has given access to a relationship with the almighty Father, who creates, sustains, and stands outside all things. This is the astounding reality of the Christian faith. This is the framework through which we can see Jesus' life, death, and resurrection, as well as the Scriptures that bear witness to Him.

We can have some predetermined ideas about God and faith, about how to interact with one another and what God might have to say about us. Often, these are informed by philosophies, feelings, or what we have heard from others. Where should we turn to get the final word on God? Well, the beginning. Where should we turn to understand our relationship with God? Well, the relationship from the beginning. John begins his Gospel not just by giving his own testimony, his own thoughts and experiences—he relies on the testimony of Scripture, from Moses to John the Baptist.

It is clear that God is Trinity from the first verses of Scripture and that God desires to interact with His "very good" creatures, which were made in His own image. Even though the darkness overtook the hearts of fallen people, God's desire was still to be with humans. Sure, they were kicked out of the garden, but not before a promise was given—a child would come. Many children came, and they all pointed to the perfect Child.

Moses was one of those children, born under slavery to set God's people free. Moses got to experience closeness and intimacy with the Lord, talking as to a friend (see Exodus 33:11). He even desired that "all the LORD's people were prophets, that the LORD would put His Spirit on them!" (Numbers 11:29). But Moses was only able to deliver the Law to God's people (see John 1:17). The Law stood as a testimony of God's holiness and man's inescapable slavery. But One was coming to set the people free for good.

John the Baptist was one of those children. As the final prophet announcing the coming of the Light, he was a voice crying out the truth for all who would hear: "He who comes after me ranks before me, because He was before me" (John 1:15). He was pointing to the Child of promise, the eternal Son at the Father's side. The Word became flesh and brought grace upon grace.

There is no question about who God is or who we are. It is clear from the very beginning. God is love, light, freedom, truth. And we are His.

Father in heaven, thank You for making Your grace and truth so evident to us through Jesus. Set us free to understand Your plan and our purpose. In Jesus' name we pray. Amen.

WILL WE REJECT OR RECEIVE THE WORD?

He was in the world, and the world was made through Him, yet the world did not know Him. . . . But to all who did receive Him, who believed in His name, He gave the right to become children of God. (JOHN 1:10, 12)

The Bible is one long, unified letter detailing God's mission to save humanity. While some parts can be confusing, and other parts may be mystifying, the message is clear: God wants to be with His people. Now, God created the world, but He does not need the world. God loves the world, but God does not need the world to love Him back. God needs nothing—neither creation, nor a relationship with creation—to be God. God is complete and whole and holy within Himself. And God decided to create, out of His divine love and wisdom.

Creation became disjointed, alienated from its Creator. The clay pot began criticizing the potter (see Isaiah 45:9), and instead of smashing it, our Creator God decided to become the clay. The Word became the stuff He created. The Word came into the world, so that the world could come to God. This has been the consistent mission and method of God from the beginning: coming to our rescue. But the big problem is that we either fail to recognize or reject the rescue of God.

One of humanity's biggest weaknesses is our self-reliance, our yearning for self-justification. *I'll make it right. I'll do it myself,* we think. Or we find ourselves pitiable, helpless, and beyond salvation: *I'll never be good enough. No one will ever be able to help me.* These are both sides of the same coin—rejecting the rescue of our God. Jesus has come into the world, which was created through Him, with the express purpose of saving it. Will we reject or receive it?

Jesus has given us the right, the authority, to become children of the heavenly Father. The clay has been given the ability to know and love the Potter who formed it (see Isaiah 64:8). The clay (we humans who have been handcrafted out of dirt) has been given the ability to exist not only temporarily but forever made into God's children. Greater than Pinocchio becoming a real boy, we have become really human—connected to our Creator, children of God, loved now and forever, destined for eternity.

We can reject this message of good news and hope, but we are rejecting ourselves and our own worth if we reject the grace and love offered to us in this Word. We can receive this message of acceptance, and we will find ourselves in the center of God's story. Will we reject or receive the Word?

Lord God, give us eyes to recognize Your Word in our lives. Enable our hearts to receive Your love and grace in Jesus. Empower us to live now and forever as Your children. Amen.

WE ARE HELD TOGETHER BY THE ETERNAL WORD MADE FLESH

For the law was given through Moses; grace and truth came through Jesus Christ. (JOHN 1:17)

God answers the same old problems in new and confounding ways. Throughout Scripture, it's not that we discover certain things that make sense; we discover that everything makes perfect sense in light of God's Word. John 1:1–18 details how God's Word has made known God's ways and God's will throughout time.

Jesus is the eternal Word.

God's Word is continually at work in the Scriptures. From the very first pages, it is God speaking that makes things happen. "And God said" (Genesis 1:3). The Trinity is visible in those first three verses as the Spirit hovers, as God creates, and as the Word breaks forth. The Word of the Lord is so overwhelming that the Israelites are scared to hear directly from this Word anymore (see Exodus 20:19). They preferred the voice of the prophet (Moses) over the voice of Power, so that's how God delivered His Word from that time until the birth of Christ. Hebrews 1 makes this clear: "God spoke to our fathers by the prophets, but in these last days He has spoken to us by His Son . . . through whom also He created the world" (Hebrews 1:1–2).

Jesus creates all things.

If Genesis didn't make it clear, the witness of the Scriptures is that Jesus is not only eternal but He is also Co-Creator. The psalmist sings, "By the word of the LORD the heavens were made, and by the breath of His mouth all their host" (Psalm 33:6). The New Testament carries forward this theme as well: Jesus Christ is He through whom all things were made and through whom we exist (see 1 Corinthians 8:6), the one through whom all things were created. "All things were created through Him and for Him. And He is before all things, and in Him all things hold together" (Colossians 1:16–17).

Jesus becomes human.

The first promise after the fall was for a son to come (see Genesis 3:15)—a son of Eve, fully human. His attention on Abraham and Abraham's descendants demonstrated that the blessing of God would come through a combination of Abraham's descendants and God keeping His covenant (see Genesis 12:1–3). King David's throne was promised to be both fulfilled by a human yet divinely protected (see 2 Samuel 7:13). How would this combination of two separate and distinct realities: the temporal and mortal smash together with the eternal and divine? This is the mystery of the Word made flesh (see John 1:14). This is the mystery of Scripture—a mere Word that will endure throughout time and beyond time.

The New Testament upholds this paradox—that Jesus is most certainly God and also most certainly human. God's Son, Jesus, "was descended from David according to the flesh" (Romans 1:3). "When the fullness of time had come, God sent forth His Son, born of a woman, born under the law" (Galatians 4:4). "Since therefore the children share in flesh and blood, [Jesus] partook of the same things, that through death He might destroy the one who has the power of death" (Hebrews 2:14).

In Jesus, all things come together and are held together. That means us too. That means our lives, our futures. We are held together by the eternal Word made flesh.

Oh God, please hold us together by the power of Your Word. Speak to us and refresh our faith today and forever. In Jesus' name we pray. Amen.

WHY DID THE WORD BECOME FLESH?

The Word became flesh and dwelt among us, and we have seen His glory, glory as of the only Son from the Father, full of grace and truth. (JOHN 1:14)

One of the most compelling things about this section of Scripture is that it leaves us with more questions than answers, more wonderings and amazement than simple solutions. Here are some questions that arise from John 1:1–18.

What does it mean to call Jesus the "Word"?

Imagine learning how to speak like an ant. Getting down on your hands and knees, talking to them. It would be humiliating. This is what it means that Jesus is the Word. Jesus is the one who has humbled Himself, becoming obedient to the Father and making God known in the world. God frequently reveals His will and accomplishes it through His spoken word. In Genesis 1, we repeatedly read, "And God *said*, 'Let there be,'" and there was. The prophets frequently said, "Thus *says* the Lord." And Jesus Himself said, "Truly, truly I *say* to you" (emphases added). We also see the power of Jesus' spoken word in His miracles, the words He used to heal the sick, drive out demons, still storms, and raise the dead. This Word is God breaking into space and time through the Word. And that Word is personal, a person, God Himself. We call Jesus the Word, and we affirm His place within the Trinity and His eternal role of making God known to us creatures.

Why did Christ have to become flesh?

Faith is not merely spiritual. Faith is physical too. Faith is physical because life is physical. God designed this world to be a holding together of opposites: the breath of life with dust of the ground, God above it all with His creation. Jesus became flesh because words weren't enough. Words could be enough, but a faith filled only with words becomes cerebral. It doesn't embrace all of what it means to be a human.

This is why we celebrate Baptism and Holy Communion. God doesn't only give us the Word; He has joined it to water. We have received the body and blood of Christ in simple bread and wine. These sacraments are the physical experience of grace, forgiveness, and salvation. Jesus came in the flesh so that we could "taste and see that the LORD is good" (Psalm 34:8), so that we could see with our eyes and touch with our hands that we have fellowship with the Father and life in Christ (see 1 John 1:1–3). God created us for a physical life and all the experiences that come along with it. Eating and drinking and celebrating and finding value in our work are blessings from God that demonstrate the value of our physical lives (see Ecclesiastes 3:12–13). Our flesh is temporary, and the joys that accompany this physical life are temporary too. But they are meant to point us to the eternal reality: God intends to redeem our flesh. Just as there is already Jesus' physical body in heaven, so our physical bodies will be remade!

Dear God, thank You for sending us Your Word, Your Son in the flesh, to redeem our flesh. We cling to You, to Your Word, and to the promise of resurrection in Christ. Amen.

HOLDING THE LIGHT IN OUR HANDS

The light shines in the darkness, and the darkness has not overcome it. (JOHN 1:5)

Christmas memories for me always evoke a cold winter night leading to a warm church, where I was entrusted with a half-melted candle. I got to hold fire in my hands! While the pastor read John 1:1–18, we would sing "Silent Night," and I would stare at the flickering flame of my candle, entranced by the glow. The Word became flesh and made His dwelling among us.

We humans get to behold the glory of God. We humans get to see and hear God's goodness. God has made it possible to hold in our hands the impossibly big reality of His existence. God comes to us in ways that we can grasp—literally. Like a child holding a candle, we can approach the God who has the power to burn down everything yet allows us to be enthralled at His presence. We have been allowed into the presence of God through Jesus Christ.

John 1:1–18 is the appointed reading for Christmas Day. While there are no shepherds or angels, this text is the heavenly perspective on the incarnation of Christ. It is the backstory of the coming of Christ, the eternal viewpoint, the reason and purpose behind it all. Without this, Christmas provides for people only the "warm and fuzzy" feelings of nostalgia. Without this, Christmas is just another day off from work. Without this, we have no right to become children of God, opening the present of faith around the tree of life, the blood-stained cross.

We've spent our first week with Jesus, celebrating the eternal plan of light and life, grace and truth. We see the mission of Jesus unfolding throughout the Gospels, but more than that, "where meek souls will receive Him still" (*LSB* 361:3), we see Jesus' light and life each day in our lives. The Word at the beginning is the same Word giving meaning and purpose to mundane moments and special occasions alike.

As John bore witness to the Light, so do we. We glorify God. We hold on, like giddy kids, entrusted with this burning light, which is the presence of Christ. We bear witness to what the Light is doing in the world, what the Light of men is doing in our lives. "No one has ever seen God" (John 1:18), but we testify to the only God, at the Father's side, who has made Him known to us. And this is the Light that the darkest days and nights—the deepest pains and hurts—will never overcome.

Lord Jesus, we praise You for coming among us, for bringing glory to heaven and earth in Your birth, Your death, and Your resurrection. We praise You for shining Your light into the darkness and bringing us into the eternal light of God's love. Amen.

THE ANNUNCIATION TO MARY

Week 2—Luke 1:26–38

In the sixth month the angel Gabriel was sent from God to a city of Galilee named Nazareth, to a virgin betrothed to a man whose name was Joseph, of the house of David. And the virgin's name was Mary. And he came to her and said, "Greetings, O favored one, the Lord is with you!" But she was greatly troubled at the saying, and tried to discern what sort of greeting this might be. And the angel said to her, "Do not be afraid, Mary, for you have found favor with God. And behold, you will conceive in your womb and bear a son, and you shall call His name Jesus. He will be great and will be called the Son of the Most High. And the Lord God will give to Him the throne of His father David, and He will reign over the house of Jacob forever, and of His kingdom there will be no end."

And Mary said to the angel, "How will this be, since I am a virgin?"

And the angel answered her, "The Holy Spirit will come upon you, and the power of the Most High will overshadow you; therefore the child to be born will be called holy—the Son of God. And behold, your relative Elizabeth in her old age has also conceived a son, and this is the sixth month with her who was called barren. For nothing will be impossible with God." And Mary said, "Behold, I am the servant of the Lord; let it be to me according to your word." And the angel departed from her.

GOD'S STRANGE BUT PERFECT TIMING

In the sixth month the angel Gabriel was sent from God to a city of Galilee named Nazareth, to a virgin betrothed to a man whose name was Joseph, of the house of David. And the virgin's name was Mary. (LUKE 1:26–27)

It had been around four hundred years since the voices of the prophets had fallen silent at the close of the Old Testament. In that time, God's people had experienced incredible upheaval: the exiles returned to Judah and rebuilt the temple under the Persians, then Alexander the Great and his Greek Empire crushed the Persians, taking control of Israel and Judah. When Alexander died suddenly, his realm was divided into four kingdoms, two of which vied for control of Canaan. As pressure to adopt Greek culture and religion intensified in Jerusalem, a group of Jewish leaders, the Maccabees, rose up and gained independence once again for the Israelites. But it was a short amount of time before an upstart group of generals and leaders on the Italian peninsula gained traction and began to form their own empire to bring the known world under their heel. The people of God once again came under the rule of another outside force—Rome.

Persians, Greeks, Romans. The people of God between the Old and New Testaments experienced a loss of autonomy and self-rule. They endured the struggle of their culture being transformed by those who did not follow God. It harkens back to the words of the psalmists, "How long, O Lord?"

How long must foreigners rule? How long must the ways of God be forgotten? How long must we suffer under the ways of the godless?

The Maccabees had given the people a respite amid this period of subjugation. In short memory, the people longed for freedom that had been experienced under them.

It was in this time that God's plans for the Messiah came to fruition. The promise given in Genesis 3:15 entered into the world: "I will put enmity between you and the woman, and between your offspring and her offspring; He shall bruise your head, and you shall bruise His heel."

The offspring who would mortally bruise the head of the serpent was coming into the world. Gabriel announced to Mary, a simple girl, that the longed-for Messiah was coming through her. God will do His work in and through her.

Into this tumultuous period, the Son of God became incarnate. Not into a palace or even through the great temple in Jerusalem—His royal blood, the line of David, came through His virgin mother. There would be no marching armies, courtiers, or great halls for this King. Instead, He came to a family in the despised town of Nazareth.

God put His power on display through the time and place of the coming of His Son. Why not send the Messiah when David ruled the land? When Solomon the Wise built the Israelite Empire into a world power and constructed the great temple? Why not give a son to Josiah, the king who returned to the ways of God after years of the people drifting away? No. God puts His power on display by coming at a time when His people were helpless. They experienced the rule of others, the power of outside forces. Would the Messiah not come as the Maccabees had to free them from this rule? No. God sends His Son in the line of David to save His people from their sins. He would be born of a virgin and enter into the world to declare the power of the God who sent Him.

Heavenly Father, thank You for sending Jesus in Your perfect, unexpected time. Amen.

PART OF THE PLAN

And he came to her and said, "Greetings, O favored one, the Lord is with you!" (LUKE 1:28)

God keeps His promises. Remember Genesis 3:15: "I will put enmity between you and the woman, and between your offspring and her offspring; He shall bruise your head, and you shall bruise His heel."

This was not some spur-of-the-moment idea. This was God's plan all along. Before He created the world, before the fall of humanity at the sins of Adam and Eve, God knew how He would redeem His creation. The plan was always to send His Son.

At just the right time, in God's plan, Jesus is conceived—not of a sinful father and mother, who would pass their sinful nature on to their child, but instead of a virgin who conceives a sinless child by the power of the Holy Spirit. God is keeping the promises He made to His people over the years: "And he said, 'Hear then, O house of David! Is it too little for you to weary men, that you weary my God also? Therefore the Lord Himself will give you a sign. Behold, the virgin shall conceive and bear a son, and shall call His name Immanuel'" (Isaiah 7:13–14).

Jesus was now fully God and fully man. Even in the womb He is Immanuel, God with us. To save the created world, God does not force it to join Him under its own power. Instead, even in conception, He steps down. It was always what was going to happen.

Creation could not save itself. From the first promise to Gabriel's message, God takes action to save. Humanity needed a perfect Savior, an unblemished sacrifice. God chose Mary to be the first step of that promise, becoming incarnate. A young woman chosen to be blessed and so bless others. In the whole of time and womanhood, here was the virgin from whom the Savior would be born.

Creation's natural ways, built by the Creator, would be used to deliver this perfect Son. This Son would step perfectly into an imperfect world. He would walk in the dirt of our world. He would experience the pain, sorrow, and brokenness of fallen creation, all while remaining sinless Himself. From His conception to His ascension, Jesus would remain perfect.

That perfect life would not sit on a shelf. It wouldn't become a trophy of self-righteousness. Instead, Jesus uses His perfect life as the tool of salvation. In Baptism, Jesus wrapped us in His perfect righteousness, in which we can stand before God through all eternity. It is the perfect gift of sacrifice that we all needed. This was all part of the plan.

Heavenly Father, thank You for Your perfect plan and Your perfect Son, whose sacrifice makes me perfect forever. Amen.

NO SHORTCUTS

And the angel said to her, "Do not be afraid, Mary, for you have found favor with God. And behold, you will conceive in your womb and bear a son, and you shall call His name Jesus." (LUKE 1:30–31)

If you've ever taken a shortcut for the wrong reasons, you've probably felt the repercussions. In third grade, we had a new PE teacher, Mr. Bender. On the first day, he had us running some laps around the ball field. A couple of friends began cutting their laps through the middle of the field. Mr. Bender's back was turned, and I thought, *This is a great idea. Less running.* As I made the turn, Mr. Bender looked our way. After getting a talking-to about cutting the field, a couple of laps were added to our run. To add insult to injury, which church did Mr. Bender and his family end up attending that Sunday? Mine, where my dad was the pastor. Had to relive cutting that lap in front of my parents.

But that is usually what happens with shortcuts we take out of laziness. There is something ahead of us that appears hard and strenuous, and our sinful nature kicks in. We think, *I can cut this short and not put in the work.*

For Jesus, there could be no shortcut. The plan for salvation could not come around by any half measures. Jesus had to be born into our world as a human. His mission called for Him to take our sin on His shoulders; how could He do that without having first walked through the world with us?

When Gabriel announced to Mary that she would carry the Son of God, it was not only an announcement for her but for all creation. God was instituting His plan. Over the many years between Adam and Eve's creation and Jesus' conception, there would be no shortcut. He will not destroy the world to remake it without redeeming it.

It would have been easier. It would have taken less pain and effort for Jesus to simply come as deity and bring the armies of heaven to wipe out all those who rebelled against the Father. Easier, but there would be none who would remain. If God had decided that avoiding the pain and suffering of sending His Son into the world would be easier, then it would have meant the doom of humanity. It would have meant our doom. But that was never the mission. The mission was that Jesus would come and live among us. That His blood would cover us in redemption. Jesus skips the shortcut. God declares the mission has begun through an angel to Mary. He puts the world on notice: Redemption is coming. The time is at hand.

Dear Lord, thank You for skipping the shortcuts and coming to live among us. Amen.

RESPONDING TO AN ANGEL'S MESSAGE

And Mary said to the angel, "How will this be, since I am a virgin?" (LUKE 1:34)

The angel Gabriel's visit to Mary is an event unique in Scripture. It should be! The Savior of the world has been announced. But where else do we see the elements of this announcement connecting through the rest of the Bible?

In the book of Daniel, specifically 8:15–17 and 9:20–23, this same angel Gabriel appears to deliver God's message. Gabriel appears to give Daniel insight and wisdom. But also notice that Daniel and Mary have similar reactions to Gabriel's appearance: fear. Often in Scripture, the appearance of an angel is quickly followed up with the reassurance, "Do not be afraid!" These are not the sweet, gentle cherubs of renaissance paintings and porcelain statues. These are the mighty messengers of God. Their holiness and purity make our sin and wretchedness stand out in terror. Only the message of God's forgiveness through Christ can bring the peace they promise.

Gabriel's message of a Savior to Mary would have been well known to her. Mary would have encountered the prophecies of the Messiah from the prophets and writings of the Old Testament. While it seemed strange that she would be the one to bear the Savior, Isaiah had prophesied that "the virgin shall conceive and bear a son, and shall call His name Immanuel" (Isaiah 7:14).

The prophecies also declared that this would be a son in the line of David. This lines up with the prophecy of Nathan to David in 2 Samuel 7:11–16 (and again in Isaiah chapters 9 and 16). Mary, the descendant of David, would bear a son whose bloodline would be of the line of David.

If an angel appeared to you, do you think you might have a few questions? Especially if, as in Mary's case, the message seemed impossible? A virgin would give birth. Only a few verses earlier in Luke 1:18, Zechariah asks similarly about the possibility of his wife, Elizabeth, having a child in her old age. Mary was looking at the impossible. Zechariah at the improbable. But both ask questions of the Lord's plan. In a similar situation (see Genesis 18:10–15), Sarah laughs when God promises a child in her old age. But to the impossible situation of Mary Gabriel explains that this child will be conceived by the miraculous power of the Holy Spirit (see Matthew 1:18–20). While Zechariah questioned from unbelief, and Sarah laughed at God's plan, Mary is blessed by the answer to her question. God has chosen her to bring the Savior into the world.

Heavenly Father, help me always respond to Your Word in faith. Amen.

UNEXPECTED COMPLICATIONS

In the sixth month the angel Gabriel was sent from God to a city of Galilee named Nazareth, to a virgin betrothed to a man whose name was Joseph, of the house of David. And the virgin's name was Mary. (LUKE 1:26–27)

Gabriel's announcement to Mary seems clear-cut at first, but when we look more closely at it, some questions come to the surface.

Why does Luke start this passage with the phrase, "In the sixth month" (Luke 1:26)?

Six months before visiting Mary, God sent the angel Gabriel to Jerusalem to deliver His answer to the long-forgotten prayers of a priest named Zechariah. Gabriel announced that God was granting Zechariah and his wife, Elizabeth, a son (see Luke 1:5–20). That son was John the Baptist, the forerunner who prepared the way for Jesus' ministry.

How was Mary able to find favor with God (1:28)?

Mary was conceived in sin and born a sinner, like each descendant of Adam and Eve—like each of us. God showed her favor not because of anything she was or did, but purely by His undeserved grace and mercy alone. He shows that same favor to all of us by giving His Son to save us from our sins.

Why was Mary troubled by the angel's greeting (1:29)?

Like every other sinful believer who is visited by an angel, Mary was troubled because her sinful condition came to mind in the presence of the holy angel. Since every sinner in Scripture who encounters an angel is filled with terror, her first thought may well have been that God had sent this angel to punish her, not to give her good news. That is why Gabriel reassured her with the words "Do not be afraid Mary, for you have found favor with God."

Was Mary expressing unbelief when she asked Gabriel, "How will this be?" (1:34)?

When Gabriel told Zechariah that his wife, Elizabeth, would conceive a son, Zechariah responded, "How shall I know this?" (Luke 1:18), a question filled with unbelief and skepticism because of his advanced age and that of his wife. Mary's question was one of faith, asking how this conception would take place. Was there anything she would need to do to bring it about?

What does "The Holy Spirit will come upon you" and "the power of the Most High will overshadow you" mean (1:35)?

Gabriel responded to Mary's question with the assurance that Mary did not need to do anything; God the Holy Spirit would do all the work for her and in her. He would conceive Jesus in her womb by His divine power. The same is true for our salvation. We don't need to do anything—indeed, we can't do anything to create or sustain saving faith in us. The Holy Spirit Himself creates and sustains our faith through His Word and Sacraments.

What did Mary mean when she said, "I am the servant of the Lord" (1:38)?

Mary was expressing her faithful submission to God's will for her life. Even if accepting His will would result in her neighbors judging and condemning her for becoming pregnant before her marriage to Joseph.

Gracious Father, thank You for favoring me and being with me always for Jesus' sake. Amen.

HE STEPPED DOWN INTO OUR WORLD

The child to be born will be called holy—the Son of God. (LUKE 1:35)

It is so strange that God would create. Think about that. God is all knowing, everywhere, and has enormous, unlimited power in His hands. And what does He do with all of that? He creates. When Gabriel announces to Mary that she will bear the Savior, God is announcing that His creation is worthwhile. This Son of God would be fully God and yet fully human. What an incredible blessing to us as creation that God would become what He created.

Jesus joins us in the physical world. God's plan for salvation does not involve some hidden, spiritual means to ascension or knowledge. Instead, with two feet firmly planted on the planet He created, Jesus would walk, talk, eat, and live among His people. All because God would come to a young woman and say that she had been chosen. Just a normal Hebrew girl, through whom God would work His plan for salvation. Jesus would grow up in a family with brothers and sisters, adopted by a father who believed the angel's announcement as well. He would experience the ups and downs of everyday life among family and friends. He would be hungry or tired at times. He would experience all of the things that come with our daily human life. Yet He would still remain our Savior. God's Son came to meet us where we are.

The life of Jesus is the center of our life as Christians. Through the weekly readings we hear in church, we can follow how His life played out here on earth. We can even hear this passage in the Advent and Christmas seasons, as well as part of the feast day of the Annunciation. But even more, Jesus' life plays out in our weekly rhythms of worship.

Working among His creation has always been God's way. In worship, He meets His people in the proclaimed Word. The bread and wine are a physical mystery wherein His Son is present in a way that we can reach out and touch. Each time we see a Baptism and remember ours, we remember that God uses the simple water He created long ago to claim us as family members in His kingdom.

Jesus' life on this earth was both extraordinary and ordinary. It is one of those strange paradoxes of a God who would step down into His creation. He would work miracles and turn religious teaching on its head. Yet He grew up as the earthly son of a carpenter. As a member of a family, He worked around the house and played with His siblings. The announcement of a Savior to Mary meant so many great things, but most of all, it meant the extraordinarily ordinary Savior had come for His people.

Lord Jesus, thank You for stepping down into our world to be our Savior and our Brother. Amen.

JOSEPH'S DREAM

WEEK 3—MATTHEW 1:18–25

Now the birth of Jesus Christ took place in this way. When His mother Mary had been betrothed to Joseph, before they came together she was found to be with child from the Holy Spirit. And her husband Joseph, being a just man and unwilling to put her to shame, resolved to divorce her quietly. But as he considered these things, behold, an angel of the Lord appeared to him in a dream, saying, "Joseph, son of David, do not fear to take Mary as your wife, for that which is conceived in her is from the Holy Spirit. She will bear a son, and you shall call His name Jesus, for He will save His people from their sins." All this took place to fulfill what the Lord had spoken by the prophet:

"Behold, the virgin shall conceive and bear a son, and they shall call His name Immanuel"

(which means, God with us). When Joseph woke from sleep, he did as the angel of the Lord commanded him: he took his wife, but knew her not until she had given birth to a son. And he called His name Jesus.

BIRTH STORIES

Now the birth of Jesus Christ took place in this way. (MATTHEW 1:18)

Parents never forget the story of their child's birth. The day I was born, my father got pulled over by a police officer as he raced my mother to the hospital through the snow. As for my own children, when it came time for my wife to deliver our firstborn, we were able to comfortably walk to the hospital right across the street on a quiet summer's evening.

In contemporary Western culture, such stories are merely fond recollections. But in traditional cultures, the circumstances of a child's birth spoke volumes about the child's character and purpose. The Bible records in Genesis 25 that Jacob and Esau wrestled in Rebecca's womb, foreshadowing the perennial strife between their descendants, the Israelite and Edomite peoples. Exodus 2 tells how, as an infant, the prophet Moses was hidden in a basket on the riverbank among the reeds, until he was "drawn out" (a Hebrew pun on the name *Moses*). Later, God would use Moses to draw out His people from the Sea of Reeds (known popularly as the Red Sea).

For Matthew and his ancient Judean audience, the birth of Jesus also spoke volumes about His character and God's purpose for His life. Matthew's words in verse 18 reflect this expectation, that somehow the Christ's birth would foreshadow the fulfillment of God's promises to Abraham and David. Yet the story begins with scandal.

When it came time for Mary and Joseph to consummate their marriage and move in together, Joseph discovered that his betrothed wife was already pregnant. Although Matthew adds for our sakes that this pregnancy was worked by the Holy Spirit, Joseph had no such knowledge. For his part, a quiet divorce was a merciful reaction. In ancient Judean culture, their marriage was already in legal effect. Had Mary's presumed infidelity become public knowledge, she would have been ostracized by her community, or even stoned to death amid public outrage (see Leviticus 20:10; John 7:53–8:11).

By the end, Joseph accepts Mary into his home. By custom, this signaled that the bride had been found to be a virgin. This meant that Jesus would receive the status of being Joseph's natural heir, and if Mary was Joseph's first wife, then Jesus would be entitled to a double portion of the family estate as his firstborn. "A just man" would never so wantonly squander the patrimony of his own family—but by the testimony of God's angel, Joseph knew that Jesus was not the son of another man.

Their betrothal fulfilled, it was highly unusual for Joseph and Mary to abstain from sexual intimacy until the birth; this required mutual consent and a worthy purpose (Exodus 21:10; 1 Corinthians 7:5). With the angel's testimony, however, their conduct up to the time of Jesus' birth left no doubt about His origins, and these events pointed to how Jesus would "save His people from their sins." Jesus was conceived by the power of the Holy Spirit and the will of God the Father. On the third day from His crucifixion, Jesus would again receive life by the power of the Holy Spirit and the will of God the Father—immortal, resurrected life (see Romans 1:4) as God's "firstborn from the dead" (Revelation 1:5).

Heavenly Father, thank You for bringing Joseph to accept his place in the life of Your Son, our Savior, Jesus. Amen.

NOT BY HUMAN HEROISM

Her husband Joseph, being a just man and unwilling to put her to shame, resolved to divorce her quietly. (MATTHEW 1:19)

Iron Man is a favorite superhero in my family. Tony Stark by no means came from humble beginnings, but what ultimately makes him Iron Man is not the wealth, technology, or intelligence he inherited from his parents. These advantages did not mold him into a hero, let alone a virtuous man. What ultimately makes him a hero is his heroic decision: in the face of cruel inevitability, he makes the hard choice that no one else can.

As much as we admire heroes, Jesus is *not* this sort of figure. His story is not at the intersection of chance and courage, as if He boldly took up the mantle of John the Baptist. Nor did He one day work up the gumption to speak out against corruption to die as a catalyst for change. Neither did Jesus convince heaven of His worthiness, as if the dove at His Baptism was a kind of Nobel Peace Prize. No, Jesus was Messiah from *conception.*

Like Moses, Samuel, and other major figures from the Bible, the account of Jesus' birth shows that He didn't choose His own path in life; He was put on it by God. Remarkably, however, with Jesus, God acted immediately, despite Jesus' own parents. Moses' mother, Jochebed, hid him in a basket to protect him from the Egyptians (Exodus 2). Samuel's mother, Hannah, promised God that she would give her child to the priests if God would only cure her infertility (1 Samuel 1). In each case, God blessed the parents' desires. With Jesus, however, His parents' desires are reversed! Mary maintains her virginity, and yet the Spirit causes her to conceive. Joseph decides to divorce his wife, and yet God brings the family together.

No other prophetic figure is so radically and uniquely from God. Matthew does not go into detail about Mary, Joseph, or the heavenly messenger (unlike Luke in chapter 2, Matthew does not describe any light and glory or fear and trembling). Matthew gives just enough background for us to know that Jesus came, in the words of another evangelist, neither from "the will of the flesh nor of the will of man, but of God" (John 1:13). Matthew uses narrative instead of a prose prologue, but for him, that's the big idea behind the Christmas story.

And it's crucial because of how Jesus' story would seem to end. When He hung there on the cross, crying, "My God, My God, why have You forsaken Me?" (Matthew 27:46), it seemed like the prevailing powers of greed and violence were in control of Jesus' story—not God. But just as He did at Christmas, God would once more reverse human plans and purposes on Easter. The Judean authorities meant to discredit Jesus, but God would vindicate Him through the resurrection. The Romans meant to break the Judean spirit, but God would conquer even the dynasty of Julius Caesar through His risen King. Jesus began His natural life with no help from the flesh and will of man, and Jesus would begin His immortal life in just the same way: no heroic decision of man, but the gracious providence of God. And even as the Messiah would surrender Himself, God would be victorious.

Heavenly Father, thank You for Your perfect, unexpected plan that Jesus fulfilled completely. Amen.

A NATION IN LABOR PAINS

You shall call His name Jesus,
for He will save His people from
their sins. (MATTHEW 1:21)

Waking from his dream, what did Joseph think about his newly adopted son? The name *Jesus* was a common variation of *Joshua.* Like many traditional Hebrew names, it had a transparent meaning built on the Hebrew name of the Israelite God: "Yahweh is help" (*Y'ho + shua*). The name may have originally referred to Yahweh answering a mother's cry for help to bring her and her child safely through the birthing process—a much riskier proposition until only very recently in human history. But the angel didn't say "God will save your family from a perilous childbirth." The messenger was explicit: saving their *whole people* was the reason behind this name.

Faithful men like Joseph believed that Israel, as a people, was suffering for their sins. The vast territory of King David's twelve-tribe confederation had been reduced to a fragment of just one tribe's ancestral land: the tribe of Judah. While the Judeans were grateful to live and worship in this small parcel around the city of Jerusalem, life in Judea fell far short of God's promises to Abraham and David. Israel existed only as a conquered people.

After liberation from slavery to Egypt, they had become the subjects of the Assyrians—then the Babylonians, then the Medo-Persians, then the Macedonians, then the Seleucids, and then finally the Romans. The prophets knew why this was happening: it was God's righteous wrath "for our sins, and for the iniquities of our fathers" (Daniel 9:16), and men like Daniel would intercede for "the sin of [God's] people Israel" (Daniel 9:20). Israel would begin to implement the prophets' reforms, only to quickly slide back into corruption, getting crushed again by another giant empire.

Would God's promises ever truly be realized? Israel was "like a pregnant woman," bearing the pain for hope of what lay on the other side—but, as one prophet said, "we were pregnant, we writhed, but we have given birth to wind" (Isaiah 26:18). So, in a sense, the whole people of Israel *was* praying that Yahweh would help them amid a perilous childbirth.

Israel was hoping for the birth of a king: a messiah who would rescue them from the enemies that God had sent to punish them for their sins. Israel needed a king who would establish a new kingdom of Israel, one that wouldn't fall into sin and destruction all over again. *Jesus* was to be that king. Mary and Joseph hadn't expected Him, but Israel had prayed for Him for generations.

And Jesus would achieve this victory in the most surprising way: by letting Himself die in submission to God's will, and then being raised from the dead on the third day. *Resurrection* is Israel's new birth (see John 16:21; Romans 8:22). Through resurrection by the power of the Holy Spirit, Jesus renewed the kingdom of Israel as the kingdom of heaven, what we call the church (see Ephesians 1:20–2:6). This renewed kingdom of the church has been saved from Israel's sins, sharing in the Messiah's resurrected life of power and righteousness.

Gracious Father, hear our prayers for help as we await Jesus' second coming. Amen.

ABRAHAM AND ISAAC (REPRISE)

And her husband Joseph, being a just man and unwilling to put her to shame, resolved to divorce her quietly. (MATTHEW 1:19)

Like many Hispanic firstborns, my father gave me his first name. This is a common tradition in many cultures, a way for families to pass the torch to the next generation. Joseph gave his name to his son, Jesus' brother Joses (a variation of *Joseph*; cf. Mark 6:3; 15:40), but Jesus received neither name nor blood from Joseph. He was the answered prayer of the nation, not His nuclear family. He stood as the Son of God and the Son of Israel or, as Matthew put it in the genealogy, "the son of David, the son of Abraham" (Matthew 1:1).

The title "son of David" in Matthew 1:1 was a standard term for the awaited Messiah who would inherit King David's throne (see Matthew 20:29–21:9). But it was unusual, if not unique, to use "son of Abraham" as a title for an individual. *All* Israelites considered themselves to be the son of Abraham as a collective (Deuteronomy 26:5). The events of Jesus' birth, however, make Him "son of Abraham" in a larger sense: He is a new Isaac, the branch of Israel's family tree that inherits the promise.

Abraham is described in Genesis 15 as a just but childless man who had resolved to make his servant Eliezer his heir. God spoke to Abraham, however, in a dream and promised to give him a legitimate son, who would go on to be a great nation. Abraham's wife, who had never been able to conceive, went on to miraculously bear a son: Isaac. After another dream from God, Abraham got up first thing in the morning to do as he was instructed: to send away his female servant and the child he had fathered by

her (Genesis 21). Finally, Abraham had one more dream from God, in which he was told that Isaac's birth required a firstfruits offering (Genesis 22). Abraham again got up early, taking Isaac with him. As Abraham clasped dagger in hand and Isaac lay bound on the altar, God's angel intervened at the last moment to stay Abraham's hand, providing a substitute to save Isaac.

In God's providence, history repeats itself with Joseph. All these events are condensed into one fateful night, and they take a surprising turn: Joseph had resolved to send Mary and her child away first thing in the morning, but at the last moment, God's angel intervened in a dream, commanding Joseph to accept the child and promising that He would go on to save the nation. Jesus is the new "son of Abraham" who embodies the entire nation—and all God's promises.

But lest this all seem very nationalistic, the very next thing that Matthew tells us is that foreign astrologers from the East arrived in Judea to pay homage to the new Messiah (see Matthew 2:1). They are not rejected in Jerusalem as unwelcome outsiders but rather guided by God's light in the sky to their destination. This episode recalls the final part of God's promise to Abraham: "In your offspring shall all the nations of the earth be blessed" (Genesis 22:18). Jesus the Son of Abraham embodies Israel to save Israel. But as Israel flourishes, all the nations of the world are invited to be "grafted in" (Romans 11:17).

Holy Father, thank You for revealing Your Son's salvation to believers of all nations through the entire Scripture, and to me. Amen.

WHY DIDN'T THEY NAME JESUS "IMMANUEL"?

"Behold, the virgin shall conceive and bear a son, and they shall call His name Immanuel" (which means, God with us). (MATTHEW 1:23)

It always struck me as odd that even though the angel commands Joseph to name the child "Jesus," the prophecy quoted by Matthew reads "Immanuel." Why didn't they name Him that? In fact, when you look at the original prophecy in Isaiah 7, it seems to have little to do with the birth of Jesus.

Back in the days when Israel still existed as an independent nation, the northern and southern tribes broke into two distinct kingdoms: Samaria and Judah. Samaria entered into an alliance with a foreign nation, and the two put military pressure on Judah to force them into joining their coalition. God sent the prophet Isaiah to Judah's King Ahaz to exhort him to stand firm and resist the temptation to enter into any such foreign alliances.

Ahaz rejected Isaiah's counsel and sent an envoy to the most brutal regime of the known world: the Neo-Assyrian Empire. Ahaz pledged that Judah would serve Assyria as a vassal state if Assyria would defeat Samaria and their allies. Defeat them they did, but the Assyrians' merciless program of destruction, deportation, and resettlement left the Northern Kingdom unrecognizable. Not only had Judah all but exterminated their fellow Israelites, their new vassalage meant they had also committed themselves to the idolatry of Assyrian paganism.

God sent Isaiah to Ahaz again, this time with a stern rebuke: the Assyrians would not be easy masters, and in the end, they would come for Judah too. Judah was to be reduced to wasteland and wilderness, fit only for wandering herdsmen (see Isaiah 7:21–25). Judah would be devastated, but God would extend His gracious presence around a small remnant by sending the promised Messiah: "Behold, the virgin shall conceive and bear a son, and shall call His name Immanuel" (Isaiah 7:14).

No one saw it coming. It was only after Jesus' resurrection that Matthew could see this Easter egg hidden in Christmas. Even amid Roman oppression and devastation, God had extended His presence around a small remnant of His people in the congregation formed by His Messiah. And the Spirit would give the last evangelist an even deeper insight: Jesus was *literally* Immanuel: "The Word was God. . . . And the Word became flesh and dwelt among us" (John 1:1, 14).

Gracious Father, thank You for sending Your Son to be God with us. Amen.

HE SAVED HIS PEOPLE FROM WHAT AND FOR WHAT?

She will bear a son, and you shall call His name Jesus, for He will save His people from their sins. (MATTHEW 1:21)

Tuesday, we considered how the angel's description of Jesus' mission to "save His people from their sins" meant that as "son of David" He would save Israel as a *kingdom* from their political adversaries, which God had previously appointed for their judgment. Thursday, we saw how Matthew has deliberately shaped his account of Jesus' birth to parallel the story of Abraham: as "son of Abraham," Jesus was also to save Israel as a *people*, preserving the family line of Abraham the way that Isaac did so many centuries earlier.

These claims, however, were immediately scandalous to first-century Judeans because not only had Jesus been executed by the Romans as a criminal but He had died unmarried and childless. If Jesus was to be the founder of a new kingdom in the royal line of David, then the sun had already set on His dynasty. If Jesus was to be the branch of Abraham's family line that would inherit and realize God's promises to their ancestors, then His family tree had already fallen.

The resurrection and ascension of Jesus, therefore, did not rescue the old ways of being a kingdom or being a nation: they meant complete transformation. The names *Immanuel* and *Jesus* pointed not to Israel's mere survival but to its *rebirth* as the church. It's not enough to say that this new Israel appoints its rulers through ordination and multiplies its numbers through Baptism, as if the church merely has quirky rituals for the same basic categories of politics and family.

Through Jesus, the church does politics and family in fundamentally different ways. Yes, Christians must participate in earthly politics, but not because they dream of leadership or because they adhere to a certain political philosophy. Jesus didn't save Israel by exposing corruption or legislating reforms: He did it by loving His political opponents more than He loved winning. Similarly, Christians must honor their earthly familial duties as sons and daughters, husbands and wives, and fathers and mothers. But we do not go along with the rest of the world, neither idolizing our families to the neglect of everyone else around us nor searching for surrogate families in networks of individuals with similar ideas and preferences. Jesus said His mother and brothers were those who spent their time imitating and listening to God (see Matthew 12:48–49).

Heavenly Father, thank You for Your Son's perfect salvation and for my place in Your holy family of believers. Amen.

THE FIRST CHRISTMAS

WEEK 4—LUKE 2:1–20

In those days a decree went out from Caesar Augustus that all the world should be registered. This was the first registration when Quirinius was governor of Syria. And all went to be registered, each to his own town. And Joseph also went up from Galilee, from the town of Nazareth, to Judea, to the city of David, which is called Bethlehem, because he was of the house and lineage of David, to be registered with Mary, his betrothed, who was with child. And while they were there, the time came for her to give birth. And she gave birth to her firstborn son and wrapped Him in swaddling cloths and laid Him in a manger, because there was no place for them in the inn.

And in the same region there were shepherds out in the field, keeping watch over their flock by night. And an angel of the Lord appeared to them, and the glory of the Lord shone around them, and they were filled with great fear. And the angel said to them, "Fear not, for behold, I bring you good news of great joy that will be for all the people. For unto you is born this day in the city of David a Savior, who is Christ the Lord. And this will be a sign for you: you will find a baby wrapped in swaddling cloths and lying in a manger." And suddenly there was with the angel a multitude of the heavenly host praising God and saying,

"Glory to God in the highest,
and on earth peace among those
with whom He is pleased!"

When the angels went away from them into heaven, the shepherds said to one another, "Let us go over to Bethlehem and see this thing that has happened, which the Lord has made known to us." And they went with haste and found Mary and Joseph, and the baby lying in a manger. And when they saw it, they made known the saying that had been told them concerning this child. And all who heard it wondered at what the shepherds told them. But Mary treasured up all these things, pondering them in her heart. And the shepherds returned, glorifying and praising God for all they had heard and seen, as it had been told them.

A DIFFERENT MANGER SCENE

And Joseph also went up from Galilee, from the town of Nazareth, to Judea, to the city of David, which is called Bethlehem, because he was of the house and lineage of David. (LUKE 2:4)

When we picture where Jesus was born, we usually imagine something that looks like the nativity scenes on our mantels at Christmastime—an open-walled stable with no houses in sight, surrounded by a menagerie of animals.

But Jesus' birth likely looked a little different than that. And while we can't know for sure just what His birth looked like, we can certainly paint a more accurate picture based on what we know about the events and time surrounding His birth.

Jesus was born in Bethlehem—not Nazareth, where Mary and Joseph were from and where Jesus would grow up—because His parents traveled there for a census. Caesar Augustus issued a decree that a census should be taken to determine the tax to be charged to pay for wars that the Roman military, who were governing the land, had undertaken. This governmental order served to fulfill Micah's prophecy about the coming Savior: "From you [Bethlehem] shall come forth for Me one who is to be ruler in Israel, whose coming forth is from of old, from ancient days" (Micah 5:2).

Mary and Joseph were both from the lineage of David, so they went to David's hometown of Bethlehem to register. But, by the time they arrived, the town was completely full of other visitors who were also there to register!

When Scripture tells us that there was "no place for them in the inn," we might think that all of the motels in town were booked up. But the Greek word we translate as "inn" is used only one other place in Luke: the Upper Room in which Jesus celebrated the Last Supper with His disciples.

So it is more likely all the upper rooms (think guest rooms) in Bethlehem were occupied when Jesus was born. Instead, Mary and Joseph would likely have tried to stay with a relative, who would have only had the structure that sheltered their animals available. This wasn't a traditional stable—it was more likely a cave or a grotto, kind of like today's garage. This room would have been connected to the house, but livestock still would have stayed there.

While Jesus' birth did not look like our nativities make it look, His birth was still incredibly humble. He was not born in a lavish palace surrounded by servants, nor was He lovingly placed in a cradle.

The Savior of the world, the only perfect human to ever exist, the Son of God who would die to save all humanity, was born in a side room, surrounded by animals, and laid to rest in a feeding trough—for you.

Jesus, Savior of the world, thank You for humbling Yourself by becoming a human. Amen.

JESUS' HUMBLE BIRTH

And she gave birth to her firstborn son and wrapped Him in swaddling cloths and laid Him in a manger, because there was no place for them in the inn. (LUKE 2:7)

Jesus' birth was incredibly humble in many ways. Not only was He born surrounded by animals in an offshoot of somebody's house but He was also born in a humble city.

Bethlehem was the home city of King David, one of Israel's most renowned kings. But despite David's status as king, his hometown was still regarded as small and humble! The prophet Micah describes it like this: "But you, O Bethlehem Ephrathah, who are too little to be among the clans of Judah" (Micah 5:2). The Ephrathites were a small clan in the tribe of Judah, so they were likely regarded as somewhat insignificant. Jesus being born in this relatively unknown town makes His birth all the more humble.

After Jesus was born, the first people to know this good news were shepherds in a nearby field. Shepherds were not highly esteemed in the culture at this time; they were seen as working-class citizens. The fact that these lowly shepherds were the first to hear about the birth of Jesus solidifies Jesus' humble birth!

Shepherds have been an important part of the Bible's story from Genesis to Jesus. Many of Scripture's greatest men of faith had been shepherds, including Abel, Abraham, Isaac, Jacob, at least ten of the twelve sons of Jacob (who formed the twelve tribes of Israel), Moses, and King David. David had likely shepherded his father, Jesse's, flocks on the very same hills where these shepherds heard of Jesus' birth!

When Samuel was going to anoint David as king, David had to be called in from the fields where he was watching his father's sheep. David's humble beginnings as a lowly shepherd were replaced with God's plan for him to become king of Israel. Similarly, God chose these humble shepherds to be the first people to hear of the birth of the Savior of the world—the Savior who had been promised for generations!

The humility of Jesus' birth was amplified by the sign that was given to the shepherds for how they would recognize Him. They were told to look for a baby in swaddling cloths in a manger. Likely, no other baby would have been found in such a poor, lowly place, so this sign served as an indication of where they could physically find this baby.

Jesus, the Savior of the world, God in flesh, was born in a humble city, laid in a humble manger, and known first by humble shepherds.

God, thank You for sending Your Son, Jesus, to be the Savior of the world. Help us to be humble as His birth was humble. Amen.

JESUS' LIFE OF HUMILITY

When the angels went away from them into heaven, the shepherds said to one another, "Let us go over to Bethlehem and see this thing that has happened, which the Lord has made known to us." (LUKE 2:15)

For the past two days, we've talked a lot about Jesus' humility—how the way He entered this world as a human was incredibly humble. But the humility that was present in Jesus' life did not end at His birth. Rather, it extended throughout His ministry and still today.

Jesus, the eternal Son of God, humbled Himself to become human and share His life with us. This humility continued throughout His life as He began His public ministry, interacting with people from all walks of life. Throughout His entire ministry, Jesus tends to focus on people who would have been regarded as humble, second-class, unclean, or unwanted.

Jesus healed lepers, who were completely cast out from society. He forgave a woman who had been with many men who weren't her husband. His feet were washed by a woman who was a prostitute. He ate with tax collectors. He healed blind beggars. He offered salvation to the Gentiles and Samaritans.

All of these situations would have been radical for the time. No one talked to Gentiles, prostitutes, or tax collectors. But Jesus did. No one dared to touch a person with leprosy. But Jesus did.

Jesus constantly interacted with the humblest and lowest people in society. And not only interacted—loved. Jesus ate with, forgave, and showed compassion to people who would have been ignored or hated. Even though He was the Son of God, He did not consider anyone unworthy of the love of God.

Before His crucifixion, Jesus washed His disciples' feet, an act that would have only been done by the lowest servant in a household. At His death, Jesus was nailed to a cross, which was a punishment fit for a lowly criminal. His grave was not His own. When He rose, some of the first people He appeared to were women, who would have been regarded as lower status.

Still today, Jesus loves the humblest people. He loves us sinners, who constantly forsake Him. Despite all of our shortcomings and failures, Jesus forgives us and shows us compassion, just as He did to the people He encountered during His time here on earth.

May we likewise show compassion and love to those around us, even though we may see them as undeserving of God's love. Jesus did not deny anyone His love, but instead treated them differently—better—than the world would have treated them. The love of Jesus was not hindered by social status or cultural perception but instead, it was amplified by the fact that He chose to love even the humblest.

Jesus, teach us to show compassion to the humble like You do. Amen.

PROCLAIMING GOD'S PRAISES

*Glory to God in the highest, and
on earth peace among those with
whom He is pleased!* (LUKE 2:14)

When the angels proclaimed the good news to the humble shepherds, they proclaimed the glory of God! This humble birth that occurred in an insignificant town surrounded by animals was proclaimed by angels—God's messengers, who are present at important events throughout Scripture.

Throughout Scripture, angels fulfill many different duties. First, angels are often messengers for God, proclaiming something that would happen. The angel Gabriel told Mary that she would bear a son who would be the Savior of the world (see Luke 1:26–33).

Second, angels often praise God for His goodness, mercy, and grace. The psalmist calls upon the angels to praise God: "Bless the LORD, all His hosts, His ministers, who do His will!" (Psalm 103:21). This psalm also indicates that angels serve God and do His will; they obey Him.

When the angels announce the birth of Jesus to these shepherds, they are proclaiming the greatest event in all of history—the birth of the Savior that had been promised to God's people for generations. Prophets throughout the Old Testament were pointing to this Savior, who would redeem God's people. Isaiah prophesies: "For to us a child is born, to us a son is given; and the government shall be upon His shoulder, and His name shall be called Wonderful Counselor, Mighty God, Everlasting Father, Prince of Peace" (Isaiah 9:6).

Jesus was this child, who would fulfill every promise that God had made to His people, and the angels are simply proclaiming that He is here!

This amazing child is born today in Bethlehem! A Savior, who is Christ the Lord!

This good news was and is truly the best news for all of God's people. After Jesus' death, the apostles continued to spread this Gospel across the world by "preaching good news of peace through Jesus Christ" (Acts 10:36). We, today, continue to spread this Gospel too.

And, at the end of days when Jesus comes back to redeem the earth, both we and the angels will proclaim the goodness of God! In Revelation, we get a glimpse of what that will look like:

"Then I looked, and I heard around the throne and the living creatures and the elders the voice of many angels, numbering myriads of myriads and thousands of thousands, saying with a loud voice,

"'Worthy is the Lamb who was slain, to receive power and wealth and wisdom and might and honor and glory and blessing!'" (Revelation 5:11-12).

Praise be to God for His mercy and goodness that have been present throughout all time!

God, our Father, may we proclaim Your Gospel and goodness like the angels. Amen.

PONDERING GOD'S GREAT TREASURES

But Mary treasured up all these things, pondering them in her heart. (LUKE 2:19)

Many Christians outside of the Roman Catholic Church don't focus on Mary, the mother of Jesus, much. But today, I want to invite us to focus on this incredible figure in the salvation story.

Toward the end of the account of Jesus' birth, we see Mary "treasur[ing] up all these things, pondering them in her heart." It's likely that the first two chapters of Luke's Gospel came from the recollections of Mary when Luke interviewed her as he was compiling the account of Jesus' life.

Imagine Mary, a relatively young woman, who had just given birth without ever having been with her fiancé, Joseph, holding her newborn son. Nine months before, an angel had come to her to say that she would bear the Savior of the world. And now, she was holding this tiny baby, with animals surrounding her. She has to lay Him in a feeding trough, a manger. It is unlikely that this is how Mary had pictured she would bring God's Son into the world.

But thanks be to God that our plans are not His plans. His ways are higher than our ways. Mary's life likely did not go how she dreamed it would, but God used this ordinary woman to fulfill His promise to redeem the world and save His people.

So Mary, holding her son whom she knows is from God, treasured up all these things in her heart. Through the years she ponders them, rolling them around in her mind. And when Luke interviews her years later, she has the benefit of hindsight and can realize the full significance of all these miraculous events that unfolded over the years.

Mary had seen her son converse with the leaders of the church at just twelve years old. She had seen Jesus perform incredible miracles. She had seen her firstborn son brutally killed on a cross. And then, three days later, she had seen Him alive in the flesh again. Then, a few short weeks on earth after His resurrection, Mary saw her son ascend to heaven to be with His Father.

All of those precious memories of the first moments in Jesus' life, including the incredible events surrounding His birth, Mary treasured up. She held them close. She might not have fully recognized the significance of them at the time, but she knew He was God's Son, so they were surely important.

Lord, help us treasure Your good gifts just as Mary treasured up these things in her heart. Amen.

JESUS' AMAZING BIRTH AMONG US

And the angel said to them, "Fear not, for behold, I bring you good news of great joy that will be for all the people." (LUKE 2:10)

The story of Jesus' birth is miraculous yet humble, ordinary yet extraordinary. When we celebrate Christmas, Jesus is, of course, at the heart—but it's easy to forget the incredible circumstances that led to and surrounded His birth, as well as the implications it has for us today.

The true thrill of Christmas is the fact that our loving God and Creator so loved the world that He sent His only Son as a human to redeem it and be His people's Lord and Savior. But surrounded by trees and tinsel, presents and pie, we can forget just how amazing Jesus' birth was. We can become distracted by everything our culture has made Christmas and forget the true circumstances that we should be celebrating and honoring.

Jesus, the Son of God, chose to humble Himself as a human. He was born surrounded by animals and laid in their feeding trough. He knew what it meant to live without the luxuries of life and to suffer want. His voluntary coming among us and sharing of our life serves to show His boundless love for us. No matter what we may encounter in this life, Jesus understands our temptations and struggles. And we can remember that He came to bring restoration and peace to the world—maybe not in the way we expect, but in the way that God intends, according to His plan.

When Jesus comes again on the Last Day, He will remove all the problems and pains that trouble us. He will forever remove death, pain, sin, and suffering from His creation, and we will enjoy perfect, eternal lives in His glorious presence. We will praise Him for all our days, overjoyed to be made perfect in His presence.

Christmas reminds us of the world-changing life our Savior actually lived among us. We can always find a place at His manger, gazing in wondrous awe at the Lord of all creation who came here for you—for the world. In Baptism, we are made His children. During Holy Communion, we actually receive the very body and blood that Christ came to offer on the cross for our salvation. In a mysterious yet very real way, we tangibly come into contact with God, who loves and forgives us. And by reading His Word, we can get to know our Savior and our God through what He reveals to us in Scripture. May we continue to revel in the joy of Christmastime all year round!

Thanks be to You, God, for sending Your Son to redeem the world. Help us maintain the joy of Christmas all year. Amen.

THE VISIT OF THE WISE MEN

WEEK 5—MATTHEW 2:1–18

Now after Jesus was born in Bethlehem of Judea in the days of Herod the king, behold, wise men from the east came to Jerusalem, saying, "Where is He who has been born king of the Jews? For we saw His star when it rose and have come to worship Him." When Herod the king heard this, he was troubled, and all Jerusalem with him; and assembling all the chief priests and scribes of the people, he inquired of them where the Christ was to be born. They told him, "In Bethlehem of Judea, for so it is written by the prophet:

"'And you, O Bethlehem, in the land of Judah,
are by no means least among the rulers of Judah;
for from you shall come a ruler
who will shepherd My people Israel.'"

Then Herod summoned the wise men secretly and ascertained from them what time the star had appeared. And he sent them to Bethlehem, saying, "Go and search diligently for the child, and when you have found Him, bring me word, that I too may come and worship Him." After listening to the king, they went on their way. And behold, the star that they had seen when it rose went before them until it came to rest over the place where the child was. When they saw the star, they rejoiced exceedingly with great joy. And going into the house, they saw the child with Mary His mother, and they fell down and worshiped Him. Then, opening their treasures, they offered Him gifts, gold and frankincense and myrrh. And being warned in a dream not to return to Herod, they departed to their own country by another way.

Now when they had departed, behold, an angel of the Lord appeared to Joseph in a dream and said, "Rise, take the child and His mother, and flee to Egypt, and remain there until I tell you, for Herod is about to search for the child, to destroy Him." And he rose and took the child and His mother by night and departed to Egypt and remained there until the death of Herod. This was to fulfill what the Lord had spoken by the prophet, "Out of Egypt I called My son."

Then Herod, when he saw that he had been tricked by the wise men, became furious, and he sent and killed all the male children in Bethlehem and in all that region who were two years old or under, according to the time that he had ascertained from the wise men. Then was fulfilled what was spoken by the prophet Jeremiah:

"A voice was heard in Ramah,
weeping and loud lamentation,
Rachel weeping for her children;
she refused to be comforted,
because they are no more."

HEROD THE GREAT
AND THE MAGI

*Now after Jesus was born in Bethle-
hem of Judea in the days of Herod the
king, behold, wise men from the east
came to Jerusalem.* (MATTHEW 2:1)

The Roman Empire was expansive. It included all the lands around the Mediterranean Sea and extended far across what we call the Middle East today. This included the ancient Persian Empire in the east, where wise men were very famous. These were not kings, but highly educated advisors to kings. The Persian name for them was *magi*. In the Old Testament, Daniel and his three friends Shadrach, Meshach, and Abednego had been trained as magi when they were taken to Babylon as young men (see Daniel 1 and 2). In time, Daniel was promoted to an administrative position over all the magi and other officials (see Daniel 6:28). Being astrologers, the magi carefully studied the stars and noted the special star that appeared at Jesus' birth.

King Herod the Great ruled Israel at this time. He had assisted Augustus in the Roman civil war against Marc Antony and Cleopatra. When Augustus became emperor of Rome, he rewarded Herod by making him ruler over the land of Israel and giving him the title of king. Herod received the nickname "the Great" because of the massive building projects he undertook, especially enlarging and beautifying the temple in Jerusalem.

In his early years, Herod was a promising ruler, but as he grew older, he became more and more paranoid that rivals would assassinate him. He ordered two of his sons executed at the instigation of his relatives. He also had his favorite wife killed when she was accused of having an affair, along with her father and brother, whom Herod had appointed as Israel's high priest. With this background, it is not at all surprising that all Jerusalem was troubled when the wise men arrived looking for a child who had been born King of the Jews.

When Herod died, Caesar Augustus divided his kingdom into four parts. Herod's son Archelaus was given the regions of Judea and Samaria, which he ruled in his father's place. Joseph did not return to Bethlehem because Archelaus was cruel and vindictive. Caesar Augustus recalled him early in his reign and replaced him with a succession of Roman procurators, or military governors—one of which would be a man named Pontius Pilate.

Instead of returning to Bethlehem, Joseph brought his family to Mary's hometown of Nazareth where another of Herod's sons, Herod Antipas, was ruling Galilee. Jesus was raised there and learned to be a carpenter alongside His father Joseph.

*Our gracious Father, at the right time,
You brought Your Son, Jesus Christ, into our
world. Yet the leaders of the world rejected
Him and tried to kill Him. Thank You for
faithful believers like the Wise Men and Joseph
and Mary who protected Him and worshiped Him. Guard us from all enemies and
strengthen us in faith that we may trust and
serve You without fear all the days of our lives.
We pray in Jesus' name. Amen.*

PROVIDING ALL OUR NEEDS

But when [Joseph] heard that Archelaus was reigning over Judea in place of his father Herod, he was afraid to go there, and being warned in a dream he withdrew to the district of Galilee. And he went and lived in a city called Nazareth, so that what was spoken by the prophets might be fulfilled, that He would be called a Nazarene. (MATTHEW 2:22–23)

Matthew wrote his Gospel for the Jewish people, as an answer to the objections about Jesus being the promised Messiah that ran through the Jewish community. It was important for him to demonstrate that Jesus fulfilled all the prophecies about the Christ in the Old Testament. One great stumbling block for Jews was that Jesus was known as Jesus of Nazareth because He was raised in that town in the northern region of Galilee. In fact, above His head on the cross stood the title, "Jesus of Nazareth, King of the Jews."

At the time Matthew wrote his Gospel account, many Jews were rejecting Jesus based on the very passage the chief priests brought to Herod to identify the birthplace of Jesus: Micah 5:2. It reads, "But you, O Bethlehem Ephrathah, who are too little to be among the clans of Judah, from you shall come forth for Me one who is to be ruler in Israel, whose coming forth is from of old, from ancient days." John records a dispute among the Jews over this very fact. "When they heard [Jesus'] words, some of the people said, 'This really is the Prophet.' . . . But some said, 'Is the Christ to come from Galilee? Has not the Scripture said that the Christ comes from the offspring of David, and comes from Bethlehem, the village where David

was?' So there was a division among the people over Him" (John 7:40–43).

So Matthew includes this passage in his Gospel to explain that Jesus was indeed born in Bethlehem but raised in Nazareth because of King Herod's response to the visit of the Wise Men. He also includes two prophecies (see 2:15 and 2:18) to reassure the Jews this was all part of God's plan.

This passage highlights God the Father's providential care and protection of Jesus—and of each of us. In Herod, we see Satan's hatred of Jesus and his desire to destroy Jesus' mission from the very beginning. But God knew Satan's plots and the thoughts of man, and He sent an angel to warn Joseph in a dream to take the Christ Child and flee Bethlehem for Egypt. Nothing stands in the way of God the Father accomplishing our salvation through Jesus Christ.

When Joseph and Mary fled to Egypt, a large party of Jews were already living in cities like Alexandria. In fact, the Jewish historian Josephus wrote that more Jews lived in Egypt at the time than in Israel itself. It is likely the holy family's trip and their stay in Egypt were funded by the gold, frankincense, and myrrh the Wise Men had brought to Jesus—another example of God the Father providing for His Son.

Heavenly Father, we deserve nothing but punishment and death for our sins, but for Jesus' sake, You graciously forgive us and make us Your own. Protect us from the enemies who would harm us: Satan, the world, and our own sinful nature. Fill us with Your Holy Spirit, protect us, and provide all our needs as Your Son, Jesus, leads us to our heavenly home. In Jesus' name. Amen.

SATAN'S TREACHEROUS PLANS

Then Herod, when he saw that he had been tricked by the wise men, became furious, and he sent and killed all the male children in Bethlehem and in all that region who were two years old or under, according to the time that he had ascertained from the wise men. (MATTHEW 2:16)

Ever since the serpent slithered into the Garden of Eden in Genesis 3, the battle has been on between Satan and God. Since he was completely overpowered by God from the start, Satan turned against the man and woman God had made in His own image. Even then, the devil could not force them to disobey God. He could only use his cunning to tempt them. Of course, he was successful, and Adam and Eve ate the forbidden fruit. But that very day, God promised a Savior, the seed of the woman who would crush the serpent's head.

Many times throughout the Old Testament, Satan tried to destroy the line leading to that seed. But God worked through believers like Noah, Abraham, Isaac, Jacob, Moses, and Joshua to save His people and keep the line leading to Christ intact.

Now that the Savior is born, Satan again intensifies his efforts to cut Him off, using, in this case, the paranoia of King Herod. We see something of the cunning of the serpent in Herod's private audience with the Wise Men. He asks when the star appeared to learn the age of the child. He tells them to report back to him when they find the Christ Child, so he, too, can go and worship Him. It would not be surprising if the Wise Men naively thought Herod was being sincere.

If God had not warned the Wise Men to *not* return to Herod, and if He had not warned Joseph to rise in the night to immediately flee with Jesus and Mary, Satan might well have succeeded. But Christ's time to die had not yet come, and Satan's plans were foiled again.

In the coming weeks, we will see Jesus combat Satan repeatedly. Twice in the Gospels, Satan stirs people to seek Jesus' death (when His neighbors in Nazareth tried to hurl Him off the cliff upon which their town was built (see Luke 4:28–30), and when the crowds in Jerusalem tried to stone Him to death (see John 10:30–39). But Jesus feared no enemies. He knew He could trust His Father to provide for His needs and protect Him and dedicated Himself to fulfilling His mission to save us from our sins.

Only on the day of God's choosing, Good Friday, would Satan see Jesus put to death on the cross. But he would see his apparent triumph turn to complete defeat when Jesus rose victorious on the third day. Even more, he would learn that Jesus Christ provided a way of salvation for all of Adam and Eve's children through that bitter suffering and dying for our sins—rising to life again to deliver us from death, Satan, and hell.

Holy Father, thank You for protecting Jesus from Satan's wrath through Herod, delivering Him unto death on the cross, and raising Him victorious from the grave on the third day. Give us, Your children, confidence that You are always with us, protecting us every day as You lead us to paradise for Jesus' sake. We pray in His holy name. Amen.

JOY AMID OUR GRIEF

Then was fulfilled what was spoken by the prophet Jeremiah: "A voice was heard in Ramah, weeping and loud lamentation, Rachel weeping for her children; she refused to be comforted, because they are no more." (MATTHEW 2:17–18)

Matthew wrote his Gospel to convince the Jewish people that Jesus was the Savior promised throughout the pages of the Old Testament. In this passage, we see him quoting many Old Testament passages. Two that particularly jump out deal with Rachel weeping for her children. This is pulled together from two Old Testament passages.

In Genesis 35, Jacob is leading his family across the Promised Land toward Bethlehem.

> **Then they journeyed from Bethel. When they were still some distance from Ephrath, Rachel went into labor, and she had hard labor. And when her labor was at its hardest, the midwife said to her, "Do not fear, for you have another son." And as her soul was departing (for she was dying), she called his name Ben-oni; but his father called him Benjamin. So Rachel died, and she was buried on the way to Ephrath (that is, Bethlehem).** (Genesis 35:16–19)

Rachel's suggested name, *Ben-oni*, means "son of my sorrow." To spare Benjamin from always being thought of as the cause of his mother's death, Jacob changed it to *Benjamin*, which means "son of the right hand."

The prophet Jeremiah later picked up on Rachel weeping over her child to speak of the Babylonian exile of the people of Judah. "Thus says the LORD: 'A voice is heard in Ramah, lamentation and bitter weeping. Rachel is weeping for her children; she refuses to be comforted for her children, because they are no more'" (Jeremiah 31:15).

The descendants of Benjamin lived in the kingdom of Judah, and these children of Rachel were led off into exile with the people of Judah by the Babylonians, weeping and grieving as they were driven along the same road Rachel traveled when she died in childbirth.

Matthew uses this prophecy to recapture the grief and sorrow that struck the village of Bethlehem when Herod ordered the execution of the boys of Bethlehem.

Yet this passage from Jeremiah does not end with the weeping, but God's great comfort of His people, assuring them that after their exile, the sons and daughters of Judah will return to once again inhabit the land of Judah.

Likewise, because of Jesus' life, death, and resurrection, these young boys of Bethlehem who had been circumcised into God's covenant with Abraham, Isaac, and Jacob will be raised with us to eternal life when Jesus returns and the sorrow of their death will be turned to joy and laughter, all because of Jesus Christ.

Heavenly Father, You know our times of sorrow and grief. Comfort us through Your Son, Jesus Christ, who has conquered sin, death, and hell that we may live in hope and cheer, knowing He will raise us to eternal life when He returns. In Jesus' name. Amen.

WHOSE FAULT?

Now after Jesus was born in Bethlehem of Judea in the days of Herod the king, behold, wise men from the east came to Jerusalem, saying, "Where is He who has been born king of the Jews? For we saw His star when it rose and have come to worship Him." When Herod the king heard this, he was troubled, and all Jerusalem with him. (MATTHEW 2:1–3)

It is hard to read this account without wondering why God led the Wise Men to Herod when He knew Herod would respond in fear and jealousy, murdering the innocent boys of Bethlehem. Could not God have used the star to guide them directly to the house in which Jesus was without first stopping over at Herod's palace?

God certainly could have done that, but God is full of mercy and love—even for a wicked king like Herod. God wanted to let Herod and the Wise Men together hear the good news that a Savior had been born. Had the Wise Men followed the silent star directly to the house, they would not have heard Micah's prophecy, which explained the presence of the star and the true identity of the child born King of the Jews. That His origins were from of old, from ancient times. That this child King was actually the eternal Son of God.

The Lord wanted the Wise Men to know this—but He also wanted Herod and all the members of the court to hear this as well. God wanted to lead Herod to repentance and faith, to humble himself to recognize that his Lord and Savior was here during his reign.

Herod's murderous response was his own—God was in no way responsible for Herod's rejection of his Savior and for attempting to murder Him as a rival. When Herod died and faced his judgment before the Lord, he had absolutely no excuse that he was totally unaware. The news had disturbed and troubled him. That turbulence of his heart was answered by God's prophetic message through Micah. Herod simply chose to close his ears and his heart and to cunningly play the devil's part. Pretending to be sincere, he professed faith in the Christ Child, asking the Wise Men to find Him and report back so he, too, could go worship Him. If only Herod had been sincere—the boys of Bethlehem would have survived, and Herod himself would have been forgiven and given eternal life.

Lord God, You do not desire the death of any, but that every person turns to You in repentance and trusts in Jesus Christ for salvation. Forgive me for not always responding to Your Gospel in repentance and faith. Cleanse and forgive me for Jesus' sake. Fill my heart with love for my enemies so I may seek their welfare and share the Good News of Your salvation with them. In Jesus' name. Amen.

GOD IS ALWAYS WATCHING, PROTECTING

Behold, an angel of the Lord appeared to Joseph in a dream and said, "Rise, take the child and His mother, and flee to Egypt, and remain there until I tell you, for Herod is about to search for the child, to destroy Him." And he rose and took the child and His mother by night and departed to Egypt and remained there until the death of Herod. (MATTHEW 2:13–15)

Many times, we live our lives feeling secure and safe. If enemies are plotting against us, we aren't aware. We may, indeed, not have any human enemies plotting against us, but the Bible tells us our spiritual enemies—the devil, the unbelieving world, and our own sinful nature—are constantly plotting against the church and against us.

This passage reminds us that our God and Father is well aware of these plots, and nothing can harm us unless He permits it. And He would only permit that harm if He plans to work something good for us or for others through it. Even when we go through times of sickness or suffer from the choices of others, God is working to strengthen our faith and touch those around us—even our human enemies. No matter what is happening, we can live in freedom and security because our God is with us, guiding all things for our good (Romans 8:26–39).

This is why God gathers us together for worship each week. There, He can remind us through Word and Sacrament that He is always with us. He carefully watches all that happens and guides everything for our good. His Word encourages us when we are fearful. His work in Baptism reminds us that He has washed away our sins, adopted us as His own sons and daughters, and given us His Holy Spirit as a guarantee of the eternal life He has prepared for us. And in Holy Communion, He gives the very body and blood Jesus sacrificed on the cross to save us, and He reassures us He will always be with us to guide us to our heavenly home.

Heavenly Father, encourage me to trust You whenever I face danger or learn of people plotting against me. Give each of us believers courage to share the Good News of Jesus Christ, confident that You will keep us safely by Your Holy Spirit. We pray in Jesus' name. Amen.

TWELVE-YEAR-OLD JESUS IN THE TEMPLE

Week 6—Luke 2:40–52

And the child grew and became strong, filled with wisdom. And the favor of God was upon Him.

Now His parents went to Jerusalem every year at the Feast of the Passover. And when He was twelve years old, they went up according to custom. And when the feast was ended, as they were returning, the boy Jesus stayed behind in Jerusalem. His parents did not know it, but supposing Him to be in the group they went a day's journey, but then they began to search for Him among their relatives and acquaintances, and when they did not find Him, they returned to Jerusalem, searching for Him. After three days they found Him in the temple, sitting among the teachers, listening to them and asking them questions.

And all who heard Him were amazed at His understanding and His answers. And when His parents saw Him, they were astonished. And His mother said to Him, "Son, why have You treated us so? Behold, Your father and I have been searching for You in great distress." And He said to them, "Why were you looking for Me? Did you not know that I must be in my Father's house?" And they did not understand the saying that He spoke to them. And He went down with them and came to Nazareth and was submissive to them. And His mother treasured up all these things in her heart.

And Jesus increased in wisdom and in stature and in favor with God and man.

A STUDENT OF THE WORD

Now His parents went to Jerusalem
every year at the Feast of the
Passover. And when He was twelve
years old, they went up according
to custom. (LUKE 2:41–42)

If you are reading this passage of Scripture from the perspective of a twenty-first-century Christian, most mentions of Jewish observances and traditions likely go right over your head. Christians do not observe different festivals multiple times a year, and we do not travel to a singular temple in Jerusalem for worship.

But in Jesus' day, Jewish males were required to travel to Jerusalem for three festivals each year—Passover, Pentecost, and the Festival of Booths. We hear in Luke that Joseph and Mary faithfully brought Jesus to the Passover each year, most likely in addition to the other two aforementioned festivals.

Jesus, as a twelve-year-old Jewish boy, would now become a bar mitzvah, which means "a son of the covenant." This new title would allow Him to join His earthly father, Joseph, in the Courtyard of the Men, bringing Him closer to the temple building and giving Him access to the temple courts and teachers there. (Before turning twelve, Jesus would have had to stay with Mary in the Courtyard of Women, which was located farther away from the temple.)

Since it took Mary and Joseph three days to find Jesus when He went missing, we can assume the temple isn't the first place they went to look for Him. Like us, they might have assumed a twelve-year-old boy would have wanted to watch the horse and chariot races at the Hippodrome or wanted to see the Roman soldiers quartered at the Antonio Fortress. After all, Jerusalem was a major metropolis compared to Jesus' tiny hometown of Nazareth!

However, Jesus was in His Father's house—the temple courts—listening to the teachers and, perhaps more surprisingly for a child, answering the scribes' questions! This is not exactly the first place you'd imagine a boy to go in a major city—and certainly not what you would expect a child to do in a culture that did not value children or their opinions.

We might also be surprised to hear that Jesus is interested in learning about the Scriptures and God when He Himself is God! In many ways, Jesus set aside His divine omniscience to learn the same way we humans do—including memorizing portions of Jewish Scripture, which He has clearly mastered based on the scribes' amazement at His answers.

Jesus' commitment to learning from teachers of the faith—amid a city of potential distractions and despite His status as the Son of God—serves as a great example for us, who struggle to attend weekly worship, who neglect to read our Bible daily, and who are prone to think we know all there is to know about Scripture. Let us turn to Jesus, the perfect example, when we don't study His Word as we should.

Jesus, help me to forever be a student of the Word, just as You were. Amen.

LEARNING THE THINGS OF GOD

And He said to them, "Why were you looking for Me? Did you not know that I must be in My Father's house?" (LUKE 2:49)

J esus studying the Word of God and learning from earthly teachers and scribes seems a little counterintuitive to us. *Isn't He the Son of God? Wouldn't He already know all this stuff?*

Yes, and yes! However, Jesus, in His divine wisdom, became fully God and fully man. To accomplish our salvation, He humbled Himself, setting aside His divine power and knowledge. He lived in that state of humiliation from conception through His death. Only when He rose again on the third day was He exalted, taking up His full divine power and knowledge. So at twelve years old, Jesus learned to memorize portions of God's Word just like you and I must.

For many of us in our day-to-day life, learning the things of God is the last thing on our mind—we have work to finish, kids to pick up and put down, friends to check in on, dinners to cook, yards to mow, and houses to clean.

But for Jesus, His main priority was to study the Scriptures and spend time with God. Throughout His earthly ministry, Jesus often withdrew alone to pray (see Luke 5:16; 6:12; 9:18). In His darkest hour in the Garden of Gethsemane, Jesus poured out His soul to His Father in prayer (see Matthew 26:36–46). Even though He was (and is) the Son of God, He still desired communion with Him and used prayer as an avenue to that end.

In our daily lives, we should strive to spend as much time alone with God as possible. That will look different for everyone, and it might differ for you in different seasons of life. Whether you listen to an audio reading of the Bible on your commute home or find time in the evenings to read Scripture by yourself, it's important to follow the example of Jesus and spend time with your heavenly Father.

When Jesus was tempted in the wilderness in Matthew 4:1–11, He quoted Scripture to deter Satan. And when Satan twisted God's Word in an attempt to sway Jesus, Jesus rebutted him with even more Scripture. Satan's lies are no match for the truth of God.

Likewise, when we are tempted by the evil one, we can use Scripture—especially Scripture we have memorized—to remind ourselves of God's promises and deter Satan from discouraging us. When Satan speaks lies that you are not worthy, that you've done too many bad things, that God could never love you, pray the truth of Scripture over and again to be reminded that Christ purchased and won you as His child—forever.

God, thank You for giving us Your Word to study and memorize. Fill me with Your Spirit. In Jesus' name. Amen.

PREPARING TO SHARE

*And all who heard Him were
amazed at His understanding
and His answers.* (LUKE 2:47)

W e often think of Jesus' earthly mission only as the culmination of His ministry at the cross. And while we should always keep our eyes focused on the cross and the salvation He won for us there, we should also look to the three years of Jesus' ministry that led up to that moment for some important notes about Jesus' mission.

After Jesus started His public ministry, He spent most of His time doing two main things: performing miracles (healing the sick, casting out demons) and teaching about the kingdom of God. Arguably, His teaching about the kingdom of God was the most important because it showed His disciples and followers why He came—even if they didn't understand it at the time.

In this scene in the temple, Jesus is preparing for that part of His important three-year ministry. He is listening to the teachers there, yes, but He is also teaching them. In fact, "All who heard Him were amazed at His understanding and His answers."

Some twenty years later, He likely debated and corrected some of those very same teachers! The scribes and Pharisees—who so vehemently opposed Jesus' ministry, who were so focused on their rituals and laws that they forgot about God, who put Jesus to death—were learning from the very Son of God! Yet they failed to see His divinity and sentenced Him to death for blasphemy instead.

Jesus' teaching of these stubborn scribes, even at this early age, reminds each of us likewise to be continual students of God's Word. By studying the Scriptures each day, we grow in our knowledge of our Savior and more deeply understand how powerful the grace He gives us is. May we never have hard hearts like these teachers, who were so focused on their traditions that they missed the fulfillment of the prophecies they so diligently studied!

The goal of our Bible study should always be twofold: to grow in understanding of God and to be able to share the Gospel clearly with others. Our mission on earth is similar to Jesus' mission—to spread the Gospel to the ends of the earth! Studying and memorizing Scripture gives us a framework to share the Good News and helps us to be prepared for any scenario we may face in the mission field.

May our minds be open to receiving the knowledge of God's Word from the Holy Spirit, and may our hearts be open to sharing that Good News with those around us at every opportunity.

*Jesus, help us to prepare and share the
Good News of Your Gospel always. Amen.*

WHAT IT LOOKS LIKE TO LOVE GOD'S WORD

I have stored up Your word in my heart, that I might not sin against You. (PSALM 119:11)

Psalm 119 is well known for being the longest recorded psalm in the Bible. Because of that, it's likely that few of us have ever read it all the way through in one sitting! Before reading the rest of this devotion, I invite you to read Psalm 119 in its entirety.

One of the main points of this passage from Luke—which, hopefully, you have gathered from this week's previous devotions—is that Jesus loved studying the Word of God. This psalm speaks exactly to that same love, and it beautifully describes Jesus' love for the Scriptures that He demonstrated at the temple.

While we don't know exactly who wrote this psalm, the author clearly had a devout love for God's Word and meditated on it day and night. We can look to this author and to Jesus as examples in the faith of what it looks like to love God's Word.

Today, slowly read through each of the selected verses from Psalm 119, and then see if the paraphrase provided helps you better understand the verse.

"I have stored up Your word in my heart, that I might not sin against You" (v. 11).

I keep Your word close to me at all times so that I don't sin against You.

"Make me understand the way of Your precepts, and I will meditate on Your wondrous works" (v. 27).

Help me understand Your laws, and then I will meditate on all the good You have done in my life.

"Incline my heart to Your testimonies, and not to selfish gain!" (v. 36).

Make my heart open to Your Word instead of the things that I want.

"Teach me good judgment and knowledge, for I believe in Your commandments" (v. 66).

Give me wisdom to make good choices. I believe Your Law is good for me!

"Your hands have made and fashioned me; give me understanding that I may learn Your commandments" (v. 73).

You are the God who created me. Please help me understand Your Law better.

"You are my hiding place and my shield; I hope in Your word" (v. 114).

You, God, are my refuge and place of peace. You protect me, and I place my hope in You.

"Great peace have those who love Your law; nothing can make them stumble" (v. 165).

Those who obey Your Law have everlasting peace, and nothing can cause them to falter.

Lord, give me a lasting love for Your Word. Amen.

WHY DID IT TAKE SO LONG?

And when the feast was ended, as they were returning, the boy Jesus stayed behind in Jerusalem. His parents did not know it, but supposing Him to be in the group they went a day's journey, but then they began to search for Him among their relatives and acquaintances, and when they did not find Him, they returned to Jerusalem, searching for Him. (LUKE 2:43–45)

After studying this text for four days this week, you might still be wondering: how in the world did Mary and Joseph not realize they had left Jesus behind in Jerusalem? And why did it take them so long to find Him after they realized He was missing? He was their oldest son—how is this possible? The answer is maybe more simple than you might think!

Mary and Joseph likely didn't realize they had left Jesus behind for a few potential reasons. Their family had traveled to Jerusalem with relatives and friends—His parents likely assumed that Jesus was with His cousins or friends! And by this point, Mary and Joseph also likely had other children besides Jesus, so perhaps they were wrangling His little brothers and sisters and assumed their twelve-year-old was disciplined and able to take care of Himself.

This doesn't mean that Mary and Joseph were negligent parents, and it certainly doesn't mean that Jesus was disobedient. Rather, it's more likely that Mary and Joseph simply assumed Jesus would have been with their group—and Jesus says they should have known He "must be in My Father's house" (Luke 2:49). This misunderstanding between the two parties led to Jesus missing for a few days.

It likely wasn't until the families gathered together in the first evening to stop for the night that they realized Jesus was not there. Can you imagine the fear that was in their hearts when they realized their eldest son wasn't in their travel group?

Now why did it take them three days to find Jesus after they realized He was missing? As previously mentioned, they likely didn't notice Jesus wasn't with them until they stopped for the evening. Traveling alone at night would have been dangerous for the pair, so it is also likely they waited until the morning to head back to the city to find Jesus.

Keep in mind that Mary, Joseph, and Jesus had to walk all the way from Nazareth to Jerusalem, which was about sixty or seventy miles and likely took them about a week to walk there and a week to walk back. They had walked around ten miles that first day, so they wouldn't want to walk that far at night where there was the potential to be robbed.

So—day one that Jesus was missing was the travel day when they thought He was in their company. Day two was spent rushing back to Jerusalem and searching as much as they could before dark. Day three is when they finally found Him in the temple.

These small details in the story do matter. Jesus, Mary, and Joseph were real people who lived real lives here on earth. Praise God for the families He gives us—here on earth and in heaven!

Father, thank You for sending Your Son to live a perfect life here on earth to save us. Amen.

GROWING THE LOVE OF GOD'S WORD

And Jesus increased in wisdom and in stature and in favor with God and man. (LUKE 2:52)

This passage clearly demonstrates Jesus' love of the Scriptures—a love He wants to impart to us. God gifted us His Word to make us wise unto salvation and to instruct us on the right and wrong ways to go. We desperately need God's Word; our inherent sinful desires lead us to believe our moments of temptation are the right decisions.

Scripture also helps us treasure the eternal things of heaven more than the things of this earthly life. Remember Psalm 119? The author clearly treasured God's Word above all else—he meditated on it day and night and continually asked God to make His will known through the Scripture.

How can we maintain this love of God's Word? By attending corporate worship at church each week. Church today is similar to Jesus' going to the temple—it's where God speaks to us directly through His Word and our pastor explains that Word through a sermon. Confession and Absolution, Communion, and the Prayers of the Church are all integral parts of the worship service that draw us closer to Christ.

In addition, gathering with the community of believers encourages us and holds us accountable. When we surround ourselves with fellow Christians, we can abide together. As we live out our lives together, we can lean on one another in the hard times that we will inevitably face. Turning to fellow Christians in addition to God's Word can give us great comfort in this broken world.

In church, we also have the opportunity to go to Bible class to learn Scripture, where we are asked questions and also have the opportunity to ask questions to grow as Christians. With each question, we grow in our knowledge and understanding of Scripture. Voicing our fears, doubts, and questions among fellow Christians helps us learn and grow in our faith!

Just as Jesus grew in wisdom of God's Word, we, too, should strive to that same goal. We will never exhaust Scripture—there is always more to learn! We have our whole lives to dig deeper into Scripture. Throughout the many seasons we'll face in life, we can be comforted, disciplined, and encouraged through Scripture. God has given us His Word to do those very things, and we are blessed to live in a time where we have such wide access to the Bible. Scripture has been translated into nearly every language, and many of us likely own multiple Bibles.

May we always have a heart that is open to growing in wisdom and stature with the Lord!

Father, may we always seek to learn more about Your Word, which You have gifted to us. In Jesus' name. Amen.

JOHN THE BAPTIST

Week 7—Matthew 3

In those days John the Baptist came preaching in the wilderness of Judea, "Repent, for the kingdom of heaven is at hand." For this is he who was spoken of by the prophet Isaiah when he said,

> "The voice of one crying in the wilderness:
> 'Prepare the way of the Lord;
>   make His paths straight.'"

Now John wore a garment of camel's hair and a leather belt around his waist, and his food was locusts and wild honey. Then Jerusalem and all Judea and all the region about the Jordan were going out to him, and they were baptized by him in the river Jordan, confessing their sins.

But when he saw many of the Pharisees and Sadducees coming to his baptism, he said to them, "You brood of vipers! Who warned you to flee from the wrath to come? Bear fruit in keeping with repentance. And do not presume to say to yourselves, 'We have Abraham as our father,' for I tell you, God is able from these stones to raise up children for Abraham. Even now the axe is laid to the root of the trees. Every tree therefore that does not bear good fruit is cut down and thrown into the fire.

"I baptize you with water for repentance, but He who is coming after me is mightier than I, whose sandals I am not worthy to carry. He will baptize you with the Holy Spirit and fire. His winnowing fork is in His hand, and He will clear His threshing floor and gather His wheat into the barn, but the chaff He will burn with unquenchable fire."

Then Jesus came from Galilee to the Jordan to John, to be baptized by him. John would have prevented Him, saying, "I need to be baptized by You, and do You come to me?" But Jesus answered him, "Let it be so now, for thus it is fitting for us to fulfill all righteousness." Then he consented. And when Jesus was baptized, immediately He went up from the water, and behold, the heavens were opened to Him, and he saw the Spirit of God descending like a dove and coming to rest on Him; and behold, a voice from heaven said, "This is My beloved Son, with whom I am well pleased."

A STIRRING PROPHET

In those days John the Baptist came preaching in the wilderness of Judea, "Repent, for the kingdom of heaven is at hand." (MATTHEW 3:1–2)

A man wandered in the wilderness outside of Jerusalem. There were those who followed him and were his disciples. He went about declaring the coming of the King and His kingdom. He practiced Baptism as a central tenet of following God. His message was simple: "Repent, for the kingdom of heaven is at hand" (Matthew 3:2). What he did would give him his title: John the Baptizer.

Isaiah had prophesied about the ministry of John. He had declared that there would be one in the desert who proclaimed, "In the wilderness prepare the way of the Lord; make straight in the desert a highway for our God" (Isaiah 40:3). With Tiberius reigning as Caesar in Rome, Pontius Pilate the Roman governor in Judea and Samaria, and Herod Agrippa on the puppet throne in Galilee, John would walk in the wilderness declaring the coming of a heavenly ruler and a dominion that would never end. Because of this message John would catch the ear of the powerful secular and religious rulers.

It is strange that the message of a wandering wilderness preacher could cause such a stir. His wardrobe was camel skin, and his diet was locusts and honey. This was not a powerful ruler sitting in the halls of palaces, waited on by advisors and servants. John was a simple man living in the wild. But his message of the coming Messiah, the call to repentance, and Baptisms were drawing crowds. They were leaving their homes and trekking into the wilderness to be baptized in the Jordan River.

Hope drew them out. Hope of the Messiah, finally on the way.

The people of Israel had long heard the story of the coming Messiah. Prophets had laid the building blocks for centuries of an unfinished narrative that would one day be fulfilled. All the while, God's people had wondered and wandered. Living in the land God had promised them was never enough, and they were always quickly drawn astray by the glint of the idols that surrounded them. They had experienced exile brought on by invading nations, separation from their families, homes, and the temple of God. Kings had come and gone, many of them doing evil in the sight of the Lord. After a time, the invaders came and stayed. Greeks came and imposed their society and language. Rome followed with their brutal methods of colonization. God's people longed for the promised Savior.

John's message of repentance and the Kingdom struck home. Crowds gathered and disciples began to follow him. But all the while, he pointed to something greater, the Promised One who was coming. John was the promised prophet, the one who would lay the final groundwork for the Messiah. So it would be when one day in the Jordan, John looked among the crowd and saw a modest carpenter approaching him. Yet this was no regular man of Israel—angels and shepherds had proclaimed His birth. Magi had followed a star from the East to bring Him gifts. After a long line of prophets and priests, John would not only proclaim the Messiah—he would touch Him.

Lord Jesus, move my heart to repentance and true faith with John's words, "Repent, for the kingdom of heaven is at hand." Amen.

A POWERFUL CONTRAST

But when [John] saw many of the Pharisees and Sadducees coming to his baptism, he said to them, "You brood of vipers!" (MATTHEW 3:7)

John the Baptist was a fascinating man. He was a wilderness holy man who dressed and acted the part. Just look at Matthew 3:7–11:

> But when [John] saw many of the Pharisees and Sadducees coming to his baptism, he said to them, "You brood of vipers! Who warned you to flee from the wrath to come? Bear fruit in keeping with repentance. And do not presume to say to yourselves, 'We have Abraham as our father,' for I tell you, God is able from these stones to raise up children for Abraham. Even now the axe is laid to the root of the trees. Every tree therefore that does not bear good fruit is cut down and thrown into the fire. I baptize you with water for repentance, but He who is coming after me is mightier than I, whose sandals I am not worthy to carry. He will baptize you with the Holy Spirit and fire."

The local religious leaders show up, and he calls them snakes! Foretold as the voice declaring the way of the Lord, he did not endear himself to those who held the reins of religion.

Now, contrast this with how he encounters Jesus in verses 13–15: "Then Jesus came from Galilee to the Jordan to John, to be baptized by him. John would have prevented Him, saying, 'I need to be baptized by You, and do You come to me?' But Jesus answered him, 'Let it be so now, for thus it is fitting for us to fulfill all righteousness.' Then he consented."

John knew the Messiah when he saw Him, but the religious leaders who had thought themselves important because of their status and power he calls snakes. Yet John humbled himself before the carpenter from Galilee. John knew who held the true power and authority. This unassuming man from Nazareth was, in fact, God incarnate.

Could you imagine what John must have felt as Jesus asked to be baptized? It is clear in his answer. He asks Jesus to baptize him, not the other way around. Yet the Savior gives one of many gifts—He sets an example for His followers. He, the Prince of Peace, God with us, the Word, steps into the waters of the Jordan to be baptized.

In this moment, the great exchange of Baptism takes place. Instead of a sinful person stepping in to be washed clean, the sinless Savior steps into the flowing river to take on the sins of all who enter the waters of Baptism. Heaven opens, and God declares that this is His Son, His most loved. The Holy Spirit lands on Jesus, sealing the trinitarian declaration. Jesus has come. He is baptized to show those who would believe in Him that the exchange will be complete. It echoes the scene as the apostle John would explain it in his Gospel: "Behold, the Lamb of God, who takes away the sin of the world!" The perfect sacrifice had arrived. Not powerful or religious men making their way down from important cities but instead a carpenter from the countryside, humbly requesting to be baptized.

Lord Jesus, in Your humble Baptism You empowered Baptism to be a cleansing fountain for me and for all. Amen.

JESUS' BAPTISM IS OUR BAPTISM

And behold, a voice from heaven said, "This is My beloved Son, with whom I am well pleased." (MATTHEW 3:17)

Jesus' Baptism holds importance for us today. Through this act, He empowers Baptism to be the sacrament in which we rejoice! Jesus' own act brings us peace and joy, which can be found in our washing as He baptizes us with water and the Word. Not only this, but John the Baptist's declaration that one would come to baptize with "the Holy Spirit and with fire," alongside the Holy Spirit appearing as a dove, directly foreshadows the Day of Pentecost. Fire and the Spirit would come upon the baptized that day. The act of Jesus walking into those waters of the Jordan to be baptized by John continues today.

God declares over Jesus, "This is My beloved Son, with whom I am well pleased." At the start of His public ministry, God makes sure everyone knows who Jesus is. This is not another prophet, priest, or earthly king. This is the Messiah. He has come with purpose and mission to walk the road to the cross and the empty tomb.

Our sins are taken away. The sacramental nature of Baptism might appear transactional, yet it is not. Instead, it is a gift that transforms and changes us. It takes one identity and gives us a new one. Too often, the temptation for Christians is to try to find the fuel for the Christian life within themselves: *If only I could be better, do better, love better—then God might love me.* Or maybe it falls to the other side of the road: *I am not better and can never be. God could never love me.* This work of Jesus proclaims otherwise. We are called to follow Him in His Baptism because of the assurance He gives us. As the waters rush over Jesus and God declares His love for Him, He says the same thing for us.

You are a saint. Not because of what anyone says about you but because of what God says about you. Jesus' Baptism not only launched His earthly mission but it conveys upon you the identity He gained for you on the cross. His Baptism grants you yours. In the mysterious combination of Jesus' work, the Word, and water, God conveys to you the identity of son or daughter of the King. Any question about how you could ever be good enough is erased. You are. Why? Jesus made it so when the water washed you clean.

The work that Jesus does in His Baptism is of endless benefit to us. New identity is gifted to us as water and the Word washes away our sin. These rushing waters carry those who were once far off and bring them into the family of God. It anchors the baptized in an unyielding grip of grace that cannot be broken. It is a gift that we did not deserve but that God gives freely. As Jesus approached John the Baptist, He knew what He was doing. Even as He took steps in His earthly mission and ministry, He was working across time and space. Through the Holy Spirit, the waters of every river, stream, lake, pool, and font used to baptize men, women, and children into the kingdom of God are connected back to the waters of the Jordan where the Savior humbled Himself to be baptized for us.

Lord Jesus, thank You for taking up my sins in Baptism so that I may truly be God's own child. Amen.

JESUS' BAPTISM THROUGHOUT SCRIPTURE

Then Jesus came from Galilee to the Jordan to John, to be baptized by him. (MATTHEW 3:13)

Scriptures foretold the coming of John the Baptist. The prophet Isaiah speaks about the voice in the desert:

> Comfort, comfort My people, says your God. Speak tenderly to Jerusalem, and cry to her that her warfare is ended, that her iniquity is pardoned, that she has received from the LORD's hand double for all her sins. A voice cries: "In the wilderness prepare the way of the LORD; make straight in the desert a highway for our God. Every valley shall be lifted up, and every mountain and hill be made low; the uneven ground shall become level, and the rough places a plain. And the glory of the LORD shall be revealed, and all flesh shall see it together, for the mouth of the LORD has spoken." (Isaiah 40:1–5)

Malachi speaks of this coming prophet as well: "Behold, I send My messenger, and he will prepare the way before Me. And the Lord whom you seek will suddenly come to His temple; and the messenger of the covenant in whom you delight, behold, He is coming, says the LORD of hosts" (Malachi 3:1).

Yet, John was still ignored. His outward appearance and message of repentance did not resonate with the standing religious power brokers or the lofty political elite. In fact, even as John does exactly what God calls him to do, it would be the ruler Herod who would first imprison him (see Matthew 11:2) and go on to behead him (see Matthew 14:1–12) because of the specific call to repentance John laid before him.

John was the voice calling in the desert. His ministry, prophesied in the Old Testament, came to fulfillment when Jesus walked into the Jordan with him. He had begun the process of declaring the kingdom of God and preparing hearts for repentance. The valleys of the hearts of men and women had been raised up, the hills had been made low. People were beginning to see the need they had for a Savior, even as that Messiah waded into the flowing waters.

Paul proclaims the Good News of Jesus for us using baptismal language:

> How can we who died to sin still live in it? Do you not know that all of us who have been baptized into Christ Jesus were baptized into His death? We were buried therefore with Him by baptism into death, in order that, just as Christ was raised from the dead by the glory of the Father, we too might walk in newness of life. For if we have been united with Him in a death like His, we shall certainly be united with Him in a resurrection like His. (Romans 6:2–5)

John is sent to declare the way of the Lord, the Messiah who has come to rescue the world. Yet he did not expect that the Baptism that day would be one in which Scriptures would also declare salvation. Jesus' Baptism rings through the rest of Scripture as a hope for His people.

Jesus Christ, the whole of Scripture proclaims Your mission of forgiveness. Fill me with faith, peace, and joy. Amen.

UNITED IN PURPOSE AND MISSION

Immediately He went up from the water, and behold, the heavens were opened to Him, and he saw the Spirit of God descending like a dove and coming to rest on Him. (MATTHEW 3:16)

The whole scene of the Baptism of Jesus seems like it could be taken right out of a movie. A wilderness preacher proclaims his message to gathered crowds. Powerful men whose status is threatened seek to make trouble for this baptizer. He is unsurprised by their attacks and rebukes them quickly with a sharp tongue. Then the gathered people begin to part as a simple carpenter's son makes His way up to the front. For the first time in a long time, the preacher is speechless. He insists that he cannot baptize this man. It is this man whom his message has been referring to all the while—but after a word, this prophet enters the water to baptize the Messiah.

That in and of itself would make a wonderful scene. Get the cameras in the right spot, make sure the sound is set, lighting at the perfect time of day. How incredible! God had this plan all along. This would make a worthwhile piece of the overarching redemption story God has been crafting since the fall. It is powerful and surprising. The prophet would be so reverent of a simple man from Nazareth while insulting the powerful. The waters flow over this man in Baptism and the start of the next chapter of the story begins.

But God didn't leave it there.

"And when Jesus was baptized, immediately He went up from the water, and behold, the heavens were opened to Him, and he saw the Spirit of God descending like a dove and coming to rest on Him"

(Matthew 3:16). The Holy Spirit comes to rest on Him. God's Spirit descends from heaven, appearing as a dove. Here, standing before the people was the physical presence of God united in human form. It was as Isaiah had foretold: "And the Spirit of the LORD shall rest upon Him, the Spirit of wisdom and understanding, the Spirit of counsel and might, the Spirit of knowledge and the fear of the LORD" (Isaiah 11:2).

In that river stood God Incarnate, united with the Spirit, which had hovered over the waters. Jesus' ministry would begin. A triune Father, Son, and Holy Spirit, three yet one, united in purpose and mission. Mark writes that Jesus would proclaim, "The time is fulfilled, and the kingdom of God is at hand; repent and believe in the gospel" (Mark 1:15). It would be easy to think of "at hand" in the modern idea of "close by" or "almost within reach." But what if, instead, we viewed it as Jesus was plainly saying the kingdom of God could be touched. The kingdom is wherever the King is reigning.

Here, in Jesus, for the first time, the kingdom of the Trinity could be touched. Father and Spirit united through the Son in physical form. The Father on high as Creator, the Son incarnate walking among His people, the Spirit ever present with wisdom and truth. The importance of the Holy Spirit's descent onto Jesus in His Baptism cannot be overstated. It is the declaration that God will move among His people. His Messiah has arrived, and His Spirit is with Him.

Lord Jesus Christ, You are God Incarnate, my Savior, and my God. Amen.

AN OLD BAPTISMAL FONT

Then Jerusalem and all Judea and all the region about the Jordan were going out to him, and they were baptized by him in the river Jordan, confessing their sins. (MATTHEW 3:5–6)

After seminary studies, a young man received his first call to start a new church. The call came from, of all places, the church at which his wife had been confirmed. He would arrive and spend time in this church, getting to know the lay of the land before stepping out in the venture of bringing together a new congregation amid a quickly growing community down the road.

One day while sitting in his office at the mother church, the senior pastor called the young pastor into his office. There, sitting in the corner, was a baptismal font. It was nothing special. Made of stained wood and a metal bowl, it appeared to be a run-of-the-mill, ordinary font. Then the senior pastor told its story.

An unknown Lutheran church had closed its doors some years before. A local layman had asked to take the font so that he could hold it for the possibility that one day it could be used again. It sat in his garage for years, unused. At the time of his death, it still sat collecting dust among other odds and ends. But as his things were being cleaned out by his family, the font was discovered by his sister and brother-in-law.

They took the font and cared for it, remembering his intentions. They sanded and re-stained it. Then they heard their church would be planting a new congregation. With joy, they contacted their pastor, bringing the font to his office. He, in turn, told its story to the church planter. A simple font of wood cared for by saints over the years would once again be put into use.

It had a story. For from the waters over the years, heaven had come down to earth and claimed the hearts, bodies, and minds of sinners, transforming them to saints. It had been the focal point of the growth of the family of God for generations, and it would be once again. Nothing special, but everything extraordinary. This new church would carry it in and out of a school cafeteria as they met for worship. It would maintain its central role in the church, a tool used to usher in the kingdom of God.

Why is this baptismal font so extraordinary? It will never sit under the flying buttresses of a cathedral. It is unlikely its waters will ever be poured over the head of someone overly rich or famous. But, nestled into a neighborhood, it will be a welcoming doorway to the saints. Just as the Jordan was all those years ago.

Jesus' Baptism gives importance to this simple font. For when He entered the waters and came up again, He gave importance to every drop of water that would be used for that purpose. A congregation will celebrate Jesus' Baptism time and again as they baptize infants, children, and adults. The Spirit will reach down through the waters of that simple font just as it descended onto Jesus in the Jordan.

Through His Baptism, Jesus blesses simple things to be used as tools to convey His saving grace.

Lord Jesus, thank You for using the water in humble fonts to wash away our sins, give us Your Holy Spirit, and make us Your brothers and sisters. Amen.

THE TEMPTATION IN THE WILDERNESS

WEEK 8—LUKE 4:1–13

And Jesus, full of the Holy Spirit, returned from the Jordan and was led by the Spirit in the wilderness for forty days, being tempted by the devil. And He ate nothing during those days. And when they were ended, He was hungry. The devil said to Him, "If You are the Son of God, command this stone to become bread." And Jesus answered him, "It is written, 'Man shall not live by bread alone.'" And the devil took Him up and showed Him all the kingdoms of the world in a moment of time, and said to Him, "To You I will give all this authority and their glory, for it has been delivered to me, and I give it to whom I will. If You, then, will worship me, it will all be Yours." And Jesus answered him, "It is written,

> "'You shall worship the Lord your God,
>   and Him only shall you serve.'"

And he took Him to Jerusalem and set Him on the pinnacle of the temple and said to Him, "If You are the Son of God, throw Yourself down from here, for it is written,

> "'He will command His angels concerning You,
>   to guard You,'

and

> "'On their hands they will bear You up,
>   lest You strike Your foot against a stone.'"

And Jesus answered him, "It is said, 'You shall not put the Lord your God to the test.'" And when the devil had ended every temptation, he departed from Him until an opportune time.

FAMILIAR TEMPTATIONS, FAMILIAR GROUND

And Jesus . . . was led by the Spirit in the wilderness for forty days, being tempted by the devil. (LUKE 4:1–2)

The conflict between God and Satan has gone on since the day the angel disobeyed God and lost his place in heaven. When God created humanity, Satan won his first temptation contest with Adam and Eve in the Garden of Eden. Now he comes to trip Jesus up and derail God's plan of salvation.

The contrast between these temptations could hardly be more stark. Adam and Eve were well-fed in a lush garden paradise, but Jesus has been fasting for forty days and nights in a barren wilderness. Adam and Eve gave in after one temptation, but Jesus faithfully obeyed God through forty days of temptation.

But there were great similarities as well: Adam and Eve had only God's Word to stand on, and Jesus stood on that same Word alone. And maybe most important, the whole destiny of our human race rested in their hands alone. Adam and Eve's failure in Eden brought sin, suffering, death, and damnation to all their offspring who would follow after them. Had Jesus failed and fallen to Satan's temptation, our eternal doom would be sealed and our sin forever inescapable.

But this wilderness in which we find Jesus driven by the Holy Spirit is familiar. It is the same place through which God drove His people long ago when He was leading them from slavery in Egypt to the Promised Land. During those forty years, Satan tempted the people of God, and he tripped them up over and again. They griped because they were hungry. They didn't trust God to provide water for them. They grew tired of manna and wanted meat. They grew tired of wandering and wanted it all to be done.

Not so with Jesus. He willingly entered this wilderness after being baptized. He faced the test which we so often fail. He didn't go there as our example—though we can certainly learn from Him how to resist Satan with the Word of God. He went as our Champion, our Substitute, to perfectly obey for each time we yield to temptation and follow our evil desires instead of resisting them and honoring God instead.

Lord Jesus, thank You for resisting Satan's temptations for us all. Give me grace to stand firm when I am tempted. Amen.

INTENSE TEMPTATIONS

And He ate nothing during those days. And when they were ended, He was hungry. (LUKE 4:2)

Jesus was not just tempted at the end of His forty days in the wilderness; Luke tells us He was tempted the entire time. Satan hit Him from all sides, maybe enough to keep Jesus so focused that He didn't really notice how hungry He was becoming. But after forty days, Jesus felt His hunger strongly.

That's when Satan's last three temptations came. Just as with Eve, Satan started with a question to raise doubt. He had asked Eve, "Did God really say . . . ?" He insinuates to Jesus, "If You are the Son of God." There was a lot behind that statement. *"If You are the Son of God, then why did Your Father leave You out here to starve? Forty days—He has forgotten all about You. Fine Savior You will be if You die of hunger, forgotten and alone!"*

That temptation had worked with the children of Israel—time and again. They had felt abandoned, forgotten. But not Jesus. When Satan tempted Him to turn stones into bread, Jesus answered "It is written, 'Man shall not live by bread alone'" (Luke 4:4). He took this passage from Deuteronomy where Moses in his farewell sermon had reminded the children of Israel how God had faithfully cared for them all through those forty years in the wilderness. Jesus trusted His Father still and had no reason to doubt.

Good enough, but if Jesus leaned too far on trusting His Father, maybe Satan could get Him to fall the other direction. There was a challenging road ahead for Jesus—something Jesus knew much more clearly than Satan. Rejection, bitter betrayal,

denial, scorn, ridicule, and the brutality of humanity were all ahead of Him. "Bow down and worship me, and all these kingdoms are Yours—without the suffering, without the pain, without the needless heartache."

But Moses' words from Deuteronomy arose in Jesus' mind: "You shall worship the Lord your God, and Him only shall you serve" (Luke 4:8).

One final temptation remained. So Jesus trusted His Father oh, so much, eh? Would He be willing to prove it? Satan took Jesus to the highest point of the temple and told Him to throw Himself down. He even quoted a psalm promising God would send His angel so Jesus would not even touch His foot against a stone. It seemed the perfect trap. If Jesus refused to jump, it would look like He didn't really trust His Father after all.

But Jesus didn't have to prove Himself to Satan. He knew that God, His Father, knew how much He trusted Him. Jesus resisted again with the Word from Deuteronomy: "You shall not put the Lord your God to the test" (Luke 4:12).

Satan's time of temptation was through, for now. He would withdraw to await a more opportune time—a time when Jesus was fixed to a cross. When the Jewish chief priests and crowds of passersby would shout, "If You are the Son of God, come down from the cross!"

Lord Jesus, thank You for overcoming Satan's temptation with God's Word. Strengthen me when I am tempted. Amen.

A LIFE OF TEMPTATION AND OBEDIENCE

And when the devil had ended every temptation, he departed from Him until an opportune time. (LUKE 4:13)

Does it seem strange that Jesus' public ministry had only just begun with His Baptism, but then immediately the Spirit led Him away from the people of Israel, out into the wilderness, to fast and be tempted by Satan? Wouldn't that temptation have been better later on, after He had more time teaching and preaching?

The New Testament often refers to Jesus as the Second Adam. The first thing we read after the creation of Adam and Eve in Genesis 2 is their temptation and fall to the serpent in Genesis 3. Their temptation and fall took place right away, at the start of their work for God and His kingdom. It is fitting that Jesus should likewise begin His ministry, His work for the kingdom of God, by going to battle against Satan's temptation for them and for all of us, their offspring.

More than that, Jesus has come as their Substitute and their Savior. They were tempted, so He, too, must be tempted. They were filled with sin, so He must take that sin upon Himself and give them His righteousness, obedience, and perfect holiness.

Jesus' earthly mission is to destroy the works of Satan. And what are those works of Satan? Through his successful temptation, Satan had made Adam and Eve and all their descendants objects of wrath. Satan put creation under a curse by his temptation. The fallen angel turned sinners from God and locked them in the chains of sin, death, and separation. To destroy that work, Jesus came to provide Himself as our Substitute. In place of our sin and disobedience, Jesus offered His life of perfect obedience. From womb to tomb. He faithfully did all His Father commanded and resisted all of Satan's temptations. On the cross, He would offer God a life of complete and full obedience.

But even when Satan withdrew from Jesus, that didn't mean he never tried to tempt Him again. He kept tempting Jesus through the people and circumstances before Him. We will see Jesus face threats and persecution from the Pharisees and the Jewish leaders. His sanity will be questioned by His own family. Great crowds will try to crown Him as their king and deter Him from His mission to the cross. His disciples will encourage Him to turn from His path and avoid the shame of the cross. But Jesus will never fail, never stray, never slip. His perfect obedience clear to the cross and to death would seal Satan's destruction—and win our eternal salvation.

Lord Jesus, You faithfully walked the path of Your Father's will without ever straying. Your obedience and innocent suffering and death has won eternal life for all of us. Thank You for all eternity. Amen.

TEMPTATION THROUGHOUT SCRIPTURE

And Jesus, full of the Holy Spirit, returned from the Jordan and was led by the Spirit in the wilderness for forty days, being tempted by the devil. (LUKE 4:1–2)

In this week, when we consider the temptation and successful obedience of our Lord, Jesus Christ, it is fitting to look at other Bible passages to see what God's Word says about the temptations we face.

Genesis 3:1–7

We have already looked at Adam and Eve's fall when Satan successfully tempted Eve to disobey God, and both Adam and Eve eat the forbidden fruit in the Garden of Eden. This first temptation added two more enemies and their temptations: (1) the world of sinners who tempt us to disobey and follow our own wicked desires, and (2) our own sinful nature that makes evil look good and good look evil. These three enemies seek our eternal separation from God: the devil, the world, and our own sinful nature.

Job 1–2

In the first two chapters of Job, Satan joins the angels who stand before God. When God points out Job's great faith and godliness, Satan accuses Job of serving God only because of the wealth God gave him. When God gives him permission, Satan takes away all Job's wealth and kills all his children. Then Satan asks to ruin Job's health and God permits him. We can't understand why God permits suffering and temptation, but it is always to drive us away from self-confidence, to find our forgiveness, peace, and strength in God Himself alone.

1 Chronicles 21

God described King David as a man after His own heart (see 1 Samuel 13:14). Yet Satan successfully tempted David, inciting him to order a census of Israel's army, which displeased God and brought a plague upon Israel. Yet during that plague, God stopped the angel and accepted David's plea for forgiveness on the very site where his son Solomon would build the first temple.

1 Corinthians 10:13

The New Testament has many promises to make about temptation. Paul wrote to the Corinthians, "No temptation has overtaken you that is not common to man. God is faithful, and He will not let you be tempted beyond your ability, but with the temptation He will also provide the way of escape, that you may be able to endure it."

Hebrews 2:18

Finally, the letter to Hebrews assures us that Jesus is here to help us whenever we are tempted. "For because He Himself has suffered when tempted, He is able to help those who are being tempted." Also check out Hebrews 4:15: "For we do not have a high priest who is unable to sympathize with our weaknesses, but one who in every respect has been tempted as we are, yet without sin." Jesus not only overcame Satan's temptation for us, but He is present to help us in all our times of temptation.

Lord Jesus, Your perfect obedience has won pardon for all of my sins. Strengthen me to honor You with my obedience. Amen.

SATAN'S SUBTLE TEMPTATIONS

*The devil said to Him, "If You are
the Son of God. . . ."* (LUKE 4:3)

The idea of Jesus, the eternal Son of God, being tempted by an angel He once created seems strange and raises a number of questions:

How many temptations did Satan lay before Jesus?

From Matthew, we may get the impression that Satan only came to Jesus at the end of the forty days and offered three temptations. Luke makes clear in verse 2 that Satan was there through all forty days, tempting Jesus. The last three were just given to us for examples of the kinds of temptations Satan had brought to Him before.

What was Satan trying to accomplish with his repeated words "If You are the Son of God"?

When we sinners are challenged, we often get defensive and are more likely to think we must meet the challenge to prove we are who we say we are. This temptation failed with Jesus because He knew who He was and didn't need to prove it to Satan or anyone else.

What was the crux of the temptation of making the stone become bread?

Jesus was extremely hungry at the close of the forty days. Satan was implying that God had abandoned Jesus and He would die if He did not take matters into His own hands. Jesus quoted God's Word and promises, showing where His confidence lay.

What was Satan trying to accomplish when he showed Jesus all the kingdoms of the world?

He was offering Jesus a compromise. Satan would hand over the kingdoms he had taken from God if Jesus would bow down to him. Jesus repeated Moses' command to worship the Lord and serve Him only.

Why did Satan want Jesus to throw Himself down from the temple pinnacle?

This builds somewhat on the first temptation. Since Jesus did not doubt His Father's providence when He was hungry, the devil tried to goad Him to doing something reckless, like jumping off the temple to prove He really trusted in His Father. In fact, it was a pretty smart temptation: if Jesus did not jump, it might appear He didn't trust His Father—especially since Satan provided a psalm verse to back it up. But Jesus cut through to the heart when He quoted Moses again, "Do not put the Lord to the test."

What does Luke mean when he closes the reading with the words "When the devil had ended every temptation, he departed from Him until an opportune time"?

In the following days, months, and years, Satan would try many times to sidetrack or derail Jesus in His ministry. One such time is when Jesus first announces His coming death and Peter tries to deter Him. Another is when Jesus is hanging on the cross, and the Jewish leaders repeat Satan's words from these temptations: "If You are the Son of God, come down from the cross."

Lord Jesus, thank You for resisting Satan's temptations and saving all of us. Amen.

THE BATTLE RAGES ON

And when the devil had ended every temptation, he departed from Him until an opportune time. (LUKE 4:13)

Each of us faces temptations from Satan, the sinful world around us, and from the desires of our own sinful nature. Satan has thousands of years of experience tempting sinners, and he knows every vulnerability a person can have. We are surrounded by sinful people and a culture that preys on our doubts, insecurities, and loneliness, as well as celebrating wickedness. It celebrates sinful indulgence, mocking restraint and moral values. And deep inside, our own sinful natures torment us with desires that are so strong and attractive. By our own power and strength, we are helpless to stand against these enemies. Our minds are too easily clouded, and our sinful desires work against us.

But Jesus teaches us to use God's Word and prayer to combat Satan. Because of the power of God's Word and the Holy Spirit working through that Word, the prince of darkness cannot stand against the power of God in these gifts. Scripture promises us, "No temptation has overtaken you that is not common to man. God is faithful, and He will not let you be tempted beyond your ability, but with the temptation He will also provide the way of escape, that you may be able to endure it" (1 Corinthians 10:13). Through His Word, He gives us the proper perspective to perceive the lie and the spiritual danger in Satan's promises and helps us resist the temptations.

That is why God calls us to gather together in congregations to aid and assist one another, and to receive His strength for the fight. In worship, God empowers us for our fight against Satan.

Confession and Absolution assures us of His forgiveness for the temptations to which we have yielded before, and it assures us of God's mercy and help for the next time we fight. The reminder of our Baptism in Confession draws us to our Baptism, in which God continues to drown our old, sinful nature so the image of Christ can arise in us, and we can lead obedient, faithful lives. And in Holy Communion, God gives us the very body and blood of our Savior to help us stand firm and faithful.

Satan did not give up on tempting Jesus after these forty days were over. He waited for an opportune time and kept coming after our Lord until Jesus triumphantly proclaimed, "It is finished!" and gave up His spirit. We, too, will face temptations throughout our lives, even up to our death bed. But our God is faithful, and He will uphold us with His Word and Sacraments and His powerful Spirit. Use the Word of God and His wondrous gift of prayer to keep a constant vigil against the evil one.

Lord Jesus, empower me to resist Satan's temptations, and forgive me whenever I fall. Amen.

THE BEGINNING OF JESUS' GALILEAN MINISTRY

WEEK 9—MATTHEW 4:12–17

Now when [Jesus] heard that John had been arrested, He withdrew into Galilee. And leaving Nazareth He went and lived in Capernaum by the sea, in the territory of Zebulun and Naphtali, so that what was spoken by the prophet Isaiah might be fulfilled:

"The land of Zebulun and the land of Naphtali,
   the way of the sea, beyond the Jordan, Galilee of the Gentiles—
the people dwelling in darkness
   have seen a great light,
and for those dwelling in the region and shadow of death,
   on them a light has dawned."

From that time Jesus began to preach, saying, "Repent, for the kingdom of heaven is at hand."

GALILEE OF THE GENTILES

Now when [Jesus] heard that John had been arrested, He withdrew into Galilee. (MATTHEW 4:12)

John the Baptist had been gathering great crowds of people in the wilderness, preaching a singular message: "Repent, for the kingdom of heaven is at hand" (Matthew 3:2). People from Jerusalem, Judea, and the region around the Jordan River went out to hear John, confess their sins, and be baptized. Even Jesus went to be baptized by John before fasting in the wilderness for forty days and being unsuccessfully tempted by Satan.

The time was coming for Jesus to begin His public ministry and He was preparing. As He recovered from His wilderness fast, He heard the news that John had been arrested for speaking truthful, condemning words, calling adulterous Herod Antipas—ruler over Galilee and Perea and son of King Herod the Great—to repent. John's arrest signals that Jesus' time has come. The forerunner's course is run; he has prepared the way, gathered disciples, and pierced the hearts of the people. Now Jesus would continue where John left off, carrying on the same message, saying, "Repent, for the kingdom of heaven is at hand" (Matthew 4:17). Indeed, with Jesus' very presence, the kingdom of heaven is here.

Whereas people left their homes to hear John in the wilderness, Jesus left His home in Nazareth to travel to the people. He came to Capernaum by the sea, in the territory of Zebulun and Naphtali. And in doing so, Jesus fulfilled prophecy:

> But there will be no gloom for her who was in anguish. In the former time
> He brought into contempt the land of
> Zebulun and the land of Naphtali, but in the latter time He has made glorious the way of the sea, the land beyond the Jordan, Galilee of the nations. The people who walked in darkness have seen a great light; those who dwelt in a land of deep darkness, on them has light shone. (Isaiah 9:1–2)

Indeed, the lands of Zebulun and Naphtali had experienced great darkness. The Assyrians had overtaken them when they conquered the Northern Kingdom of Israel in 722 BC. These two tribes made up Israel's northern border: they were the first to fall victim to Assyria's dominion. But long before Assyria exiled them, these "lost tribes" of Israel had already fallen away from Yahweh and instead lived and worshiped like their pagan neighbors.

This is where Matthew records that Jesus, the Messiah, starts His public ministry: in Galilee of the Gentiles, home of unbelievers "dwelling in the region and shadow of death" (4:16). He comes to the unexpected and the unexpecting. Jesus would have His day with Jewish rulers and political leaders. But first, as John is arrested, Jesus comes to villagers—to workers, families, and the sick. To people who perhaps hadn't gone out to hear John. And Jesus brings the same message that He brings to all people, one of repentance and kingdom hope.

Lord Jesus, just as You left Your home to proclaim Good News to all people, come and make Your home with us today. Amen.

JESUS' FIRST WORDS

From that time Jesus began to preach, saying, "Repent, for the kingdom of heaven is at hand." (MATTHEW 4:17)

First words are important. Consider the first words you spoke (or heard) when you met your spouse or current employer. They set the tone and can often leave a lasting impression. Or consider the opening lines of a speech—if you don't capture your audience's attention from the start, you face an uphill battle. And in a book, the first words should engage your readers so they keep reading. First words matter.

So we're wise to pay attention to Matthew's first recorded words of Jesus as He starts His public ministry: "Repent, for the kingdom of heaven is at hand." Short and concise. No preambles, disclaimers, or apologies. Just the same message that John the Baptist had already been sharing. In these words, we hear both Law and Gospel proclaimed. With seemingly contrasting ideas, Jesus tells one complete story for our lives.

Repent—turn from your sins, the ways contrary to God's will, and seek forgiveness. Why? Because the kingdom of heaven is at hand; Jesus is here with all the good gifts He brings to those who follow Him. Turn from your ways to follow Jesus' ways. For Jesus' ways offer you grace, mercy, forgiveness, healing, and new life. "Repent, for the kingdom of heaven is at hand." Words of both Law and Gospel ready to meet each hearer's ear.

For the hardened heart, these words declare war because repentance requires surrender. In Greek, *repent* is a military word meaning "about-face." It is to go back, retreat, relinquish your current mission. The King of heaven will claim those who belong to Him. Those who wish to have no part in Him will have their wish fulfilled and experience the absence of the King's gifts. They'll know a place of bad news, captivity, blindness, and oppression (see Luke 4:18). A place without rescue because the King they rejected has come to reign.

But for the lost soul, Jesus' words point the way home. For the wearied heart, the words are a healing balm. For the hopelessly anxious, they're the reason to hold on. Jesus is here and He knows the way forward: "Repent, for the kingdom of heaven is at hand."

As the Holy Spirit works in our lives, we obediently take Jesus at His first words. And we act on them over and again because "if we say we have no sin, we deceive ourselves, and the truth is not in us. If we confess our sins, He is faithful and just to forgive us our sins and to cleanse us from all unrighteousness" (1 John 1:8–9). Each time we repent, we receive forgiveness and experience the kingdom of heaven at hand.

Lord Jesus, give us ears to hear and hearts to receive Your message of repentance so that we may experience the kingdom of heaven. Amen.

THE KINGDOM OF HEAVEN IS HERE

And leaving Nazareth He went and lived in Capernaum by the sea, in the territory of Zebulun and Naphtali, so that what was spoken by the prophet Isaiah might be fulfilled . . . "the people dwelling in darkness have seen a great light, and for those dwelling in the region and shadow of death, on them a light has dawned." (MATTHEW 4:13–14, 16)

Long ago, at many times and in many ways, God spoke to our fathers by the prophets, but in these last days He has spoken to us by His Son" (Hebrews 1:1–2). With Jesus' arrival on the scene, God's people no longer need signs and prophecies to foretell God's plan. Here, Jesus clearly reveals His mission as He declares the kingdom of heaven is at hand. The kingdom of heaven—with a reigning king—is something Israel's people had longed for, generation after generation. Matthew's primarily Jewish audience would recognize the significance of chapter 4, verses 15 to 16, which speak of Jesus fulfilling Isaiah's prophecy of the long-awaited Messiah: a king who would bring light to those living in darkness and comfort to those in the shadow of death.

Our ears should also perk up as we read about the "people dwelling in darkness who've seen a great light." These words come just four verses before a common Advent and Christmas reading: "For to us a child is born, to us a son is given; and the government shall be upon His shoulder, and His name shall be called Wonderful Counselor, Mighty God, Everlasting Father, Prince of Peace" (Isaiah 9:6). The Son of God's mission is in action: He takes on human flesh and is born a child, a son. "And

being found in human form, He humbled Himself by becoming obedient to the point of death, even death on a cross" (Philippians 2:8).

In His saving mission here on earth, our Savior is both mighty and peaceful, everlasting and mortal. And by His death and resurrection, "God has highly exalted Him and bestowed on Him the name that is above every name, so that at the name of Jesus every knee should bow, in heaven and on earth and under the earth, and every tongue confess that Jesus Christ is Lord, to the glory of God the Father" (Philippians 2:9–11). God will soon declare Christ's lordship over all, but for now, in Matthew 4, we get a first announcement of fulfilled prophecy, hope-filled words in action, a victorious king ushering in His unending kingdom through repentance and, ultimately, His own death.

For three years, Jesus will spend most of His time in this northern region of Galilee. He'll travel town to town, teaching in synagogues, streets, and on hillsides while accepting invitations to eat and sleep in people's homes. At least three times a year, Jesus will also go to Jerusalem in the southern region of Judea and teach in the temple courts. Jesus comes as a king for all people—and with a message all people need to hear. No matter where you live or what your family history holds, whether a learned scholar or blue-collar worker, Jesus comes to you. And now in these last days, He has spoken to us in His owns words: "Repent, for the kingdom of heaven is at hand."

Lord Jesus, thank You for coming with a mission to establish Your kingdom. We confess that You are Lord and King, to the glory of God the Father. Amen.

TIMES OF REFRESHING

Repent therefore, and turn back, that your sins may be blotted out, that times of refreshing may come from the presence of the Lord. (ACTS 3:19–20)

Even after Jesus' public death and documented resurrection, many Jewish people still did not believe that Jesus was the Christ, the one foretold by the prophets. They continued to live by the Torah's rules and rituals, going to the temple and relying on a priest to act as intercessor between them and God. Because if any unholy person approached the presence of the Lord in the temple, they would die. Yahweh demands holiness, just as He is holy, and the Jewish people were careful to follow suit—even marking the most holy place in the temple with a veil they wouldn't cross. The only time anyone went behind the curtain was on the Day of Atonement, when the high priest carried the blood of the lamb for the cleansing of the people's sins. "For it is the blood that makes atonement by the life" (Leviticus 17:11). "And without the shedding of blood there is no forgiveness of sins" (Hebrews 9:22).

Despite their unbelief, people were fascinated with Jesus' disciples—even after Jesus ascended into heaven—because they could perform miracles. Continuing the way of Jesus, the disciples traveled town to town, coming to the people, and God continued to meet hurting, broken people with His loving kindness.

In Acts 3, Peter and John heal a man who was born without the ability to walk. The people run to Peter and John in wonder and amazement, and Peter explains that Jesus gave them the power to heal the man. He goes on to accuse these Jewish people of killing Jesus, the author of life, the Messiah foretold by the prophets. And proclaiming the same message as John the Baptist and Jesus, Peter says, "Repent therefore, and turn back, that your sins may be blotted out, that times of refreshing may come from the presence of the Lord" (Acts 3:19–20).

No sin is beyond God's merciful hand of forgiveness, not even killing Jesus. And as long as you draw breath in this world, it is not too late to do an about-face and turn back to God when you hear the call to repent. For the kingdom of heaven is at hand, that is, times of refreshing from the presence of the Lord.

No longer must the Jewish people make sacrifices to make amends for their sin. No more should they fear being in the presence of the holy God. As they yelled, "Crucify!" Jesus' outstretched body and shed blood became the ultimate sacrifice, atoning for all their sins and the sins of the whole world. As Jesus breathed His last, the veil in the temple was torn, and the separation between God and man was no more. Now, because of Jesus, all people can approach the throne of God with confidence, receiving mercy and finding grace to help in time of need (see Hebrews 4:16).

So repent. The sacrifice has been made. Times of refreshing in God's presence are yours.

Lord Jesus, forgive me of all my sins and grant me times of refreshing that come in Your presence. Amen.

71

THE KINGDOM OF HEAVEN

The kingdom of heaven is at hand. (MATTHEW 4:17)

This passage is focused on the kingdom of heaven—it's the good news at the heart of the reading. The reason we go through the uncomfortable work of repentance is for the reward of the kingdom. In fact, Matthew uses the phrase "kingdom of heaven" or "reign of heaven" thirty-two times throughout his Gospel—and he's the only New Testament author to do so (although others use "kingdom/reign of God"). So what is the kingdom of heaven anyway? And what does it mean that the kingdom of heaven is at hand?

The kingdom of heaven is characterized by the salvific work of Jesus. And it is precious. Jesus describes the kingdom of heaven throughout Matthew's Gospel through various parables (see Matthew 13, for example). The kingdom of heaven is like a mustard seed—though smallest among the seeds, it grows to be a very large tree that provides shade and shelter. The kingdom of heaven is like a little bit of leaven that is worked into flour and makes the whole dough rise. And again, the kingdom of heaven is like treasure hidden in a field or fine pearls, worth all of a man's fortune to buy. Or it's like a net thrown into the sea that gathers all kinds of fish and the fisherman sorts the good from the bad—just like a farmer sorts the weeds from the crop at the harvest.

The kingdom of heaven might start small, like a little ounce of faith, but its very presence changes the outcome of the story. It's worth sacrificing everything for! And it's at the very end that the kingdom's value is fully revealed.

As Jesus speaks of the kingdom of heaven, we experience the now and not-yet reality of our life in Him. With Jesus' very presence on earth, He ushers in the Kingdom. The Kingdom is here because Jesus is here, and the kingdom of heaven is about Christ's reign. And yet the kingdom of heaven is not fully realized until the Last Day—when Christ returns to make all things new. It's a reality we can hold onto now while also being a promise we cling to for the days ahead. And while we wait for the Kingdom to be fully realized, we can be confident that the kingdom work is already happening because Jesus has already come, bringing repentance and restoring us to new life in Him.

Yes, the kingdom of heaven is about the salvific work of Jesus. It comes in big ways and small ways. But in every way, it brings forgiveness, healing, peace, restoration, and times of refreshment. When we experience this new creation-reality, we're experiencing the kingdom of heaven now—and getting a foretaste of what is to come.

Lord Jesus, expand the kingdom of heaven within me in big and small ways, that I may yearn all the more for Your reign to fully come. Amen.

CONFESSION AND ABSOLUTION, PUBLIC AND PRIVATE

From that time Jesus began to preach, saying, "Repent, for the kingdom of heaven is at hand." (MATTHEW 4:17)

Repent. This word has been central to this week's reading. As is true in the time of John the Baptist and Jesus, repentance is also our right response to the Spirit's convicting work in our life. We confess our wrongdoing, receive God's forgiveness in Jesus, and live in the kingdom of heaven—a kingdom that abides by God's ways in service to Him and love to our neighbors. Confession and absolution, repentance and forgiveness. This is the ongoing rhythm of the life of the Christian. It's also the ongoing rhythm of the church.

Each time we gather for worship, we have the opportunity to once again answer Jesus' call to repent, for the kingdom of heaven is at hand. As we confess our sins and hear the pastor absolve us, we soak in Christ's forgiveness for us and the new life that is ours. But too often, church is the only place we practice repentance. While there is rich beauty and healing in corporate confession, there is also great freedom and nourishment that comes from individual confession, whether repenting to the person we've offended or privately to a pastor. It can be humbling and uncomfortable to approach this person with our remorse, but there is healing power and shared humanity in looking another person in the eye—as Peter and John do for the lame man in our Acts 3 reading—and really seeing the other person. The confessor's eyes are filled with regret, sorrow, and pain for their sin, but their trusted absolver has eyes of compassion, care, and knowing humility. Forgiveness brings times of refreshment in God's presence, both for the confessor and the absolver. It's one of the Lord's sweet gifts to us. Are we taking advantage of and using this gift?

While no fancy words are needed, sometimes having a form to follow can be helpful, especially when we practice individual confession and absolution for the first time. *Luther's Small Catechism with Explanation* has one such example to follow and ends with this life-giving prayer: "Lord Jesus Christ, I give You thanks that my sins are forgiven before Your Father in heaven. By the Holy Spirit, give me grace to trust in Your promises and so live in the freedom and peace that You have won for me in Your death and resurrection. Amen" (p. 313).

Imagine how a relationship could change when sins are confessed and forgiveness is given. Imagine the impact on families who practice both parents and children giving and receiving forgiveness from each other. And imagine how the Body of Christ would be shaped if more of us engaged in individual—perhaps mutual—confession and absolution. Times of refreshment in the presence of the Lord would multiply as we usher in more of the kingdom of heaven among us.

Lord Jesus, give me humility and the opportunity to seek forgiveness from someone I've offended. Amen.

CALLING OF THE TWELVE

WEEK 10—LUKE 5:1–11, 27–32

On one occasion, while the crowd was pressing in on Him to hear the word of God, He was standing by the lake of Gennesaret, and He saw two boats by the lake, but the fishermen had gone out of them and were washing their nets. Getting into one of the boats, which was Simon's, He asked him to put out a little from the land. And He sat down and taught the people from the boat. And when He had finished speaking, He said to Simon, "Put out into the deep and let down your nets for a catch." And Simon answered, "Master, we toiled all night and took nothing! But at Your word I will let down the nets." And when they had done this, they enclosed a large number of fish, and their nets were breaking. They signaled to their partners in the other boat to come and help them. And they came and filled both the boats, so that they began to sink. But when Simon Peter saw it, he fell down at Jesus' knees, saying, "Depart from me, for I am a sinful man, O Lord." For he and all who were with him were astonished at the catch of fish that they had taken, and so also were James and John, sons of Zebedee, who were partners with Simon. And Jesus said to Simon, "Do not be afraid; from now on you will be catching men." And when they had brought their boats to land, they left everything and followed Him. . . .

After this He went out and saw a tax collector named Levi, sitting at the tax booth. And He said to him, "Follow Me." And leaving everything, he rose and followed Him.

And Levi made Him a great feast in his house, and there was a large company of tax collectors and others reclining at table with them. And the Pharisees and their scribes grumbled at His disciples, saying, "Why do You eat and drink with tax collectors and sinners?" And Jesus answered them, "Those who are well have no need of a physician, but those who are sick. I have not come to call the righteous but sinners to repentance." . . .

The next day again John was standing with two of his disciples, and he looked at Jesus as He walked by and said, "Behold, the Lamb of God!" The two disciples heard him say this, and they followed Jesus. Jesus turned and saw them following and said to them, "What are you seeking?" And they said to Him, "Rabbi" (which means Teacher), "where are You staying?" He said to them, "Come and you will see." So they came and saw where He was staying, and they stayed with Him that day, for it was about the tenth hour. One of the two who heard John speak and followed Jesus was Andrew, Simon Peter's brother. He first found his own brother Simon and said to him, "We have found the Messiah" (which means Christ). He brought him to Jesus. Jesus looked at him and said, "You are Simon the son of John. You shall be called Cephas" (which means Peter).

JESUS CHOOSES TWELVE DISCIPLES

After this He went out and saw a tax collector named Levi, sitting at the tax booth. And He said to him, "Follow Me." And leaving everything, he rose and followed Him. (LUKE 5:27–28)

The historical context of Jesus' selection of the twelve apostles is of great significance and relevance. The biblical account of Jesus choosing these men to be His closest companions and representatives is a profound event in the history of Christianity, and it holds great theological significance for our understanding of the church and our faith.

The context surrounding Jesus' ministry during this period was one of great religious and political upheaval in Israel. The Jewish people had spent centuries after their return from Babylon being dominated by the Persians and the Greeks, who sometimes oppressed them and tried to force them to reject God's ways. Now they were under the rule of the Roman Empire and were deeply longing and intently looking for a savior to free them from their oppression. Many religious leaders and groups vied for the people's attention and loyalty, including the Pharisees and the Sadducees.

In this environment, Jesus began His ministry, preaching the Good News of the kingdom of God, performing miracles, and teaching with authority. He quickly gained a large following, including many who were frustrated with the religious leaders of their time and looking for something different. As Jesus' popularity grew, He also attracted the attention of the religious and political leaders who saw Him as a threat to their power.

Jesus chose twelve men to be His apostles out of this extensive group of followers. These men would be the eyewitnesses to His ministry, death, and resurrection, and their testimony would be the foundation on which He would build His church and inspire the writing of the New Testament of the Bible. Jesus did not choose them because they were wise or exceptionally gifted; Jesus chose a large number of fishermen, a tax collector despised by the people, and a zealot who favored the forced overthrow of Rome. He even chose a man from Judea who would be a thief and eventually betray Him, Judas Iscariot.

These men lived with Jesus for three years, traveling with Him, eating and drinking with Him. They went on missionary journeys in groups of two and received private instruction from Jesus. They were present at the Last Supper. Through the testimony of these men, we have the privilege of hearing Jesus' most important words and teachings.

Lord, thank You for reminding us that the church is not a human institution but a divine one based on Your grace, mercy, and calling. Thank You that the message of salvation through faith in Jesus Christ is for all people, regardless of their background or circumstances. Thank You for calling me. Amen.

A PERSONAL CALLING

Nathanael said to Him, "How do You know me?" Jesus answered him, "Before Philip called you, when you were under the fig tree, I saw you." (JOHN 1:48)

The main overall message of Luke 5:1–11, 27–32 and John 1:35–51 is about the call to repentance and faith in Jesus Christ as the Son of God. In Luke 5, the calling of the first disciples—Simon Peter, James, and John—to become fishers of men highlights the importance of sharing the message of salvation through Jesus with others. Similarly, in Luke 5:27-32, the story of the calling of Matthew, a tax collector, emphasizes the grace and forgiveness of God offered to all, regardless of their past sins. In John 1:35–51, the testimony of John the Baptist and the calling of the first disciples by Jesus emphasizes the belief in Jesus as the promised Messiah and the Son of God—and the importance of confessing faith in Him as the only way to salvation. Overall, these passages remind all people of the call to repentance and faith in Jesus, as well as the call to share this message with others.

The message of these three passages is also a personal calling to faith in Jesus Christ. Through these readings, we see how Jesus personally calls each of His apostles, including Simon Peter, Andrew, Philip, Nathanael, James, John, and Levi (also known as Matthew).

One of the key themes in these passages is the idea of personal calling. Jesus calls each apostle in a unique and personal way, whether through the testimony of John the Baptist, an encounter on the streets, or a miraculous catch of fish. This personal calling serves as a reminder that each of us has a unique role in the church and God's plan for salvation.

Another critical theme is faith in Jesus Christ. These passages show how the apostles come to believe in Jesus as the Son of God and the Messiah. Nathanael, for example, is initially skeptical of Jesus, but his faith is solidified through a powerful encounter with Jesus in which Jesus reveals something Nathanael had done in private. This serves as a reminder that true faith in Jesus Christ is not based on human wisdom or understanding but on the work of the Holy Spirit in our hearts.

Furthermore, the example of Peter's confession of Jesus as Lord and his recognition of his own sinfulness highlights the importance of repentance and humility in our faith. Peter, a fisherman, initially begged Jesus to depart from him as he recognized his own unworthiness. This serves as a reminder that true faith in Jesus involves acknowledging our own sinfulness and turning to Him in repentance.

Thank You, Lord, for Your personal calling and for giving us faith in Jesus Christ through Your means of grace. Thank You for reminding us that each of us has a unique role to play in the church and Your plan for salvation. Please help us to remember the importance of repentance, humility, and the work of the Holy Spirit in our faith journey. Help us to respond to Jesus' call in our lives, believe in Him, and follow Him as His disciples. Amen.

MORE THAN A RANSOM PAYMENT

Getting into one of the boats, which was Simon's, He asked him to put out a little from the land. And He sat down and taught the people from the boat. (LUKE 5:3)

The accounts in Luke 5 and John 1 that we study this week serve as powerful reminders of Jesus' mission and the nature of His calling. Through the calling of Simon Peter, James, John, Levi, Nathanael, and the other disciples, we see that Jesus was not simply sent to pay the ransom for our sins through His death on the cross. Instead, He was also sent to be a prophet and teacher, sharing the Good News of salvation through faith in Him and training His disciples to continue His mission. These passages remind us that faith comes from hearing the Gospel and that Jesus' calling and training of the Twelve was essential for the establishment of the New Testament church.

In Luke 5:1–11, we see Jesus calling Simon Peter, James, and John to be His disciples. These fishermen were going about their everyday work when Jesus came to them and said, "Put out into deep water and let down the nets for a catch." Despite their initial reluctance, they trusted Jesus and caught abundant fish. This miraculous catch provided for their physical needs and served as a sign of the spiritual abundance that would come through the power of Jesus' Word, which they would preach.

In Luke 5:27–32, we see Jesus reaching out to Levi, a tax collector, and inviting Levi to follow Him. This was a bold move because the Jewish people despised tax collectors for their association with their Roman occupiers. Yet Jesus saw Levi and called him to repentance and new life. This Levi is Matthew, who wrote the first Gospel to the very Jewish people who had previously despised him.

John 1:35–51 tells the story of Jesus calling His first disciples, including Nathanael, who initially had doubts about Jesus because of His hometown. But when Jesus revealed His knowledge of Nathanael's whereabouts, he exclaimed, "Rabbi, You are the Son of God! You are the King of Israel!" (v. 49). Nathanael's faith in Jesus was rooted in the revelation of who Jesus was: the Messiah, the Son of God.

All of these accounts demonstrate that Jesus was not only sent to pay the ransom for our sins but also to be a prophet and teacher to the Jews. He came to share the Good News of salvation through faith in Him and to train His disciples to continue His mission. Jesus reached out to individuals, not just nameless faces in a crowd, and called them to faith and repentance. This is important to remember as we think about Jesus' calling and mission and consider our own roles as unique and precious children of God.

Dear Lord Jesus, we thank You for calling us to faith individually and for Your mission to bring salvation to the world. We also ask for Your guidance and wisdom in our roles as children of God so that we may always devote ourselves to sharing what the apostles have given us, as You have taught us. We pray for the strength to follow You wholeheartedly and for the courage to reach out to those around us with the Good News of the Gospel. Amen.

PASSING DOWN THE FAITH

And Jesus said to Simon, "Do not be afraid; from now on you will be catching men." (LUKE 5:10)

I find great comfort in the understanding that throughout Scripture, God has called prophets and apostles to make disciples and continue His mission. This passing down of faith from generation to generation and the task of leading the church is a vital part of our faith and heritage.

The Old Testament is full of examples of God calling prophets to lead His people. Moses, for example, was called by God to lead the Israelites out of Egypt and into the Promised Land, and Moses had an aide named Joshua who led Israel's next generation there. God also called Isaiah, Jeremiah, and Ezekiel to be His prophets, each with a unique message for the people of their time. These prophets were not just called to speak God's Word but also to train and mentor others in the ways of God.

In Luke 5:1–11, we see Jesus calling Simon Peter, James, and John to be His disciples, and they leave their fishing boats to follow Him. In Luke 5:27–32, Jesus reaches out to Levi, a tax collector, and invites him to follow Him. This shows us that Jesus calls all types of people, regardless of their background or profession, to be His disciples and to continue His mission.

In John 1:35–51, Jesus calls His first disciples, including Nathanael, and reveals to them who He truly is: the Messiah, the Son of God. Jesus calls and trains the twelve apostles, who would later become the leaders of the early church. These apostles were tasked with spreading the Good News of salvation through faith in Jesus and continuing His mission of bringing salvation to the world. This shows us that being a disciple of Jesus involves not only following Him but also sharing His message with others.

This tradition of calling and training disciples continued throughout the early church. Paul, for example, was called by Jesus to be an apostle to the Gentiles, and he spent his life training and mentoring others such as Timothy and Titus in the ways of God. This shows us that being a disciple of Jesus involves not only following Him but also mentoring others in their faith.

As we reflect on these biblical examples, we are reminded of the importance of passing down our faith from generation to generation and of the role we play in continuing Jesus' mission. We are called to be His disciples and to reach out to others with the Good News of the Gospel. We are called to train and mentor others in the ways of God, just as the prophets, apostles, and early church leaders did before us.

Dear Lord Jesus, we thank You for calling us to be Your disciples and for entrusting us with the task of continuing Your mission. We pray for wisdom and guidance as we strive to share Your message with others and to train and mentor others in the ways of God. Give us the courage to follow You wholeheartedly and the strength to carry out Your mission in our generation. Amen.

TRUSTING JESUS AT HIS WORD

And when He had finished speaking, He said to Simon, "Put out into the deep and let down your nets for a catch." (LUKE 5:4)

Peter, James, and John had spent a long and fruitless night fishing, only to be met with the command of Jesus to cast their nets once again. Despite their doubts and fears, they obeyed—and were blessed with a catch so great that their nets began to break and their boats started to sink. Luke 5 provides a rich biblical, historical context for the significance of fishing at night and its connection to the work of God's kingdom, trust, and provision.

But why were they so hesitant to lower their nets again?

During Jesus' time, the fisherman would fish at night for several reasons. First, fish were known to be more active and plentiful at night, making it a more productive time for fishing. Second, in that day, the nets were made of linen, easily spotted by fish in the clear waters during daylight. In the darkness of night, they would be invisible to the fish. The darkness provided cover for the fisherman to cast their nets without being seen by the fish, making it more likely for them to catch a bountiful harvest. Third, the temperature of the water would be cooler at night, making it more comfortable for the fish to come closer to the surface, increasing the chances of catching them. Fourth, in some areas, the fisherman would use the stars to navigate and locate the fish.

Fishing at night was a practical decision for fishermen to catch more fish and make a living, but in this story, it takes on a deeper significance as a symbol of the work of God's kingdom. The darkness provides cover for the fisherman, just as the darkness of sin can cover us. But through the light and guidance of Jesus, we can see and receive the blessings that God has in store for us.

Just as the fishermen, we, too, may feel lost and alone in the darkness of sin and despair. But just as they were able to catch a great haul of fish with the guidance of Jesus, we, too, can find hope and salvation through Him. Through the fishermen's actions, we see a reflection of our own struggles and difficulties in life.

We also see in this story the importance of trust. The disciples, despite their doubts and fears, trusted Jesus and were blessed with a great catch. In the same way, we are called to trust in Jesus, even when it may seem frustrating, difficult, or impossible. The Holy Spirit will do the work of bringing sinners to faith, and it is our job to share the Good News with others.

Heavenly Father, we give You thanks for the example of the fishermen in the Gospel of Luke. We ask that You guide us in our own struggles and difficulties, that we may trust in You as the fishermen did in Jesus. We confess our sins and ask for Your forgiveness, through Jesus Christ our Lord. Amen.

THE CALL TO FOLLOW JESUS

They said to him, "Rabbi" (which means Teacher), "where are You staying?" He said to them, "Come and you will see." (JOHN 1:38-39)

As we read in the Gospels of Luke and John, Jesus begins to gather His twelve disciples. These Bible passages are fitting for the Epiphany season, where we focus on Jesus revealing His identity as the Son of God and the promised Savior. The Epiphany season reminds us that Jesus is not just a figure from the history pages two thousand years ago but that He is present in our lives today. In fact, all of these readings can be heard as the Gospel reading during the Sundays of Epiphany.

As we have been studying in Luke 5:1–11, Jesus calls Simon, James, and John to leave their fishing business and follow Him. They leave everything behind and become His disciples, the foundation of His church. Similarly, in John 1:35–51, Jesus calls Philip and Nathanael, who were likely working in other professions, to become His disciples. These men were not just followers but chosen by Jesus to be His apostles—to be the foundation of His church—and through whose writings we have the New Testament and know about Jesus. Through them, He comes to us today and speaks to every part of our lives and experiences.

This call to follow Jesus is not just for the first disciples but for each one of us as well. Jesus calls us to leave behind our own pursuits and follow Him, sharing His salvation with our family, friends, acquaintances, and coworkers. He calls us to be His disciples, His followers, and to be a part of His church.

As we are gathered during our weekly worship, we are reminded, through the church's seasons and the liturgical calendar, of the call to follow Jesus and share His message of salvation with those around us. This call to repentance and faith applies to our daily lives today—we are called to show the love of Christ to those in our families, communities, and workplaces. As we strive to live out our faith in our daily lives, we are reminded that Jesus is with us, encouraging us and guiding us on our journey.

Jesus is the only way to salvation, and through His death and resurrection, we have the opportunity to have our sins forgiven and gain eternal life. This call to follow Jesus is a call to salvation. It is a call to repentance and faith. It is a call to be baptized into the death and resurrection of Jesus Christ, to be united with Him and to receive the gift of the Holy Spirit.

Dear Lord Jesus, thank You for calling us to be Your disciples. Help us to have the courage to leave behind our own pursuits and follow You, sharing Your salvation with those around us. Give us the strength and guidance we need to be Your witnesses in the world. Amen.

THE SERMON ON THE MOUNT, PART 1

Beatitudes, and Salt and Light

WEEK 11—MATTHEW 5:1–16

Seeing the crowds, He went up on the mountain, and when He sat down, His disciples came to Him.

And He opened His mouth and taught them, saying:

"Blessed are the poor in spirit, for theirs is the kingdom of heaven.

"Blessed are those who mourn, for they shall be comforted.

"Blessed are the meek, for they shall inherit the earth.

"Blessed are those who hunger and thirst for righteousness, for they shall be satisfied.

"Blessed are the merciful, for they shall receive mercy.

"Blessed are the pure in heart, for they shall see God.

"Blessed are the peacemakers, for they shall be called sons of God.

"Blessed are those who are persecuted for righteousness' sake, for theirs is the kingdom of heaven.

"Blessed are you when others revile you and persecute you and utter all kinds of evil against you falsely on My account. Rejoice and be glad, for your reward is great in heaven, for so they persecuted the prophets who were before you.

"You are the salt of the earth, but if salt has lost its taste, how shall its saltiness be restored? It is no longer good for anything except to be thrown out and trampled under people's feet.

"You are the light of the world. A city set on a hill cannot be hidden. Nor do people light a lamp and put it under a basket, but on a stand, and it gives light to all in the house. In the same way, let your light shine before others, so that they may see your good works and give glory to your Father who is in heaven."

THE CROWDS GATHER

Seeing the crowds, He went up on the mountain, and when He sat down, His disciples came to Him. And He opened His mouth and taught them. (MATTHEW 5:1–2)

By the time of this passage, Jesus has spent several months in ministry. Crowds have already begun to form around Him. Wherever He goes, people congregate to hear the teachings of this new rabbi. In the ancient Near East, the rabbinical system was in full effect: young Jewish boys would memorize Scripture, grow in their knowledge of the law, and if they were the best at that, then they would have the chance to follow their rabbi as he taught around the countryside. Those young men who did not make the cut often took up the family trade.

Yet, as we see in previous chapters, Jesus was calling disciples from among these working men. He would even call a tax collector! But Jesus was not a simple rabbi. He was the Messiah, come to usher in the kingdom of God. Not only would the way in which that ministry happened be different, calling the disciples He did, but so, too, would be His teaching.

For generations the people of God (the Jewish nation) had lived in the Promised Land. They had conquered and been conquered. They had experienced times of plenty, and they had experienced seasons of scarcity. At the time of Jesus, under Roman rule, they looked for the promised Messiah to be a ruler who would free them from their subjugation and usher in an Israelite Empire that had not been seen since the days of David and Solomon.

When Jesus came on the scene, there seemed to be some hope that this might finally be that king, arrived in glory. The crowds gathered because of how He spoke to them, and they could sense the power and authority He carried. Just as He called disciples in a new way, so, too, would He teach them the true ways of His kingdom.

Instead of simply teaching and arguing the laws, Jesus spoke to their fulfillment. His teaching would not look solely to obedience for obedience's sake, but instead, He began teaching those who gathered around Him the ways of the kingdom of God.

Thus it was when Jesus climbed the mount to give His sermon. Instead of declaring how God would wipe away the Romans or how He would achieve power, He said things like "Blessed are the poor in spirit, for theirs is the kingdom of heaven" (Matthew 5:3) and "Blessed are the peacemakers, for they shall be called sons of God" (Matthew 5:9). For generations, the people had been waiting to hear from a person who would kick out their invaders. Instead, they heard how they would become salt and light to the world.

The Sermon on the Mount still holds difficult and joyous truth for us today. However, it can be easy to see the whole biblical narrative and forget what it might have sounded like to those original hearers in their day. Jesus had come, and He was gathering crowds, but He subverted the ideas of what not only a rabbi but what the Messiah might and would be.

Lord, open my ears and my mind to hear and understand Your teaching. Amen.

CONVENTIONAL WISDOM TURNED ON ITS HEAD

Blessed are the poor in spirit, for theirs is the kingdom of heaven. (MATTHEW 5:3)

Take a moment and re-read through the Scripture for this week. Notice that as Jesus teaches, He promises eight blessings to Christians in Matthew 5:1–11. Here they are:

"Blessed are the poor in spirit, for theirs is the kingdom of heaven.

"Blessed are those who mourn, for they shall be comforted.

"Blessed are the meek, for they shall inherit the earth.

"Blessed are those who hunger and thirst for righteousness, for they shall be satisfied."

"Blessed are the merciful, for they shall receive mercy."

"Blessed are the pure in heart, for they shall see God.

"Blessed are the peacemakers, for they shall be called sons of God.

"Blessed are those who are persecuted for righteousness' sake, for theirs is the kingdom of heaven. Blessed are you when others revile you and persecute you and utter all kinds of evil against you falsely on My account."

Each promise seems to turn conventional wisdom on its head. Why would anyone want to be poor in spirit? mourning? meek or merciful? Yet Jesus takes these and promises blessings to those who live in such a way. In Christian history, these have been known as the Beatitudes. Named for the Latin reading of these verses, *beati sunt* translates to "blessed are." These teachings of Jesus form a foundation of promise given to those who would be part of the kingdom of God. Some of these promises are states that the Christian should strive for: to be meek, to be hungry and thirsty for righteousness, to be pure in heart, and to be merciful peacemakers. Others are thrust upon them by the world in which they live, such as mourning and persecution. But in all these things, Jesus promises that there will be blessing instead of curses.

After sharing the blessing that will come to those who follow Him in the Kingdom, Jesus describes what His followers will be: salt and light. Those who experience or seek the actions of the Beatitudes will share the blessings they receive with those around them. Their lives will season the world around them, adding a taste of the kingdom of God to their friends, family, and neighbors. Also, they will be light into the world. As the moon reflects the sun, so, too, the life of the Christian blessed by Jesus will shine the light of the King to those around them.

Jesus turns seeming burdens into blessings. The ways of the kingdom of God are not the ways of the world. The Beatitudes also offer a barometer for followers of Jesus. Are we seeking the ways in which God has told us His blessings will come? Have pride and a haughty spirit taken control? Return to the promises of Jesus. This work of sanctification is a central piece of the life of a Christian, from cradle to grave. When feeling far from the blessing of God or cut off from connection to Him, often we can identify where we have strayed from His ways. Here, these verses show the ways of the Savior in which we Christians should strive to live each day, seeking to be blessed so that we may be salt and light to all those around us.

Lord Jesus, thank You for this wisdom. Give me a repentant heart with true reverence and a delight to be part of Your wondrous kingdom. Amen.

USING OUR GIFTS TO GOD'S GLORY

Blessed are the meek, for they shall inherit the earth. (MATTHEW 5:5)

Have you ever experienced false humility? Imagine this scenario: You have a project that must get done (for work, school, around the house, or whatever best fits your life). Now this project falls into a giftedness set that you have. You not only enjoy the work on the project, but you can sense that it is in your wheelhouse. Once it is complete, someone comes along, sees your hard work and the talent you have for it, and says, "Wow! This is so impressive!" How do you respond? You might want to avoid pride, so you brush it off as not that big a deal. Or maybe you speak to how anyone could do it—you're not *that* special. If you really want to get spiritual about it you say, "You know, the Lord is good."

It is good to avoid selfish pride—it can lead to many issues. But false humility is not the solution; it is the rut on the other side of the road. It denies the giftedness you have been given. Instead of a look-at-me! type of pride, you now are living in a woe-is-me type of pity. As a poor miserable sinner, nothing you touch can produce something good, so deflect, deflect, deflect.

Look at what Jesus does in the Beatitudes. He puts forth actions the believer should take and then promises blessing for those things. It is a direct correlation between them. Those with poor spirits are promised the kingdom of heaven. The meek are blessed with inheriting the earth. The merciful shall receive mercy, and so on it goes. Jesus promises blessing for the actions of the Christian as they follow Him in their earthly life. Not only that, but this blessing not only produces gifts for the believer but it empowers them to be salt and light to the world. These blessings are invitations to spread it around and be a part of God's work here on earth!

Followers of Jesus could quickly trip themselves up by trying to justify their blessing with a type of false humility. "Oh, me, blessed? Sure, I guess. But really the greatest blessing I could ever receive is what I have in my Baptism, so it's not really a big deal." Those words are technically true. The greatest gift Jesus gives is salvation and eternal life. However, look at what James says: "Every good gift and every perfect gift is from above, coming down from the Father of lights, with whom there is no variation or shadow due to change" (James 1:17).

God loves giving His children gifts! Jesus' earthly mission is to defeat sin, death, and the devil. He does that through His work on the cross and the empty tomb. Too often it is easy to think that the greatest gift is the only gift. Yet Jesus' mission doesn't end there. He wants to bless His people. He shows them that—through His blessings—they no longer only experience His kingdom but they can share the kingdom of God with others! And what about those days when the actions don't match up? The Christian returns, poor in spirit, with repentance to the Savior for forgiveness—and blessings of the Kingdom quickly follow.

Jesus, my Savior, guard me from pride and false humility. Instead, let me thankfully share the gifts and abilities You have given me to glorify Your holy name. Amen.

NOT-SO-RADICAL TEACHINGS

You are the salt of the earth. (MATTHEW 5:13)

Jesus has a knack for presenting Scripture in a new light—or, better to say, their original form, which only appears to be new because it has been so lost by the time He is teaching. Looking at this section of Scripture, we once again find that to be true.

The Beatitudes hinge on the idea of being lowly in spirit. This seems to be a foundational promise that can be seen in being merciful, meek, pure in heart, and in peacemaking. Here Jesus reminds the crowds of the words of the prophet Isaiah.

Isaiah 57:15

"For thus says the One who is high and lifted up, who inhabits eternity, whose name is Holy: 'I dwell in the high and holy place, and also with him who is of a contrite and lowly spirit, to revive the spirit of the lowly, and to revive the heart of the contrite.'"

Isaiah 61:1

"The Spirit of the Lord GOD is upon Me, because the LORD has anointed Me to bring good news to the poor; He has sent Me to bind up the brokenhearted, to proclaim liberty to the captives, and the opening of the prison to those who are bound."

Isaiah 66:2

"All these things My hand has made, and so all these things came to be, declares the LORD. But this is the one to whom I will look: he who is humble and contrite in spirit and trembles at My word."

These words would then be taken up by the saints who wrote the Epistles. Deeply rooted in the life of the Christian should be these ways of the Beatitudes, that they keep showing up even after Jesus has ascended.

Acts 5:41

"Then they left the presence of the council, rejoicing that they were counted worthy to suffer dishonor for the name."

2 Corinthians 7:10

"For godly grief produces a repentance that leads to salvation without regret, whereas worldly grief produces death."

1 Peter 1:22

"Having purified your souls by your obedience to the truth for a sincere brotherly love, love one another earnestly from a pure heart."

James 4:9–10

"Be wretched and mourn and weep. Let your laughter be turned to mourning and your joy to gloom. Humble yourselves before the Lord, and He will exalt you."

Revelation 21:4

"He will wipe away every tear from their eyes, and death shall be no more, neither shall there be mourning, nor crying, nor pain anymore, for the former things have passed away."

The Beatitudes should not be a surprise to any, yet they often appear as radical teachings of Jesus. Throughout Scripture, both Old Testament and New, these ideas play a part in the sanctification of God's people. Jesus is declaring them unto His disciples so that they would return to these words, that they would be blessed. Teachings found here only feel radical because they are so counter to the sinful heart, which is convinced that the blessing comes instead from pride, vain desire, and self-satisfaction.

Lord Jesus, thank You for faithfully proclaiming and teaching the truths of Your kingdom. Give me grace to remain in that kingdom and teaching forever. Amen.

WHAT DOES IT MEAN TO BE BLESSED?

And [Jesus] opened His mouth and taught them, saying: "Blessed are...." (MATTHEW 5:2–3)

Take a moment to ponder this question: What does it mean to be blessed? In the margin of this devotion, in a journal, on a scrap piece of paper, or on your phone, write down your answer. Try not to think too hard. In your life, what does it mean to be blessed? Fight the urge to write the "Sunday School" answer. In a moment this devotion will discuss that.

What was your answer? Did it deal with monetary wealth? Having your needs met or perhaps a bounty of relationships with family and friends? Being blessed is a subjective ideal. It may mean something different to each person. Some wish to have their financial needs cared for during their lifetime. Others may seek blessing through people or fulfillment in work. All of these things are, in fact, blessings! Everything we have and will receive is a gift from God. It is good to recognize those things as blessings.

Jesus declares specific blessings for specific things in the Beatitudes. Read Matthew 5:1–11 again. In the same place you wrote down your answer of what it means to be blessed, write down the specific blessings Jesus promises to His people. These are the blessings of the kingdom of heaven. Jesus' declaration of these blessings is a promise that the Christian does not have to wait until the resurrection to experience the Kingdom. It is happening all around them.

The blessings given in the Sermon on the Mount are the ways of the kingdom of God. It is tempting to view these things as something that will one day be received instead of realizing that, through Jesus' work on the cross, we have access to them right now. It is important to draw a distinction between these gifts and our salvation. We Christians are not *earning* the kingdom of God through these things. No, we are instead experiencing the benefits of being a citizen of that kingdom now.

It is not perfect. Jesus knows the hearts of His listeners, both those physically present and those who experience it through the Scriptures. He knows that there will be struggles to remain in these blessings. It cannot be fully known until, as He says in Matthew 5:12, "Your reward is great in heaven." But these blessings are not reserved for that time. Instead, they are a part of the life of the saints here and now. It is as the apostle Paul writes to the church in Corinth: "For now we see in a mirror dimly, but then face to face. Now I know in part; then I shall know fully, even as I have been fully known" (1 Corinthians 13:12).

The Kingdom is at hand. It has been brought near. So, too, are its blessings to those who believe in the Messiah. Jesus gives access to the storehouses of heaven for His followers. The life of the Christian is blessed—and not just by the earthly gifts God gives. It is also, and to a greater extent, by the blessings of the Kingdom.

Jesus Christ, thank You for giving us the Kingdom now, even though we wait until Your return to see that Kingdom fully come. Until that day, give me grace to live as Your child through faith. Amen.

SPIRITUAL POVERTY

Blessed are the poor in spirit, for theirs is the kingdom of heaven. (MATTHEW 5:3)

How does one establish a "poor spirit"? It doesn't seem to be something that would be conducive to life in this world. In Matthew 5:3, the Greek word used for "poor" is *ptōchos*. A study of that word also includes the idea of begging or asking for alms. What, then, does it mean to be poor in spirit? It means to recognize that we have nothing and can only receive the spiritual salvation we need from outside ourselves.

Just prior to his death, Martin Luther had a note in his pocket that included the German phrase for "We are all beggars." Standing before God, it is right to recognize that we have no spiritual riches that we can use to pay the debt we owe. We are all beggars before the righteousness of God. In that realization, becoming poor in spirit, there is a great blessing: the kingdom of God. In that moment of spiritual beggary, the Holy Spirit transforms the heart to find that there is a way to return to the Creator: through His Son.

It is important that in the list of blessings, Jesus starts with the most important one. There is nothing we can do, except come as spiritually bankrupt people to the foot of a loving God. In this, He displays all the blessings He himself will promise in the following verses.

Then how does one establish a "poor spirit"? John gives this explanation: "If we say we have no sin, we deceive ourselves, and the truth is not in us. If we confess our sins, He is faithful and just to forgive us our sins and to cleanse us from all unrighteousness" (1 John 1:8–9). Confession brings a person to the point quickly. Looking over the works that have, or have not, been done shows the need for a Savior. It will bring to light the bankruptcy of the soul. God, however, does not leave His people there. Jesus is faithful. He quickly brings with Him the absolution promised on the cross, the right of every citizen of the kingdom of God.

Confession and Absolution should be a cornerstone practice of every Christian. This happens weekly as the local church gathers in worship. As one of my elders, Jon, often tells me, "The worship service is not a time for us to serve God, but the time where He comes and serves us." Confession and Absolution is one of these times. From steepled stone sanctuaries and quaint rural church buildings to everything in between, as the saints assemble, Confession and Absolution delivers this promised blessing from the Beatitudes. It is the gateway into all the other blessings that follow.

Jesus' forgiveness, granted on the cross, is both final and ongoing. He knew His people. He knew that they would be fickle and foolishly drawn away from Him by all kinds of idols and lusts. Instead of condemning, He declares that those who come understanding the reality of their sin would inherit the Kingdom. It is the first blessing among blessings. No person is perfected until the resurrection. Jesus knows that His saints will struggle with sin until death or His return, so He promises a blessing: come as a beggar, leave with the Kingdom. This opens the door to blessing upon blessing.

Lord Jesus, You made Yourself poor that I may be rich. Take my spiritual poverty, cleanse me of my sin, and give me Your eternal righteousness. Amen.

THE SERMON ON THE MOUNT, PART 2

Christ Fulfills and Interprets the Law

WEEK 12—MATTHEW 5:17–48

Do not think that I have come to abolish the Law or the Prophets; I have not come to abolish them but to fulfill them. For truly, I say to you, until heaven and earth pass away, not an iota, not a dot, will pass from the Law until all is accomplished. Therefore whoever relaxes one of the least of these commandments and teaches others to do the same will be called least in the kingdom of heaven, but whoever does them and teaches them will be called great in the kingdom of heaven. For I tell you, unless your righteousness exceeds that of the scribes and Pharisees, you will never enter the kingdom of heaven.

You have heard that it was said to those of old, "You shall not murder; and whoever murders will be liable to judgment." But I say to you that everyone who is angry with his brother will be liable to judgment; whoever insults his brother will be liable to the council; and whoever says, "You fool!" will be liable to the hell of fire. So if you are offering your gift at the altar and there remember that your brother has something against you, leave your gift there before the altar and go. First be reconciled to your brother, and then come and offer your gift. Come to terms quickly with your accuser while you are going with him to court, lest your accuser hand you over to the judge, and the judge to the guard, and you be put in prison. Truly, I say to you, you will never get out until you have paid the last penny.

You have heard that it was said, "You shall not commit adultery." But I say to you that everyone who looks at a woman with lustful intent has already committed adultery with her in his heart. If your right eye causes you to sin, tear it out and throw it away. For it is better that you lose one of your members than that your whole body be thrown into hell. And if your right hand causes you to sin, cut it off and throw it away. For it is better that you lose one of your members than that your whole body go into hell.

It was also said, "Whoever divorces his wife, let him give her a certificate of divorce." But I say to you that everyone who divorces his wife, except on the ground of sexual immorality, makes her commit adultery, and whoever marries a divorced woman commits adultery.

Again you have heard that it was said to those of old, "You shall not swear falsely, but shall perform to the Lord what you have sworn." But I say to you, Do not take an oath at all, either by heaven, for it is the throne of God, or by the earth, for it is His footstool, or by Jerusalem, for it is the city of the great King. And do not take an oath by your head, for you cannot make one hair white or black. Let what you say be simply "Yes" or "No"; anything more than this comes from evil.

THE DISCIPLES AND THE CROWD

Seeing the crowds, He went up on the mountain, and when He sat down, His disciples came to Him. (MATTHEW 5:1)

As far as we know, no one was taking attendance at the Sermon on the Mount. No precise records exist to tell us who was there. But there were two distinct groups of people who heard what Jesus said.

The first is disciples. Matthew 5 opens with the statement that Jesus saw the crowds, went up on a mountain, and sat down. Then His disciples came to Him.

When we hear *disciples*, we may instinctively think of the Twelve. At this point in the narrative, however, Matthew has not introduced the Twelve yet. So far, Matthew has named only four: two sets of brothers, Simon Peter and Andrew, along with James and John. The disciples who listened to Jesus' Sermon on the Mount may have been the Twelve, or it may have been a broader group of disciples.

The word *disciple* means "learner" or "pupil." Jesus was regarded as a rabbi, or a Jewish teacher, and rabbis attracted disciples—students who wanted to learn from a rabbi. Other people in the Gospels had disciples, including John the Baptist (see Matthew 9:14) and the Pharisees (see Matthew 22:16). The book of Acts also uses the term *disciple* in a sense broader than the Twelve. Acts 6:1 says, "The disciples were increasing in number." Acts 21:16 describes "disciples from Caesarea" and even names one, calling Mnason of Cyprus "an early disciple."

The other people in the audience were apparently people outside the circle of disciples. At the end of the Sermon on the Mount, we read, "And when Jesus finished these sayings, the crowds were astonished at His teaching" (Matthew 7:28).

The second group, the crowds, were distinct from the disciples. The disciples may have emerged from the crowds, but the disciples were no longer part of the crowds. A disciple of Jesus repents of sin and turns to Jesus for the gift of forgiveness. By contrast, the crowds in the Gospels are usually spiritual searchers who have not yet come to faith. Jesus once described the crowds as "harassed and helpless, like sheep without a shepherd" (Matthew 9:36). The crowds were often clamoring for a miracle. When Jesus taught them, He spoke in parables (see Matthew 13:35).

So while the crowds may have been listening in and were amazed at Jesus' teachings, the Sermon on the Mount was spoken directly to Jesus' disciples. Jesus presented clear teachings, expounding on the Old Testament Law with divine authority. As believers, when we read His words, we read them as disciples—not as part of the crowd.

Lord Jesus, I sit at Your feet to learn from You. Be my Teacher and, by the power of Your Holy Spirit, lead me to submit myself to Your authority and to live under Your Law and Your grace. Amen.

"BUT I SAY TO YOU"

You have heard that it was said to those of old. . . . But I say to you. . . . (MATTHEW 5:21–22)

Can you think of a time when you did the bare minimum? Sometimes we do just enough to complete the task, but no more. You study *just* enough to get a passing grade on a test. Or you fix up the house *just* enough for it to sell.

In this second portion of the Sermon on the Mount, Jesus taught that the bare minimum isn't good enough when it comes to keeping God's Law. In Jesus' audience, many people were being taught to aim low. After hitting a low target, they felt a false sense of security that they were righteous in God's eyes.

In Matthew 5:17–48, Jesus raised the bar with teachings on anger, lust, divorce, oaths, retaliation, and love for enemies. For all six topics, Jesus framed His teachings with a formula: "You have heard that it was said. . . . But I say to you. . . ."

You have heard that it was said. Many faulty interpretations in Jesus' day missed the full intent of God's Commandments. These false interpretations didn't go far enough. They stopped short of God's full intent for how His people should live. Jesus taught that murder is more than killing, adultery is more than a physical act, and love is to be extended beyond those who are kind to you. The religious teachers of Jesus' day taught only the bare minimum—only enough to earn a passing grade in society's eyes.

But I say to you. By contrast, Jesus taught a fuller understanding of God's Law. He taught a righteousness that exceeded that of the scribes and Pharisees (see Matthew 5:20). Jesus presented a way of living that goes beyond the bare minimum and strives to love others to the fullest extent possible. In the six mini-lessons of Matthew 5:17–48, Jesus taught reconciliation, self-restraint, faithfulness, honesty, peacemaking, and unconditional love.

And best of all, Jesus embodied these teachings for our sakes. While we can seek to obey God's Law to a certain extent, none of us can reach the level of obedience that Jesus teaches. That's why Jesus came to personally fulfill the Law and the Prophets (see Matthew 5:17). By His perfect life, He surpassed the bare minimum and loved us to the maximum extent, giving His life on the cross for our sins. Jesus talked the talk, and He walked the walk.

Jesus is the Savior who goes above and beyond. His perfect life goes above our ability to keep God's Law. His love goes beyond our capacity to comprehend.

Lord Jesus, You reveal the heart of God. The Word of the Lord pours forth from Your lips, and so I look to You for spiritual understanding and knowledge. Amen.

JESUS FULFILLED THE LAW AND THE PROPHETS

*Do not think that I have come to
abolish the Law or the Prophets;
I have not come to abolish them but
to fulfill them.* (MATTHEW 5:17)

Jesus stated that He came not to abolish the Law but to fulfill it. He fulfilled the Law by living a perfect life and being the perfect sacrifice for our sins.

Jesus lived a perfect life! This is called His active righteousness.

None of us can live a perfect minute, much less a perfect life! We are sinful people through and through. We're like Paul, who lamented his sinful condition in Romans 7. Paul wrote, "For I know that nothing good dwells in me, that is, in my flesh" (Romans 7:18). Like you and me, Paul failed endlessly in overcoming his sinful nature. "For I do not do the good I want, but the evil I do not want is what I keep on doing" (Romans 7:19).

Can you relate? Have you tried to overcome a bad habit, or restrain your anger, or control your tongue, only to fail again? We struggle daily in the battle against sin.

Jesus was different. Hebrews 4:15 says Jesus "in every respect has been tempted as we are, yet without sin." Satan tested Jesus in the desert. Jesus passed with a perfect score. The Pharisees and scribes tried to trap Jesus in a contradiction, but they were searching for flaws that didn't exist. Jesus always conducted Himself with consistency and integrity. He lived a perfect life, fulfilling the Law by His active righteousness.

Jesus also fulfilled the Law by His death. This is His passive righteousness.

Philippians 2:8 declares that Jesus "humbled Himself by becoming obedient to the point of death, even death on a cross." Because of our sins, we deserve eternal punishment. Out of His great love for us, Jesus suffered in our place. He satisfied the wrath of a holy and righteous God by dying the death that our sins warrant.

It should have been you on the cross. It should have been me. Our sins should separate us from God forever, just as Jesus experienced alienation from His Father on the cross. But because of Jesus, our sins do not separate us from God.

Jesus came not to abolish the Law but to fulfill it. He fulfilled the Law by living the perfect life that we could not live. And He fulfilled the Law by dying in our place. Jesus accomplished His mission by holding Himself to the highest standard possible, the standard of complete adherence to God's Law.

Lord Jesus, by Your righteousness, I am declared righteous before our heavenly Father. Thank You for this gift beyond description. Comfort me with the reassurance of righteousness today and every day. Amen.

HOW PERFECT IS GOOD ENOUGH?

You therefore must be perfect, as your heavenly Father is perfect. (MATTHEW 5:48)

Sometimes we get caught in a comparison trap. *I'm not as bad as that person,* we might think. But the standard of goodness is never another person. The standard is always God. He's perfect, and nothing less than perfection is enough for Him.

To those who trust in their own goodness, James 2:10 says, "For whoever keeps the whole law but fails in one point has become guilty of all of it." When it comes to obeying God's Law, it's an all-or-nothing proposition.

Think of it this way. You can pop a balloon by smashing it with a sledgehammer or by pricking it with a needle. It doesn't matter how large an object strikes the balloon. Either way: POP!

Or think of it this way. You're climbing up a mountain, clutching a long chain. If one link breaks off, you're falling. Even if the other links remain intact, one broken link spells disaster.

The same is true for God's Law. In our eyes, there are little sins and big sins. Some sins have worse earthly consequences than others. Murder has more devastating consequences than stealing a bag of chips. But even a small sin has big consequences before the Lord. God is perfect, and only perfection is permitted in His presence.

The prophet Isaiah felt his inadequacy in the presence of God. In a vision of God's throne room, the prophet exclaimed, "Woe is me! For I am lost; for I am a man of unclean lips, and I dwell in the midst of a people of unclean lips; for my eyes have seen the King, the LORD of hosts!" (Isaiah 6:5).

Isaiah was a man of God. He was also a sinner and was broken by God's Law.

Only one thing could rescue Isaiah from his despair. It wasn't trying harder to satisfy the demands of the Law. It wasn't making a stronger case to justify or excuse away his sin. Isaiah's only hope was God's gift of forgiveness. In the vision, an angel touched his lips with a coal and declared, "Behold, this has touched your lips; your guilt is taken away, and your sin atoned for" (Isaiah 6:7).

God gives us something better than coal against our lips. He gives us the body and blood of Christ, in, with, and under the bread and wine of the Lord's Supper that touches our lips each week—the Savior who lived a perfect life on our behalf and died a sacrificial death for us. Through Jesus, your guilt is taken away and your sin atoned for.

Lord Jesus, You are my only hope. I am a lawbreaker. But through Your sacrifice on my behalf, I am loved and forgiven. Thanks be to God! Amen.

WHAT IS JESUS
REALLY SAYING?

If your right eye causes you to sin,
tear it out and throw it away. For
it is better that you lose one of your
members than that your whole body
be thrown into hell. (MATTHEW 5:29)

Does Jesus really want us to tear out our eyes?

A literal fulfillment of Matthew 5:29 would be gruesome—and would miss the point tragically. Sometimes Jesus spoke in nonliteral language. As the Master Teacher, He used many forms of communication to drive home His point. Many times, Jesus used overstatement to emphasize a key teaching. An overstatement is literally possible but should not really be done.

Jesus does not want us to gouge out our eyes, nor does He want us to cut off our hands, as the passage also states. Jesus does not intend for us to harm the body that God gave us. However, Jesus wants us to take sin seriously and to do everything within reason to curb sin in our lives.

Ultimately, what curbs sin in our lives is the Holy Spirit. He changes our hearts so that our desires align more closely with God's desires for us. God's Word teaches us, "If we live by the Spirit, let us also keep in step with the Spirit" (Galatians 5:25). By His grace, God deposits His Spirit into our hearts, so that we may renounce ungodliness and walk according to God's ways.

In the text from Matthew 5, Jesus achieves a shock factor. He's putting things in perspective. Losing an eye or a limb would be devastating— perhaps you or someone you know has suffered a physical loss like that. But as awful as it would be to lose an eye or a limb, any physical loss is to be preferred over the loss of salvation. If anything weakens our faith and pulls us away from God, the price is too high to pay. Nothing is of greater value than life forever with God.

Specifically in this passage, Jesus is forbidding lust. We might think, "One lingering glance at an attractive physique. What's the harm?" Sin can be a slippery slope. One sin leads to another. And before you know it, you've drifted from God and His loving embrace and have ended up in the embrace of another.

Keep your eye. Keep perspective. And be kept by God's grace.

Lord Jesus, by Your Spirit, drive out every impure thought in me and grant protection against anything that endangers my relationship with You. I am Yours. Amen.

BEING A GOOD NEIGHBOR

*You have heard that it was said,
"You shall love your neighbor and
hate your enemy." But I say to you,
Love your enemies and pray for
those who persecute you, so that
you may be sons of your Father who
is in heaven.* (MATTHEW 5:43–45)

My neighbor texted me the other day. My family had just added a dog to our household. We left the dog in the backyard while all of us were at work or school. My neighbor's text was gentle: "Please don't be upset with me, but there is a dog that has been barking all morning next to the fence." From my office, I texted an apology and said we'd keep the dog inside during the day going forward. "We want to be good neighbors," I texted. My neighbor assured me that he considered us to be good neighbors.

The second tablet of the Ten Commandments teaches us to be a good neighbor. Commandments 1–3 are all about loving God. Commandments 4–10 are all about loving your neighbor. A man once asked Jesus, "And who is my neighbor?" (Luke 10:29). Through the parable of the Good Samaritan, Jesus taught that your neighbor is every person who crosses your path.

Being a good neighbor includes the things Jesus spoke about in Matthew 5.

Being a good neighbor includes restraining anger. Angry thoughts lead to hurtful actions and words. Our world could use more kindness, just as God has shown kindness to us in His Son, our Savior.

Being a good neighbor includes seeing others the way God sees them. Lustful thoughts do not contribute anything good to another person's life.

God sees us as whole people, loved on account of Christ.

Being a good neighbor includes the people closest to you—yes, the people in your household are also your neighbors! And so Jesus teaches us to honor marriage vows, as He is faithful and committed to us at all times.

Being a good neighbor includes follow-through for all commitments. Jesus teaches us that a plain yes or no binds you to your word.

Being a good neighbor includes treating others according to God's standards, not according to what we think they deserve. "We love because He first loved us" (1 John 4:19). Our primary motivation for loving others is not that they love us. Our primary motivation is that God loves us, and He has given us His Son.

Where do we receive strength to do all these things? In worship, we confess to God our failure to love and serve our neighbor perfectly, and He abundantly pardons and forgives us through His Word and Sacraments. He pours out His Spirit and enables us to love one another.

Because God loves us, we can love others. We can be good neighbors.

Lord Jesus, by Your grace, help me to be a good neighbor—loving, pure, and merciful—as You are all of those things and more to me. Amen.

THE SERMON ON THE MOUNT, PART 3

Giving, Prayer, and Fasting

Week 13—Matthew 6:1–18

Beware of practicing your righteousness before other people in order to be seen by them, for then you will have no reward from your Father who is in heaven.

Thus, when you give to the needy, sound no trumpet before you, as the hypocrites do in the synagogues and in the streets, that they may be praised by others. Truly, I say to you, they have received their reward. But when you give to the needy, do not let your left hand know what your right hand is doing, so that your giving may be in secret. And your Father who sees in secret will reward you.

And when you pray, you must not be like the hypocrites. For they love to stand and pray in the synagogues and at the street corners, that they may be seen by others. Truly, I say to you, they have received their reward. But when you pray, go into your room and shut the door and pray to your Father who is in secret. And your Father who sees in secret will reward you.

And when you pray, do not heap up empty phrases as the Gentiles do, for they think that they will be heard for their many words. Do not be like them, for your Father knows what you need before you ask Him. Pray then like this:

Our Father in heaven,
hallowed be Your name.
Your kingdom come,
Your will be done,
    on earth as it is in heaven.
Give us this day our daily bread,
and forgive us our debts,
    as we also have forgiven our debtors.
And lead us not into temptation,
    but deliver us from evil.

For if you forgive others their trespasses, your heavenly Father will also forgive you, but if you do not forgive others their trespasses, neither will your Father forgive your trespasses.

And when you fast, do not look gloomy like the hypocrites, for they disfigure their faces that their fasting may be seen by others. Truly, I say to you, they have received their reward. But when you fast, anoint your head and wash your face, that your fasting may not be seen by others but by your Father who is in secret. And your Father who sees in secret will reward you.

PRACTICING THE LAW

Beware of practicing your righteousness before other people in order to be seen by them. (MATTHEW 6:1)

Giving, praying, and fasting aren't really public acts in the same way they used to be. We donate online, round up at the grocery store, or throw our loose change in a bucket. We pray by ourselves, in our head—unless we're the one called on at the annual family gathering. And fasting? We can hardly conceive of missing a meal. So certain are we of Christ being our righteousness that it is hard to imagine feeling obligated to put our own "righteousness" into action like this.

But a prophet like Moses has finally come (see Deuteronomy 18:15), and it is time for God's people to listen. In the first part of the Sermon on the Mount (Matthew 5:1–16), Jesus taught the people what "blessed" really looked like: repenting and receiving God's forgiveness, which He has come to bring. In the second part (Matthew 5:17–48), last week, Jesus taught His followers how to use the Ten Commandments as a guide for daily life in the Kingdom. Now Jesus moves into three important Christian disciplines: giving, praying, and fasting. It becomes clear that just as blessings and commandments were misunderstood, so were these religious practices.

First-century Jews had an obligation to practice the Law, to do what was outlined in the Old Testament. Even Jesus said, just a little earlier, "Let your light shine before others" (Matthew 5:16). These weren't optional: "*When you,*" He says. It's not "*If you.*" While we might not hear these words and be immediately challenged by them, His original audience would have been shocked. Jesus is addressing real issues people really face,

and throughout this week, we will see how these words very much apply to us too.

Jesus does something very important here. He places these practices into a category most people miss: worship, not witness. Basically, do these actions demonstrate how good we are, or are these the fruits of an intimate relationship with the Father? Where people were concerned with fulfilling the letter of the Law, Jesus offered the Spirit of the Law—a proper relationship to our Creator, centered in the Word.

We care about how we look in front of others, and apparently, that is a universal human truth. But there is something we should consider before all else. How are we looking in front of God? Whose approval ultimately matters? Should we look to religious experts, peers, relatives? Or should we look to the Father, who is ready to bless us when we meet with Him? Your Father sees you. How do you look?

Jesus, we look to You for our righteousness, for our wholeness, for our worth. Remind us who You are and how Your grace is changing us to be more like You. In Your name we pray. Amen.

GIVING, PRAYING, AND FASTING

When you give to the needy, sound no trumpet before you. (MATTHEW 6:2)

God isn't keeping a scorecard, even if we'd like Him to. Giving, praying, and fasting are not about the number of people helped, number of words said, or quantity of things we've given up. Jesus is teaching us that these are not really works of righteousness at all. Our faithfulness is not a way to impress God—or even the people around us. But if that's what we're seeking, Jesus notes, that's what we will get. The favor of others, while not the real goal of our walk with Christ, can be a nice thing to enjoy. We feel good when people think highly of us. We feel great when we're respected. But if we're working for mere outward appearances, then we are working against God. Basically, we can seek our reward in the opinions and goodwill of others, or we can enjoy closeness with God.

Jesus describes for His followers three ways of worship—reverent routes of relational intimacy with God. Giving is not an awesome display of how helpful we can be to others. It is a demonstration of trust, a recognition of "All that we have is Thine alone" (*LSB* 781:1), a bold declaration that God will provide for me and through me. We will hear more about the nature of God's provision in Matthew 6:25–34, but Jesus promises that God will meet us in our giving, because our God is a giving God.

Praying, as well, is not joining big words together to sound smart; it is simply demonstrating trust that our God is holy and powerful—and that God will provide for my physical and spiritual needs, now and forever. So memorable was this simple prayer of worship that still today the Lord's Prayer is prayed in public worship and private homes, and it has been taught as the guide of proper prayer in catechisms throughout the ages. God will meet us in prayer, because we can find God in His Word.

Lastly, fasting is not a chance to inform everyone of how serious we take our faith. It is simply giving up things that we rely on to worship the only thing we truly need. While it is nice to hear "I can't believe how much you trust God!" we want to experience the faithfulness of our Father in heaven, even if we're the only ones who know what else we're missing. Man does not live by bread alone, and fasting reminds us our God is the Provider.

We can worship God, or we can woo others. Jesus does not allow us room for both.

Father in heaven, we worship You. Make our lives an offering to You, to bring glory to You alone. In Jesus' name we pray. Amen.

HIDDEN IN CHRIST

When you pray, go into your room and shut the door and pray to your Father who is in secret. (MATTHEW 6:6)

If a tree falls in the middle of a forest, and no one is there to hear it, does it make a sound? If a Christian prays or gives money or fasts, and no one is there to notice, does it really count? The God who has revealed Himself to us through nature and the Scriptures points us to a hidden faith. While the world looks for signs, symbols, and demonstrations, Jesus tells us our relationship with God isn't merely a thing to be noticed outwardly. Our faith is a secret celebration too.

This is a central part of Jesus' mission. Jesus came hidden in a poor family, in a poor community, in an unimportant province of Rome. He had very few material possessions, and when He was at the point of great popularity, Jesus would go into seclusion. Although He performed miracles, Jesus was not about the show. Jesus was about the Kingdom coming. The power and wisdom of God was hidden in weakness and foolishness—something that would be astounding and unbelievable to many, and offensive to most everyone else (see 1 Corinthians 1:18).

Therefore, it should not come as a surprise to us that the hidden God desires a hidden closeness with His people. After all, Jesus fasted before He was famous, prayed before He displayed His power, and gave away everything He had, up to His very life, for the people of God. This is true hallowedness—what comes from the Father. This is the kingdom of God, coming to us. This is God's will, namely that our lives are hidden in the righteousness and faithfulness of Christ.

In the best sense, then, it doesn't matter if the world ever sees our giving, our praying, or our fasting. We want the world to see Jesus. We want the world to know how much Jesus has given (see John 15:13), how Jesus is praying for us at the right hand of the Father (see Romans 8:34), how Jesus is providing a Meal that will quench our appetites forever (see John 6:27).

Jesus forsook the world and all its glory to share with us the same closeness He has with our Father in heaven. To join Jesus on His mission means we enjoy a rich relationship with God by receiving the gifts of Jesus—giving, praying, and fasting. As Paul says, "Your life is hidden with Christ in God" (Colossians 3:3). And that is the best place to be found.

Father in heaven, we seek You, that we may be found by You. We cling to Christ, and we ask that You enable us to hear You in Your Word today. In Jesus' name. Amen.

PROPER GIVING, PRAYING, AND FASTING

Truly, I say to you, they have received their reward. (MATTHEW 6:16)

God works in unseen ways. "Blessed are those who have not seen and yet have believed" (John 20:29). Moses reiterates this unseen blessing to God's people as they prepare to enter the Promised Land: "The secret things belong to the LORD our God, but the things that are revealed belong to us and to our children forever, that we may do all the words of this law" (Deuteronomy 29:29). The apostle John reminds us as well, "And now, little children, abide in Him, so that when He appears we may have confidence" (1 John 2:28). God has shown His love in Christ, and He has made clear through the whole of Scripture the purpose of giving, praying, and fasting.

Proper giving

The Scriptures constantly talk of a giving that is unmotivated by receiving. "One gives freely, yet grows all the richer; another withholds what he should give, and only suffers want" (Proverbs 11:24). Or look to the chapter on love: "If I give away all I have . . . but have not love, I gain nothing" (1 Corinthians 13:3). The reward of giving is not the return on investment, but the relationship with our Father. Consider Zacchaeus in Luke 19, who gave away a great deal of his wealth. Jesus does not rejoice in his generosity, but in the restoration of his relationship with God. Jesus declared, "Today salvation has come to this house" (v. 9). Proper giving is when we live out what God gives.

Proper praying

The beautiful brevity of the Lord's Prayer reminds us, "God is in heaven and you are on earth. Therefore let your words be few. For a dream comes with much business, and a fool's voice with many words" (Ecclesiastes 5:2–3).

Throughout the prayer, Jesus reminds us to pray in the spirit of the Scriptures. "You shall not take the name of the LORD your God in vain" (Exodus 20:7), but "in your hearts honor Christ the Lord as holy" (1 Peter 3:15). We refuse to reject God from being king over us (see 1 Samuel 8:7), and we celebrate His rule over all kingdoms (see Psalm 2). We join Jesus in the Garden of Gethsemane as He prays, "Not My will, but Yours, be done" (Luke 22:42). We pray with the wise Agur, "Give me neither poverty or riches; feed me with the food that is needful for me" (Proverbs 30:8). We ask for forgiveness (see Psalm 32; 51; 103), and we pray against the power of temptation that is too great for us (see 1 Corinthians 10:13). We pray the Spirit of protection over all our paths, and that the Lord will keep our "going out and [our] coming in from this time forth and forevermore" (Psalm 121:8).

Proper fasting

God's people fasted as they mourned and grieved (see 2 Samuel 12, for instance). But Isaiah 58 stands as the Old Testament description of godly fasting. "In the day of your fast you seek your own pleasure. . . . Is such the fast that I choose, a day for a person to humble himself?" (Isaiah 58:3, 5). No, the point of a godly fast is "to loose the bonds of wickedness . . . to break every yoke . . . to share your bread" (Isaiah 58:6–7). Proper fasting is a demonstration and a sharing of our reliance on God above all earthly things.

O God, we want to please You, to make You happy. Help us to find delight in following You, even as we rejoice that You delight in us. In Jesus' name we pray. Amen.

QUESTIONS ABOUT GIVING, PRAYER, AND FASTING

And your Father who sees in secret will reward you. (MATTHEW 6:18)

Our lives are on display these days, but they rarely showcase Christ. We show how good or blessed or whole our lives are (and if our lives truly are, thank God!). This passage challenges us, however, to reflect on what is seen and what is unseen.

What is the reward we would receive from our Father in heaven?

First, let's say what the reward is not. It is not forgiveness or eternal life—these are gifts, given by God's grace through the merits of Jesus Christ. The reward, as I see it, is celebration and joy. Salvation provides relief, but living out our relationship with Christ produces joy. Christians are still prone to worry, fear, anxiety, resentment. Living out the life God intends us to live, however, produces joy, peace, and love in the Holy Spirit (see Galatians 6:8).

What are hypocrites?

A hypocrite is someone who says one thing and does another. We've all met one—and we've all been one. A hypocrite puts himself or herself under judgment by their own words, even if they fail to see it. The opposite is someone who is consistent in word and deed, someone whose walk matches their talk. We avoid hypocrisy by looking for God's approval over the approval of others.

How can you keep your left hand from knowing what your right hand is giving?

This is a figure of speech, but the concept is this: we give not to remember and record our own actions. A moment that may be forgettable to me might just be the difference in someone else's day. Likewise, another person's generosity toward me might not be a big part of their day, but it means the world to me. Don't worry about whether you're on record—just give what God is calling you to give.

Why should we pray if God already knows what we need?

Our prayers do not inform God about something He doesn't already know. They remind us that God is our helper when we feel helpless, and He has a plan to help us through difficulties in our life. Prayer gives us a chance to thank and praise God, and to pray for others. And when we pray, God aligns our will to His will, helping us accept difficult things, and giving us peace when we lay things in His hands that are too big for us to understand.

Does Jesus require Christians to fast?

It is not a requirement, but it is an expectation in the Scriptures. If God expects it, what would be our motivation to avoid it? Not only are there health benefits to fasting (and many of us have had to do it for medical reasons); fasting can help bring spiritual clarity. Fasting is helpful during times of repentance (Advent and Lent) and other times in life when considering big life changes (changing jobs, facing death, and so on). The idea of fasting is to let the hunger pangs that would normally drive us to food drive us instead to pray with more intensity to God as we seek His guidance and help—for Him to strengthen our faith and confidence in Him.

Gracious God, You have given us all we need through Your Son, Jesus Christ. Empower me to live in a way that declares my faith and confidence in You. For Jesus' sake. Amen.

REMEMBERING THE CURSE AND THE SAVIOR WHO REVERSES IT

When you fast, anoint your head and wash your face, that your fasting may not be seen by others but by your Father who is in secret. (MATTHEW 6:17–18)

Imagine a delicious quiche or a thick stack of buttermilk pancakes calling your name; Sunday morning is a great time for brunch. But it is also a perfect time for fasting. After fresh baked goods got me sleepy and distracted on Sunday mornings, I began this practice of fasting for myself. It changed me. My focus went from food to faith. From innocent mindlessness to intentionality. From distracted to prepared.

It is interesting to note that this is the appointed reading for Ash Wednesday, the day that marks the beginning of the Lenten journey. Lent is often filled with fasting, with preparing our hearts and minds for the presence of Christ and the celebration of Easter. Ash Wednesday itself is the remembrance of the original curse: "You are dust, and to dust you shall return" (Genesis 3:19). If you remember, however, there is more to the curse. Our eating and working are cursed too. Adam and Eve are also kicked out of God's presence, permanently changing their ability to speak to their Creator. Think about it: we give up our food, we return to God what we take from this cursed soil, and we seek God in prayer. We remember the curse when we fast, give, and pray.

This demonstrates the Christian paradox of holding together suffering and joy in our worship. We joyfully pray, give, and fast. We joyfully suffer the loss of our time, money, and resources because we know that God can do infinitely more with our lack than we can do with our abundance. We remember the curse, because we remember the Son who has destroyed the serpent and has brought us back into the presence of our Creator by becoming a curse on the cross for us.

Christian worship embraces Jesus' words in many ways, and we follow His command to examine our motives and our thoughts as we put them into practice. We pray together, whether we pray from Scripture, pray the prayers of others, or pray from our own hearts during worship. Consider adding prayer requests from your congregation's worship service into your personal prayers throughout the week. We also give, offering back to God and His church what we have first received from Him. But it's more than that. As people serve coffee (and maybe some baked goods), as people warmly greet new and old friends, as people serve others during worship, there is a Spirit of generosity and hospitality. And we fast. Join with the ancient church by fasting before receiving Holy Communion; let your hunger pangs drive you to hunger and thirst for Christ's body and blood to nourish your soul and body.

Holy Father, cleanse us from all our sin and purify us, so that we are prepared for all the ways You are calling us to live as witnesses of Your love. In Jesus' name. Amen.

THE SERMON ON THE MOUNT, PART 4

Treasures in Heaven, Do Not Be Anxious

WEEK 14—MATTHEW 6:19–34

Do not lay up for yourselves treasures on earth, where moth and rust destroy and where thieves break in and steal, but lay up for yourselves treasures in heaven, where neither moth nor rust destroys and where thieves do not break in and steal. For where your treasure is, there your heart will be also.

The eye is the lamp of the body. So, if your eye is healthy, your whole body will be full of light, but if your eye is bad, your whole body will be full of darkness. If then the light in you is darkness, how great is the darkness!

No one can serve two masters, for either he will hate the one and love the other, or he will be devoted to the one and despise the other. You cannot serve God and money.

Therefore I tell you, do not be anxious about your life, what you will eat or what you will drink, nor about your body, what you will put on. Is not life more than food, and the body more than clothing? Look at the birds of the air: they neither sow nor reap nor gather into barns, and yet your heavenly Father feeds them. Are you not of more value than they? And which of you by being anxious can add a single hour to his span of life? And why are you anxious about clothing? Consider the lilies of the field, how they grow: they neither toil nor spin, yet I tell you, even Solomon in all his glory was not arrayed like one of these. But if God so clothes the grass of the field, which today is alive and tomorrow is thrown into the oven, will He not much more clothe you, O you of little faith? Therefore do not be anxious, saying, "What shall we eat?" or "What shall we drink?" or "What shall we wear?" For the Gentiles seek after all these things, and your heavenly Father knows that you need them all. But seek first the kingdom of God and His righteousness, and all these things will be added to you.

Therefore do not be anxious about tomorrow, for tomorrow will be anxious for itself. Sufficient for the day is its own trouble.

TRUST GOD TO PROVIDE

Do not lay up for yourselves treasures on earth, where moth and rust destroy and where thieves break in and steal, but lay up for yourselves treasures in heaven, where neither moth nor rust destroys and where thieves do not break in and steal. (MATTHEW 6:19-20)

Any time you read a portion of the Sermon on the Mount, it's important to consider what Jesus has been teaching before this moment to understand the context.

In the Sermon on the Mount, Jesus is speaking to His disciples—those whom He is equipping and preparing to spread the Gospel after His ascension. We as Christians today have the same mission as the disciples who were learning directly from Jesus, so we can take each lesson to heart and apply it to our lives today.

In the first part of the sermon (week 11 in this devotional), Jesus taught the blessings for those who repent and receive God's forgiveness, which He came to bring. In the second part (week 12), He taught how to use the Ten Commandments as a guide for daily life in the Kingdom. Next (week 13), Jesus taught the right way to undertake three important Christian disciplines: giving, praying, and fasting. This week, Jesus turns our attention from earthly treasures to storing up heavenly treasures and teaches us to overcome fear and anxiety.

So what do these previous teachings have to do with treasures and anxiety? And what can we learn by considering the greater context of Jesus' teachings here?

Looking at these previous teachings in the Sermon on the Mount, we can see that Jesus is teaching His disciples about how the Ten Commandments, a tenet of the Jewish faith, impact their new life in the kingdom of God. In this new kingdom, God provides for His people just as He did during the exodus from Egypt and throughout their time in the Promised Land.

So we don't need to be anxious or worried about God providing for us, even if that provision might look different than we anticipated. But additionally, we do not need to fret about our salvation. Gone are the days of sacrifices and ritual washings—now our salvation is rooted in Jesus!

In Mark 6:8-9, Jesus counsels His disciples against taking possessions with them on their travels together: "He charged them to take nothing for their journey except a staff—no bread, no bag, no money in their belts—but to wear sandals and not put on two tunics." Clearly, Jesus wanted His disciples' focus to be on their mission, not on their provisions. In the Sermon on the Mount, He offers them the comfort that their (and our!) heavenly Father will provide for all their needs. Rejoice in this truth today!

God our Father, thank You for providing for all of our needs for Jesus' sake. Amen.

SWITCHING OUR PERSPECTIVE

No one can serve two masters, for either he will hate the one and love the other, or he will be devoted to the one and despise the other. You cannot serve God and money. (MATTHEW 6:24)

In this passage, Jesus wants us to reassess our relationship with our possessions. He makes a shocking claim in verse 24—that we cannot serve both God and money.

For most of us, our possessions are at the forefront of our minds almost all the time, even if we don't realize it. The car needs a new set of brakes. My iPhone screen cracked, so I need a new one. The roof needs replacing after a hailstorm. I need that pair of shoes I just saw an influencer post about on Instagram.

God entrusts earthly possessions to us so they can assist us to bring glory to God by serving those around us. And we should be good stewards of those possessions! But there is a fine line between taking care of those items and prioritizing them more than God.

We often think of our possessions in relation to us: *I need X so I can be/have/do Y.* But Jesus invites us to switch our perspective. Instead, we should ask how our possessions can serve God's kingdom and then focus our attention on the heavenly treasures God gives us freely—grace, forgiveness, life everlasting. These free gifts are greater than any physical possession we have here on earth! By switching our focus to gratefulness for God's goodness, we can use our possessions to pour out God's love on a world that desperately needs it.

If we focus on serving the Lord rather than our possessions, we will be free of anxiety about them because He promises to provide for all our needs.

God provides for the birds of the air and the lilies of the field—and they don't work for a paycheck! They display God's splendor and majesty without toiling. How much more can we exalt the Lord with what He has given us?

Relying on God to provide for our needs is very difficult for most of us. We like to have the control and knowledge that everything will work out. We diligently save for retirement, budget our paycheck to account for our spending, and squirrel away savings for a rainy day. But what would happen if we surrendered all of that to God? What if we gave away more than we spent? How different would our lives look?

As you consider the relationship you have with money, ask God to give you a spirit of generosity and a total reliance on Him to fill all of your needs. Ridding your heart of greed, selfishness, and materialism is a lifelong journey that will only ever be completed in heaven, but our heavenly Father is gracious and merciful to sanctify us through the Holy Spirit in this life. We can be free of the love of money only through His grace and mercy. Thanks be to God!

Holy Spirit, continue to sanctify me to make me more generous toward Your kingdom and those around me. In Jesus' name. Amen.

JESUS TREASURED US ABOVE ALL THINGS

And He withdrew from them about a stone's throw, and knelt down and prayed, saying, "Father, if You are willing, remove this cup from Me. Nevertheless, not My will, but Yours, be done." (LUKE 22:41-42)

When Jesus calls us to treasure Him above all else, it's hard for us to actually do that. We're torn by the worries and ways of this world, waffling between loving God and loving it. But Jesus, the perfect Son of God, perfectly fulfilled the command to treasure God above all else.

Jesus emptied Himself of all His heavenly treasure when He became man and lived among us. He gave up His seat at the right hand of God to become a human on earth—born of a woman, crucified for our sins, and raised three days later for our salvation. Above all else, Jesus treasured the will of God.

He poured Himself out in life and in death because He treasured us—you!—as His own brothers and sisters, heavenly treasures that would be made fit for heaven by His life, death, and resurrection. We don't deserve the grace and mercy afforded to us, but Jesus still willingly gave up His life for us sinners. We are His precious treasure!

Jesus truly sought the kingdom of God first above all else. Throughout His ministry here on earth, He met the needs of the people around Him. He healed diseases, drove out demons, performed miracles, and proclaimed the kingdom of God to all. He perfectly embodied the will of God. Every action, word, and deed proclaimed the glory of His Father.

In the Garden of Gethsemane, before His crucifixion, Jesus prayed to His heavenly Father to "remove this cup from Me." For us fallible humans, we would likely end our prayer there. We might pray something that sounds like "God, give me what I want. Amen."

But Jesus was totally focused on fulfilling His Father's mission. He followed up His ask with an addition foreign to us—complete surrender: "Nevertheless, not My will, but Yours, be done." Even though the cup that was before Him would be unthinkably painful, He surrendered His will to God, trusting that His Father would provide.

And He did! Through the life and death of Jesus, God worked salvation for all humanity. Through the ultimate sacrifice of Jesus, God provided a way back to Himself for His people.

Throughout Jesus' entire earthly ministry, He surrendered Himself to and fulfilled the will of God. He completely surrendered Himself because He so completely treasured the will of God and treasures us as His brothers and sisters. Thanks be to God for His Son, Jesus, who lived the perfect life that we couldn't so we could enjoy a perfect life with Him in eternity!

Jesus, thank You for treasuring the will of God above all else. Help us do the same. Amen.

GOD'S PROFOUND PROMISE

When Jesus heard this, He said to him, "One thing you still lack. Sell all that you have and distribute to the poor, and you will have treasure in heaven; and come, follow Me." But when he heard these things, he became very sad, for he was extremely rich. (LUKE 18:22–23)

I t's one of the most gut-wrenching stories in Scripture. But it also contains one of the most profound promises of God.

In Luke 18, Jesus encounters a rich young ruler. This man asks Jesus what he has to do to inherit eternal life. Jesus tells him, "You know the commandments: 'Do not commit adultery, Do not murder, Do not steal, Do not bear false witness, Honor your father and mother'" (18:20). To this, the rich young ruler replies that he has kept all of these commandments since his youth. Jesus then continues: "One thing you still lack. Sell all that you have and distribute to the poor, and you will have treasure in heaven; and come, follow Me" (18:22).

This ask devastates the young man— "he became very sad, for he was extremely rich" (18:23). You can almost picture him turning away from Jesus, head down and shoulders bent, grieving this monumental command from Jesus as he slowly walks away.

Seeing this young man's reaction, Jesus proclaims how difficult it is for the rich to enter the kingdom of heaven—harder than a camel going through the eye of a needle! The disciples then rightfully ask: "Then who can be saved?" (18:26). We all have wealth of some kind. What does that mean for us?

Then we hear one of the most misapplied verses in the Bible. To answer the disciples' question, Jesus responds, "What is impossible with man is possible with God" (18:27).

This verse is not saying that God will help us pass our math exam, fix our marriage, or find a new job. God can certainly perform miracles in our lives, but this verse is not talking about anything other than salvation. What is impossible with man (being saved and inheriting eternal life) is only possible with God.

Without God, we would never be able to treasure His will above all else. Without God, we would be consumed with worry about our possessions. Without God, we would selfishly hoard our money for ourselves. Without God, we would not be able to seek first the Kingdom and His righteousness.

We can be relieved of our constant striving, our anxious thoughts, our worries about tomorrow. Through His death and resurrection, Jesus has ensured our salvation. By His Holy Spirit, we are made new each day and are sanctified by His Word. We can rest in the promises of God.

Thanks be to God for doing the impossible— saving sinful human beings like you and me!

Jesus, thank You for doing the impossible. Amen.

SERVANTS OF MONEY

Keep your life free from love of money,
and be content with what you have,
for He has said, "I will never leave
you nor forsake you." (HEBREWS 13:5)

When we think about being a servant of money, we might have a character like Scrooge McDuck in mind—wearing a top hat and monocle, diving into his pool of gold coins, hoarding his possessions for himself and living a life of luxury.

When we look at our own lives, we like to justify ourselves and list all the ways we *aren't* servants of money. We drive a creaky used car. We don't live in the nice subdivision. We buy our clothes at thrift stores. We tithe 10 percent to the church. We go on only one vacation a year to the most affordable destination.

We think to ourselves, *I'm not a servant of money! That verse is meant for the ultrarich, the upper class, the 1 percent. I don't live in excess—in fact, I live a modest life compared to those around me.*

The truth is, we are all servants to money in some way.

We can be servants to money by constantly worrying about how much money we have saved. We can be servants to money by following our budget so closely that we forsake opportunities for giving. We can be servants to money by buying items outside of our means. We can be servants to money by coveting items we see promoted by influencers and people we want to emulate.

One aspect of Satan's temptation of Eve was the lure of rising up from being subservient to God and becoming the master of her own fate. But that is a lie.

God created us to be His servants. That life is a life of pure delight with value and meaning. We were created to live a life in harmony with God! If we aren't servants of God, something else will sneak in to take His place. That something will become our god, and we will live our lives in service to it—whether we recognize it or not.

Being a servant of money means we focus all our attention and energy on amassing and protecting our wealth—even if that means we never use that money to improve our lives or the lives of other people. Such a life is empty and meaningless in the end.

But God offers a better life. He asks us to trust Him completely with our finances, resting in the knowledge that He will provide for His children. This doesn't mean we should live a life where we don't work or eat or live in a home. It means we should, each day, offer up our money to God in service of Him. May we use the gifts God has given us to further His kingdom.

Father, help me to surrender my money to You every day. Amen.

SURRENDERING TO GOD

For the Gentiles seek after all these things, and your heavenly Father knows that you need them all. But seek first the kingdom of God and His righteousness, and all these things will be added to you. (MATTHEW 6:32–33)

Money and possessions are good gifts from God, protected by the Seventh Commandment (You shall not steal). But Jesus reminds us that we must keep these things in their proper place—they serve us so that we may faithfully serve God and our neighbor.

Whenever we raise them to replace God, our lives will be filled with anxiety and fear because we really don't have control over the future. Surrendering our finances to God is not easy because it means we are letting someone else be in control—and His plans might not match our plans for the future.

We set aside money for a comfortable retirement. But do we trust God to provide for us in that season of life? We buy excess groceries, so we have an overflowing pantry. But do we trust God to provide for our daily bread? We tithe 10 percent each week. But do we trust God enough to surrender more of our income to Him if we are called to do so?

I once heard a pastor ask what would happen if we gave away more money (to church, to missionaries, to those in need) than we think we can afford. This isn't to say we should not pay our bills or buy food—but to ask ourselves where our priorities lie. If we commit to surrendering more of our money to God, our budget and life would be built around that, not the other way around.

When we live confident in God's providence as Jesus reminds us in the Fourth Petition of the Lord's Prayer (Give us this day our daily bread), anxiety flees and we focus on working for the Lord and the people He has brought into our lives. When we surrender our money to God, we learn to rely on Him for our every need.

This surrendering of our money and our lives is reinforced in worship, especially in the gathering of our offerings to the Lord's service. If you don't already, when the offering is being collected, say a prayer thanking God for His financial gifts to you, and surrender them back to God for use in His kingdom. (You can do this whether you give online or in person!)

At the end of the service, when the pastor says, "The Lord bless you and keep you" (*LSB*, p. 166) as part of the Benediction, we hear another reminder of God's providence. He provides for all of our needs here on earth, and we can confidently rest in His promises to never leave us or forsake us.

Father, give us trust that You will keep us, and give us a spirit of generosity and surrender. In Jesus' name. Amen.

THE SERMON ON THE MOUNT, PART 5

Judging Others; Ask, and It Will Be Given; The Golden Rule

Week 15—Matthew 17:1–14

Judge not, that you be not judged. For with the judgment you pronounce you will be judged, and with the measure you use it will be measured to you. Why do you see the speck that is in your brother's eye, but do not notice the log that is in your own eye? Or how can you say to your brother, "Let me take the speck out of your eye," when there is the log in your own eye? You hypocrite, first take the log out of your own eye, and then you will see clearly to take the speck out of your brother's eye.

Do not give dogs what is holy, and do not throw your pearls before pigs, lest they trample them underfoot and turn to attack you.

Ask, and it will be given to you; seek, and you will find; knock, and it will be opened to you. For everyone who asks receives, and the one who seeks finds, and to the one who knocks it will be opened. Or which one of you, if his son asks him for bread, will give him a stone? Or if he asks for a fish, will give him a serpent? If you then, who are evil, know how to give good gifts to your children, how much more will your Father who is in heaven give good things to those who ask Him!

So whatever you wish that others would do to you, do also to them, for this is the Law and the Prophets.

Enter by the narrow gate. For the gate is wide and the way is easy that leads to destruction, and those who enter by it are many. For the gate is narrow and the way is hard that leads to life, and those who find it are few.

HOW SHOULD WE DEAL WITH OTHERS?

Judge not, that you be not judged. (MATTHEW 7:1)

After His Baptism, Jesus began His three-year public ministry. Most of the time He traveled around the northern region of Galilee. He taught in their synagogues on the Sabbath, then went from village to village, preaching the good news that God's kingdom was at hand.

Jesus' preaching was very different from what the Jews normally heard from their rabbis or teachers. Jesus preached with authority. He confronted people for their sin and called for them to repent. He revealed God's love and concern for them.

Jesus also performed miracles—healing the sick, giving sight to the blind and strength to the lame. As time went by, His popularity grew, and large crowds began to gather around Him. One day, Jesus led His twelve disciples up to the top of a hill, and again, a large crowd gathered to hear Him. Rather than speaking to the entire crowd, Jesus turned to His disciples, to those who already believed in Him, and He preached His Sermon on the Mount.

The very first part of Jesus' sermon is the key to understanding all of it. "Blessed are the poor in spirit, for theirs is the kingdom of God" (Matthew 5:3). Everything starts with us believers recognizing our sin and unworthiness. We have nothing to offer God. When we come to Him in humility and true, sincere repentance, He forgives our sins and makes us part of His kingdom.

Jesus goes on throughout the sermon to teach us, as forgiven children of God, what it means to live as subjects in His kingdom. In the second part, He teaches us the proper use of the Ten Commandments. God did not give them to us as guides for us to earn heaven but to show how we are meant to treat one another. Seeing how we fail to live up to God's demands, the Commandments drive us to the Savior God sent to save us, Jesus Christ. Next, Jesus teaches where we forgiven believers receive the power to live the life that pleases God. He teaches about proper giving, prayer, and fasting. Then Jesus turns our attention from earthly treasures to serving God in faith, storing up heavenly treasures, and learning how to overcome fear and anxiety.

This week, we turn to the part of Jesus' sermon where He teaches us how to deal with others, especially when we encounter believers who are caught up in sin.

Holy Father, I am a sinner You rescued by sending Your Son, Jesus Christ, to die in my place. Give me the same love and concern for others that You have for me. In Jesus' name. Amen.

CORRECTING A CHRISTIAN BROTHER OR SISTER CAUGHT IN SIN

So whatever you wish that others would do to you, do also to them, for this is the Law and the Prophets. (MATTHEW 7:12)

Early in Jesus' Sermon on the Mount, He identified the work of believers in the world. We are to be the salt of the earth and the light of the world. Just as salt preserves meat from decay, the Good News of Jesus we share with sinners preserves them from eternal death in hell. And as light guides our feet away from danger along safe paths, the Gospel of Jesus guides us away from Satan's snares and leads us safely to our heavenly home.

Now, He advances that thought by discussing how we should respond when we find a brother or sister, a fellow believer, who is caught in sin or a sinful behavior. Obviously, when a Christian is actively engaged in sin, his or her witness to the world is compromised; their salt is less preserving, and their light is dimmed significantly.

Before we approach our brother or sister, though, Jesus charges us to look deep inside. First, we need a reality check. We must recognize our own guilt and sinfulness (the log in our eyes) so we will not come at them with hypocritical pride or arrogance. Instead, realizing of ourselves we are poor in spirit, we approach them in true humility and genuine concern for their eternal welfare.

Jesus knew how difficult it is for us to walk in this humility, how difficult to find the courage to speak to someone who is in the wrong, and how difficult to find the wisdom, care, and tact to confront them properly. So Jesus encourages us to pray, giving us three bold and great promises. If we ask, God the Father will give us the concern, tact, and wisdom we need; if we seek His help and favor, we will find the help for which we are looking. If we knock, God will open the door to us. Jesus further encourages us that we can be confident our Father will give us these good gifts because even our earthly fathers, who are sinners, give good gifts to their children out of love.

Finally, Jesus gives us the Golden Rule to guide how we interact with others: "Whatever you wish that others would do to you, do also to them" (Matthew 7:12). Think of this in relation to a brother or sister believer caught in sin. If you were trapped in a sin that was driving you away from Christ, how would you want another Christian to approach you? In judgmental pride, condemnation, and condescension? No, in meekness, gentleness, and genuine concern for your eternal salvation.

Heavenly Father, keep me humble and repentant, fill me with genuine love and concern for my brothers and sisters in Christ, and give me the wisdom and tact to lovingly help any who have lost their way. In Jesus' name. Amen.

HE CAME TO SAVE, NOT TO CONDEMN SINNERS

Enter by the narrow gate. For the gate is wide and the way is easy that leads to destruction, and those who enter by it are many. For the gate is narrow and the way is hard that leads to life, and those who find it are few. (MATTHEW 7:13–14)

Of all the people who ever lived on this earth, Jesus of Nazareth alone had the right to judge people. He is the Son of God and the only perfect man who always obeyed God's Law without ever once slipping into sin and disobedience.

But Jesus did not come into the world to condemn sinners. He came in meekness and humility to save sinners by taking our sin and guilt upon Himself and suffering the wrath and punishment of God in our place. He was gentle with sinners—like the Samaritan woman at the well (John 3), or the woman that the Jews brought to Him who had been caught in adultery (John 8). Jesus could rightfully have condemned her, but instead told the crowds, "Let him who has no sin be the first to cast a stone at her" (John 8:7). Jesus called all people to repent and believe the Good News that God loved them and sent Him to save them from their sin.

Jesus showed His concern for every facet of our life. He healed the bodies of the sick and fed them to show He is concerned about our physical needs. He reached out repeatedly to Judas, whom He knew would betray Him, longing to lead him to repent of that sin and find the forgiveness Jesus would freely give.

Finally, Jesus' earthly mission was to save us from our sins by taking those sins upon Himself and enduring the punishment for those sins on the cross. He rose from the dead and established His church by pouring out the Holy Spirit ten days after His ascension so that He could find sinners, call them to repentance, and forgive all their sins by the Gospel.

On the Last Day, He will return to earth. He will raise all the dead and all people will stand before Him for judgment. Those who believed in Him will live with Him in the perfect, glorious new heaven and new earth. Those who rejected Him will be punished eternally in hell. The Good News is that Jesus carried every sin of all people of all time to the cross and paid the full price. So God offers forgiveness to each and every person.

Lord Jesus, thank You for Your perfect love for us, and for suffering Your Father's wrath in our place. Give us loving hearts that care about our neighbors who are dying without You, that we may share the Good News of Your salvation. Amen.

WHAT DO THE SCRIPTURES SAY ABOUT JUDGING?

Judge not, that you be not judged. For with the judgment you pronounce you will be judged, and with the measure you use it will be measured to you. (MATTHEW 7:1–2)

One of life's most difficult challenges is having healthy relationships with other people. Our sinful nature turns each of us inward, seeking our own pleasures, our own welfare. It is not within us sinners to look upon other people with genuine, selfless love and concern. Only God can give us a loving and tender heart.

The Bible has much to say about how God would have His Christian children treat one another. In James we read,

> Do not speak evil against one another, brothers. The one who speaks against a brother or judges his brother, speaks evil against the law and judges the law. But if you judge the law, you are not a doer of the law but a judge. There is only one lawgiver and judge, He who is able to save and to destroy. But who are you to judge your neighbor? (James 4:11–12)

Only Jesus Christ is the true, righteous Judge. Only He knows the thoughts, desires, and motivations that lie behind the outward words and actions a person does. So we must leave all judgment and punishment to Him. The enemies of Jesus learned this when they brought a woman caught in adultery to trap Him.

> And as they continued to ask Him, He stood up and said to them, "Let him who is without sin among you be the first to throw a stone at her." And once more He bent down and wrote on the ground. But when they heard it, they went away one by one, beginning with the older ones, and Jesus was left alone with the woman standing before Him. (John 8:7–9)

Jesus gave us the golden rule as a guide to remind us how to treat one another. "So whatever you wish that others would do to you, do also to them, for this is the Law and the Prophets" (Matthew 7:12).

It is a helpful way for us to understand and live out the Commandments God has given to guide our living and teach us to recognize which of our desires arise from our sinful nature, and which are from God. Of course, whenever we look at ourselves in the mirror of God's Law, our sin stands out and terrifies our conscience. But Jesus reminds us there is a narrow door for our salvation. It is not the door of our good works or good intentions. It is His cross and empty tomb. "Jesus said to him, 'I am the way, and the truth, and the life. No one comes to the Father except through Me'" (John 14:6).

Lord Jesus, thank You for laying down Your life on the cross and taking it up again on the third day. You are the narrow door who alone leads me to the Father. Guide me each and every day to do unto others as I would have them do to me. Amen.

DIFFICULT THINGS TO UNDERSTAND ABOUT JUDGING AND FORGIVENESS

Do not give dogs what is holy, and do not throw your pearls before pigs, lest they trample them underfoot and turn to attack you. (MATTHEW 7:6)

Christians today often misinterpret Jesus' command, "Judge not, that you be not judged" (Matthew 7:1). If we take it to the extreme, we turn a blind eye to everyone who is sinning and leave them without warning because Jesus commanded us not to judge.

Clearly, this is not Jesus' intention. He asks us to draw a distinction between things we should judge and things we should not. Within His church, Christ charged us to discipline openly unrepentant sinners. That is, when a believer is openly sinning and acknowledges that God's Word clearly says his behavior is wrong, but he refuses to repent and change his living, then we are to discipline him by withholding Communion and proceeding to excommunication if he persists.

When Christ forbids us from judging, He is speaking of behavior that we take offense at. Especially when our feelings are hurt and we think we know their hidden thoughts and motives, concluding they have hurt us intentionally. This kind of judging involves things that are beyond our ability to know—that is, the secret thoughts and desires in other people's hearts. The Eighth Commandment directs us to assume others have good and kind motives in their heart for the actions they do—even if they offend and hurt us. But when a person is openly sinning and not repentant for it—then we are to gently confront their sin. There can be no good motive to slander someone, steal, or commit adultery.

Perhaps the most confusing verse in this passage is verse 6 where Jesus says, "Do not give dogs what is holy, and do not throw your pearls before pigs, lest they trample them underfoot and turn to attack you."

Jesus is speaking of the fallout that can result when we hypocritically judge our Christian brothers and sisters—especially when we self-righteously point out the speck in their eye while ignoring the log in our eyes. These believers are the holy pearls. Improperly judging or excommunicating an innocent Christian is casting that believer to the unbelievers (dogs and pigs) and causing an offense that may destroy their faith.

Finally, in Matthew 7:9-11, Jesus asks, "Or which one of you, if his son asks him for bread, will give him a stone? Or if he asks for a fish, will give him a serpent? If you then, who are evil, know how to give good gifts to your children, how much more will your Father who is in heaven give good things to those who ask Him!"

Living this kind of life may seem difficult, but it is an example of Jesus using exaggeration to build confidence in us that whenever we pray to God, He will always give us good gifts. We all know our human parents are sinners who are not perfect. Yet if we asked them for bread or a fish, we are confident they won't give us a stone, or a serpent. If we can have that kind of confidence in our parents who are sinful, how much more can we ask of our heavenly Father in prayer with all boldness and trust?

Heavenly Father, please give us what we need to honor Your name and treat our fellow Christians with humility and genuine love. In Jesus' name we pray. Amen.

GOD'S GIFT OF HEALING FOR SHATTERED RELATIONSHIPS

Ask, and it will be given to you; seek, and you will find; knock, and it will be opened to you. For everyone who asks receives, and the one who seeks finds, and to the one who knocks it will be opened. (MATTHEW 7:7–8)

Living in peace with other Christians is difficult, especially when we are offended by things they say or do. Christ strongly encourages us to approach our brothers in genuine love, humility, and concern for their eternal well-being. Doing that requires God's help, so He invites us to pray—particularly when we must confront a brother or sister caught up in sin, and especially when that sin has deeply hurt or offended us.

As we go forward through Jesus' life, we will see a few times when the disciples will deeply offend one another, and great disputes will break out. Especially when brothers James and John try to take the seats at Jesus' right and left hand. Or when the disciples argue about which of them is greatest. Similar disputes break out in our congregations today, threatening to splinter and divide us. We see people leave the church for years and decades because of a hurt—real or perceived.

In worship each week, God takes the "log out of our eyes" as we confess our sins and recognize that we are sinners, just the same as our brothers and sisters in Christ. Our Kyrie prayer, "Lord, have mercy," after Confession and Absolution, is a great example of the asking, seeking, and knocking Jesus taught us to do. For in the Kyrie, we ask God to empower us to live in peace and love with one another.

The Bible readings and sermons remind us of the price Jesus paid for our sins. In Holy Communion, Christ gives us His body and His blood, providing us not only forgiveness and peace but also the strength we need to love one another as much as we love ourselves. And when we gather side by side at the Lord's Table, Christ unites us into one body—loving and caring for one another, especially those brothers and sisters caught in sin or struggling against it.

Living and working side by side with sinners is difficult. But Christ has made the way for us and strengthens us to live in peace through His Word and Sacraments.

Heavenly Father, bless our times when we gather together for worship. Bring Your Son, Jesus Christ, before our eyes, that we may find pardon and peace and share Your wonderful gifts with all people. In Jesus' name. Amen.

THE SERMON ON THE MOUNT, PART 6

A Tree and Its Fruit; I Never Knew You; Build Your House on the Rock

WEEK 16—MATTHEW 7:15–29

Beware of false prophets, who come to you in sheep's clothing but inwardly are ravenous wolves. You will recognize them by their fruits. Are grapes gathered from thornbushes, or figs from thistles? So, every healthy tree bears good fruit, but the diseased tree bears bad fruit. A healthy tree cannot bear bad fruit, nor can a diseased tree bear good fruit. Every tree that does not bear good fruit is cut down and thrown into the fire. Thus you will recognize them by their fruits.

"Not everyone who says to Me, 'Lord, Lord,' will enter the kingdom of heaven, but the one who does the will of My Father who is in heaven. On that day many will say to Me, 'Lord, Lord, did we not prophesy in Your name, and cast out demons in Your name, and do many mighty works in Your name?' And then will I declare to them, 'I never knew you; depart from Me, you workers of lawlessness.'

"Everyone then who hears these words of Mine and does them will be like a wise man who built his house on the rock. And the rain fell, and the floods came, and the winds blew and beat on that house, but it did not fall, because it had been founded on the rock. And everyone who hears these words of Mine and does not do them will be like a foolish man who built his house on the sand. And the rain fell, and the floods came, and the winds blew and beat against that house, and it fell, and great was the fall of it."

And when Jesus finished these sayings, the crowds were astonished at His teaching, for He was teaching them as one who had authority, and not as their scribes.

LIVING AS FOLLOWERS OF CHRIST

Thus you will recognize them by their fruits. (MATTHEW 7:20)

Now Jesus concludes His Sermon on the Mount, which we have been studying for the last six weeks. In the first part of the sermon, week 11 in this devotional, Jesus taught about the blessings for those who repent and receive God's forgiveness, which He has come to bring. In the second part, week 12, He taught us how to use the Ten Commandments as a guide for daily life in the kingdom of God. During week 13, Jesus taught the right way to undertake three important Christian disciplines: giving, prayer, and fasting. In week 14, Jesus turned our attention from earthly treasures to storing up heavenly treasures and taught us to overcome fear and anxiety. Last week, week 15, Jesus turned our focus to how we should deal with others, especially when it comes to confronting people in their sin.

In this final section, Jesus warns us about false teachers who will arise in the church. He gives a familiar picture of the drastic difference for those who conduct their lives by His teachings and those who reject them. On the Last Day, we will all be judged by our "fruits." Those who obey Jesus' teachings, particularly repenting of their sins and believing in Him as their Savior, will be blessed with eternal life in Christ. Those who reject Jesus here on earth will be condemned to hell.

From the previous teachings in the Sermon on the Mount, we learned what it looks like for believers to live life as followers of Christ. Jesus has given us guidelines for what it looks like to bear good fruit!

First, we live in daily confession and repentance. Regarding Baptism, Martin Luther says in the Small Catechism, "The Old Adam in us should by daily contrition and repentance be drowned and die with all sins and evil desires, and that a new man should daily emerge and arise to live before God in righteousness and purity forever" (Small Catechism, Baptism, Fourth Part). Every day, we die to our old self in repentance, and rise again in Christ because of our Baptism.

Then, as we go about our daily lives, God makes us the salt of the earth and gives us strength to proclaim His goodness through our works. Our lives are guided by the Ten Commandments and Jesus' teachings on them. Additionally, our lives are marked by faith and trust in His provisions, not anxiousness or concern with our physical belongings.

With this in mind, we have a framework for what it looks like to live as a follower of Christ, so we can have confidence that we will be counted among the "good fruit," or those who built their house on the rock.

Heavenly Father, drown the old Adam in me and raise me up in my Baptism daily. Amen.

BEWARE FALSE TEACHERS

Beware of false prophets, who come to you in sheep's clothing but inwardly are ravenous wolves. (MATTHEW 7:15)

In this closing portion of the Sermon on the Mount, Jesus teaches His followers how to recognize the differences between true teachers and false teachers who will arise in the church.

The first item to note here is that Jesus says false teachers *will* be present in the church. These false prophets will prophesy, cast out demons, and do mighty works in the name of Jesus (see Matthew 7:22), but they will not enter the kingdom of heaven. This is a sober warning to all of us to be on the lookout for false teachers.

The next item to note is that Jesus says these false teachers will be present *in the church*. These are not leaders in cults or different religions—these are leaders in the Christian Church, who claim to preach in Jesus' name. However, they are wolves in sheep's clothing, disguising their false beliefs under the guise of Christianity.

How can we identify these false teachers? Jesus tells us to judge these false prophets by their fruits. When Jesus talks about the fruit a person bears, He is often referring to their works. But when He talks about clergy, pastors, and teachers, He is speaking about their teachings even more than their deeds. We must especially pay attention to what they teach about Jesus Christ (being God and man, the promised Savior), and His mission (to save sinners by His death and resurrection). If they turn the focus off of Jesus to themselves, or to our works, then they are false teachers.

Sadly, these false teachers will not just deceive Christians who aren't careful—they are really deceiving themselves into thinking they teach the truth. In reality, they are serving Satan, devouring the sheep, and they neither know Christ as He really is nor are they known by Christ as true believers. Their fate is eternal destruction in hell.

Jesus closes this portion of the Sermon on the Mount by showing us how important it is that we build our lives on His teachings. For those who do so, nothing in life will be able to shake them, not even Christ's judgment when He returns. But for those who refuse, their lives will crumble and, without true faith in Christ, they will perish in hell eternally. Think of how haunting an ending that is for the hearers.

Usually, pastors end their sermons with the Gospel, but Jesus ended this sermon with the Law—letting it resound in the ears of His hearers. Their reaction to Him and His teachings will determine their eternal destiny. If they repent and believe, they will be saved. If they reject Him and His teachings, they will suffer eternally.

Thanks be to God for His grace, freely given to us undeserving sinners!

Holy Spirit, guide my heart and keep me far from false teachers. Surround me with faithful pastors and teachers all my days. Amen.

JESUS' POWER AND AUTHORITY

And when Jesus finished these sayings, the crowds were astonished at His teaching, for He was teaching them as one who had authority, and not as their scribes. (MATTHEW 7:28–29)

False teachers who pose as true teachers have been in the world since Satan slithered into the Garden of Eden. They fill the pages of the Old Testament and are equally noticeable in the New Testament. The Epistles of Peter, John, and Jude especially warn against false teachers.

During Jesus' ministry, He exposed the false teaching of the priests, scribes, and Pharisees. He warned the people about them and exposed their hypocrisy and foolishness. They taught that people could earn heaven by man-made works and laws, and Jesus knew the great danger they posed for God's people—the broad, easy way that leads to destruction. So He faced their persecution and opposition to continue teaching the truth.

The people to whom Jesus preached recognized that He had a different kind of power and authority than the scribes: "And when Jesus finished these sayings, the crowds were astonished at His teaching, for He was teaching them as one who had authority, and not as their scribes" (Matthew 7:28–29). Perhaps the false teachers of the time also recognized His power and felt threatened by it, as well as the sway Jesus held with the people.

In the end, the false teachers rose against Him, condemned Him to death, and handed Him over to Pontius Pilate. They shouted for His death and pressured Pilate to condemn Him. Even though Pilate found no fault in Jesus, the false teachers were so threatened by Jesus' teaching that they convinced Pilate to crucify Jesus.

Yet Jesus' warning at His trial called them to repent: "But I tell you, from now on you will see the Son of Man seated at the right hand of Power and coming on the clouds of heaven" (Matthew 26:64). Even the tearing of the temple curtain when He died (see Matthew 27:51) was God's direct warning to the priests. The priests would be the only ones in the temple to witness it, since only priests and Levites were able to enter the temple itself.

Jesus warned His followers not to be impressed by these false teachers and their power and popularity. In the same way, He warns us from being impressed by big TV evangelists who build huge ministries and are widely applauded. We need to examine their teachings about Jesus and salvation and discern whether they are faithful to Christ and His teachings. Thanks be to God for all of the faithful pastors and church workers who proclaim Christ's death and resurrection until He comes!

Jesus, hold me fast to You, the true teacher with all power and authority. Amen.

JESUS IS LORD

For I was hungry and you gave Me no food, I was thirsty and you gave Me no drink, I was a stranger and you did not welcome Me, naked and you did not clothe Me, sick and in prison and you did not visit Me. (MATTHEW 25:42–43)

Jesus offers a terrifying statement in Matthew 7:21: "Not everyone who says to Me, 'Lord, Lord,' will enter the kingdom of heaven, but the one who does the will of My Father who is in heaven." When we read this verse, many Christians start to wonder if they will be counted among those who are cast into hell on the Last Day. How can we know that we are saved?

The truth is, there will be self-proclaimed "Christians" who will not enter heaven. They will have called Jesus Lord but will not have done the will of God. They will not have repented of their sin and trusted in Jesus Christ alone as their Savior. They will be counted among the goats on the Last Day.

Just saying "Jesus is Lord" does not guarantee your faith. We read in Matthew 8:29 that even demons recognized Jesus as God: "And behold, they cried out, 'What have You to do with us, O Son of God? Have You come here to torment us before the time?'" As James similarly writes, "Even the demons believe—and shudder!" (James 2:19). Blind acknowledgment of Jesus as God does not equal true faith.

But hear this: we are not saved by our works.

When Jesus speaks about doing what He teaches, He is talking about genuine, saving faith, which puts His words into practice like trees bearing fruit. This is in stark contrast to those who speak His name but don't believe.

Our genuine faith in the Son of God can't help but be expressed in good works that speak to the goodness of our Good Father! "In the same way, let your light shine before others, so that they may see your good works and give glory to your Father who is in heaven" (Matthew 5:16). Our good works do not save us, but they allow us to proclaim the glory, grace, and mercy of God to those around us.

Jesus, thank You for perfectly obeying God's Law in my place and taking my sins to the cross to be forgiven. Amen.

FALSE PASTORS

On that day many will say to Me, "Lord, Lord, did we not prophesy in Your name, and cast out demons in Your name, and do many mighty works in Your name?" And then will I declare to them, "I never knew you; depart from Me, you workers of lawlessness." (MATTHEW 7:22–23)

When reading this passage, one question that comes to mind is this: *How can false prophets prophesy, cast out demons, and perform mighty miracles in Jesus' name?* If they're false prophets, how are they able to do these things that we usually associate with those who are believers in Christ? How can we discern false prophets?

These are difficult questions, and they might make us worry that the pastors who baptized us, confirmed us, or gave us Communion were actually false leaders despite the fact that their outward acts make it seem like they're really true teachers. And if they possibly were, does that mean our Baptism is invalid? Or that we didn't really receive Holy Communion?

First, let's talk about how false prophets can perform these miracles. It is not our faith that has the power to do these things, but God working through Christ's name and His Word. Pastors are ordinary men called to an extraordinary vocation— to faithfully preach the Word of God to His people. God works powerfully through pastors, but the pastors themselves are not the source of that power.

That is why we can be confident we received the new birth in Baptism and Christ's body and blood in Holy Communion whether the pastor who officiated believed it himself or not. God's Word makes these Sacraments valid—not the pastor's character or faith. So even if you were baptized by an unbelieving pastor, your Baptism is valid because of Christ's Word and the faith the Spirit created through that Word and Sacrament.

Just because such a leader performed works through which God saves people does not mean he will escape punishment. Pastors are saved only by faith, not the works of ministry they perform.

So it's true, then, that false teachers could cast out demons, prophesy, or perform miracles in Jesus' name, and still be false teachers. But it's only because God is working through His Word that they proclaim to perform these mighty acts! We still need to discern whether they are false prophets by comparing their teachings to what is in the Word of God. That is the true barometer for discerning between false prophets and true teachers.

We don't know exactly why God would choose to use false teachers to work through. Many of God's actions are a mystery to us humans; many of them don't make sense, based on our perspective. There are many things about God that we will never understand on this side of heaven, but we can be confident that His Holy Spirit will sustain us in our faith until we see Him face to face.

Holy Spirit, keep me close to God all my days until You call me home. Amen.

PREPARING FOR CHRIST'S RETURN AND JUDGMENT

And when Jesus finished these sayings, the crowds were astonished at His teaching, for He was teaching them as one who had authority, and not as their scribes. (MATTHEW 7:28–29)

Jesus' words in this entire Sermon on the Mount (and throughout Scripture) expose our sin and show us our Savior. In the Sermon on the Mount, we hear some of the most marvelous depictions of grace, but we also hear some of the most serious condemnations. As you read this portion of Scripture, find rest in the moments of grace and mercy, and run to the Father in confession and repentance in moments of conviction.

This set of verses also teaches us how to live in love and service to God and one another. We should seek to "bear fruit in keeping with repentance," as John the Baptist said in Matthew 3:8. Our faith is lived out in the fruit of our actions. We are not saved by our works, but they are the outpouring of Christ in us. May we always bear good fruit and build our house on the rock!

However, Jesus also cautions us against listening to and believing in false teachers who distort God's Word and minimize the importance of Christ's work. When Christ's work is minimized, the importance of our works is greatly exaggerated. This can lead to false prophets preaching a false gospel—one that places the focus on what we can do to earn salvation, not what Christ has already accomplished for us through His life, death, and resurrection.

When we consider all these things, it is important to keep Judgment Day in mind. That can be a scary thought—no one wants to think about dying!—but for us Christians, the Last Day will be a glorious day in which we are united with our heavenly Father and begin our eternal life in His presence. We do not want to be so focused on the external impression we give others that we neglect repentance and faith. None of us want Christ to say "I never knew you" on that Last Day. We want to be welcomed into heaven with some of the most comforting words in all of Scripture: "Well done, good and faithful servant" (Matthew 25:21).

The Scripture readings and the sermon we hear each week in the worship service allow us to hear Jesus' words, understand His teachings, and learn how we can practice the things Jesus teaches in this and His other sermons.

May God use this Scripture to draw you closer to Him in daily confession, repentance, and forgiveness! Our heavenly Father graciously waits to forgive our sins and increase our faith day by day through His Holy Spirit.

Father, draw me closer to You each day through confession and repentance. In Jesus' name. Amen.

JESUS HEALS THE SICK

WEEK 17—MATTHEW 8:1–17

When He came down from the mountain, great crowds followed Him. And behold, a leper came to Him and knelt before Him, saying, "Lord, if You will, You can make me clean." And Jesus stretched out His hand and touched him, saying, "I will; be clean." And immediately his leprosy was cleansed. And Jesus said to him, "See that you say nothing to anyone, but go, show yourself to the priest and offer the gift that Moses commanded, for a proof to them."

When He had entered Capernaum, a centurion came forward to Him, appealing to Him, "Lord, my servant is lying paralyzed at home, suffering terribly." And He said to him, "I will come and heal him." But the centurion replied, "Lord, I am not worthy to have You come under my roof, but only say the word, and my servant will be healed. For I too am a man under authority, with soldiers under me. And I say to one, 'Go,' and he goes, and to another, 'Come,' and he comes, and to my servant, 'Do this,' and he does it." When Jesus heard this, He marveled and said to those who followed Him, "Truly, I tell you, with no one in Israel have I found such faith. I tell you, many will come from east and west and recline at table with Abraham, Isaac, and Jacob in the kingdom of heaven, while the sons of the kingdom will be thrown into the outer darkness. In that place there will be weeping and gnashing of teeth." And to the centurion Jesus said, "Go; let it be done for you as you have believed." And the servant was healed at that very moment.

And when Jesus entered Peter's house, He saw his mother-in-law lying sick with a fever. He touched her hand, and the fever left her, and she rose and began to serve Him. That evening they brought to Him many who were oppressed by demons, and He cast out the spirits with a word and healed all who were sick. This was to fulfill what was spoken by the prophet Isaiah: "He took our illnesses and bore our diseases."

HE TRAVELED THE COUNTRYSIDE, HEALING THE SICK

When He came down from the mountain, great crowds followed Him. (MATTHEW 8:1)

Dealing with sickness and disease has been a part of the world since Adam and Eve took a bite of the fruit in the garden. It has brought with it heartache and sorrow as healthy bodies are destroyed. Whole continents have been ravaged by various diseases. It is as much a fact of life as death and taxes. It was not the way in which humanity was created to be, but it is now a part of existence on planet earth.

In Jesus' day, there were already doctors and medicines used for combating illness. Luke was himself a doctor—"Luke the beloved physician greets you" (Colossians 4:14)—and Jesus would remind His followers that it is the sick in need of a doctor, not the healthy (see Matthew 9:12). While not up to the standards expected of modern-day hospitals and doctors' offices, there were those who cared for the sick. Their abilities would have been limited by the time they lived in, herbal remedies, basic surgical techniques, and limited availability. Healers did the best they could, but it often wasn't enough.

Jesus, however, came and healed completely. Miraculously. He traveled the countryside, healing the sick. His healing even touched the lives of those whom modern medicine cannot heal: people living with leprosy and paralysis. There was no need to stay overnight in a hospital or work on recovery. When Jesus healed a person, they were made whole again. It wasn't as if there was time needed for the legs to adjust to their new mobility or for scars to heal.

Here was the Word made flesh. Jesus was the Word spoken in the beginning to create. There He stood among those whom our fallen creation afflicted. He spoke, and they were re-created. It was not just a healing, it was making people whole again—their physical bodies returning to the way they were supposed to be, without ailment. As soon as the Word spoke, it happened—(re)creation happening before the eyes of the people.

The crowds began to follow Jesus. They traversed the countryside, navigated the thoroughfares of cities, and walked the streets of small towns, all so that they might get a glimpse of the power and authority with which this wandering rabbi spoke. His teachings were incredible, and He backed them up with His actions. This was not a charlatan planting people in the audience to be "healed." They were the outcast and downtrodden. Those that the crowds often walked past on the other side of the street. This man spoke over them, and they were healed.

The crowds grew. The work of Jesus continued. They came to see the marvelous and were not disappointed.

Lord, may I marvel as the crowds did at the works Your Son has done. May I open my eyes to see the work He has done, is doing, and will accomplish in my life. In Jesus' name. Amen.

THE BODY IS AN IMPORTANT PART OF LIFE

When He came down from the mountain, great crowds followed Him. . . . And when Jesus entered Peter's house, He saw his mother-in-law lying sick with a fever. He touched her hand, and the fever left her, and she rose and began to serve Him. (MATTHEW 8:1, 14–15)

There is a simple, heretical thought that has existed for generations: the spiritual is greater than the physical. Councils have been called, creeds written, and doctrines honed all to battle this false idea. But it is an easy lie to believe. Look at the world that surrounds humanity. There is death, starvation, warfare, injustice, and evil upon evil. The preacher of Ecclesiastes ponders, "I saw under the sun that in the place of justice, even there was wickedness, and in the place of righteousness, even there was wickedness" (3:16). Is there not a longing to leave behind this earthly vision and find another, more serene spiritual realm? Wise men and mystics have hunted for this ascension to nirvana, if only the spirit could overcome the physical form.

Then why does Jesus heal people from physical ailments? If the whole purpose of this earthly life is for a person to grow toward their own spiritual ascension, why would Jesus heal the sick that He came across in His time of ministry? Because the physical is also a part of the created being. Often the spiritual overrules the physical, but has the day ever changed from good to bad when all you needed was a snack or a nap? Don't the physical things of this world bless the soul as well? Why does a song, vibrations hitting a membrane in the ear, alter the state of mind? If you think this idea is silly,

then look no further than the words of Scripture to see its validity: "And whenever the harmful spirit from God was upon Saul, David took the lyre and played it with his hand. So Saul was refreshed and was well, and the harmful spirit departed from him" (1 Samuel 16:23).

Jesus knows that the spirit and the body are not two separate pieces. They are, instead, a united whole. He cares deeply for those who are in physical distress because He knows that their body is an important part of their life. He doesn't speak of some spiritual day when they get to separate from the body but instead declares the beauty and worthiness of the physical world through His healing of body and mind. Not only that, He returns purpose to those who have struggled. Look at Peter's mother-in-law in the verses above. The fever leaves, and she begins to serve! Jesus healed her not just to remain but to love her neighbors. As Jesus heals, He declares that His new heaven and new earth will be one united in a perfected resurrection of body and spirit.

Heavenly Father, may I rejoice today in the person You created me to be. Help me see the joy of this physical world, even as evil appears to surround me. May I be used as an instrument of Your kingdom to others today. As I have been healed, may I take Your healing to my neighbors. In Jesus' name. Amen.

THE RESURRECTION OF THE BODY

That evening they brought to Him many who were oppressed by demons, and He cast out the spirits with a word and healed all who were sick. This was to fulfill what was spoken by the prophet Isaiah: "He took our illnesses and bore our diseases." (MATTHEW 8:16–17)

Through the code of Jewish Law, many people who had varying types of ailments and illnesses were prohibited from being touched. Yet here Jesus reaches out not only to heal but to physically touch those who were sick. In this He fulfilled the words of the prophet Isaiah: "Surely He has borne our griefs and carried our sorrows; yet we esteemed Him stricken, smitten by God, and afflicted" (Isaiah 53:4).

A lie believed by many people is that they must be made well before they can be loved by God. If only they could be a little more well-behaved, a little healthier, a little more—fill in the blank. But Jesus takes on the sickness of mankind. He takes on Himself the sinful, fallen world and gives back true healing. As He traveled the countryside, His miracles gave testament to the resurrection that was to come.

Every week, churches around the world confess the Apostles' Creed. In it, there are two simple lines that state belief in the resurrection of the body and in the life everlasting. Core to the beliefs of every Christian person are these two ideas that were put in the simplest creed, written for people to remember the most basic, most important, tenets of the faith: "I believe in . . . the resurrection of the body, and the life everlasting" (*LSB*, p. 159).

As Jesus healed the sick, He was the one who declared the importance of resurrection and the life everlasting. This was a cornerstone of His ministry. He would have a never-ending kingdom in which the fall would be undone. Sinful nature would be removed, and there would be a resurrection in which creation would be put back into the perfect state in which it had been created. In taking on the sins of mankind, He also took on the sinful brokenness that was encountered by the entrance of illness and disease. He would reach out and touch those who had been deemed unclean. But in a miraculous moment, He would transfer His cleanliness to their affliction.

Here, once again, was a glimpse of the kingdom that is coming. This carpenter's son, by every person with leprosy healed and every paralyzed person who walked, was proclaiming the day in which there would be no more sickness and no more tears. Instead of seeing a day of spiritual fulfillment, Jesus was declaring that all would once again be made right. Bodies and spirits restored. His joy was not just in fire insurance from the pits of Sheol but in the whole redemption of the world. It will all be made new in the resurrection with a life that will never end.

Heavenly Father, help me to long for the day when Jesus returns—when the resurrection is declared over my body to walk in the life everlasting. Lord, open my eyes to see that life begins now. Through the saving work of Your Son, I am already on this journey. May I see the world as He did. In Jesus' name. Amen.

CENTURIONS

When Jesus heard this, He marveled and said to those who followed Him, "Truly, I tell you, with no one in Israel have I found such faith. I tell you, many will come from east and west and recline at table with Abraham, Isaac, and Jacob in the kingdom of heaven, while the sons of the kingdom will be thrown into the outer darkness. In that place there will be weeping and gnashing of teeth." And to the centurion Jesus said, "Go; let it be done for you as you have believed." And the servant was healed at that very moment. (MATTHEW 8:10–13)

These verses show that Jesus came to seek and save the lost. He would start with the people of Israel, but He was here to save the world—everyone. A Gentile centurion heard about the work of Jesus and called for Him to heal his servant. Another Roman centurion makes this declaration of who Jesus is after His death: "And when the centurion, who stood facing Him, saw that in this way He breathed His last, he said, 'Truly this man was the Son of God!'" (Mark 15:39). Roman centurions play a role throughout the New Testament. Here is another example:

At Caesarea, there was a man named Cornelius, a centurion of what was known as the Italian Cohort, a devout man who feared God with all his household, gave alms generously to the people, and prayed continually to God. . . . "Can anyone withhold water for baptizing these people, who have received the Holy Spirit just as we have?" And [Peter] commanded them to be baptized in the name of Jesus Christ. Then they asked him to remain for some days. (Acts 10:1–2, 47–48)

The story of Cornelius in the book of Acts is an incredible testament to the saving grace Jesus came to deliver to all people. Both Cornelius and Peter had dreams. Cornelius, the Gentile centurion, dreamed of Jesus telling him to call for Peter to come minister to his household. Peter, on the other hand, has a dream showing him that there is no longer a separation between clean and unclean—that all people are worthy of the Gospel.

Why the connection of Roman centurions? These were the battle commanders of the Roman army. They would have had command of between eighty and one hundred men (a century). Why would this one Roman profession be important enough for Jesus to have encountered them and Scripture to mention them throughout the New Testament?

Centurions kept law and order. They would have been seen as the oppressors of Israel, violently stamping out any rebellion. When Jesus heals the servant of a centurion, when the centurion at the cross is the one to confess the nature of Jesus, and when Peter baptizes the household of Cornelius, it would have been a clear message: Jesus came to save all people, even *those* people.

There is no person on earth who is outside the love shown by the work of Jesus. The example of centurions is Jesus' firm exclamation point that "God did not send His Son into the world to condemn the world, but in order that the world might be saved through Him" (John 3:17).

Lord, may I have eyes like You to see that You have come to save all people. I rejoice that I have been saved through Jesus and pray that more would come to know the Good News of His life, death, and resurrection. In Jesus' name. Amen.

"IF YOU WILL"

And behold, a leper came to Him and knelt before Him, saying, "Lord, if You will, You can make me clean." (MATTHEW 8:2)

Leprosy is a devastating disease. It eats away at the flesh until a person finally succumbs and dies. But it also robs that person of physical human connection because it is spread through contact. No hugs from family or friends. No brushing past people in the marketplace. No firm handshake to close a deal. It not only creates a physical sickness but removes physical touch and adds an element of mental struggle as well.

Matthew does not tell his readers how long this man with leprosy had been dealing with the disease. What would be known is that because of the laws of Israel, he would have had to remove himself from the general population so that the disease would be quarantined. This man had been living for some time away from others. If he kept any company, it would have been with other people who had leprosy.

Is it not strange, then, that when he approaches Jesus, he simply says, "Lord, if You will, You can make me clean"? Not a question or a request, but a statement. A bold one at that. The declaration is that Jesus has the power. The leper is not questioning *if* it is in Jesus' power; he is stating, "You have the power, if it is in Your will." It is an incredibly different sentiment.

This is not a new idea to those who have followed God over the centuries. It harkens to the stories of the Old Testament: Noah trusted God and built an ark. Joseph saw the intention of evil turned to good. David believed in a sling against a giant. Esther lived courageously in faith and saved her people. Three men stood before a king and declared, "If this be so, our God whom we serve is able to deliver us from the burning fiery furnace, and He will deliver us out of your hand, O king. But if not, be it known to you, O king, that we will not serve your gods or worship the golden image that you have set up" (Daniel 3:17–18).

A man with leprosy now stood in the long line of saints who trusted God above their own knowledge, hopes, and well-being. He saw the Word made flesh and could have begged for the Messiah to return his health. He could have tried to force Jesus into healing him by pointing to the crowds—they had come to see a miracle, after all. There are any number of ways this afflicted man could have approached Jesus.

Instead, he proclaimed the power and authority that Jesus possesses. Not "*if* You can make me clean" but "You *can* make me clean." There is no doubt in this man. He bowed down before Jesus, knowing exactly who He was. And when Jesus heard his declaration, He simply responded with two powerful words: "I will."

May we come to Jesus with our uncleanness and declare this same thing. May we all hear the "I will" that is the gift of the cross and the empty tomb.

Dear Jesus, show me the places in my life where I need Your power and authority to heal me, body and spirit. May I come to You and simply declare, "If You will, You can make me clean." Amen.

TODAY, NOT ONE DAY IN THE FUTURE

That evening they brought to Him many who were oppressed by demons, and He cast out the spirits with a word and healed all who were sick. (MATTHEW 8:16)

Miracles in the Bible are fun. Why? They are clear moments where the supernatural reaches out and touches the natural. People get sick, people die. But when Jesus comes along, things are different. The easy notion is to get focused on the extraordinary work that Jesus did as the Word made flesh. It was incredible. Today, even a simple surgical procedure takes weeks or even months to heal from. Yet Jesus was fully healing people who had diseases with no known cure. He did it by touching them. He did it by speaking their health into existence.

But what was Jesus continuing to teach by doing these miracles? That He cares about the ordinary. He could have looked into the eyes of the man with leprosy and said, "I won't today, but one day you will have the resurrection, so until then, life is just going to be terrible." But He didn't. When the centurion showed up presenting a greater faith than many of the people of God, He could have said, "Listen, you're Roman. Wait until My time here is done, then the Kingdom will be for you." But He didn't. Peter's mother-in-law had a fever, and He could have said, "Keep hydrated and rest. I'll see you next week." But He didn't.

No! Jesus came in and healed. He healed the man with leprosy, whose life was transformed. He healed the servant of the centurion because He came for all people. He healed Peter's mother-in-law to bring her sickness to an end. He cares for people. Not someday down the road, but today.

Not when there is some great awakening, but when there's a fever on a Saturday. He is teaching His people that even though there will be a new heaven and a new earth at His second coming, He cares for people now.

Temptation arises for followers of Jesus to just wait. The world is a tough place. Maybe it would be better to cloister believers in a safe place where they can be unhindered by the world. Or perhaps to not care about this earthly life and only focus on what is to come. But the life everlasting, the life of the Kingdom, doesn't start when you die—it starts when you are made alive in the waters of your Baptism! It comes with the spoken and read Word. It comes in humble bread and wine that are joined to Jesus' body and blood.

These miracles are the steadfast love of God for His people. They declare that He loves ordinary people, in their ordinary lives, going about ordinary tasks. He will heal them to make their lives better, to pull them away from suffering, to give them new purpose. Christians, then, must care about this life, the gift that it is even amid a fallen world. Rejoice! You are not living in the waiting room to eternal life. Jesus has brought the kingdom of God down to this imperfect world. Follow His example.

Lord, may I follow Jesus in my daily life. May I remember that this life is not waiting for the beginning of the next but that I am already redeemed. Help me declare the praises of Jesus to a world in need. In Jesus' name. Amen.

NICODEMUS'S VISIT

WEEK 18—JOHN 3:1–21

Now there was a man of the Pharisees named Nicodemus, a ruler of the Jews. This man came to Jesus by night and said to Him, "Rabbi, we know that You are a teacher come from God, for no one can do these signs that You do unless God is with him." Jesus answered him, "Truly, truly, I say to you, unless one is born again he cannot see the kingdom of God." Nicodemus said to Him, "How can a man be born when he is old? Can he enter a second time into his mother's womb and be born?" Jesus answered, "Truly, truly, I say to you, unless one is born of water and the Spirit, he cannot enter the kingdom of God. That which is born of the flesh is flesh, and that which is born of the Spirit is spirit. Do not marvel that I said to you, 'You must be born again.' The wind blows where it wishes, and you hear its sound, but you do not know where it comes from or where it goes. So it is with everyone who is born of the Spirit."

Nicodemus said to Him, "How can these things be?" Jesus answered him, "Are you the teacher of Israel and yet you do not understand these things? Truly, truly, I say to you, we speak of what we know, and bear witness to what we have seen, but you do not receive our testimony. If I have told you earthly things and you do not believe, how can you believe if I tell you heavenly things? No one has ascended into heaven except He who descended from heaven, the Son of Man. And as Moses lifted up the serpent in the wilderness, so must the Son of Man be lifted up, that whoever believes in Him may have eternal life.

"For God so loved the world, that He gave His only Son, that whoever believes in Him should not perish but have eternal life. For God did not send His Son into the world to condemn the world, but in order that the world might be saved through Him. Whoever believes in Him is not condemned, but whoever does not believe is condemned already, because he has not believed in the name of the only Son of God. And this is the judgment: the light has come into the world, and people loved the darkness rather than the light because their works were evil. For everyone who does wicked things hates the light and does not come to the light, lest his works should be exposed. But whoever does what is true comes to the light, so that it may be clearly seen that his works have been carried out in God."

THE JEWISH GROUPS JESUS ENCOUNTERED

Now there was a man of the Pharisees named Nicodemus, a ruler of the Jews. (JOHN 3:1)

In John 3, Jesus is approached by a man named Nicodemus who was a Pharisee and a ruler of the people. The Pharisees are one of many groups of religious leaders Jesus encounters in His ministry. One of the challenging things about reading the Gospels is keeping track of these different groups, remembering their differences of belief and focus, and remembering who belongs to which group.

When Jesus encountered Nicodemus's group, the Pharisees, the conversation centered upon the external following of Jewish laws and customs. The Pharisees looked good on paper, but their hearts were often more concerned with how righteous they appeared than how righteous they truly were. The Pharisees were laypeople who were particularly devoted to the teachings of another group, known as the scribes. Several Pharisees are named in the New Testament including this same Nicodemus, as well as Joseph of Arimathea—they both care for Jesus' body in burial. Perhaps most notably, the apostle Paul had been trained as a Pharisee.

The Pharisees were allied with the scribes, who copied manuscripts to preserve them. The scribes were considered experts in Jewish law. They tended to be teachers as well, but they did not have a full understanding of the Old Testament. They viewed it as a series of laws by which the people of Israel could earn heaven. They failed to see it was really about the coming Messiah, who would win salvation for all sinners. The Pharisees were dedicated to the teachings of the scribes. On one occasion of Jesus' teaching, the people remarked that Jesus taught "as one who had authority, and not as the scribes" (Mark 1:22).

When Jesus encountered the group called the Sadducees, the conversation centered upon their mistaken beliefs. Most crucially, the Sadducees did not believe in life after death. They were considered conservative because they only held the first five books of the Hebrew Bible as authoritative Scripture (Genesis through Deuteronomy). Since they did not see obvious references to the resurrection from the dead, heaven and hell, or angels in the books of Moses, they rejected these teachings. Whenever the Gospels refer to the chief priests, it is likely they belong to the party of the Sadducees.

The people of Israel were like sheep without a shepherd because these three groups only seemed to care about showing off their righteousness and fighting with each other for supremacy. They believed one's relationship with God depended on how one lived their life. These groups condemned anyone who was not living up to their standard of righteousness. When Jesus encountered the scribes, Pharisees, or Sadducees, He rebuked and corrected their false teachings—often in the presence of the very people these religious leaders were supposed to care for.

The antagonism between Jesus and these religious leaders is central to the story of the Gospels. The scribes, Pharisees, and Sadducees end up forming a temporary alliance against Jesus, their common enemy. Jesus predicts exactly what will happen in this very text from John 3. Jesus, the Son of Man, will be lifted up on the cross to give eternal life to all who believe in Him.

Lord Jesus, You faced many enemies from many factions in Your earthly life, and Your church and the world suffer many factions today. Bring unity and peace to Your one, holy, universal church. Amen.

TEACHING ISRAEL'S TEACHER

[Nicodemus] came to Jesus by night and said to Him, "Rabbi, we know that You are a teacher come from God, for no one can do these signs that You do unless God is with him." (JOHN 3:2)

When Nicodemus came to Jesus by night, he revealed his conviction that Jesus came from God. Jesus would not have been able to perform the miraculous signs and wonders He was doing unless He was from God. Well done, Nicodemus. Many of his fellow Pharisees believed Jesus came from Satan. Yet there was much that Nicodemus did not understand. Nicodemus did not understand God's kingdom. He did not understand God's character—how God rules and reigns by grace upon grace, not burden upon burden.

Jesus responded that Nicodemus must be born again to see the kingdom of God, but Nicodemus didn't understand. After discussing Baptism, Jesus pointed Nicodemus toward the cross where He would be lifted up to give eternal life to those who believe in Him. Jesus used Moses lifting up the serpent in the wilderness (see Numbers 21:8–9) as a comparison to help Nicodemus understand, but Nicodemus's confusion remains.

We then hear from this passage what is perhaps the most well-known verse in the entire Bible—John 3:16. This verse is beloved for good reason. It points us to the hope of eternal life that is given to us because of God's love. That love is shown in Jesus, who was sent to give His life for us so that we might have eternal life.

Yet the following verse, verse 17, is perhaps more emblematic of this passage and clarifying for Nicodemus. It proclaims that Jesus did not come into the world to condemn the world, but that through Jesus and His death and resurrection, the world might be saved.

Jesus confused the religious leaders because they believed the kingdom of God was about power and control, proving one's own righteousness, and forcing others to live more strictly. Jesus pointed Nicodemus toward the reality that in the kingdom of God, God chooses to reign and rule through love, not condemnation—through sacrifice, not self-righteousness. The kingdom of God is not about showing off righteousness and heaping up burdens upon God's people to condemn them. The kingdom of God is Jesus bearing those burdens out of love, removing the condemnation out of love. And we enter into that kingdom of God through water and the Spirit—through Baptism.

Lord Jesus, thank You for the gift of Baptism that brings us into Your kingdom and gives eternal life. Be patient with us when we are confused. Keep our eyes fixed upon You and Your Word and teaching. Amen.

THE HEART OF JESUS' MISSION

For God so loved the world, that He gave His only Son, that whoever believes in Him should not perish but have eternal life. (JOHN 3:16)

Jesus' mission connects to this reading in many different ways. Why did Jesus come to earth as a human being? Jesus came to save the world by His death and resurrection because of God's love for all people. Jesus came to bring the kingdom of God to earth, to usher in God's reign and rule. Jesus came to be light shining in darkness. Jesus came to seek and to save the lost. Each of these is apparent in our reading for the week.

God so loves the world that He sent Jesus to be lifted up on the cross. By faith in Jesus, and through His death and resurrection, we have eternal life. Jesus brings the kingdom of God to earth and provides a way for us to enter into His kingdom—by being born of water and the Spirit in Baptism. Jesus is the light shining in the darkness, beckoning Nicodemus (and all of us) to come to Him, for the darkness cannot overcome Him.

Perhaps most interesting is that Jesus came to seek and save the lost. Nicodemus was lost and confused, but he was supposed to be Israel's teacher. How much more were the people of Israel confused if their teachers were? Yes, Jesus frequently had altercations with the religious leaders, but He was trying to save them because He knew they were lost. He knew they were leading people astray. He knew they were focused on all the wrong things. He knew they were dwelling in darkness.

Many of the scribes, Pharisees, and Sadducees rejected Jesus. Many conspired against Jesus to put Him to death. Yet Nicodemus stood out among these. In John 7, Nicodemus seeks to defend Jesus, encouraging his fellow religious leaders not to condemn Jesus before giving Him a fair and honest trial. Nicodemus is shouted down. In John 19, Nicodemus, along with Joseph of Arimathea, takes care of Jesus' burial. Joseph provides the tomb and Nicodemus provides the spices for burial.

Nicodemus saw Jesus carry out His mission to be lifted up, given, and sacrificed so that we might have eternal life. Nicodemus honored Jesus by caring for His body, even after Jesus proclaimed in John 19:30, "It is finished."

Of course, Jesus' burial was of short duration. He rose on the third day. Jesus appeared to Mary Magdalene, the eleven remaining apostles, and hundreds of other people before ascending into heaven.

Lord Jesus, thank You for coming into our world out of love for us. Thank You for bearing the weight of sin and death so that we might have eternal life. Strengthen us to share Your love with the world. Amen.

MOSES' BRONZE SERPENT

And as Moses lifted up the serpent in the wilderness, so must the Son of Man be lifted up, that whoever believes in Him may have eternal life. (JOHN 3:14–15)

Nicodemus initially stated to Jesus that they knew He came from God. But did they really? Throughout John's Gospel, the various religious leaders struggle and argue over the question of where Jesus came from. Jesus had even clarified this Himself in John 8:42, saying, "If God were your Father, you would love Me, for I came from God and I am here. I came not of my own accord, but He sent Me."

Still, in John 9, as Jesus heals a blind man, the Pharisees (Nicodemus's religious group) are divided on Jesus' origins. Some argue that Jesus can't be from God because He does not keep the Sabbath. Others take Nicodemus's logic that a sinner, one not from God, could not perform such miraculous signs.

Many of the miraculous signs Jesus performed might remind us of the miraculous signs performed for Israel in Exodus and Numbers. In this passage from John 3, Jesus invites us to consider a story from Numbers 21. God had delivered the people of Israel out of Egypt, out of the house of slavery. On their way to the Promised Land, the people frequently grumble against God and against Moses. Often, they complain about the food and lack of water. On numerous occasions, they long to go back to Egypt.

On one such occasion, the Lord sends fiery serpents among them. These serpents bite the people, and they repent, asking Moses to pray for God to take the serpents away. The Lord commands Moses to make a serpent and set it on a pole that will be lifted up for everyone to see. Moses makes a serpent out of bronze, puts it on a pole, and lifts it up. Everyone who had been bitten by the serpents and looked up at the bronze serpent was healed. But anyone who did not look up was not healed and died.

Jesus says in this text, "And as Moses lifted up the serpent in the wilderness, so must the Son of Man be lifted up, that whoever believes in Him may have eternal life" (John 3:14–15). Whoever looked to the serpent lifted up on the pole lived. Whoever looks to Jesus, lifted up on the cross, lives eternally.

God provided a way for the Israelites to live. They could not save themselves. If any refused to believe Moses, if they refused to look up to the serpent on a pole, they died. Their salvation was from God, and their deaths were their own fault. God likewise provides a way for all people to live eternally through Jesus' death on the cross. We cannot save ourselves. God provides salvation and eternal life in Jesus. Those who refuse to look to Jesus and believe are much like those Israelites who died from fiery serpent bites, refusing the salvation God freely provided for each one of them. In Jesus, He offers salvation to every one of us.

Jesus, we know and trust that You are from the Father. Keep our eyes lifted up to You and the power of Your cross. Amen.

NICODEMUS'S CONFUSION

Jesus answered him, "Truly, truly, I say to you, unless one is born again he cannot see the kingdom of God." (JOHN 3:3)

Probably the most confusing part of this passage involves a word Jesus uses that has two meanings. Our English translations have a hard time with such ambiguous words. Jesus says, "Truly, truly, I say to you, unless one is born again he cannot see the kingdom of God." The Greek word in question is translated as "again." Nicodemus takes Jesus quite literally with this meaning and notes the absurdity of being physically born a second time. But if you look in your Bible, you may have a footnote that shares how this word could also be translated as "from above."

Jesus clarifies for Nicodemus what it means to be born again, born from above, by adding in verse 5, "Truly, truly, I say to you, unless one is born of water and the Spirit, he cannot enter the kingdom of God."

Nicodemus would have been familiar with John the Baptist and his ministry. John had been baptizing people in the Jordan River, drawing the attention of religious leaders from Jerusalem such as Nicodemus. In Matthew and Luke's Gospels, both record John the Baptist proclaiming to the religious leaders and crowds, "I baptize you with water for repentance, but He who is coming after me is mightier than I, whose sandals I am not worthy to carry. He will baptize you with the Holy Spirit and fire" (Matthew 3:11). When Jesus is baptized by John, the Holy Spirit descends upon Jesus. It's unclear if Nicodemus would have known about Jesus' Baptism. Regardless, Nicodemus had plenty of evidence to connect being born again/ from above and the water and Spirit of Baptism, but he is utterly confused by what Jesus says in John 3.

Why does Nicodemus not make the connection? Is it because he, like the other Pharisees, had rejected John's message in Matthew 3:2 ("Repent for the kingdom of heaven is at hand")? Since John's Baptism was for repentance, I wonder if Nicodemus felt it was superfluous to him. Did he and the other Pharisees consider themselves already prepared for the kingdom of God because of their own obedience and righteousness?

In this way, the setting of this reading takes on a compelling color. Nicodemus comes to Jesus by night, in the darkness. Nicodemus likely wants to keep this meeting with Jesus a secret, hence the hour, but Nicodemus is clearly in darkness regarding the kingdom of God.

Later in the reading, we hear about such light and darkness and are encouraged along with Nicodemus to come to the light, to abandon the evil works of darkness and bask in the true light that shines in the darkness—Jesus. That is precisely what Nicodemus did on Good Friday after Jesus' death.

Lord Jesus, thank You for being light in our darkness. Continue to draw us to You and Your light that no darkness can overcome. Amen.

LIFTED UP

And as Moses lifted up the serpent in the wilderness, so must the Son of Man be lifted up, that whoever believes in Him may have eternal life. (JOHN 3:14–15)

In the church you attend, I am guessing there is a cross. Indeed, there may be more than one. In many churches, the cross stands as the focal point of the architecture. The cross is often lifted up, drawing our eyes to it.

Jesus proclaims in this reading, "So must the Son of Man be lifted up, that whoever believes in Him may have eternal life." Later in John's Gospel, Jesus tells us, "And I, when I am lifted up from the earth, will draw all people to Myself" (John 12:32).

When a church places the cross as the central focus of its architecture, it draws people to the cross. We lift up our eyes to the lifted-up Jesus and behold the one who gives us eternal life by His death and resurrection. We receive from the cross forgiveness, salvation, and peace with God.

Another focal point in many congregations is the baptismal font. In Baptism, we are united with Jesus in a death and resurrection like His. In Baptism, we are united with the lifted-up Jesus and the triune name of God, the name of the Father and of the Son and of the Holy Spirit, is placed upon us. In our Baptism, we receive the sign of the cross upon our foreheads and hearts to mark us as ones redeemed by Christ the crucified. Our Christian lives begin in the name of God and with the sign of the cross.

As we gather for worship, we have numerous opportunities to remember our Baptism and remember the cross. Worship services begin with the Invocation, the invoking of God's name, which was placed upon us in Baptism. As that triune name is invoked, the sign of the cross is made.

We confess our sins and receive Absolution, forgiveness for our sins. This forgiveness is given, again, in the triune name of God and with the sign of the cross.

We profess our faith in the triune God in the words of one of the three Creeds (Apostles', Nicene, or Athanasian). Our hymnal suggests making the sign of the cross at the end of the Creeds.

And our worship services close with the Benediction where the name of God is placed on us once again with the sign of the cross in blessing.

John 3 highlights being born of water and the Spirit in Baptism as well as Jesus being lifted up on the cross. We are constantly reminded of Baptism and the cross in our worship services.

Dear Jesus, thank You for giving Your life for us so that we would not perish but have eternal life. Thank You for the gift of Baptism, which brings us into Your eternal kingdom and family. Thank You for reminding us of Baptism and the cross each time we worship. Amen.

JESUS CALMS STORMS
AND DRIVES OUT DEMONS

WEEK 19—MATTHEW 8:23–34

And when He got into the boat, His disciples followed Him. And behold, there arose a great storm on the sea, so that the boat was being swamped by the waves; but He was asleep. And they went and woke Him, saying, "Save us, Lord; we are perishing." And He said to them, "Why are you afraid, O you of little faith?" Then He rose and rebuked the winds and the sea, and there was a great calm. And the men marveled, saying, "What sort of man is this, that even winds and sea obey Him?"

And when He came to the other side, to the country of the Gadarenes, two demon-possessed men met Him, coming out of the tombs, so fierce that no one could pass that way. And behold, they cried out, "What have You to do with us, O Son of God? Have You come here to torment us before the time?" Now a herd of many pigs was feeding at some distance from them. And the demons begged Him, saying, "If You cast us out, send us away into the herd of pigs." And He said to them, "Go." So they came out and went into the pigs, and behold, the whole herd rushed down the steep bank into the sea and drowned in the waters. The herdsmen fled, and going into the city they told everything, especially what had happened to the demon-possessed men. And behold, all the city came out to meet Jesus, and when they saw Him, they begged Him to leave their region.

JESUS' POWERFUL WORD

And they went and woke Him,
saying, "Save us, Lord; we are
perishing." (MATTHEW 8:25)

What's a task you've done a hundred times? Not just any task but one that requires skill and training, one that you've mastered from years of practice?

Many of Jesus' disciples made their livelihood as fishermen. They were experts of the sea, and the Sea of Galilee was their main waters for operation. The Sea of Galilee—a rather small lake—resembles an upside-down pear shape with hills and sharp cliffs lining the perimeter. It's the world's lowest freshwater lake, coming in at 686 feet below sea level. Like any skilled angler, the disciples would be very familiar with its 13-mile length (north to south) and 8-mile width (east to west). They'd know the most productive parts of the lake to fish and which areas to avoid. Just as you know how to navigate the specifics of a well-practiced job, they'd known the Sea of Galilee like the back of their hand since they were boys.

So the disciples' response as they travel the Sea of Galilee during a storm should surprise us. This certainly wasn't the first storm they'd encountered on the waters. The lake's low-lying position surrounded by hills makes unexpected storms common. They'd seen strong storms before, but this time, the storm was so big they were convinced they'd die. They were terrified, yet somehow Jesus was sleeping through the commotion. The disciples wake Him up and say, "Save us, Lord; we are perishing." The fishermen ask the carpenter to take the helm. Jesus rebukes the wind and the sea—and both the blustery wind and boisterous waves instantly calm. When Jesus speaks, creation responds.

The storm makes Jesus' journey across the water nearly impossible. Then, coming to the other side, Jesus encounters two demon-possessed men "so fierce that no one could pass that way" (v. 28). With the simple command "Go" (v. 32), Jesus frees the men and sends the formidable demons into a herd of pigs who rush off a steep bank and drown in the Sea of Galilee. Nothing in all of creation, nor minions of the devil, can stand in Jesus' way.

Jesus, the one who creates all things and holds all things together, has authority over all things (see Colossians 1:16–17). And everyone in this passage—Jews, Gentiles, and demons—recognizes that to some extent. The demons possessing the men know right away they're in the presence of the Son of God, the one with power to torment and condemn them. After the Gentile herdsmen flee the countryside, their community recognizes Jesus as a man of great power and begs Him to leave the region. And the disciples don't lean on their own expertise but come to Jesus to save them from the storm, marveling that wind and sea obey Him. Do you recognize Jesus' authority over your daily life and work?

Lord Jesus, help me trust in the power of Your Word to hold all things together in my life. Amen.

AWE OR FEAR?

And the men marveled, saying, "What sort of man is this, that even winds and sea obey Him?" (MATTHEW 8:27)

What sort of man is this, that even winds and sea obey Him?" The disciples marvel in wonder at who their rabbi might be. The demons answer their question, crying out, "What have You to do with us, O Son of God? Have You come here to torment us before the time?" (Matthew 8:29).

In these two replies to Jesus, we see how all people will respond in His presence: either in awe and trust or in fear and disgust. For when faced with Jesus' offer of salvation in light of our mortality, there's no room for apathy. Not really. On the Last Day—the day the demons foretell as a time of torment—the Savior will return to earth with great glory; every knee shall bow and every tongue confess that Jesus Christ is Lord. Some will confess this to their salvation and saving faith in Jesus' victory; but others to their damnation, refusing to believe in Jesus' authority over all.

Last week's reading from John 3:17–18 reminds us why Jesus came to earth:

> For God did not send His Son into the world to condemn the world, but in order that the world might be saved through Him. Whoever believes in Him is not condemned, but whoever does not believe is condemned already, because he has not believed in the name of the only Son of God.

God sent Jesus into the world to make Himself known. The Word became flesh and dwelled among us. In His humanity, Jesus is known as just a carpenter from Nazareth, son of Joseph and Mary. But as the divine God-man, Jesus calms the storms and shuts up demons with the sound of His voice. Jesus comes to save the world and reveal His Father's love. And His authority cannot be denied; it demands a response.

How do we respond to Jesus' authority in the world? Does it cause us to believe or to grumble? How about when Jesus' authority exposes our depravity and need for a Savior? Like the demon-possessed men, we are ensnared in sin, and we are in need of freedom. *What have You to do with me, O Son of God? Will You condemn me too?* we may wonder. Jesus, however, comes not to condemn but save—to proclaim good news to the poor and to set the captive free (see Luke 4:16–21). He exposes the darkness and brings in Himself the true source of light (see John 3:19–21).

Jesus' authority over all creation is made prominently clear in this passage. Do you respond in awe or fear?

Lord Jesus, thank You for coming to save the world, not condemn it. Save me. Amen.

JESUS CAME TO REDEEM

I will put enmity between you and the woman, and between your off-spring and her offspring; He shall bruise your head, and you shall bruise His heel. (GENESIS 3:15)

God cursed Adam and Eve, the land, and all of creation when they fell into sin. But He didn't banish Adam and Eve from the garden without also making a promise for redemption, a way back into His presence. Jesus came into the world to redeem: to overcome Satan, to take back what was lost in Eden, and to bring all of creation back into a right relationship with God. In this week's reading we get a foretaste of the full plan that is to be revealed. On the cross, Jesus will crush Satan's head. In His death and resurrection, He will defeat sin, death, and the power of the devil. Here, we get a glimpse—Jesus makes clear that He has power over even a fierce storm and thousands of scary demons. We see that God's promised redemption isn't just for people; it's for His whole created world—for land, plants, animals, and all created beings.

Romans 8:22 says, "For we know that the whole creation has been groaning together in the pains of childbirth until now." Hurricanes, earthquakes, tornadoes, and storms of all kinds ravage the earth. Wildfires, droughts, and disease remind us that this world is not as it should be. When the world shakes, who can stand against it? We're reminded of our helplessness when extreme weather hits, praying it'll graciously pass over our home. We can't stop the winds from swirling or the waters from rising. We do our best to take shelter or flee. But really, we're at the mercy of the storm. Or so it seems.

Jesus has mercy on His disciples. When He calms the winds and waves, the sea is stilled in an instant. This goes against all naturally occurring weather patterns. It's a supernatural soothing for a creation groaning in pain, crying out to its Creator. Even the demons know the Son of God and cry out in their torment. Jesus casts out the demons into unclean animals and frees the men in distress. Satan may have used a serpent in the garden to tempt God's people to sin. But here Jesus directs both demons and animals according to His will. "If God is for us, who can be against us?" (Romans 8:31).

So we can say confidently with Paul:

Who shall separate us from the love of Christ? Shall tribulation, or distress, or persecution, or famine, or nakedness, or danger, or sword? . . . No, in all these things we are more than conquerors through Him who loved us. For I am sure that neither death nor life, nor angels nor rulers, nor things present nor things to come, nor powers, nor height nor depth, nor anything else in all creation, will be able to separate us from the love of God in Christ Jesus our Lord. (Romans 8:35, 37–39)

Lord Jesus, thank You for redeeming me and all of creation through Your death and resurrection. I look forward to the day when all will be made new. Amen.

GOD WIELDS HIS POWER THROUGH HIS SPOKEN WORD

And He said to them, "Why are you afraid, O you of little faith?" Then He rose and rebuked the winds and the sea, and there was a great calm. (MATTHEW 8:26)

How do you envision these words of Jesus to His disciples: "Why are you afraid, O you of little faith?" Are they gentle and tender like a parent comforting a scared, young child? Are they inquisitive and probing like a teacher helping a student grow in understanding? Are they reprimanding and motivating like a coach pushing his team to be better? The Bible doesn't say. But it's not the first time God asks His people a question when they're distressed. In doing so, God reveals something about Himself and His relationship with those He loves.

Job had been a faithful follower of God, living according to God's commands. When Job lost everything—all his children, his livelihood, good health, and his grieving wife turned against him—he had some questions for God. He was upset and began to doubt God's goodness. Had God forgotten about His servant Job? When Job questions God, God responds with questions of His own: "Where were you when I laid the foundation of the earth? Tell me, if you have understanding" (Job 38:4). God responds to Job's questions by pointing to who He is as Creator—the One who shut in the sea and made clouds its garment; the One who said, "Thus far shall you come, and no farther, and here shall your proud waves be stayed" (Job 38:11). When Job sees life as out of control and chaotic, God reminds Job that He thoughtfully ordered every detail of creation and has power over it. As Job learns an important truth about His Creator, God redeems Job's life, blessing him with even more abundance than before.

How does God wield His power? Through His spoken Word. "In the beginning was the Word, and the Word was with God, and the Word was God. . . . All things were made through Him, and without Him was not any thing made that was made" (John 1:1, 3). In the beginning, God created the heavens and the earth. God spoke, and light appeared. He spoke again, and formed the sky, the dry land and plants, the sun, moon, and stars, and every living creature upon the earth. With His Word, the whole world was formed. And with His Word, the world continues to spin.

So why are you afraid, O you of little faith?

God is the Creator who was, who is, and who will be. The One who has always controlled the clouds, winds, and water. When Jesus calms the storm, He reveals Himself as the Creator. The One who is both majestic and gentle, wielding both great power and great care—all for the sake of His people.

As God asserts His power over creation, Job, Jesus' disciples, and all people throughout time have opportunity to praise the Lord. We join voices with the psalmist by declaring: "Bless the LORD, O my soul! O LORD my God, You are very great! You are clothed with splendor and majesty. . . . He lays the beams of His chambers on the waters; He makes the clouds His chariot; He rides on the wings of the wind. . . . You make springs gush forth in the valleys; they flow between the hills" (Psalm 104:1, 3, 10).

Lord Jesus, You are indeed very great! My soul blesses You, my rock and my refuge. Amen.

WHERE CAN I FIND JESUS?

The LORD is near to the broken-hearted and saves the crushed in spirit. (PSALM 34:18)

If God has control over the wind, waves, and demons, why can the world around us be so out of control and cause such great pain and destruction?

It's easy to find ourselves feeling like Job—confused by the hardship and suffering that seem to be ever coming our way. We love Jesus and even make time for devotions with Him! So why is life so hard? As soon as I pull out my list of reasons why things in this world aren't right, God's words to Job sound in my mind. Was I there at the foundation of the world? No. Am I Creator God? No, I am His creature. I don't know the will or the ways of our God fully. I don't know why He allowed sin to enter the world and all His beloved creation to reap the consequences. I don't know how He can continue to watch creation groan and people die.

But I do know that God is loving, gracious, and long-suffering. He's proven that time and again. He wants all men to be saved and come to the knowledge of this truth. And He did not spare His own Son but gave Himself up as a ransom for all. Because of Jesus, I don't get what I rightly deserve as a result of my sin—death.

So alongside our questions of "why," let's learn to also ask "where?" Where is God in the face of suffering? Where is God as injustice abounds? Where is God in the storm?

Our God does not avoid suffering but steps into it, taking on the worst of its form. We find our mighty, Creator God hanging on a cross, dying to pay the price for our broken world. God does not ignore the state of creation or even declare it beyond repair. Rather, "God so loved the world, that He gave His only Son, that whoever believes in Him should not perish but have eternal life" (John 3:16). God so loved the world that He chose to save it. For God so loves you.

I don't know why God allows storms to rage, but I do know our God is in the boat. And when He makes His presence known, we learn more about Him as our Savior. I don't know why people are tormented by demons of all kinds, but I do know "The LORD is near to the brokenhearted and saves the crushed in spirit." Our God has crushed the serpent's head. He hears the cries of His people and steps into our hurt. And He promises to come again to make all things new—a new heaven and new earth with no mourning, crying, or pain. God speaks and His words accomplish their purpose. God makes promises and sees them through. So I'll ask "why" and "where" and cling to the truth that our God is faithful and He is near. He's in the boat.

Lord Jesus, when I ask why, remind me where to find You—in Your Word and in Your church. Amen.

ALL WE REALLY NEED

Jesus said to them again, "Peace be with you. As the Father has sent Me, even so I am sending you." And when He had said this, He breathed on them and said to them, "Receive the Holy Spirit." (JOHN 20:21–22)

Jesus offers peace to His disciples in this week's reading and throughout the four Gospel accounts. Somehow, even though the disciples physically walked with Jesus, witnessed His miracles, and even saw His risen body, they continually needed reassuring. They needed peace for each new day in this world. In John's Gospel account, the last thing Jesus does with the disciples is give them peace through the receiving of the Holy Spirit.

Imagine all the final things Jesus could have equipped His disciples with: answers to theological questions, a Mary Poppins-like bag that could provide for any physical need, supernatural strength and uncompromised immune systems so they'd never get tired or sick—but instead, He leaves them with the Spirit of peace. That's what they need to take on the world.

Where do you first turn to for peace? When life is hard or seems out of control, when you're afraid or not sure how to get to the other side, what do you do? Do you run an internet search for the answer? Consumer social media or a news outlet on repeat? Do you push further, work longer, and try harder? Do you find a comforting food or drink and zone out for a while? We all have ways we seek to soothe our soul when things seem beyond our control.

But perhaps recognizing that things are beyond our control is exactly what we need to do to bring us once again to the reality that God is God, and we are not. To ask the Carpenter to take the helm. While we might be able to provide temporary relief, only Jesus can give us peace that's not from this world, peace that surpasses our understanding, peace that doesn't depend on our circumstances.

When we cry out to God to save us, He responds by giving us His peace. We experience this every time we gather for Divine Service. As we sing the Kyrie, "Lord, have mercy. Christ, have mercy. Lord, have mercy" (*LSB*, p. 204), we join with all the people who have ever cried out to the Lord to save them. And He does. As we hear the pastor deliver God's words of forgiveness to us, we breathe in the comfort of new life, a balm to our souls. As he proclaims God's saving work, our spirits can calm, being reminded again that Jesus enters chaos to restore order. And as we receive Jesus' body and blood in Holy Communion, we are tangibly reminded that Christ is near, Christ is here. In this Meal, Jesus brings His life and salvation to those of us who are doubting or afraid. Yes, Jesus continues to give His followers what they need for this life: His Spirit of peace.

Spirit of Peace, bring us comfort and assurance for each new day in You. In Jesus' name. Amen.

JESUS RAISES A DEAD GIRL AND A YOUNG MAN

Week 20—Mark 5:21–24, 35–43; Luke 7:11–17

And when Jesus had crossed again in the boat to the other side, a great crowd gathered about Him, and He was beside the sea. Then came one of the rulers of the synagogue, Jairus by name, and seeing Him, he fell at His feet and implored Him earnestly, saying, "My little daughter is at the point of death. Come and lay Your hands on her, so that she may be made well and live." And He went with him.

And a great crowd followed Him and thronged about Him. . . .

While He was still speaking, there came from the ruler's house some who said, "Your daughter is dead. Why trouble the Teacher any further?" But overhearing what they said, Jesus said to the ruler of the synagogue, "Do not fear, only believe." And He allowed no one to follow Him except Peter and James and John the brother of James. They came to the house of the ruler of the synagogue, and Jesus saw a commotion, people weeping and wailing loudly. And when He had entered, He said to them, "Why are you making a commotion and weeping? The child is not dead but sleeping." And they laughed at Him. But He put them all outside and took the child's father and mother and those who were with Him and went in where the child was. Taking her by the hand He said to her, "Talitha cumi," which means, "Little girl, I say to you, arise." And immediately the girl got up and began walking (for she was twelve years of age), and they were immediately overcome with amazement. And He strictly charged them that no one should know this, and told them to give her something to eat. . . .

Soon afterward He went to a town called Nain, and His disciples and a great crowd went with Him. As He drew near to the gate of the town, behold, a man who had died was being carried out, the only son of his mother, and she was a widow, and a considerable crowd from the town was with her. And when the Lord saw her, He had compassion on her and said to her, "Do not weep." Then He came up and touched the bier, and the bearers stood still. And He said, "Young man, I say to you, arise." And the dead man sat up and began to speak, and Jesus gave him to his mother. Fear seized them all, and they glorified God, saying, "A great prophet has arisen among us!" and "God has visited His people!" And this report about Him spread through the whole of Judea and all the surrounding country.

VICTOR OVER DEATH

Jesus said to the ruler of the synagogue,
"Do not fear, only believe." (MARK 5:36)

Jesus' popularity is rising in this week's passages. He has demonstrated His power as the Son of God and the promised Messiah through His miracles of healing the sick, cleansing people of leprosy, and driving out demons. Last week, we saw Him still a massive storm on the Sea of Galilee and drive demons out of two among the Gentile Gadarenes (see Matthew 8:23–34). While the casting out of demons is already stunning, Jesus next shows His power over death. Neither demons nor death can withstand His power, and no one can stop His care for those in need.

While we might have expected there to be more resurrections, the Gospels record Jesus raising only three people from the dead. The first is a twelve-year-old girl who has just died. The second is a young man being carried out of his village for burial. (The third, Lazarus, will be the subject of next week.)

The girl was the daughter of Jairus, a synagogue ruler. When Jairus approached Jesus, his daughter was dying, but there was still hope that Jesus could heal her if He arrived in time. Though time was short, and every moment mattered, along the way, a woman afflicted with a bleeding disorder for twelve years touched Jesus, trusting that this would heal her. Jesus, knowing her need, stopped to reassure her that her faith had healed her. Just after this exchange with the healed woman, messengers arrived to say that the little girl had died. Now it seemed there was no reason for Jesus to continue with Jairus—death had won. But Jesus told Jairus not to fear, and He went on to Jairus's house. Death would not be the final step in this journey.

Our other text, from Luke, records Jesus' victory over death when He met the widowed mother of a young man who had died that day. Being widowed meant she had no husband to support her, and now that her only son was dead, she would live in poverty. She was not looking for her son's rising that day, just his burial. But the touch and command of Jesus ended that journey with life.

On this day we can talk about the shadow of death that covers every child of Adam and Eve. As far as our eyes can see, death holds sway over all humanity. But Jesus Christ came into our world to win His victory over death. By miracles, as we see this week, and by His Easter victory, we see the defeat of death. When Jesus returns, He will raise all people for judgment, and death will be completely vanquished, never to contaminate the new heaven and the new earth.

Lord Jesus, Your power over death continues today. Therefore, help us believe and follow Your words, "Do not fear, only believe." Amen.

REACHING PAST THE MOMENT OF DEATH

And He said, "Young man, I say to you, arise." And the dead man sat up and began to speak. (LUKE 7:14–15)

Jesus holds power over death. This is the crucial truth that our texts teach this week. At the start of both texts, death seems to have the upper hand. Death outruns life, and so both the little girl and the young man die before Jesus arrives. We might fear that death will outrun our lives. If so, then the finish line of our lives will only bring death waiting for us. But Jesus shows a greater power than death. He reaches past the moment of death and returns the story to life.

When Jesus goes to raise the young girl, He speaks of death as sleeping. He even uses the same word to raise her from the sleep of death her parents had probably used many times before to wake her from sleep. What power is in both His Word and His touch. He takes her hand, as a caring parent would do to wake a sleeping child. New life begins with that touch. Then with a gentle command, "Little girl, I say to you, arise," He brings life to her. To Jesus, the sleep of death is no barrier to the gift of life.

With another touch and command, Jesus brings life to the young man. The widow's only son, her single hope, was taken far too soon. But Jesus meets the funeral procession on the road. Life and death collide on that narrow road. But the certainty of death was utterly destroyed when Jesus touched the bier. His words to the widow echo the words said to Jairus. To her, He says, "Do not weep" (Luke 7:13). What a command to give a widow on a funeral journey. But Jesus sweeps away her sorrow when He restores the young man

with the simple words, "Young man, I say to you, arise" (Luke 7:14). With that, life and hope reigned. The funeral procession turned around to become a joyful homecoming for the widow and her son.

These miracles of resurrection are not separate from us. We live in the promise of the resurrection. Jesus reassures us that death has no hold on us, and when He returns to raise us, we will live forever. A child dies in her youth, and a young man dies in the prime of his adult life. No matter for Jesus. He raises both of them and makes broken families whole. And He will raise us, restoring us forever into the whole family of the people of God.

Dear Jesus, remind us that our life journey is not a defeated procession to death, but that You have called us already from death to life eternal. Amen.

JESUS MEETS DEATH WITH HIS IRRESISTIBLE LIFE

[Jesus] said to them, "Why are you making a commotion and weeping? The child is not dead but sleeping." (MARK 5:39)

Jesus' ministry has been accelerating since Mark 1, and His enemies have been powerless to stop Him. In that first chapter, He calls disciples and does miracles of healing. However, in chapter two, He not only heals the paralyzed man but forgives his sins. The healing power shows His authority to do this divine work of forgiveness. In chapters two and three, more conflicts arise, but Jesus has an answer to each objection. Finally, in Mark 3:6, His enemies decide they must kill Him. Surely, they imagine, death will stop Him. But now in Mark 5, Jesus meets death with His irresistible life.

What a sequence of miracles. He heals the sick, forgives sins, casts out demons, and calms the stormy sea. Now, when it seems He has already done it all, Jesus raises the dead. How can His enemies outdo this? How can they argue that raising the dead is wrong? He raises a little girl, giving her back to her joyful parents. He restores a young man to his mother, a widow. Besides all this, these miracles are seen by so many. The mourners had already come to Jairus's home. The town had already turned out for the funeral procession of the young man. But the words of Jesus bring the little girl and the young man out of death as though it were a mere sleep.

Jesus' enemies will continue to rage against Him, but they have no power against Him. Death is the only threat they have. Yet Jesus has shown His power over death. Soon, He would announce His intent to die in our place. However, death will not be the end of His work. Come Easter, His tomb will be empty as He crushes death by His overwhelming life.

Each of the people Jesus raised from the dead ended up dying again. To permanently and eternally defeat death, Jesus' death had to destroy it from the inside out. His enemies did not force Him to death, but He chose to die for our sake. He suffered death on the cross and was laid in a grave, likely to the joy of His enemies. But on the third day, from inside that grave, He conquered death, rising to life again, because death could not keep its hold over Him. He has risen, never to die again, and when He returns, He will completely vanquish death and remove its hold from His creation. All believers will be raised to eternal life, and death will be gone forever.

Lord Jesus, remind us of Your overwhelming power and how You put all Your enemies beneath You for the blessings on Your people. Amen.

JESUS' MINISTRY OF HEALING

*And immediately the girl got up and
began walking (for she was twelve years
of age), and they were immediately
overcome with amazement.* (MARK 5:42)

n the wonder of Jesus' victory over death, we
see themes repeated in other parts of Scripture.

Mark 8:22, 25

"And some people brought to Him a blind man
and begged Him to touch him. . . . Then Jesus laid
His hands on his eyes again; and he opened his
eyes, his sight was restored." Jesus' ministry of
healing builds from Mark 1 through to Maundy
Thursday. While His enemies feared these miracles,
people desperate for healing saw Jesus as their only
hope. Imagine the excitement as, finally, there was
someone who could heal every disease. It didn't
matter what the illness was or how long it had
afflicted someone. Bring the sufferer to Jesus! He is
the supreme healer whose specialty is every disease
the world has known.

Mark 14:33

"And He took with Him Peter and James and
John, and began to be greatly distressed and
troubled." In the miracle of raising the little girl,
Jesus took only Peter, James, and John to Jairus's
house. Later, in Mark 9:2–8, Jesus took the same
three to the Mount of Transfiguration. They see
His divine glory but cannot tell anyone. Finally, in
the Garden of Gethsemane, Jesus again takes these
three and asks them to watch and pray with Him.
What power, glory, and sorrow they have seen.
They have watched Jesus dismiss death with a word
and glow with divine light. But finally, in the garden,
they listen as He prays to the Father, obedient to
the death that He must endure for the sake of
the world.

Matthew 9:36

"When He saw the crowds, He had compassion
for them, because they were harassed and helpless,
like sheep without a shepherd." When Jesus saw
the funeral procession, He knew the sorrow and
desperate situation of the widow. His knowledge
of her need walked step for step with His compassion for her. In Matthew 9, Jesus' ministry was
teaching the kingdom of God and healing every
disease and affliction. Whether His mercy healed
countless crowds or restored the life of one young
man, Jesus stepped forward to meet the needs
that He foreknew.

Luke 2:20

"And the shepherds returned, glorifying and
praising God for all they had heard and seen, as
it had been told them." Miracles of birth and resurrection bring joyful praise. The shepherds on
Christmas Eve saw the chorus of angels and the
newborn Messiah. What stories of joy and hope
they had to tell. So also, everyone who saw the
resurrection of the young man had reason to glorify
God. The Messiah walks among us and the dead are
raised. Let His people rejoice and give Him thanks!

*Lord Jesus, remind us of the compassion
and power that marked Your ministry, which
still protect and guide Your people today.
Amen.*

GOD WALKS WITH US

Jesus said to the ruler of the synagogue, "Do not fear, only believe." (MARK 5:36)

This week's text raises many questions:

Why did Jesus tell Jairus not to fear when word came that his daughter had died?

Messengers had just come from Jairus's house with the bitter news that Jairus's daughter had died. They asked a harsh question: "Your daughter is dead. Why trouble the Teacher any further?" All the urgency, the rushing to find Jesus and hurry Him along, all this was useless now. They expected Jairus to let go of both Jesus and any hope of life.

What a moment of choice for Jairus. Jairus was like Peter walking on the water and taking his eyes off of Jesus to notice the winds and the waves. If Jairus took his eyes off Jesus and let despair strike him as he heard his daughter had died, he would have sunk beneath waves of despair. Jesus was lifting up Jairus's faith through that tragedy. He says the same to us when we face moments of great loss, pain, and despair—"Do not fear, only believe."

How could the crowd go from loud wailing to laughing in scorn at Jesus?

These mourners were sympathetic to the families and loved ones of the deceased, but not generally emotionally involved. Some were "professional mourners," meaning they would go from grieving family to grieving family to weep and wail. They thought Jesus' words about the girl sleeping showed He was hopelessly out of touch. How could He say that the girl was sleeping? He hadn't even seen her yet. Certainly, they who had been there knew better than He did. They knew death and they knew there was no return from it.

Why did Jesus keep referring to her as being asleep?

Jesus wanted to teach Jairus—and us—to see death the way God does. It is not an insurmountable mountain. It is not a cliff that casts us straight down for eternity. No, it is similar to sleep because God has the power to bring His people back to life when He chooses. Death is a valley of the shadow, but a valley is not an endless cliff. Crossing a valley, we descend—but then we ascend again. God walks with us through the valley of the shadow to life again. It gives us great confidence and comfort to know death has no hold on us or our loved ones who have died before us. He will raise us all on the Last Day and reunite all believers together with Jesus.

Dear Jesus, what power and mercy You showed in these resurrections. Help us to keep our eyes on You alone so that our faith endures. Amen.

WE FLEE TO JESUS

And when the Lord saw her, He had compassion on her and said to her, "Do not weep." (LUKE 7:13)

Jesus has the solution for all the problems that plague us, even death. When it appears that death has spoken the final word, Jesus has new words of hope and life. We hear those in our daily reading of His Word. Also, knowing our weakness in the face of death, we gather in God's house—whether at funerals or in our weekly worship. We flee to Jesus for comfort, peace, and hope amid our terror. As Romans 6 teaches, in Baptism, God has joined us to Christ's death and resurrection so that we die to sin and rise to new life. By His death, death has lost its power over us. In Holy Communion, we receive the body and blood Jesus sacrificed in death, so that we may live in His grace, forgiveness, and resurrection.

At funerals in particular, we acknowledge that death is the result of our sin, but God has vanquished sin and death in Jesus Christ. On the Last Day, the body of the believer we lay to rest will be raised by God's power and glorified to live with God forever in the new heaven and the new earth. Even now, the souls of those who have died in faith are with Him in heaven, waiting for the resurrection of their bodies.

The Mark 5 and Luke 7 accounts are important texts of resurrection, which are included in our lectionaries (weekly schedule of Scripture readings). They are also found in our hymnody. One of the great hymns in *Lutheran Service Book* powerfully sets these accounts in poetry. Hymn 552, "O Christ Who Shared Our Mortal Life," especially notes Jesus' victorious battle against the forces of death. Stanzas 5 and 6 relate the raising of Jairus's daughter, and 7 and 8 the raising of the widow's son.

Many hymns sing of resurrection and one that especially captures images of these texts is Hymn 722, "Lord, Take My Hand and Lead Me." The song's three verses remind us of the powerful touch of Jesus, His guidance through our life, and His power to carry us even through death.

Heavenly Savior, through Your powerful Word and Sacraments, renew our faith so that we have no fear of death but trust in Your resurrection promise. Amen.

JESUS RAISES LAZARUS

WEEK 21—JOHN 11:17–44

Now when Jesus came, He found that Lazarus had already been in the tomb four days. Bethany was near Jerusalem, about two miles off, and many of the Jews had come to Martha and Mary to console them concerning their brother. So when Martha heard that Jesus was coming, she went and met Him, but Mary remained seated in the house. Martha said to Jesus, "Lord, if You had been here, my brother would not have died. But even now I know that whatever You ask from God, God will give You." Jesus said to her, "Your brother will rise again." Martha said to Him, "I know that he will rise again in the resurrection on the last day." Jesus said to her, "I am the resurrection and the life. Whoever believes in Me, though he die, yet shall he live, and everyone who lives and believes in Me shall never die. Do you believe this?" She said to Him, "Yes, Lord; I believe that You are the Christ, the Son of God, who is coming into the world."

When she had said this, she went and called her sister Mary, saying in private, "The Teacher is here and is calling for you." And when she heard it, she rose quickly and went to Him. Now Jesus had not yet come into the village, but was still in the place where Martha had met Him. When the Jews who were with her in the house, consoling her, saw Mary rise quickly and go out, they followed her, supposing that she was going to the tomb to weep there. Now when Mary came to where Jesus was and saw Him, she fell at His feet, saying to Him, "Lord, if You had been here, My brother would not have died." When Jesus saw her weeping, and the Jews who had come with her also weeping, He was deeply moved in His spirit and greatly troubled. And He said, "Where have you laid him?" They said to Him, "Lord, come and see." Jesus wept. So the Jews said, "See how He loved him!" But some of them said, "Could not He who opened the eyes of the blind man also have kept this man from dying?"

Then Jesus, deeply moved again, came to the tomb. It was a cave, and a stone lay against it. Jesus said, "Take away the stone." Martha, the sister of the dead man, said to Him, "Lord, by this time there will be an odor, for he has been dead four days." Jesus said to her, "Did I not tell you that if you believed you would see the glory of God?" So they took away the stone. And Jesus lifted up His eyes and said, "Father, I thank You that You have heard Me. I knew that You always hear Me, but I said this on account of the people standing around, that they may believe that You sent Me." When He had said these things, He cried out with a loud voice, "Lazarus, come out." The man who had died came out, his hands and feet bound with linen strips, and his face wrapped with a cloth. Jesus said to them, "Unbind him, and let him go."

JESUS WAITED TWO MORE DAYS

Now Jesus loved Martha and her sister and Lazarus. So, when He heard that Lazarus was ill, He stayed two days longer in the place where He was. (JOHN 11:5–6)

D o you remember sick days when you were young? Often on those days, a parent will give their child a little extra leniency on rules that are usually nonnegotiable. A sore throat may mean a Popsicle or ice cream for lunch. A child will be kept home from school, and parents shift their schedule around them. In many households, it means a little more time watching TV or movies as a sick child rests. One movie that played on many a screen on sick days, especially in the '80s and '90s, was *The Princess Bride*. At one point, the protagonist in dire straits is taken to Miracle Max by his friends to be healed. In his hovel, Billy Crystal as Max explains there is a difference between being all dead and mostly dead.

Jesus hears of Lazarus's illness, yet He remains where He is. Lazarus has gone from mostly dead to all dead. At that time, there were many illnesses that might present as mostly dead. Modern medicine has developed the gift of machines and techniques that fully allow healthcare workers to understand when someone is truly dead. Yet even today, there are times when what seems like the only true diagnosis ends up being only mostly dead. Jesus waits two more days, until there can be no doubt. His willingness to wait assures one thing: when He and the disciples arrive, Lazarus will be indisputably dead.

The disciples must have been confused—Mary and Martha torn between grief and hope. But Jesus waited. There would be more to come. Jesus would put on a display of power that would astonish all those around Him. But in that time, even as those He loved pled for His presence, He waited.

Dear Jesus, let me come to You with all the pleas of my heart. In those times I don't see You, when You are waiting, help me to trust in the promises You have spoken, knowing they do not disappoint. Amen.

THE RESURRECTION AND THE LIFE HAS COME

Martha said to Jesus, "Lord, if You had been here, my brother would not have died. But even now I know that whatever You ask from God, God will give You." (JOHN 11:21–22)

What would you feel? A beloved parent, sibling, child, or friend has fallen deathly ill. Within distance is a doctor who has the specific medicine needed to save this person. This doctor is also a friend. Hastily, word is sent to the physician. As you watch your loved one get weaker, you hope and pray that the doctor will arrive. In deep sorrow, death arrives. After the fact, like an insult, the healer finally arrives. Too late.

This is how Martha meets Jesus in John 11. She knew that Jesus had the power to save Lazarus. It was more than knowledge. It was conviction, belief. Yet Jesus was not there in time. What would have been your response to Jesus showing up too late? Martha responds in pain: "Lord, if You had been here, my brother would not have died."

This world is full of sorrows. Jesus will promise His followers that "in the world you will have tribulation" (John 16:33). Being a follower of Jesus does not remove this fact. Foolishly, many believe the lie that life as a Christian will be easy. Martha's pain is clear that it is not.

Martha does, however, display how to combat the troubles of this world: hope. Specifically hope in Jesus. While she knows Jesus could have healed her brother, she continues by saying to Him, "But even now I know that whatever You ask from God, God will give You." What belief!

The power in that statement is immediately followed by another exchange. In saying her brother will rise again, Martha believes it will be in the resurrection at the Last Day. It is the main point of these verses. Jesus responds, "I am the resurrection and the life" (John 11:25). In one sentence, Jesus declares that He rules over creation. Nothing, not even death, can stop Him. He will tell Martha that those who believe this will never die. He then simply asks if she does believe this. Her response is a matter-of-fact, "Yes, Lord; I believe that You are the Christ, the Son of God, who is coming into the world" (v. 27). Martha affirms that standing before her is the One who was and is and is to come, who holds in His hands the power of death and life. He not only controls it but He *is* it. What a stunning declaration of faith.

It would be easy to lose sight of this amid the action of Jesus raising Lazarus from the dead. But these verses hold within them this truth: the resurrection and the life has come. All one needs to do is believe, and that resurrection and life is theirs.

Lord, let me rejoice in the coming of Your Son, the resurrection and life. Amen.

JESUS' MISSION

Then Jesus told them plainly,
"Lazarus has died, and for your
sake I am glad that I was not there,
so that you may believe. But let
us go to him." (JOHN 11:14–15)

Jesus' mission is put on display in this week's passage. He has been wandering and teaching. Miracles have been performed; healing abounds. But here, in this passage, He makes a declaration that is the bedrock of why He has come to dwell among His creation.

It must have been strange for the disciples to hear the words of Jesus when His two days of waiting ended. Jesus says He is glad that His friend has died. Glad. That must have been strange. But Jesus knew what it would mean through what He would do in that place. Not only would He put the power and authority housed within Him on display but He would declare that He is the resurrection and the life.

It was an echo of the night at the burning bush when God declared to Moses, "I Am who I Am" (Exodus 3:14). Jesus is laying claim to the power not only to heal those living but to resurrect that which was dead. He was declaring that He is the Messiah—God and man trekking across the Near East. He was glad not at Lazarus's death but in the power to show who He was so that more would believe. This reveals Jesus' mission. Not just to reveal His power and might but for the purpose of belief. He is the resurrection and life, but not as the pagan gods would have power over those things. No. He brings the power of the Creator's love to bear for the sake of the creation.

With a simple phrase, He raised a dead man: "Lazarus, come out" (John 11:43). That was all it took. No test tubes or labs. There was no need to perform a mystic ritual in which He needed the correct ingredients and the alignments of the planets. No. He spoke, and it happened. He did it for the love of His friends. He did it for the love of His disciples. He did it for His love of the world.

Jesus shows His power in raising Lazarus; He did not seek to hold that power to Himself. Instead, His steadfast love used that power to declare who He was to the world. Even in this miraculous moment, Jesus uses this situation to point to the rescue that is coming on the cross and the eternal life that He will give to all who believe through His empty tomb.

Heavenly Father, Your Son used His power to bless us. His ministry continues to bring us to belief. In Jesus' name. Amen.

JESUS' GIFT OF ETERNAL LIFE

Now a certain man was ill, Lazarus of Bethany, the village of Mary and her sister Martha. (JOHN 11:1)

This was not Jesus' first encounter with Mary and Martha. Earlier, we read, "Now as they went on their way, Jesus entered a village. And a woman named Martha welcomed Him into her house. And she had a sister called Mary, who sat at the Lord's feet and listened to His teaching" (Luke 10:38–39).

Jesus had spent time among these women. They were His friends. It is a fascinating moment in His ministry that, outside the twelve apostles, there are named people with whom Jesus connects more than once. This provides insight into how deep the relationship would be between Jesus and this family. When the sisters sent word that Lazarus was sick, it was not some random person. It was someone with whom time had been spent. "Jesus said to her, 'I am the resurrection and the life. Whoever believes in Me, though he die, yet shall he live'" (John 11:25).

This is a cornerstone of faith reflected throughout the Bible, especially in the Epistles. Resurrection and life are deeply held beliefs by all Christians. The writers of the Epistles will latch onto this great gift that Jesus gives and extol the hope of life eternal:

"For as by a man came death, by a man has come also the resurrection of the dead" (1 Corinthians 15:21).

"When Christ who is your life appears, then you also will appear with Him in glory" (Colossians 3:4).

"Blessed be the God and Father of our Lord Jesus Christ! According to His great mercy, He has caused us to be born again to a living hope through the resurrection of Jesus Christ from the dead, to an inheritance that is imperishable, undefiled, and unfading, kept in heaven for you" (1 Peter 1:3–4).

Martha responded to Jesus in faith: "Yes, Lord; I believe that You are the Christ, the Son of God, who is coming into the world" (John 11:27). The confession of a believer is always a great gift. Not because of a decision they have made—but because of the proof of the Holy Spirit at work in their life. Jesus even declares that this confession will be the foundation on which His church is built. "Simon Peter replied, 'You are the Christ, the Son of the living God.' And Jesus answered him, 'Blessed are you, Simon Bar-Jonah! For flesh and blood has not revealed this to you, but My Father who is in heaven. And I tell you, you are Peter, and on this rock I will build My church, and the gates of hell shall not prevail against it'" (Matthew 16:16–18).

"Jesus wept" (John 11:35). A two-word verse in Scripture but well known for people of faith. They are two words that convey great depth. Jesus was not unaffected by the issue that had hit this home in Bethany and the fate of His friend. Jesus feels deeply, just as His creation does. This is reflected in this verse: "And when He drew near and saw the city, He wept over it" (Luke 19:41).

Lord, may Your Word constantly reveal to me the depth of Jesus' saving work and passion for Your creation. In Jesus' name. Amen.

WE DIE, BUT WE NEVER DIE?

Jesus said to her, "I am the resurrection and the life. Whoever believes in Me, though he die, yet shall he live, and everyone who lives and believes in Me shall never die. Do you believe this?" (JOHN 11:25-26)

Sometimes the words of Jesus are crystal clear. Other times, they can be confusing. In these verses, Jesus seems to contradict Himself. First, He says that those who believe in Him, *though they die*, which appears definitive. Even those who believe in Jesus will die. That belief does not negate death—or does it? He goes on to say that those who live and believe in Him will *never* die. Which is it?

It must be remembered that in the beginning, God created humanity as both physical and spiritual beings. These two components of our being are not separate. Instead, the physical and spiritual are intertwined. While there are medical marvels of heart, lung, and now even hand transplants, a surgeon has yet to transplant a soul. It is something both material and immaterial. Caught up in the physical realm yet somehow different than all that surrounds it. We can look to this to see what Jesus is speaking in the verses above.

Christians both will and will not experience death. It is a fact that the physical nature of humanity dies. The physical body will fade and die of illness, tragedy, or old age. While many try to find ways to extend life, physical immortality cannot be grasped. When Jesus says, "though he die," He speaks of the physical form. It will die and decay.

What, then, of the spirit? The believer's spirit will never die. Jesus looks to the thief on the cross and says, "Truly, I say to you, today you will be with

Me in paradise" (Luke 23:43). Paul writes this: "For since we believe that Jesus died and rose again, even so, through Jesus, God will bring with Him those who have fallen asleep. For this we declare to you by a word from the Lord, that we who are alive, who are left until the coming of the Lord, will not precede those who have fallen asleep" (1 Thessalonians 4:14-15). After physical death, the believer's spirit rests with Christ in paradise.

Jesus' claim of being the resurrection is the promise that one day, Christ will reunite those spirits with their risen bodies when He returns. To be fully human is to be both physical and spiritual. Thus, even that which dies (physical) will one day live again. That hope is the greatest gift of God to those who believe. Life eternal.

Dear Jesus, thank You for coming to defeat death. While there may be a time when my physical body fails me, thank You that it is not the end. I rejoice, knowing that one day in resurrection You promise a new heaven and a new earth where I will live with You as in the days of the garden. Amen.

IN THE WAITING

Martha said to Jesus, "Lord, if You had been here, my brother would not have died. But even now I know that whatever You ask from God, God will give You." Jesus said to her, "Your brother will rise again." Martha said to Him, "I know that he will rise again in the resurrection on the last day." Jesus said to her, "I am the resurrection and the life. Whoever believes in Me, though he die, yet shall he live, and everyone who lives and believes in Me shall never die. Do you believe this?" She said to Him, "Yes, Lord; I believe that You are the Christ, the Son of God, who is coming into the world." (JOHN 11:21-27)

A friend or family member lies behind the doors in surgery or in an emergency situation—and all you can do is wait. Maybe there's a screen that will give an update, but most of the time it's waiting, hoping, and praying—heart-wrenchingly held in limbo. Preparing yourself for the worst, hoping for the best.

Martha and Mary knew they had an ace in the hole. No matter how bad Lazarus got, they could always send for Jesus. He had healed so many, surely He would heal His friend. With urgency, they sent the message: "Come quick, Lazarus is dying." Then all they could do was wait. When would Jesus arrive? They watched their brother get worse and worse until finally, he took his last breath.

Yet still, Martha hoped. This was the Christ. He could do anything. When Jesus finally arrived, she said as much. And He did.

He was the resurrection and the life.

He is the resurrection and life.

You probably spend time waiting. Sure there are times, good times, when being thankful and giving God praise comes easy. But what about in the waiting?

The good news is that He knows. He prepared for you. In the waiting, He grants hope. Each week, He meets you in the bread and the wine, His body and blood for you. He met you in the waters of your Baptism. There, through the power of His Word, He claimed you and calls you friend, brother, sister.

There will be waiting. Remember, He promises this world will bring trouble. But He ends that promise by saying, "Take heart; I have overcome the world" (John 16:33).

In the waiting, don't lose sight of the fact that He is already there. Trust His promises. Confess as Martha and find that hope is always at hand.

Lord, let me trust You in the waiting. May I learn to trust Your promises in those times and see how You are good. Amen.

THE DEATH OF JOHN THE BAPTIST

WEEK 22—MARK 6:14–29

King Herod heard of [Jesus' miracles], for Jesus' name had become known. Some said, "John the Baptist has been raised from the dead. That is why these miraculous powers are at work in Him." But others said, "He is Elijah." And others said, "He is a prophet, like one of the prophets of old." But when Herod heard of it, he said, "John, whom I beheaded, has been raised." For it was Herod who had sent and seized John and bound him in prison for the sake of Herodias, his brother Philip's wife, because he had married her. For John had been saying to Herod, "It is not lawful for you to have your brother's wife." And Herodias had a grudge against him and wanted to put him to death. But she could not, for Herod feared John, knowing that he was a righteous and holy man, and he kept him safe. When he heard him, he was greatly perplexed, and yet he heard him gladly.

But an opportunity came when Herod on his birthday gave a banquet for his nobles and military commanders and the leading men of Galilee. For when Herodias's daughter came in and danced, she pleased Herod and his guests. And the king said to the girl, "Ask me for whatever you wish, and I will give it to you." And he vowed to her, "Whatever you ask me, I will give you, up to half of my kingdom." And she went out and said to her mother, "For what should I ask?" And she said, "The head of John the Baptist." And she came in immediately with haste to the king and asked, saying, "I want you to give me at once the head of John the Baptist on a platter." And the king was exceedingly sorry, but because of his oaths and his guests he did not want to break his word to her. And immediately the king sent an executioner with orders to bring John's head. He went and beheaded him in the prison and brought his head on a platter and gave it to the girl, and the girl gave it to her mother. When his disciples heard of it, they came and took his body and laid it in a tomb.

THE PROPHET AND FORERUNNER

In those days John the Baptist came preaching in the wilderness of Judea, "Repent, for the kingdom of heaven is at hand." (MATTHEW 3:1–2)

In this week's passage, we take a look at the death of John the Baptist. But to fully understand the significance of his death, we need to understand his life—who he was and what he did.

John the Baptist was related to Jesus—John's mother, Elizabeth, and Jesus' mother, Mary, were related. Many people refer to the two as cousins, but we're not sure of the exact relationship between them. Scripture only refers to Elizabeth as Mary's "relative" in Luke 1:36.

When a pregnant Mary visited a pregnant Elizabeth, Elizabeth exclaimed, "When the sound of your greeting came to my ears, the baby in my womb leaped for joy" (Luke 1:44). Even before he was born, the Spirit led John to recognize that Jesus was more than just an ordinary man!

John the Baptist was a great prophet God raised up to prepare the Jews for the coming of their Savior, Jesus. "And he went into all the region around the Jordan, proclaiming a baptism of repentance for the forgiveness of sins" (Luke 3:3). John's ministry was preparatory, particularly aimed at convicting the Jews of their sins so they would understand their need for the Savior, then baptizing them to wash those sins away and preaching about the Savior who was living unknown among them.

He preached a fiery message that didn't mince words. He referred to the crowds that came out to him as a "brood of vipers" (Luke 3:7) and encouraged them to repent and be baptized. He warned people not to rely on their status as Abraham's children but to bear good fruit.

The crowds loved John and thought he was a great prophet. Some even thought *he* was the expected Savior! But John did not waver in preaching the truth—he always shifted the focus back to Jesus. "I baptize you with water, but He who is mightier than I is coming, the strap of whose sandals I am not worthy to untie. He will baptize you with the Holy Spirit and fire" (Luke 3:16).

John's message was not popular among the Jewish leaders or King Herod. As we see in this week's passage, Herod had John beheaded, even if reluctantly. John's death foreshadowed Jesus' coming death.

Through his life and death, John preached the Gospel and preached a message of repentance, drawing God's people closer to Him. Thanks be to God for faithful servants that dedicate their lives to Him!

God in heaven, bless all preachers of Your Word. In Jesus' name. Amen.

JOHN STOOD FIRM

As [Jesus] said these things, He called out, "He who has ears to hear, let him hear." (LUKE 8:8)

Mark's mention of John's death arises as various groups of people make statements about the abundant number of miracles Jesus and His disciples are performing. Jesus sent the Twelve out in groups of two to neighboring villages with power to heal the sick and drive out demons. This was in Galilee, the northern area Herod Antipas ruled, so of course, he was interested in what was going on. His personal feeling was that Jesus was John the Baptist raised from the dead. Mark tells us Herod had imprisoned John for preaching against his marriage to his brother's wife, Herodias. Herod frequently went to the prison to hear John preach about righteousness. God's Law perplexed him—made him grow guilty and fearful—yet he liked to listen to John. Perhaps it was because John was a man of conviction. His preaching had resulted in his imprisonment, yet John never backed down. He stood firm in declaring God's Law and Gospel.

At Herod's birthday celebration, the daughter of his wife, Herodias, danced for him, and Herod enjoyed it so much he made a rash vow, promising to give her anything she asked—"up to half of my kingdom" (Mark 6:23). After consulting her mother, she requested John the Baptist's head on a platter. Herod reluctantly granted her request to save embarrassment before his guests, despite his fearful respect of John as a prophet.

John's arrest and death was probably welcome news to the Jewish religious authorities in Jerusalem because John exposed their false righteousness, hypocrisy, and greed. But they were finding Jesus to be an even greater thorn in their side. John's death fulfilled his own teaching to his disciples that Jesus must increase, and he must decrease.

John's death also foreshadowed Jesus' own death in the coming years. Before Jesus' death, He, too, was widely accepted by the crowds until they turned against Him. The message of the Gospel is sometimes not received despite initial interest.

In the parable of the sower, Jesus talks about people like Herod, who at first hear the Gospel, but then forsake it: "And the ones on the rock are those who, when they hear the word, receive it with joy. But these have no root; they believe for a while, and in time of testing fall away" (Luke 8:13). Herod seemed, at the very least, to be interested in what John the Baptist had to say, but when his reputation was at stake in front of his guests, he gave in and forsook the truth of God's Word. When Herod would later question Jesus on the morning of Good Friday, Jesus remained silent. He had not one word to add to those that John had said (see Luke 23:6–17).

May we, in times of trial, stand firm in the Gospel, no matter the consequences. Thanks be to God that He gives us the strength to withstand persecution, trial, and sword!

God, give me the strength to stand up for the Gospel no matter what. In Jesus' name. Amen.

JOHN'S DEATH AND JESUS' DEATH

Count it all joy, my brothers, when you meet trials of various kinds, for you know that the testing of your faith produces steadfastness. (JAMES 1:2–3)

By looking at the life and death of John the Baptist, we can learn more about the life, death, and resurrection of Jesus Christ. These two relatives had more in common than their genetics—their lives were connected from the beginning in the greater story of the Gospel.

Just as John was arrested and imprisoned for preaching the Gospel, Jesus would be arrested and held as a prisoner for the message He preached. Neither backed down from the truth they preached to avoid arrest, imprisonment, or death. Their steadfastness is a model for us Christians.

Just as John preached the truth and righteousness to Herod, Jesus would preach the truth to the Jewish leaders and to Pontius Pilate. Neither John nor Jesus were afraid to speak harsh truths to those in power—no matter the consequences. May we Christians seek to be truthful at all times, just like them.

Just as John was executed under a reluctant Herod who felt pressured by his wife, stepdaughter, and the crowd of dignitaries around him, Jesus would be executed under a reluctant Pilate who felt pressure from the Jewish chief priests and the crowds chanting for Jesus' crucifixion. These leaders cared more about their reputations and their political futures than they did about the truth or doing what was just and right. We Christians should not care about the opinions of others in light of the Gospel.

But by this injustice and cowardice, God's will would be fulfilled, and Jesus would be sacrificed for the sins of the world. Rising to life on the third day, He won the victory over sin and death and assured believers of their own resurrection when He returns to judge the living and the dead. John the Baptist understood this truth and preached it faithfully until his death.

John faithfully lived out his life as a disciple of Jesus—he preached the Gospel of Jesus without compromise, in the face of danger, and to all people. Jesus, knowing the fate that lay ahead of Him, did not waver in His proclamation of the Gospel, proclaiming the kingdom of God until His final breath.

May we look to the examples of Jesus and John the Baptist to strengthen our witness as we share the Gospel with those around us in our daily lives. May we not be deterred by differing views, persecution, hate, or the opinions of those around us. Thanks be to God for equipping us with everything we need—and for His grace when we fail.

Holy Spirit, give me the strength to stand firm and share the Gospel, no matter the consequences. In Jesus' name. Amen.

HEARD HIM GLADLY?

And these are the ones sown on rocky ground: the ones who, when they hear the word, immediately receive it with joy. And they have no root in themselves, but endure for a while; then, when tribulation or persecution arises on account of the word, immediately they fall away. (MARK 4:16–17)

I n the passage for this week, one perhaps surprising inclusion is that Herod "heard [John] gladly" (Mark 6:20). It's surprising for two reasons.

One, John was very critical of the marriage relationship between Herod and his brother Philip's wife, Herodias. Most of us, when someone confronts us with a difficult truth, buck back and refuse to hear it. Herod "was greatly perplexed" but still listened to him with gladness, likely because he knew that John was "a righteous and holy man." The truth of God's Word that John spoke struck a deep and profound response in him. He could see there was something different about John, so he was willing to listen to what he had to say, even if it contradicted his own personal beliefs.

The second reason this inclusion is surprising is that Herod eventually had John killed, as we see in the latter half of the passage. If he heard him gladly, why would he have him killed? We know that Herod had previously kept John safe when Herodias sought his death, so he clearly protected him up to a point—but what changed? What caused Herod to stop hearing John gladly and have him killed instead?

To gain some additional insight, we can look to the parable of the sower in Mark 4. Jesus speaks of those who have shallow roots—who rejoice to hear the Word but are eventually scorched by opposition: "And these are the ones sown on rocky ground: the ones who, when they hear the word, immediately receive it with joy. And they have no root in themselves, but endure for a while; then, when tribulation or persecution arises on account of the word, immediately they fall away" (Mark 4:16–17).

Herod seems to be one of these seeds that was sown on rocky soil. He initially heard the message John preached with gladness, despite its criticism of his life choices. He likewise endured for a while, protecting John and keeping him safe.

However, tribulation arises in the form of a dinner party, where Herod must decide between saving John or saving face in front of his guests. Herod had made a rash promise to Herodias's daughter and did not want to go back on his word or tarnish his reputation in front of his guests.

These guests were not just Herod's personal friends—they were "nobles and military commanders and the leading men of Galilee" (Mark 6:21). These were important men, with lots of political, military, and community influence. If Herod upset or offended them, they could easily ruin his political career.

So instead of standing firm in the face of tribulation, Herod gave in. He cared more about the opinion of the people who were important in the eyes of the world than the one whose opinion matters most—God. Like the seed that fell on rocky soil, he withered and fell away. John was killed.

May we be like the seeds that are sown on good soil, who gladly hear the Word, accept it, and bear much fruit.

Jesus, may I bear fruit for You all the days of my life. Amen.

WHICH HEROD?

Let every person be subject to the
governing authorities. For there is
no authority except from God, and
those that exist have been insti-
tuted by God. (ROMANS 13:1)

When you read this passage for the first time, you might have wondered which Herod is featured in this story. There seem to be a lot of them in the New Testament!

Why are there so many Herods in the Bible? Herod was the family name of a powerful dynasty. The descendants of King Herod the Great, the family patriarch, took the name Herod as their family name. In our Western context, we can think of it as a last name.

When Jesus was born, King Herod the Great was the ruler of a large region including Judah, Samaria, and Galilee. This King Herod was the one who was visited by the Wise Men looking for the King of the Jews. After their visit, Herod "saw that he had been tricked by the wise men, became furious, and he sent and killed all the male children in Bethlehem and in all that region who were two years old or under, according to the time that he had ascertained from the wise men" (Matthew 2:16). The bloody dynasty of the Herods begins here, at the birth of Jesus. King Herod had many wives, so many of his children were half-siblings.

After King Herod the Great died, his kingdom was divided between three of his sons—Antipas, Archelaus, and Philip. The Herod in this week's passage, Herod Antipas, was given Galilee and the region east of the Jordan River. His half-brother Philip had originally married Herodias, a daughter of King Herod, their stepsister. Later, she divorced

Philip to marry Herod Antipas, who was more ambitious. This is where our story picks up—with John the Baptist criticizing their relationship, which went against the Law of Moses.

Later in the Scriptures, we encounter the Herod family again at the crucifixion of Jesus. Pontius Pilate didn't want to deal with this dispute, so "when he learned that [Jesus] belonged to Herod's jurisdiction, he sent Him over to Herod, who was himself in Jerusalem at that time" (Luke 23:7). The Herod in this story is still Herod Antipas, who killed John the Baptist.

Herod Antipas was at enmity with Pilate because he was scheming to regain that territory of Judea and Samaria that his father, Herod the Great, had once ruled. When Pilate did him the favor of sending Jesus to him, Herod gave up his hostility against Pilate, and they "became friends with each other that very day, for before this they had been at enmity with each other" (Luke 23:12).

The Herod dynasty is one filled with bloodshed, betrayal, and political intrigue. In Acts 12:1-2, yet another Herod from another generation will put to death James, brother of John, the first apostle to be martyred. Pray that all your politicians and leaders would draw closer to Jesus and follow Him.

Jesus, we know that You work through all rulers, even the evil Herod family. May You still draw our leaders close to You. Amen.

THE LAST PROPHET

Finally, be strong in the Lord and in the strength of His might. Put on the whole armor of God, that you may be able to stand against the schemes of the devil. (EPHESIANS 6:10–11)

God calls very few of us to lay down our lives for the sake of the Gospel, but we can expect to face hostility when we proclaim God's Word—the message that all sinners need to hear but few truly want to. Whether our friends abandon us, or our family cuts off ties, we might encounter opposition.

By God's grace, John had fulfilled his God-given mission to prepare for Jesus. Perhaps knowing Jesus' ministry had begun and crowds were flocking to Him, John sensed his work was drawing to a close. He seemed to turn his focus to confronting Herod's sin and calling on him to repent. Like Herod, we also have to weigh carefully where we give our greatest loyalty—to God or to our own reputation and little kingdom of one. Whatever Herod stood to gain by keeping his vow, he stood to lose his eternal salvation by neglecting John's call to repent.

To faithfully serve God and follow John's example, we need the strength and encouragement that comes from God's Word and Sacraments. Sunday after Sunday, God shows us the goal and end of our life—the resurrection to eternal life that God offers us for Jesus' sake. God reminds us that nothing on earth is worth sacrificing that salvation for.

Thanks be to God that He gives us the strength for this task. We sinful humans could never perfectly live a life in sync with the Gospel, but we are blessed with a merciful, compassionate, and forgiving God. He continuously lets us sinful humans partake in the spreading of His Word, despite our sinfulness!

God also opens our eyes to our neighbors' greatest need—which is to hear the Word of God that calls them to repent of their sins and trust in Jesus as their Savior. This message is often not well received by the world, but it's a necessary message.

John the Baptist is a great example for us Christians as we journey through life, proclaiming the Gospel and preaching Christ crucified. May we stay faithful until the very end, no matter the consequences, like our brother John.

The twenty-fourth stanza of the hymn "By All Your Saints in Warfare" (*LSB* 518) perfectly sums up our journey through this passage about the faithful witness of John the Baptist, who did not shrink from threats of death throughout his life nor in the moment of death. I encourage you to find and read that particular stanza as you close out this week.

Father, thank You for the example of John the Baptist. May we faithfully proclaim the Gospel until our final breath. In Jesus' name. Amen.

JESUS FEEDS FIVE THOUSAND

WEEK 23—MATTHEW 14:13–21

Now when Jesus heard [about John the Baptist's death], He withdrew from there in a boat to a desolate place by Himself. But when the crowds heard it, they followed Him on foot from the towns. When He went ashore He saw a great crowd, and He had compassion on them and healed their sick. Now when it was evening, the disciples came to Him and said, "This is a desolate place, and the day is now over; send the crowds away to go into the villages and buy food for themselves." But Jesus said, "They need not go away; you give them something to eat." They said to Him, "We have only five loaves here and two fish." And He said, "Bring them here to Me." Then He ordered the crowds to sit down on the grass, and taking the five loaves and the two fish, He looked up to heaven and said a blessing. Then He broke the loaves and gave them to the disciples, and the disciples gave them to the crowds. And they all ate and were satisfied. And they took up twelve baskets full of the broken pieces left over. And those who ate were about five thousand men, besides women and children.

PROVIDING ALL WE NEED

Now when Jesus heard this, He withdrew from there in a boat to a desolate place by Himself. But when the crowds heard it, they followed Him on foot from the towns. When He went ashore He saw a great crowd. (MATTHEW 14:13–14)

These verses pick up from where we left off in week 22 with the beheading of John the Baptist. John's disciples buried his body and went to tell Jesus what had happened. Upon hearing the news, Jesus retreats for some quiet to an uninhabited, desolate area of the northeast shore of the Sea of Galilee (see Luke 9:10).

The crowds hear about this and follow Him to that place, wanting to sit at His feet and hear what He has to say—possibly see a miracle or be healed themselves. Jesus is deep into His public ministry, and people from all over had heard what He had been doing, so it is no surprise that they were thronging to follow Him. Although the disciples were quick to protect Jesus and urge Him to send the crowds away, Jesus feels compassion toward them. He is gracious to them and provides for them both earthly food in the form of bread and fish as well as heavenly food in the form of His Word. He wants the people to stay because He knows that His time on earth is limited—and preaching and teaching is what His Father has sent Him on earth to do.

The crowd is willing to sit and listen. They are so caught up in Jesus' marvelous words that they give no thought about where they will get dinner. From John's account of this miracle, we are told that a boy brought the five loaves and two fish that are provided to Jesus. Jesus prays a blessing, and when the disciples distribute the meal, Matthew tells us that all in the crowds ate and were satisfied (see 14:20). Not only were they all satisfied but there was much left over that was collected to share with others. Jesus provides not only what we need but even more than we need so that this love, kindness, and caring we receive can, in turn, be shared with others.

He provides the food that the people need and tells His disciples that He is the bread of life, providing for the world not just in terms of earthly needs but also feeding them for eternal glory (see John 6:35). The task of feeding such a crowd is larger than the disciples can even imagine, so they were quick to send the crowds away—but Jesus teaches them about caring for one another and trusting in Him to provide all things to those who believe.

Heavenly Father, thank You for providing all we need in Your Son, Jesus Christ. In Jesus' name. Amen.

FEEDING BOTH SOUL AND BODY

Jesus said, "They need not go away; you give them something to eat." (MATTHEW 14:16)

The crowd that follows Jesus longs for Him and the Good News that He brings. It is this yearning desire that finds the people in a desolate area with nothing to eat. Eating was not even their priority—they were simply following Jesus and most likely not even aware of what hour of the day approached. It is exactly what Jesus meant in the Sermon on the Mount when He said, "Seek first the kingdom of God and His righteousness, and all these things will be added to you" (Matthew 6:33)—including food.

The people were so absorbed in Jesus' gracious words they didn't think about their supper. But Jesus' disciples did. Knowing the vast amount of food a crowd this big would require, they asked Jesus to send the people home so they could get what they need. Jesus did otherwise. Jesus knew what they needed—food for their physical bodies and the Word of God for their thirsting souls. Having preached to nourish their souls, now He feeds their bodies. That is what He gives them; by multiplying the five loaves and two fish, He is able to sustain five thousand men plus women and children. This miracle happens without the crowds even realizing it, but the disciples are aware. There should be no surprise at this miracle. Jesus had always cared for their needs; why would He not feed this crowd? He does the same for all people, including us.

Providing the meal for the people gave them what they needed for their physical needs, but Jesus teaches His disciples that He has given them far more than what they need to meet their physical needs. Providing this food points to the spiritual food that God also provides. He gives eternal life, and when we taste and see, there is no need to spend all our effort searching for earthly food because we will have eternal food, and we can trust God to provide for our physical needs. Jesus is the bread of life, and it is through Him that we eat and are always satisfied to live our lives reflecting Him and using the baskets that are left over to continue sharing this life-saving bread from heaven.

Heavenly Father, thank You for providing all we need to support this body and life. Give us grace to share this same Good News with all the world. In Jesus' name. Amen.

GOD IS FAITHFUL TO US SO WE CAN BE FAITHFUL TO HIM

And they all ate and were satisfied. And they took up twelve baskets full of the broken pieces left over. (MATTHEW 14:20)

Martin Luther tells us in the Small Catechism that God, our Father, gives us all that we need: "clothing and shoes, food and drink, house and home, wife and children, land, animals, and all I have" (Creed, First Article). It continues to tell us why: "All this He does only out of fatherly, divine goodness and mercy without any merit or worthiness in me." In Luther's explanation of the First Article of the Creed, he focuses on the earthly things that God has given us. He acknowledges that we need these things as human creatures and that they come from God.

Why does He do all this? Jesus' mission on this earth was to show God's fatherly, divine goodness and mercy. Not only did Jesus preach it that afternoon, but He showed it by providing the people the food that they needed. As a man living in this world, Jesus demonstrated that we are to live our lives serving one another and also know that through our freedom in Christ, we are not of this world.

This passage stresses God's faithfulness to provide the food that we need for sustenance; Christ promises to take care of all our physical needs. This passage tells us how Jesus provides food for people and throughout Scripture, God provides all that we need—food, shelter, and the like, that we might be able to focus our attention on living godly lives serving one another, not fussing and fretting over from where our next meal will come. The concern the disciples have for the people and themselves is not only met but Matthew tells us that the people were completely satisfied and there was even food left over.

As Jesus provides for the crowd, He is also teaching and training the disciples to know that in the future, throughout their ministry, they can trust Him to provide for all their bodily needs so they can focus their attention on preaching Christ crucified. In the Gospel of John, we learn that Jesus spends time talking and teaching the disciples why He does these things. There are many times when Jesus does something and then He has a conversation with His disciples, asking them why they think He did what He did. All of Jesus' earthly ministry was for a reason—to point to the Father. Providing food pointed to the Father, who provides all that we need. Jesus acknowledges the Father as He looks to heaven and blesses the food, and we are to do the same daily in our lives.

Heavenly Father, thank You for providing all that we need in this life. May we look to You for all things. In Jesus' name. Amen.

A LIFE OF LOVE AND COMPASSION

When He went ashore He saw a great crowd, and He had compassion on them and healed their sick. (MATTHEW 14:14)

The passage begins with verse 12 where John the Baptist's disciples had just taken his body and buried him after Herod ordered his beheading. John the Baptist was the great forerunner of Jesus. Jesus' mother and John's mother were cousins. John was a great man of faith, and through his ministry God convicted many Jews of their sin and showed their need for a Savior. John prepared the Jews to welcome Jesus' ministry of love, forgiveness, and grace. He had baptized Jesus, which marked the beginning of Jesus' own ministry. He had pointed his own disciples to Jesus saying, "Behold, the Lamb of God, who takes away the sin of the world!" (John 1:29). When John's disciples complained that Jesus was now baptizing and all were going to Him, John answered them, "He must increase, but I must decrease" (John 3:30).

Now that John has died, Jesus' own death comes clearer. So when Jesus hears this news and wants to go away to a solitary place for a bit, it is understandable. During Jesus' earthly ministry, there were people whom we know Jesus loved dearly. We see the effect of John's beheading on Jesus here; it is similar to how Jesus responded to the death of Lazarus in John 11:35.

This is not the only time Jesus feeds a large crowd so we should not be surprised by the outcome. In Matthew 15:32–38, we will see that Jesus feeds four thousand men besides women and children. This is a relationship and Jesus clearly reveals the compassion He has for them as well. Throughout Jesus' earthly ministry, He showed compassion especially to the crowds who followed Him; Matthew specifically refers to this in Matthew 9:36 and Matthew 15:32. This compassion is shown not only to large crowds but also to individuals who were trying to have Jesus touch and heal them. We see the disciples respond with asking Jesus to ask the crowds to go away in this passage, but other times, they want the little children to go away and Jesus rebukes them, as in Mark 10:14. The disciples also ask Jesus to send away the mother of a demon-possessed daughter in Matthew 15:23.

In the final verses of this week's passage, Jesus feeds the five thousand, but He always points His work to the Father. In verse 19, it says that Jesus looked up to heaven and gave a blessing, acknowledging the thanks due to the Father and teaching us to pray. Throughout His earthly ministry, Jesus demonstrated to the people and to us today that we are to pray and give thanks for all that we receive. He does this when He heals the man who was deaf in Mark 7:34 and before raising Lazarus in John 11:41. The two most commonly known places that Jesus prays are at the Last Supper (see Matthew 26:26) where He gives His disciples His very body and blood for the forgiveness of their sins and in the Garden of Gethsemane (see John 17:1) where He prepares to suffer on the cross for our sins. We will look at these prayers in a few weeks.

Heavenly Father, thank You for having compassion on us poor, miserable sinners. Empower us to feel and show compassion to those around us. In Jesus' name. Amen.

JESUS' DEEP COMPASSION

Now when it was evening, the disciples came to Him and said, "This is a desolate place, and the day is now over; send the crowds away to go into the villages and buy food for themselves." But Jesus said, "They need not go away; you give them something to eat." (MATTHEW 14:15–16)

The word *compassion* can be defined as "to suffer together." Compassion is having an overwhelming feeling for those who are suffering. Jesus had compassion on the crowd. When we read this the first time, we might get the impression that Jesus just had compassion on them being hungry since it was nearly time to eat. But this overwhelming feeling is deeper than that.

When He first landed on this desolate shore, Jesus looked at the people and had compassion on them—He knew their suffering. Suffering more than they even realized. As Jesus looked on the crowd, He saw the sin and Law that consumed them; they were lost and afraid. He had compassion for them because their rabbis were teaching them they had to win God's favor through their own hard work and obedience—a burden no person can bear. He knew that they needed the bread of life. Jesus was there to relieve their suffering, so after teaching them of God's mercy and love for hours, He tells them to sit, and He feeds them with bread and fish and with His Word, leaving them satisfied and covered by love.

Were all the people in the crowd aware of the miracle Jesus had just performed?

The people who had gathered were such a large group and spread out throughout the area—and we are told that they were specifically sitting down.

The reality is that many, if not most, did not know what had happened. There was a sense of blind faith and trust. They had heard about the wonders Jesus had done, which is why they were following Him, to see for themselves. They did not even think about the time of day or the supplies they needed. They may have assumed that Jesus would take care of them. In the Gospel of John, the disciples get the five loaves and two fish from a boy, so the boy may have known, but the crowds certainly had no idea how much food Jesus started with. However, in Matthew, it is just the disciples who are with Jesus as He blesses the food, and they begin to distribute. This would have been a teaching moment for Jesus with the disciples. The people that were there would not have been able to grasp the magnitude of the miracle Jesus had done.

But according to John 6:14–15, some recognized the miracle. Jesus knew they intended to come and take Him by force to make Him king, so He sent His disciples away in the boat and dismissed the crowds. Then Jesus withdrew again to the mountain by Himself to pray. After spending hours in prayer, He went to them, walking on the water (Mark 6:45–52).

Heavenly Father, thank You for providing for us, even when we do not realize it. May we thank You at all times, in all circumstances. In Jesus' name. Amen.

WE CAN BE CONFIDENT IN GOD'S PROVIDENCE

Those who ate were about five thousand men, besides women and children. (MATTHEW 14:21)

As we read these verses, we are reminded of Jesus' humanity. He had a human mind, heart, and body like all of us, which required food and drink, clothing and shoes, sleep, and so on. So He understands that we also have basic, physical needs that must be met if we are to live and serve Him in this world.

We are also reminded that God does not only give us eternal bread—the spiritual gifts we need of forgiveness, peace, and eternal life—but that He also faithfully gives us physical bread, meeting all of our bodily needs. God recognizes that we need these daily, earthly materials to serve Him and be good and godly citizens as we live out our vocations.

We are reminded of this each time we pray the Lord's Prayer, which Jesus taught us to pray. When we ask our Father in heaven to give us our daily bread, we are looking to God to provide all our physical needs as Luther summarized them in his explanation of the First Article of the Creed. We are challenged to constantly turn to Jesus, the author and perfecter of our faith, for all of our needs of body and soul.

We are also shown Jesus' compassion for us. He extends to us the same compassion He extended to the crowd. He loves us like no one else can, and He performed a miracle to provide five thousand men (and additional women and children) with bread and fish so that they can be full and fully satisfied—even though the disciples wanted Jesus to send the people away to take care of themselves. How many times have we done this—made a personal conclusion about our situation and cut Jesus off before we have even asked? We try to qualify what God can do, but He proves us wrong. He feeds the crowd, and we have twelve baskets left over! How many more could He have fed that day? The answer is all of them; nothing is impossible for our God. He richly and daily provides us all that we need and more than we can even ask for.

When we gather in worship, we are reminded of our heavenly Father's concern for all aspects of our lives, not just our spiritual need for forgiveness and salvation. As He nourishes our spirits with the body and blood of His beloved Son, He nourishes and strengthens our bodies through the bread and wine. His Word reminds us that He will provide all our needs of body and soul, and His Benediction assures us that He will bless us and keep us in this life, until He brings us to live with Him in glory everlasting.

Our Father, who art in heaven, hallowed be Thy name. Thy kingdom come. Thy will be done, on earth as it is in heaven. Give us this day our daily bread. And forgive us our trespasses, as we forgive those who trespass against us. And lead us not into temptation but deliver us from evil. For Thine is the kingdom, and the power and the glory, forever and ever. Amen.

JESUS IS THE GOOD SHEPHERD

WEEK 24—JOHN 10:10–18

The thief comes only to steal and kill and destroy. I came that they may have life and have it abundantly. I am the good shepherd. The good shepherd lays down His life for the sheep. He who is a hired hand and not a shepherd, who does not own the sheep, sees the wolf coming and leaves the sheep and flees, and the wolf snatches them and scatters them. He flees because he is a hired hand and cares nothing for the sheep. I am the good shepherd. I know My own and My own know Me, just as the Father knows Me and I know the Father; and I lay down My life for the sheep. And I have other sheep that are not of this fold. I must bring them also, and they will listen to My voice. So there will be one flock, one shepherd. For this reason the Father loves Me, because I lay down My life that I may take it up again. No one takes it from Me, but I lay it down of My own accord. I have authority to lay it down, and I have authority to take it up again. This charge I have received from My Father.

THE GOOD SHEPHERD

I am the good shepherd. The good shepherd lays down His life for the sheep. (JOHN 10:11)

Israel was an agricultural country. People worked on farms, orchards, vineyards, and kept flocks and herds. Towns and villages had common sheepfolds where many different flocks were kept and protected together. Everyone had seen shepherds leading their own individual flocks out of the common sheepfolds by calling them by name and leading them out with just the sound of their voices. Jesus captures that very familiar experience to teach us His relationship to us, His sheep.

The passage of John 10:10–18 is often considered one of the key passages regarding the nature of Jesus as the Good Shepherd. This passage is understood in the context of the larger narrative of the Bible, which reveals Jesus as both fully God and fully man. In this passage, Jesus describes Himself as the Good Shepherd who is willing to lay down His life to protect the sheep and knows them intimately. When He talks in other parables about a shepherd leaving his ninety-nine sheep to go and search out the one lost sheep, He is speaking of Himself.

Here, Jesus describes Himself as the Good Shepherd who lays down His life for His sheep. This is a powerful declaration of the love and sacrifice of Jesus for humanity. Through His death on the cross, Jesus demonstrates His willingness to lay down His life for His followers, providing full salvation and forgiveness of sins. In this way, the Good Shepherd imagery in John 10:10–18 serves as a reminder of the love and grace Jesus offers to all people. Additionally, Jesus' declaration that He knows His sheep and they follow Him highlights the intimate relationship He desires to have with each of His human creatures, each of His followers. This is a call to all people to trust in Jesus as their Good Shepherd, to follow Him closely, and to rely on His guidance and protection in this life and the life to come.

Jesus not only provides for our physical needs but He also cares for our spiritual needs. He is the source of abundant life, giving us peace and joy in this life and eternal life in the next. When we follow Jesus, we are guided in the path of righteousness and protected from the forces of evil that seek to steal, kill, and destroy.

As we reflect on the imagery of the Good Shepherd, we are reminded that we are not just sheep but beloved children of God. Jesus not only calls us by name but He also knows us intimately and loves us unconditionally. We can trust in Him to lead us and provide for us—always.

Dear Lord, thank You for being our Good Shepherd, loving, guiding, and caring for us as Your sheep. Help us to trust in Your leading and provision for our lives. We acknowledge that we are Your beloved children and that You know us intimately. May we follow You closely, always relying on Your guidance and protection. Amen.

THE SHEPHERD WHO GIVES ABUNDANT LIFE

I came that they may have life and have it abundantly. (JOHN 10:10)

The main overall message of the passage of John 10:10–18 is the abundant life that Jesus Christ offers to all who believe in Him. As the Good Shepherd, Jesus is the only one who can provide eternal life to His sheep. He is the gatekeeper, the only way to the Father, and those who follow Him will always be saved and led.

Jesus describes Himself as the Good Shepherd, who lays down His life for His sheep. This is a reference to His ultimate sacrifice on the cross where He died to take away the sin of the world and to offer salvation to all who believe in Him. The Good Shepherd's love for His sheep is unconditional and selfless; through this love, we can have abundant life.

In contrast to the Good Shepherd, the passage also mentions the hireling—who does not honestly care for the sheep and runs away when danger arises. This references false teachers and prophets who lead people astray from the truth, such as the rabbis and Pharisees, the teachers who led Israel astray. Jesus warns us to beware of such people and to follow Him alone.

The passage also speaks of the sheep knowing the Good Shepherd's voice and following Him. This is a call to us to listen to Jesus and follow His teachings—not just with our ears but with our hearts. It is through consistent and dedicated Bible reading that we are able to discern the voice of Jesus since it is through this medium that Christ communicates with us. We get to have a personal relationship with Jesus and trust in Him completely. Only then can we have the abundant life that He promises.

In verses 17 and 18, Jesus declares that He has the power to lay down His life and to take it up again. This references His resurrection from the dead, confirming His deity and power over death. Jesus defeated sin and death through His death and resurrection and offers us the gift of eternal life. He also declares that no one takes His life from Him. This will be important to remember in the weeks ahead when we study Jesus' arrest, trials, and crucifixion. Neither Judas, Caiaphas, the Jewish high court, or Pontius Pilate and his soldiers have the power to take Jesus' life from Him. He must lay it down of His own free choice—and He will.

As members of Jesus' flock, we believe in the centrality of the cross and the resurrection in our salvation. Therefore, we trust in Jesus alone as our Lord and Savior and seek to follow Him in all aspects of our lives. Through faith in Him, we have the assurance of eternal life and the abundant life He promises.

Dear Lord Jesus, thank You for Your love and sacrifice on the cross. Thank You for offering us the gift of eternal life and the abundant life that You promise. Help us to listen to Your voice and to follow You so that we may have the fullness of life that You desire for us. Protect us from false teachers and prophets and guide us in Your truth. We pray for our brothers and sisters, that they may remain steadfast in their faith and continue to share the Good News with the world. In Your holy name, we pray. Amen.

OUR GOOD SHEPHERD LIVES

I am the good shepherd. I know My own and My own know Me. (JOHN 10:14)

John 10:10–18 is a beautiful passage that speaks to the heart of who Jesus is and what He came to do. In this passage, Jesus proclaims Himself to be the Good Shepherd, and in doing so, He points to His mission as our Savior.

Jesus' declaration that He is the Good Shepherd is significant because it speaks to His role as our protector too. Just as a good shepherd lays down his life for his sheep, Jesus lays down His life for us. He did this by offering Himself as a sacrifice for our sins, dying on the cross in our place. This is the ultimate act of love and protection, and it shows us just how much Jesus loves us and cares for us.

But Jesus' mission doesn't end with His death on the cross. In fact, it is through His death and resurrection that He truly exercises His protecting role as our Good Shepherd. By dying for our sins, Jesus defeated Satan and all the power of sin and death that he had over us. And by rising from the dead, Jesus demonstrated His victory over these powers and promised to always be with us to the end of the age. Jesus has made us forever safe in His mighty hand through His death and resurrection.

In this passage, Jesus also points to His divinity when He says, "No one takes it from Me, but I lay it down of My own accord" (v. 18). This statement shows us that Jesus is not just a human being but also God. He has the power to lay down His life and take it up again because He is in control of His own life. This is a powerful reminder of who Jesus is and what He came to do.

It is fitting that during the Easter season each year, we celebrate Good Shepherd Sunday. A dead shepherd helps no one. But when Jesus, our Good Shepherd, destroyed Satan and rose to life again, He promised to always be with us to the end of the New Testament age, so we are forever safe in His mighty hand. This is a message of hope and encouragement for us, reminding us that we are never alone, no matter what we face in this life. Jesus is always with us, and we can trust in His love and care for us.

John 10:10–18 is a powerful passage that points us to Jesus and His mission. It reminds us that Jesus is our Good Shepherd who lays down His life for us, and that He has made us forever safe in His mighty hand through His death and resurrection. This passage is a message of hope and encouragement for us, reminding us that no matter what we face in this life, we are never alone, and we can trust in Jesus' love and care for us.

Dear Lord, we thank You for sending Jesus to be our Good Shepherd. We thank You for the love and care that He shows us and for laying down His life for us. We ask that You help us to be like Him, loving and caring for others as He has loved and cared for us. We pray this in Jesus' name. Amen.

OUR STRONG PROTECTOR

He who is a hired hand and not a shepherd, who does not own the sheep, sees the wolf coming and leaves the sheep and flees, and the wolf snatches them and scatters them. He flees because he is a hired hand and cares nothing for the sheep. (JOHN 10:12-13)

In today's world, we can feel lost and alone. We struggle with fear and insecurity, searching for someone to guide us and protect us from harm. In John 10:10-18, Jesus says, "I am the good shepherd. The good shepherd lays down His life for the sheep." In this passage, Jesus assures us—His followers—that He is our protector and guide, just as a good shepherd takes care of his sheep.

The book of Nahum provides a similar message, declaring that the Lord is our protector. In Nahum 1:7, it says, "The LORD is good, a stronghold in the day of trouble; He knows those who take refuge in Him." Just as Jesus is our Good Shepherd, He is also our protector in times of trouble.

God's Word protects us from false teachings and helps us to remain faithful to the truth. The Lord knows His own and will ensure that we remain true to the faith, protected from those who would try to lead us astray. In John 10:11-13, Jesus says, "I am the good shepherd. The good shepherd lays down His life for the sheep. He who is a hired hand and not a shepherd, who does not own the sheep, sees the wolf coming and leaves the sheep and flees, and the wolf snatches them and scatters them. He flees because he is a hired hand and cares nothing for the sheep." Just as a good shepherd protects his sheep, so does Jesus protect His followers. He lays down His life for them, providing the ultimate sacrifice to save them from their sins.

The Lord is our stronghold in times of trouble, just as He is the Good Shepherd who lays down His life for us. Through His sacrifice, we are given the gift of salvation and the assurance of eternal life. The Word of God protects us from false teachings and helps us to remain faithful to the truth. We can take refuge in Jesus, our Good Shepherd, knowing that He will protect us and guide us on our journey.

Dear Lord, we thank You for protecting and guiding us. We thank You for sending Jesus, our Good Shepherd, to lay down His life for us. Help us trust in You, knowing that You will protect us and guide us always. We ask that You give us the strength to remain faithful to the truth, guided by Your Word. In Jesus' name. Amen.

"I HAVE AUTHORITY"

No one takes [My life] from Me, but I lay it down of My own accord. I have authority to lay it down, and I have authority to take it up again. (JOHN 10:18)

Some questions may arise when reading this text:

What does it mean that Jesus has "authority" to lay down His life and take it up again?

The term *authority* in this passage refers to the power and right to act that Jesus has received from the Father. This authority was demonstrated most clearly in His death and resurrection. By laying down His life, Jesus made the ultimate sacrifice for our sins, offering His life as a ransom for many (see Mark 10:45). In this way, He fulfilled the prophecy of the Good Shepherd, who would lay down His life for the sheep (see John 10:11).

But the story does not end with the death of Jesus. He also had the authority to take up His life again. Jesus demonstrated that authority when He rose from the dead on the third day (see Romans 8:11). The resurrection of Jesus is the cornerstone of our faith, for it demonstrates the power of God to save us from sin and death. Moreover, the fact that Jesus has risen from the dead proves that He is indeed the Son of God, who has the power to forgive our sins and give us eternal life (see Romans 1:4).

This authority of Jesus to lay down His life and take it up again is not just a historical event but also has practical implications for our lives as Christians. First, it demonstrates the love of God for us. The Father gave Jesus the power and right to lay down His life and take it up again in His resurrection so that we might be reconciled to Him and receive the gift of eternal life (see John 3:16). This love of God is unconditional and unending, and it is the foundation of our salvation.

Second, the authority of Jesus to lay down His life and take it up again reminds us of the call to follow Him and lay down our lives in service to others. As Christians, we are called to love our neighbors as ourselves, to bear one another's burdens, and to serve those in need (see Galatians 6:2; Romans 15:1). By laying down our lives in this way, we imitate the love of Christ and participate in His mission of salvation.

Finally, the authority of Jesus to lay down His life and take it up again provides us with hope and comfort in times of difficulty. Jesus has the authority to raise us from the dead to eternal life, as He raised Lazarus, the synagogue ruler's daughter, and the son of the widow from Nain. When we face trials and temptations, we can take refuge in the Lord, who has the power to rescue us and restore us to life (see Psalm 46:1). Our hope is not in this world but in the promise of eternal life with Jesus, who has the authority to lay down His life and take it up again.

Dear Lord, we thank You for the love You have shown us in sending Your Son, Jesus, to lay down His life for us. Help us follow His example and lay down our lives in service to others, confident that Jesus will raise us to new life when He returns. We pray in His name. Amen.

THE SHEPHERD CALLS US IN WORSHIP

I have other sheep that are not of this fold. I must bring them also, and they will listen to My voice. So there will be one flock, one shepherd. (JOHN 10:16)

In John 10:10–18, Jesus declares Himself to be the Good Shepherd and tells us that He has the authority to lay down His life and take it up again. This passage is a powerful reminder of who Jesus is and what He has done for us.

As the Good Shepherd, Jesus is the one who cares for and protects His sheep. In this role, He contrasts the hired hand who abandons the sheep when danger threatens. As our Good Shepherd, Jesus is willing to lay down His life for His sheep, giving up His own life to save us from our spiritual enemies.

This is a remarkable picture of Jesus' love for us. He is not only willing to lay down His life but also has the authority to take it up again, demonstrating His power over death and resurrection. In this, we see that Jesus is not just a simple shepherd—He is the Good Shepherd, the one who has been given the power and right by God the Father to save us.

For us as believers in Jesus, this means that we can have confidence in Him as our Good Shepherd. We no longer have to be afraid of the dangers of life or the power of death. Jesus has defeated our enemies and given us eternal life; we can rest in Him as our Good Shepherd who protects and guides us.

Jesus gathers us as His flock in worship so that we are all part of the Body of Christ, rather than individuals who briefly gather together then go our separate ways when worship is over. We hear Jesus' voice in worship and receive His nourishment through the Word and the Sacraments of Baptism and Holy Communion. In these, we are reminded of our identity as sheep in His flock and His protection and guidance that always go with us. As we receive the gifts of grace in these Sacraments, we are strengthened and empowered to share the Good News with others, calling them to follow Jesus as their Good Shepherd too.

This passage, read on Good Shepherd Sunday in the Easter season, is a powerful reminder of the love, protection, and guidance of Jesus, our Good Shepherd. It reminds us of His sacrifice and authority over death, encouraging us to follow Him and share the Good News with others.

Gracious and loving God, we thank You for sending Jesus, our Good Shepherd, to lay down His life for us and take it up again in His resurrection. Help us to trust in His authority and love for us and to follow Him as He leads us to our heavenly home. Strengthen us through Your Word and Sacraments and use us to share the Good News with others, calling them to follow Jesus as their Good Shepherd too. Amen.

PETER'S GREAT CONFESSION

WEEK 25—MATTHEW 16:13–20

Now when Jesus came into the district of Caesarea Philippi, He asked His disciples, "Who do people say that the Son of Man is?" And they said, "Some say John the Baptist, others say Elijah, and others Jeremiah or one of the prophets." He said to them, "But who do you say that I am?" Simon Peter replied, "You are the Christ, the Son of the living God." And Jesus answered him, "Blessed are you, Simon Bar-Jonah! For flesh and blood has not revealed this to you, but My Father who is in heaven. And I tell you, you are Peter, and on this rock I will build My church, and the gates of hell shall not prevail against it. I will give you the keys of the kingdom of heaven, and whatever you bind on earth shall be bound in heaven, and whatever you loose on earth shall be loosed in heaven." Then He strictly charged the disciples to tell no one that He was the Christ.

WERE THEIR JUDGMENTS RIGHT?

[Jesus] asked His disciples, "Who do people say that the Son of Man is?" And they said, "Some say John the Baptist, others say Elijah, and others Jeremiah or one of the prophets." (MATTHEW 16:13–14)

've seen enough!" Whether it's a sporting event that starts going the wrong direction for our team or a movie that gets predictable, we reach a point where we can start to draw conclusions. It didn't take people long to begin putting things together with Jesus. The miracles, the teachings, the authority—it was clear He was a man sent from God. They had seen enough to make their judgments of Him. But were they right?

Some thought He was John the Baptist. No, they didn't believe in reincarnation. They sensed a similar power and spiritual force; most likely, they believed the same spirit that empowered John was upon Jesus. The same energy that enlivened Elijah and Jeremiah in the Old Testament enlivened Jesus. In the eyes of the people, He was a prophet, speaking God's Word in a way they needed to hear. But the people were waiting for more.

The people of God seem to be always waiting. Waiting for the end of slavery in Exodus, waiting for the end of the forty-year wilderness wanderings in Deuteronomy, waiting for the end of Babylonian captivity in Jeremiah and, in Jesus' time, they were waiting for the end of Roman occupation in their homeland. They were waiting for the leader to come who would set them free. They were waiting on God's guy, and Jesus was looking like the right one. But not quite.

Jesus is unpredictable. Jesus doesn't operate by the "standard" of the day. All the signs and miracles were great, but the fact that Jesus would do them at the wrong times (on the Sabbath, when you shouldn't be doing anything) and at the wrong places (like the synagogue, where only "church" should happen) frustrated many of the leaders within the faith community. Jesus isn't the Savior they want—but He's the Savior Israel needs.

Jesus isn't just a prophet. Jesus, as Peter professed, is Messiah. The Anointed One—in other words, the one who will be crowned King of all kings, Lord of all lords, and King of all of God's creation. Jesus is the Leader for whom we are waiting. The question becomes for us, have we seen enough? Are we ready to profess our faith in the One who not only speaks truth, but *is* truth? Are we, like Peter, ready to follow our Leader?

Jesus, we confess that You are the Messiah, the King we need. We wait for You, and we trust in You. May Your Spirit empower us as we follow You. Amen.

THE CHRIST AND SO MUCH MORE

On this rock I will build My church, and the gates of hell shall not prevail against it. (MATTHEW 16:18)

Jesus wants to share. He shares His ministry with His unlikely band of disciples. And He promises in this passage to share His authority and His church with them too. Jesus' ministry left so many people wondering how they should define Him—what box He fit into. *Is He conservative? liberal? traditional? progressive? Is He a prophet or just a troublemaker?* Many see Him seeking religious reform, bringing a spiritual revival, re-energizing faith. But Peter picked up on something else: Messiah.

The Hebrew word *Messiah*, like the Greek word *Christ*, means "Anointed One." David became king when the prophet Samuel anointed him (see 1 Samuel 16). David was also known as a warrior. Peter picked up on the power of the prophet/priest. Peter didn't come out and say it, but he easily could have added "King" to the list. David was king, so his Son, the Christ, must also be king. Now it will become evident that Peter misunderstood the political nature of the Christ, but he saw something more. Jesus is not just strengthening believers; He is waging war. They should have seen it; they should have heard it. All Jesus' talk of "kingdoms," all the Good News proclamations—how do you extend a kingdom other than war? How do you proclaim Good News if it's not that victory will surely be won?

Jesus made it clear to His closest disciples that this was a war between heaven and earth, and He is the King leading the charge. A prophet may preach to his own people, or even, like Jonah, go to a foreign land. But a king comes to conquer, and Jesus came to storm the gates of hell. In other words, this ministry of His was going to be much more than a Sunday morning message. The ministry of Jesus is the kingdom of heaven being loosed upon earth. The kingdom of freedom conquering slavery to sin and death. The kingdom of light conquering the kingdom of darkness.

Jesus shared all this with His disciples, but He did something more: He told them they were going to be on the front lines, loosing heaven and binding hell. Jesus promised to share His authority and power with them too. They were an essential part of the King's battle strategy, to build a breach point into enemy territory. That breach point is the church, still confessing Jesus is Lord.

So a Sunday morning message is more important than we may think. A word of forgiveness, a Meal: these are fighting words. These are weapons in a war over the very souls that surround us. Remember what Jesus said: the *gates* of hell. Not the armies of hell or weapons of hell. Hell is on the defensive, because Jesus has already won. Jesus wants to share His victory with us. How can we pick up Peter's confession and join in loosing heaven and binding hell today?

The Lord reigns! You are King. We celebrate Your victory over sin, death, and hell, and we ask that You extend further and further into our hearts and world. In Your name, Jesus, we pray. Amen.

WHY STAY SILENT?

Then He strictly charged the disciples to tell no one that He was the Christ. (MATTHEW 16:20)

Jesus is the unlikely Messiah. He had no official religious training. He had no political or business connections, never led an army into battle. Jesus didn't have a famous father, nor was He a proven warrior. Since He taught and performed miracles, the category of "prophet" fit His ministry very well. But His disciples saw more than that. They were beginning to see a movement taking shape. And Jesus finally revealed to them the deeper reality. He is Messiah, the Anointed One, the Son of David, the coming King. And they are commanded not to share it with anyone. Why not?

He was doing such good things: healing, teaching, preaching, casting out demons. Jesus was doing kingdom work. And that made Him the King. The disciples were piecing it together, and Jesus confirmed their thoughts and hopes. But they couldn't tell anyone? When considering the whole mission of Jesus, this makes total sense. He was born in obscurity, unknown for thirty years, and now, misunderstood by the majority of those who met Him. Jesus saw this time for what it was: an opportunity to instruct His disciples and leave the crowds in their confusion.

The time was coming when the title *Christ* would become necessary, but Jesus still had much to accomplish. *Prophet, teacher,* and *rabbi* were still safe terms. Calling Him Christ put Him in a different category altogether. Being a prophet, He was an antagonist to the religious leaders of His day. But to be the Christ meant that He was challenging all leaders. (It later becomes clear that even the disciples did not understand what being the

Christ meant.) Yes, so many other titles work too. Prophet, Priest, Man of God, God Himself. But Jesus Christ is still how we refer to Jesus two thousand years later.

What did it mean for Jesus to take this title upon Himself? Jesus' ministry was about creating a new kingdom, challenging the earthly (and spiritual) authorities opposed to God. Jesus was subverting all rules and rulers. Jesus was ushering in a whole new time—remember His first sermon, recorded in Mark? "The time is fulfilled, and the kingdom of God is at hand" (Mark 1:15). A new time, a new kingdom, a new way of relating to God and the world: accomplished by Jesus Christ.

Saying too much can be just as detrimental as saying too little. As Jesus made clear to Nicodemus, "We speak of what we know" (John 3:11). He gave the disciples what they needed. The ongoing nature of discipleship, the slow journey of walking with Jesus, means that sometimes we believe before we see, and other times, we see before we believe. "Don't tell anyone" transforms into "Tell the world!" Where are you on the slow journey, and what do you need our unlikely Messiah to reveal to you?

Jesus, Messiah, we follow You. Whether or not we understand everything, we believe that You are the Christ, and You hold all things together. Lead us into Your kingdom now and forever. Amen.

CARRYING THIS CONFESSION

Blessed are you, Simon Bar-Jonah!
For flesh and blood has not revealed
this to you, but My Father who
is in heaven. (MATTHEW 16:17)

God's Word can reveal things to us in a way that nothing else can. As the Scriptures attest, "Your commandment makes me wiser than my enemies . . . than all my teachers . . . than the aged, for I keep Your precepts" (Psalm 119:98–100). Paying attention to the Scriptures enables us to see, hear, experience, and learn in ways that others cannot.

Plenty of people thought they knew Jesus, from those who knew that "no prophet arises from Galilee" (John 7:52), to those who thought, "Is not this Joseph's son?" (Luke 4:22). King Herod even thought Jesus was John the Baptist back from the dead (see Luke 9:7)! But there were plenty who saw Jesus by faith, those who called Him "Rabbi" (John 3:2) and "Son of David" (Mark 10:48). In this passage, Jesus' disciples demonstrate their closeness to God's Word through their understanding. They believed that one like Moses would come from among them (see Deuteronomy 18:15). They believed that a Son of David would reign forever (see Psalm 89:29). And they firmly believed Jesus was the one to whom these Scriptures pointed.

This is a common theme, especially in John's Gospel: Nathanael confesses his faith (see John 1:49); Peter says, "Lord, to whom shall we go? You have the words of eternal life" (John 6:68); and Martha shares her belief in Jesus when she calls Him "the Christ, the Son of God" (John 11:27). Peter also responded, shortly after this interaction, with "See, we have left everything and followed You" (Matthew 19:27).

The church is the gathering of those who carry this confession. Jesus says the church will be built on the rock of this confession. This is the first time in the New Testament that the concept of church is mentioned—the real kingdom of priests, the real holy nation (see Exodus 19:6). Paul reiterated this truth in Ephesians 2:19–20: "You are . . . members of the household of God, built on the foundation of the apostles and prophets, Christ Jesus Himself being the cornerstone."

The church is where God's kingdom is breaking through against the "domain of darkness" (Colossians 1:13), where the gates of hell will not prevail, where the spiritual war will be fought. Professing the name of Jesus is the battle cry, and we pick up our armor (see Ephesians 6:10–20). It is not an easy thing to be the church of Jesus, but it is the best thing. It is not obvious what the church is, but once the arrows start flying, the power of the church is realized.

Jesus shares its real power: forgiveness of sins. The Word of God, proclaimed and professed by God's people, culminates in this ultimate triumph: you are set free. After all, that is how God identifies Himself: "I am the Lord your God, who brought you out . . . of slavery" (Exodus 20:2). To be brought out of slavery is to be brought into freedom. And "if you abide in My word, you are truly My disciples, and you will know the truth, and the truth will set you free" (John 8:31–32). Where are we seeing God's freedom break through in us?

Jesus, we cling to Your Word. Build us up in the strength of Your might and fill us with Your Word. Set us free and extend Your freedom through us. Amen.

CHALLENGING QUESTIONS

I will give you the keys of the kingdom of heaven, and whatever you bind on earth shall be bound in heaven, and whatever you loose on earth shall be loosed in heaven. (MATTHEW 16:19)

This week's passage raises several challenging questions:

What are the keys of the kingdom, and to whom does Jesus give them?

Jesus is the door (see John 10:7-9), through whom we gain access to the Father (see Romans 5:2). And, just like a parent handing the keys to the car over to their new teenage driver, Jesus is giving the church the keys of the kingdom—that is, the power to forgive the sins of repentant sinners and to withhold forgiveness from those who will not repent. In other words, God's people have permission to bring others to Jesus. Not just permission, but authority. These "keys" are the clear Gospel message that all people can receive forgiveness and come to their heavenly Father through the life, death, and resurrection of Jesus. The church has called and appointed pastors to put these keys to work publicly in worship, to guarantee all people receive the Good News of forgiveness.

What does it mean to be bound and loosed in heaven?

Sin constricts and binds us, like a snake slowly squeezing the life out of us. The weight of sin and the struggle we face is enough to take out anyone; in fact, sin has taken out everyone. Jesus came to set us free, to unbind us from sin, death, and the devil. Jesus came to release us. Just as Jesus passed along the keys to the Kingdom, He has commanded His church to bind the sins of those who refuse to repent of their sins and to release the sins of those who confess their sins and trust Jesus as their Savior. Jesus was saying that our words have eternal impact. In the name of Jesus, we can release people from their sin. In the name of Jesus, we can cast out demons and banish evil. Our words are a very powerful vehicle; how carefully will we drive?

What was wrong with people believing Jesus was a great prophet?

To believe Jesus is merely a prophet is to believe wrongly. It is to stand on the wrong rock, to use your house key to try to start your car. It is to reject Jesus as the Christ, the King, to join with all His accusers. "The stone that the builders rejected has become the cornerstone" (Psalm 118:22) means that we are either standing on Christ or falling to our own ruin. Where will we take our stand?

Father in heaven, thank You for opening the door of heaven to all believers. Make our pastors faithful with the keys of the Kingdom. Empower us to share Your freedom and peace, in Jesus' name. Amen.

WHO DO YOU SAY HE IS?

He said to them, "But who do you say that I am?" (MATTHEW 16:15)

Written almost thirty years ago, a modern worship song titled "In the Secret," written by Andy Park, caught churches by storm—in all sorts of ways. It was catchy and memorable, while also appearing self-centered and light on theology. The chorus speaks about our desire to rejoice forever, beholding the glorious face of Christ. While the lyrics are very simple, this passage from Matthew has helped me to see another side of that song: the raw reality of being a disciple of Jesus. *I want to know Him more.*

The crowds weren't clear about this man. The disciples themselves thought they had a good understanding. But we know there's a lot more to the story, and Jesus is not telling it all at once. John puts it this way: "Now there are also many other things that Jesus did. Were every one of them to be written, I suppose that the world itself could not contain the books that would be written" (John 21:25). John is telling us that Jesus did a lot of other things, but what we need to know is written here.

Every Sunday, every time the Word of God is read, every time a hymn or song of praise is sung, every time the church gathers to worship Jesus (and take its stand against the gates of hell), Jesus is inviting us to get to know Him more through the Holy Scriptures. Even when everything stays almost exactly the same. *How can there be another sermon on the same passage?* The answer is simple: we haven't said everything that these passages say about this man and what He's done for us. We begin to realize that we are the ones changing, and He is the one staying the same.

I know who Jesus is, and yet I still need to hear over and again who He is. I know what Jesus has done, and yet I need to hear one more time what He has done for me. That's not because Jesus is changing—I am. As Paul wrote, "Now I know in part; then I shall know fully, even as I have been fully known" (1 Corinthians 13:12). We are fully known. And the crazy thing? Jesus wants us to know Him and His love more fully too.

Halfway through our year-long journey with Jesus, we get invited into a private conversation with the Christ. The fact that, in the church calendar, this reading is used on some normal Sunday in the normal (Pentecost) season of the Church Year makes perfect sense, just as the parallel passage (Mark 8:27-29) being found at the beginning of the Lenten season does. It doesn't matter when we hear it because every Sunday is an invitation to answer once again, "Who do you say I am?"

Dear Jesus, we want to know You more. We confess our abiding trust in You, and we ask You to enable us to see You. Amen.

JESUS PREDICTS HIS COMING PASSION THREE TIMES

Week 26—Luke 9:21–22, 43–45; 18:31–34

And He strictly charged and commanded them to tell this to no one, saying, "The Son of Man must suffer many things and be rejected by the elders and chief priests and scribes, and be killed, and on the third day be raised." . . .

And all were astonished at the majesty of God.

But while they were all marveling at everything He was doing, Jesus said to His disciples, "Let these words sink into your ears: The Son of Man is about to be delivered into the hands of men." But they did not understand this saying, and it was concealed from them, so that they might not perceive it. And they were afraid to ask Him about this saying. . . .

And taking the twelve, He said to them, "See, we are going up to Jerusalem, and everything that is written about the Son of Man by the prophets will be accomplished. For He will be delivered over to the Gentiles and will be mocked and shamefully treated and spit upon. And after flogging Him, they will kill Him, and on the third day He will rise." But they understood none of these things. This saying was hidden from them, and they did not grasp what was said.

JESUS' GREATER PURPOSE

And He strictly charged and commanded them to tell this to no one, saying, "The Son of Man must suffer many things and be rejected by the elders and chief priests and scribes, and be killed, and on the third day be raised." (LUKE 9:21–22)

Israel had once been a great empire. During the reign of David and then Solomon, Israel gained status and stature. Israel runs along the eastern shore of the Mediterranean Sea. Its many ports were open for trade between other great nations of the time, creating a center of commerce. If merchants wanted to convey their goods overland from North Africa into the Middle East or into Eurasia, they paid taxes to cross the roads of Israel, the only route with plentiful water. Money flowed into the coffers of God's chosen people during this time. The nation was prosperous.

Then came many terrible rulers. God's covenant with His people was forgotten, and foreign invaders decimated the land. Time and again, the people wandered far from God. Time and again, their enemies visited destruction upon them. The Persians, Greeks, and Romans were only the latest in a long line of invaders. But God's promised Messiah would come—He would set all things right.

The people watched and waited for this hero. When Jesus begins His ministry, the whispers also begin—that God has sent His Messiah. Jesus, however, proclaims a different message.

While the people longed for an earthly Savior, Jesus is an eternal one. Many wished that He would oust the Romans. Instead, Jesus privately informed His disciples that He would be killed by them. In fact, the Jewish religious rulers would be a part of His death, men who should welcome the Messiah as He establishes His kingdom. They are not supposed to be enemies of the person who brings their longed-for freedom.

But Jesus promises more. He declares that He will be put to death, but He will rise again. He did not come to defeat Rome—no, His foe is death itself. The people have too low a vision for the Messiah. They envisioned a general riding into Jerusalem on a stallion. Jesus is a carpenter content with a donkey. It does not make sense that He says that He will die. How can a warrior accomplish anything by dying?

Jesus is the Messiah that is needed, not the one for which the people hope. Every time He declares His death, He also proclaims that He will rise again. The Romans are too small a target. Jesus is going after death. The only way to defeat it is to die Himself. He begins preparing His disciples for this fact and for the joy they will find in His resurrection.

Lord, help me to remember why You came to earth. While I see the many temporal issues I have and wish You would fix them all, remind me You came for a greater purpose. Thank You for going to the cross for me. Thank You for giving me eternal life. Amen.

JESUS' MISSION

And taking the twelve, He said to them, "See, we are going up to Jerusalem, and everything that is written about the Son of Man by the prophets will be accomplished. For He will be delivered over to the Gentiles and will be mocked and shamefully treated and spit upon. And after flogging Him, they will kill Him, and on the third day He will rise." But they understood none of these things. This saying was hidden from them, and they did not grasp what was said. (LUKE 18:31–34)

The disciples do not want to even think about it—Jesus has told them He will suffer and die. Not just a light suffering either, but He will be arrested, mocked, and flogged. There may be lingering visions of the grand conqueror they believe the Messiah to be, but Jesus keeps telling them, at least three times—He will be arrested, suffer, die, and rise. Still, they do not understand.

Jesus is preparing His disciples. He knows it will take them time to fully grasp what will happen. Their notions of the Messiah and His work need to be pushed aside for the true reason Jesus has come. Only the suffering and death of the sinless Savior can save sinners.

In these passages, Jesus makes God's plan of salvation clear. In Genesis 3, at the fall of mankind, God promised a Savior. Jesus is revealing to those who follow Him that He is that promised Savior. He has not come to renew the earthly riches of the people of Israel. Instead, He is the fulfillment of the people. He is the treasure that has finally come after so many years. As He walks the countryside preaching, teaching, and working miracles, He knows His greatest purpose: He has come to die and rise again.

Notice that both of those things have to happen. Jesus does not predict His death without declaring His resurrection. It is always the cross and the empty tomb. Together they make up the greatest rescue that could ever happen. Jesus came first to take our sin and then to grant us the new life.

But, like the disciples, it is easy for us to miss the message Jesus brings. Too often we Christians want a genie, not a Savior. Someone who fixes problems and grants wishes, not the Savior come to take sin. It is good for the proclamation of His death to shake the believer out of any spiritual stupor in which he may reside.

Jesus' purpose was not to grant wishes. He did not come to make people rich. His aim was not earthly power. No—instead, a steadfast love for humanity drove Him. He repeats to His followers why He came so that one day when their eyes are opened to the truth, they will rejoice in the suffering and death that took away their sins and the resurrection that invited them into new life.

Heavenly Father, I often become distracted. Too many times I hope that You might simply grant wishes instead of being the Creator and Restorer of the universe. In those times, bring me to repentance. Let me give thanks that Jesus came to redeem sinners, of which I am one. He came to make me a saint, which my Baptism says I am. Thank You. In Jesus' name. Amen.

ALL FOR ME

And all were astonished at the majesty of God. But while they were all marveling at everything He was doing, Jesus said to His disciples, "Let these words sink into your ears: The Son of Man is about to be delivered into the hands of men." But they did not understand this saying, and it was concealed from them, so that they might not perceive it. And they were afraid to ask Him about this saying. (LUKE 9:43–45)

I think I would have been afraid too. Jesus is doing all these miraculous things: He is healing the sick, walking on water, turning water into wine. If I were a disciple, I would want the good times to roll! But here is Jesus, once again, saying that He will be delivered into the hands of men. There is a serious tone that cannot be ignored. But Jesus' suffering and death are at such odds with their expectations that they live in denial until the day those cruel events stand before them in undeniable horror.

This is the reason that Jesus has come. It is His purpose. He has to be arrested. He has to die. He has to rise again. He shares this with His disciples to prepare them—not only for His death but for afterward when He will ascend to heaven again. There will come a day when they understand. A day when it will be made clear. Jesus has given them the information—it will simply take time and the working of the Spirit for it to become knowledge.

Jesus brings that same knowledge to us today. He has laid out in Scripture the purpose for His life, death, and resurrection. But how often do we have the information but not the knowledge? It is easy enough to say, but do we perceive its meaning?

Slow down for a moment and add "for me" to Jesus' words:

Luke 9:22
"The Son of Man must suffer many things and be rejected by the elders and chief priests and scribes, and be killed, and on the third day be raised." *For me.*

Luke 9:44
"Let these words sink into your ears: The Son of Man is about to be delivered into the hands of men." *For me.*

Luke 18:32–33
"For He will be delivered over to the Gentiles and will be mocked and shamefully treated and spit upon. And after flogging Him, they will kill Him, and on the third day He will rise." *For me.*

Jesus came for you. All of this He did to save you from your sin and bring you back into relationship with God.

Lord, let me know what You have done for me through Your Son. In Jesus' name. Amen.

JESUS' PREDICTIONS ARE A SUMMARY OF THE BIBLE

And taking the twelve, He said to them, "See, we are going up to Jerusalem, and everything that is written about the Son of Man by the prophets will be accomplished." (LUKE 18:31)

While it may have been outside the knowledge of the disciples, the work Jesus came to do should not have come as a surprise. Many Old Testament prophets had spoken of what would happen to the Messiah.

- "For dogs encompass Me; a company of evildoers encircles Me; they have pierced My hands and feet—I can count all My bones—they stare and gloat over Me; they divide My garments among them, and for My clothing they cast lots." (Psalm 22:16–18)

- "Surely He has borne our griefs and carried our sorrows; yet we esteemed Him stricken, smitten by God, and afflicted. But He was pierced for our transgressions; He was crushed for our iniquities; upon Him was the chastisement that brought us peace, and with His wounds we are healed." (Isaiah 53:4–5)

- "And I will pour out on the house of David and the inhabitants of Jerusalem a spirit of grace and pleas for mercy, so that, when they look on Me, on Him whom they have pierced, they shall mourn for Him, as one mourns for an only child, and weep bitterly over Him, as one weeps over a firstborn." (Zechariah 12:10)

God's steadfast love leads to this point. There was no other way for Him to rescue His creation than to send His Son. It was the only way. But for the sake of love He does.

- "For God so loved the world, that He gave His only Son, that whoever believes in Him should not perish but have eternal life. For God did not send His Son into the world to condemn the world, but in order that the world might be saved through Him." (John 3:16–17)

As Jesus tells His disciples of His suffering, death, and resurrection, He is telling the story of the Bible. All of it points to this. It is the focal point. It is the story of a God who loved you so deeply that He would subject Jesus to torture and the cross. It is the story of a God who is all powerful and would not let death conquer His Suffering Servant. All of Scripture hinges on this proclamation. When Jesus speaks it, He is speaking the Bible summed up into a few words.

Lord may I never forget the reason Jesus came to suffer and die—because of Your love for me. May I rejoice in His resurrection because I, too, will one day be resurrected. In Jesus' name. Amen.

NOT READY FOR A SUFFERING KING

Then He said to them, "But who do you say that I am?" And Peter answered, "The Christ of God." And He strictly charged and commanded them to tell this to no one. (LUKE 9:20–21)

W hy does Jesus command His disciples to keep His identity as the Christ of God secret? Much of what Jesus does is in front of crowds of people. They follow Him from village to village. Yet in this moment, He doesn't simply request—He commands His disciples to remain quiet about the fact that He is the Christ because He will have to suffer and die.

People were not ready for the King Jesus. They had a preconceived notion of who He needed to be and what He needed to do. Even as Jesus shares the knowledge of the way of the Savior to His disciples, they cannot fathom what He has come to do. Jesus will even reprimand Peter:

> From that time Jesus began to show His disciples that He must go to Jerusalem and suffer many things from the elders and chief priests and scribes, and be killed, and on the third day be raised. And Peter took Him aside and began to rebuke Him, saying, "Far be it from You, Lord! This shall never happen to You." But He turned and said to Peter, "Get behind Me, Satan! You are a hindrance to Me. For you are not setting your mind on the things of God, but on the things of man." (Matthew 16:21–23)

If Peter could not see the need for Jesus' sacrifice, then none of Jesus' disciples or followers would either. People were unable to comprehend that this King would need to die. He was not there to establish His rule among them as an earthly ruler but instead to give the great gift of eternal life that could only be accomplished through His suffering and death.

How often do we as Christians know this truth but confess that we prefer the worldly Savior? Maybe not with our words—but in how we act. We treat Jesus not as the Savior who came to bring us back to God but the King who is here to give us power and authority. We fall in love with the idea of Jesus instead of who He actually is. This is why Jesus told His disciples to remain quiet and keep these predictions to themselves. Because people back then were the same as people today: sinners in need of salvation. We would much rather have Jesus come to give us riches than to save us from our sin.

The people of Jesus' day were not ready to hear the message of a suffering King come to save all people. Are we?

Lord, prepare my heart. Take away my desire for power and riches. Grant me a heart that welcomes the King who would suffer for my sake. In Jesus' name. Amen.

OUR SIN TOOK HIM
TO THE CROSS

The Son of Man must suffer many things and be rejected by the elders and chief priests and scribes, and be killed, and on the third day be raised. (LUKE 9:22)

don't know if I had ever cried in front of my friends before. The movie theater was dark enough that I hoped they wouldn't see me. It was 2004 and, like many church youth groups around that time, we had come to watch the only R-rated movie allowed to be viewed together: *The Passion of the Christ*. The visuals were strikingly real. All of the whipping, beating, and crucifying happening right in front of us. To this day, I still remember a line from Stuart Townend's song about the depth of God the Father's love that spoke of our sin binding Christ to the cross until everything was finished.

It's always seemed strange that people argue over who is to blame for Jesus' death. Some would say that it is the Jewish leaders who sought to remove Him as a threat to their power. Others say the blame falls on Pontius Pilate and the Romans because they were the ones who did the deed. But the answer is much more sinister than that.

I am the reason for the death of Jesus.

You are the reason for the death of Jesus.

Our sin took Him to the cross. When He shared with His disciples that He would suffer and die, He did it not out of obligation but out of love. It was the Father's love that sent the Son. It was the Son's love for His Father and for humanity that took Him down the path to the cross.

Jesus knew as He shared the plan with those who followed Him that they wouldn't understand. But the Spirit would reveal it to them someday. He told them with that knowledge—they would one day know that His sacrifice was necessary.

He didn't come to be an earthly king. He came to be the King of kings. With His work the greatest enemy would be defeated. People who were once far from God would be brought near. He knew that the disciples would be the ones to take the message out after He left them. He told them He would suffer, die, and rise again. All so that one day we would know that He had suffered, died, and rose again. That is why we gather each week in worship—to be reminded of our Savior's dying love.

He had to go to the cross. Our sin drove Him there. Our sin would hold Him there. Not because sin had power over Him but because He had power over it. He would be humiliated so we could be lifted up. He would suffer so that we could be comforted. He would die so that death would lose its sting. He would rise again so that we, too, may someday rise.

Humanity's sin would cause the Savior to suffer, die, and rise again. All because He loved us.

Dear Jesus, our sin held You to the cross. Thank You for dying to save us. Amen.

THE TRANSFIGURATION

Week 27—Matthew 17:1–13

And after six days Jesus took with Him Peter and James, and John his brother, and led them up a high mountain by themselves. And He was transfigured before them, and His face shone like the sun, and His clothes became white as light. And behold, there appeared to them Moses and Elijah, talking with Him. And Peter said to Jesus, "Lord, it is good that we are here. If You wish, I will make three tents here, one for You and one for Moses and one for Elijah." He was still speaking when, behold, a bright cloud overshadowed them, and a voice from the cloud said, "This is My beloved Son, with whom I am well pleased; listen to Him." When the disciples heard this, they fell on their faces and were terrified. But Jesus came and touched them, saying, "Rise, and have no fear." And when they lifted up their eyes, they saw no one but Jesus only.

And as they were coming down the mountain, Jesus commanded them, "Tell no one the vision, until the Son of Man is raised from the dead." And the disciples asked Him, "Then why do the scribes say that first Elijah must come?" He answered, "Elijah does come, and he will restore all things. But I tell you that Elijah has already come, and they did not recognize him, but did to him whatever they pleased. So also the Son of Man will certainly suffer at their hands." Then the disciples understood that He was speaking to them of John the Baptist.

STANDING ON THE MOUNTAINTOP WITH GOD

And after six days Jesus took with Him Peter and James, and John his brother, and led them up a high mountain by themselves. (MATTHEW 17:1)

What's the most impressive mountain range you've ever seen in person? The Rocky Mountains? The Blue Ridge Mountains? The Appalachian Mountains? A mountain range outside of the US?

The Bible contains many mountains where important events took place. Let's highlight three of them. One is Mount Sinai. There, amid thunder, lightning, and a thick cloud, Moses ascended the mountain and received the Ten Commandments. On the mountain, Moses encountered God and His great authority.

Another key mountain is Mount Carmel. There, the prophet Elijah engaged the prophets of Baal in an altar-lighting contest. The Baal prophets failed; Elijah succeeded, as God lit his sacrifice with fire from heaven. On the mountain, Elijah beheld God's great power.

A third key mountain is unnamed but was the setting of a significant event in Jesus' ministry. Scholars have suggested this mountain may have been Mount Tabor or Mount Hermon, but the Bible doesn't specify. The name of the mountain is less important than the event that transpired on it. On this mountain, Jesus' disciples saw Him in a spectacular new way.

Six days after predicting His death and resurrection, Jesus took Peter, James, and John up a "high mountain" (Matthew 17:1). There, Jesus' appearance changed. "His face shone like the sun, and His clothes became as white as light" (Matthew 17:2). This event is known as His transfiguration.

And who was there with Jesus and the three disciples? None other than two famous mountain-climbers of the Bible: Moses and Elijah! These heroes of the faith made a cameo appearance out of heaven. These revered saints once again spoke with God on the mountain. This time, God was not unseen but was visible to their eyes. They encountered God Almighty in human flesh, Jesus!

Moses and Elijah were two of the most important figures in the Old Testament. If there were a Mount Rushmore of Old Testament heroes, those two men would be on it. But Jesus eclipsed them in importance, which is why Jesus also eclipsed them in appearance on the mountain. The prophets stood in the light of Jesus, the "bright morning star" whose radiance surpasses all others (Revelation 22:16).

As His children, we stand in the light of Jesus as we read His Word, worship, pray, and live together in community with our brothers and sisters in Christ. What a privilege!

Lord Jesus, we stand in awe of Your incomparable majesty. With the saints of old and the saints of today, we bow before You and worship You as the God of glory. Amen.

PULLING BACK THE CURTAIN

[Peter] was still speaking when, behold, a bright cloud overshadowed them, and a voice from the cloud said, "This is My beloved Son, with whom I am well pleased; listen to Him." (MATTHEW 17:5)

Jesus' transfiguration proclaims His divinity. The transfiguration was a pulling back of the curtain, a display of majesty not typically seen in His earthly ministry.

In humility, God's Son clothed Himself in human flesh. He lowered Himself. Jesus "did not count equality with God a thing to be grasped, but emptied Himself, by taking the form of a servant, being born in the likeness of men" (Philippians 2:6–7). By appearances, no one would have guessed that God was walking among them. Jesus' true identity is divinely revealed to those with eyes of faith, opened by the Holy Spirit.

Jesus, God's Son, was revealed through words. He confessed His divinity on multiple occasions. He claimed to exist before Abraham (see John 8:58). He claimed to be the only way to God (see John 14:6). He said that He and the Father are one (see John 10:30).

The New Testament authors affirm the divinity of Jesus. Paul wrote in Colossians that "in Him the whole fullness of deity dwells bodily" (Colossians 2:9). In opening his Gospel, John wrote that Jesus "was in the beginning with God" and that "all things were made through Him" (John 1:2–3).

In Matthew 16, the chapter before the transfiguration account, Peter indicated that he was beginning to understand who Jesus was. People were offering a variety of opinions about Jesus' identity. Jesus asked the disciples point-blank, "But who do you say that I am?" (Matthew 16:15). Peter answered correctly, "You are the Christ, the Son of the living God" (Matthew 16:16). With those words, Peter confessed Jesus' divinity.

With words, Jesus was declared to be God. In the transfiguration, Jesus is declared to be God through an event. His glory is not just explained in words but is shown. This is your Savior: God in human flesh. He is "Son of God and Son of Man" (*LSB* 537:1).

As human, He is able to sympathize with you in your weakness. As God, He is able to strengthen you in your weakness. Jesus cares about you and He is powerful to help you in your time of need.

The almighty God of the universe stood in your place on the cross. And now by His power, He stands beside you in every trial and trouble. God Himself comes to your aid!

Lord Jesus, Son of God and Son of Man, I look to You for Your grace and goodness. You are the God who loves me and delivers me. My hope is in You. Amen.

THE NEW EXODUS

And behold, two men were talking with Him, Moses and Elijah, who appeared in glory and spoke of His departure, which He was about to accomplish at Jerusalem. (LUKE 9:30–31)

The transfiguration is mentioned in three Gospels (Matthew, Mark, and Luke) and one Epistle (2 Peter 1:16–18). Luke's account contains a unique word—Luke wrote that Moses and Elijah were talking to Jesus about His departure. The Greek word translated "departure" is *exodus.*

Moses, in particular, knew all about an exodus. The book of Exodus chronicles the Israelites' escape from slavery in Egypt. Under Moses' leadership, the Israelites left behind a lifetime of bondage and stepped into freedom. God parted the Red Sea, and they walked through on dry land, saved from Pharaoh and his army—saved for a lifetime of service to the Lord.

Jesus' transfiguration anticipated a new exodus. His people were in bondage—bondage to sin. In Romans 6:17, Paul wrote that we are "slaves to sin." Our sin imprisons us. We are captive to our impure thoughts, our foolish impulses, and our destructive behaviors. We struggle in vain to break free from the pattern of sin that grips us.

Jesus brings us out of slavery not through the Red Sea but by His crimson blood, shed on the cross. He brings us out of slavery and into freedom not through parted waters but through the saving water of Baptism. You are set free from sin. Sin is no longer the driving force in your life. God is! His grace is!

At His transfiguration, Jesus spoke with Moses and Elijah about His exodus—His imminent departure. On a dark Friday, Jesus departed from the land of the living. He breathed a final breath, and His body was placed in a tomb.

Consider the irony: In His moment of revealed glory, His transfiguration, Jesus was thinking about the inglorious treatment that awaited: torment, beating, mockery, and finally death on a cross, which "He was about to accomplish at Jerusalem" (Luke 9:31). In His moment of revealed glory, a moment of darkness was on His mind.

Peter didn't understand. He wanted to build tents for Jesus, Moses, and Elijah. Peter wanted to prolong the glory. His motto was "Let the good times roll!"

Jesus recognized that the transfiguration was a fleeting moment. He came to accomplish a specific purpose. The exodus of the cross must precede His return to heavenly glory. There would be no eternal glory for humankind without His death, purifying us from sin and transforming us for eternity.

Lord Jesus, because of Your exodus from this life on the cross, I have life forever with You. Until that day when I see You in heavenly glory, keep my heart focused on You. Amen.

EYEWITNESS TESTIMONY

For we did not follow cleverly devised myths when we made known to you the power and coming of our Lord Jesus Christ, but we were eyewitnesses of His majesty. For when He received honor and glory from God the Father, and the voice was borne to Him by the Majestic Glory, "This is My beloved Son, with whom I am well pleased," we ourselves heard this very voice borne from heaven, for we were with Him on the holy mountain. (2 PETER 1:16–18)

In Peter's day, mythology was abundant. Think of Greek and Roman mythology and the elaborate attempts of humans to explain how the world works through tales of gods and goddesses. In teaching about Jesus, Peter wasn't repeating fiction. He wasn't passing down some kind of myth, nor was he using his own imagination to concoct a new religion.

Peter's teachings were entirely different. He came face to face with God Incarnate. Peter personally saw unmistakable evidence of Jesus' divinity. Peter saw an unforgettable sight: Jesus radiating with heavenly glory.

And Peter personally heard God's voice authenticating Jesus' divinity. How did Peter know that Jesus is God's Son? God told him! No interpretation was necessary. God made it perfectly clear who Jesus was!

Jesus' transfiguration was "the prophetic word more fully confirmed" (2 Peter 1:19). Jesus fulfilled prophecy. God promised to send a Savior; Jesus is the Messiah long foretold. The Old Testament pointed ahead to Jesus. A conservative estimate is that the Old Testament contains more than three hundred specific prophecies fulfilled by Jesus' life, death, and resurrection.

Peter's Epistle is a powerful witness. As we read the Bible, we're not reading secondhand accounts or hearsay. We have the original sources! We have eyewitness testimony. Peter was there. He saw with his eyes. He heard with his ears.

As we read God's Word with our eyes and hear God's Word with our ears, we can be confident that we are encountering the real deal. Through the pages of Scripture, God speaks to us with words written by His chosen disciples and prophets. Through the Bible, we come to know God and His saving work for us in Jesus.

Lord God, You have graciously revealed Your Son to us through the faithful testimony of the prophets and apostles. Help us always to believe what You teach us and rejoice in the gift of our Savior, who fulfills Your Word. Amen.

SET APART FOR CHRIST'S SERVICE

Jesus took with Him Peter and James, and John his brother. (MATTHEW 17:1)

Why did Jesus choose Peter, James, and John to accompany Him but not the others? Sometimes more can be accomplished in smaller numbers. Jesus had many followers but only a dozen men designated as His twelve disciples. Like a master tradesman mentoring his apprentices, Jesus invested in the twelve and equipped them to extend His ministry.

From within the Twelve, Jesus strategically selected a subgroup: Peter, James, and John. These three were key leaders in the early church. With the central role they would play in spreading the faith, it was important that these three men were absolutely certain of Jesus' identity. With egos and competing agendas swirling within the Twelve, a group of three allowed for more intensive, focused training.

Peter was the disciples' spokesperson. At the first Christian Pentecost in Acts 2, Peter preached a convicting sermon through which the Holy Spirit led three thousand to faith in one day. The first half of Acts primarily chronicles Peter and his bold leadership. In addition to Peter's spoken words recorded in the Bible, we also have two Epistles bearing his name.

James and John were brothers. Known for their passion, they were called "sons of thunder" (Mark 3:17). James was the first disciple to be martyred for his faith (see Acts 12:2). No action speaks louder than the willingness to lay down your life for a cause that matters, and nothing matters more than faith in Jesus.

John was Jesus' best friend. He was the disciple "whom Jesus loved" (John 13:23). Jesus entrusted His mother to John at the cross. John wrote a Gospel, three Epistles, and the book of Revelation. He was the last surviving disciple. In his later years, he was an elder statesman who mentored key church leaders.

The transfiguration is not the only time these three were set apart to be with Jesus at an important moment. They also were with Jesus when He restored Jairus's daughter to life. They beheld His power over death. These three disciples were also with Jesus when He prayed in the Garden of Gethsemane before His betrayal. They saw His agony in the garden and His reliance on prayer.

As Christ set these men apart, He has set you apart. Through Baptism, He has designated you for service to Him. As Christ invested in these men, He invests in you. By His Spirit, He pours Himself into you. You, too, are a witness for Jesus and a key part of advancing His kingdom purposes!

Lord Jesus, as You equipped the disciples for service, equip me too, that I might declare Your goodness and lead others to know You, the world's Savior. Amen.

HE TOUCHED THEM, AND HE TOUCHES US

But Jesus came and touched them, saying, "Rise, and have no fear." (MATTHEW 17:7)

The end of the transfiguration account includes a little word that communicates a big action. After hearing the Father's voice from the cloud, the disciples fell to the ground in terror. Then we read, "But Jesus came and touched them, saying, 'Rise, and have no fear.'" Did you notice what Jesus did before He spoke? He touched them.

There's power in a simple touch. In a world shifting toward touchless experiences, it's common for people to keep their distance. But there's something special about human touch. For example, in a time of sadness, someone may comfort you with compassionate words and a hand on the shoulder. The extra touch communicates, "I'm here for you."

The text doesn't provide details about Jesus' touch. Perhaps He lifted a head with His finger. Or maybe He placed a hand on a shoulder. Or He may have grabbed a hand and helped them to their feet as He told them to rise.

He touched them.

Jesus touches us too—not with His physical hands but with means of grace that comfort us. Through Word and Sacrament when we gather in worship, He reaches into our lives and makes His presence known. Jesus touches us through His Word. Through the Words of Absolution, He speaks pardon and relief to our weary souls. Jesus touches us through Baptism. While the physical hand belongs to the pastor, it's Christ who snatches a child from the clutches of Satan and delivers that child safely into God's family. Jesus touches us through Holy Communion. The body that once shined brightly on a mountain is given to us in the Sacrament, along with the blood shed for our sins.

Our Lord comes to be with us in these simple yet powerful means of grace. His glory is hidden, but it is present. Hidden glory is not absent glory. Jesus didn't always shine brightly as He did at His transfiguration. Certainly He didn't on the cross—just the opposite. There, Christ's glory was concealed. A bloody man hanging from a criminal's cross—no one would walk by and think, "What glory to behold!"

But glory hidden is not glory absent. On the cross, the glory of God's grace was shown, along with the glory of His power to remove the stain of sin from humankind. And now in Word and Sacrament, the Lord of glory touches us with His grace, and through His healing touch, He gives us the peace that passes all understanding (see Philippians 4:7).

Lord Jesus, You have touched my life with Your grace. Thank You for all of Your gifts to me, especially the gifts of Your Word and Sacraments. Amen.

THE TRIUMPHAL ENTRY

WEEK 28—LUKE 19:28–40

And when He had said these things, He went on ahead, going up to Jerusalem. When He drew near to Bethphage and Bethany, at the mount that is called Olivet, He sent two of the disciples, saying, "Go into the village in front of you, where on entering you will find a colt tied, on which no one has ever yet sat. Untie it and bring it here. If anyone asks you, 'Why are you untying it?' you shall say this: 'The Lord has need of it.'" So those who were sent went away and found it just as He had told them. And as they were untying the colt, its owners said to them, "Why are you untying the colt?" And they said, "The Lord has need of it." And they brought it to Jesus, and throwing their cloaks on the colt, they set Jesus on it. And as He rode along, they spread their cloaks on the road. As He was drawing near—already on the way down the Mount of Olives—the whole multitude of His disciples began to rejoice and praise God with a loud voice for all the mighty works that they had seen, saying, "Blessed is the King who comes in the name of the Lord! Peace in heaven and glory in the highest!" And some of the Pharisees in the crowd said to Him, "Teacher, rebuke Your disciples." He answered, "I tell you, if these were silent, the very stones would cry out."

WHAT'S IN A NAME?

If anyone asks you, "Why are you untying it?" you shall say this: "The Lord has need of it." (LUKE 19:31)

The names and titles we give to one another say a lot about the context of our relationships, situations, and circumstances. While we receive our given names from our parents, as relationships are formed and life takes place, a wide variety of other terms and monikers find their way to connect to us.

As a student in grade school, my gym teacher saw the effort I was giving during a class and shortened my last name to "Jetz." Quite ironic, given the lack of speed God had blessed me with. In high school, my German class was a tight-knit group, and somehow the nickname "Das Chad" became my calling card. Even now, in my adult life, the wide variety of names can give you a sense of the context in which they might be used.

"Dad." "Mr. J." "Coach."

As we read Luke's account of Jesus making His way into Jerusalem, the names used to reference Jesus give us some key insight into the ways various groups viewed Him. Three different titles are assigned to Jesus throughout this text: "Lord." "King." "Teacher."

The disciples echo the term "Lord," which Jesus had directed them to use when giving them instructions. The original Greek would be translated as "supreme authority" or "master." In Jewish culture, because the name of God could not be spoken, these titles implicitly declare in the conversation that the colt was being put to use by One who had divine power. It is interesting to note that the owners are not recorded as disputing the intention nor the title of the One who was requesting.

As Jesus rides on, we see the multitude of followers who rejoice that the "King" comes in the name of the Lord. When looking at the Greek used here, it translates to "a sovereign" as an abstract term. These people were looking for a ruler, someone who would take up authority over the current rulers and establish the peaceful kingdom that they had been longing for.

Hearing and witnessing the commotion, some of the Pharisees address Jesus as "Teacher." Just your everyday, run-of-the-mill instructor. A rabbi who was getting the people all worked up, just to lead them away from their religious leaders and bring about more oppression from the Romans.

Three very different names. Three very different understandings of who this Jesus was. All giving insight into who He really is. So much so that Jesus declares, "If these were silent, the very stones would cry out" in verse 40 of this week's reading. Even creation recognizes who the Creator is.

With the benefit of hindsight, we can join the people on that road and rejoice that Jesus is all of these things and more. As our Prophet, Priest, and King, He has redeemed us by His innocent suffering and death, destroyed the power of death by His resurrection, and restores us each day through Baptism by the power of His Spirit.

Name above all names, we confess that we do not always recognize You as the promised King who comes in the name of the Lord, the Messiah who faced the suffering and death that we deserved because of our sin. By Your Holy Spirit, Your Word, and Your Sacraments, strengthen our faith that You would reign in our lives as our coming King! Amen.

YOU HAVEN'T SEEN ANYTHING YET

Blessed is the King who comes in the name of the Lord! Peace in heaven and glory in the highest! (LUKE 19:38)

In the streets of a city, ticker tape rains from the buildings. Bands play lively, spirited, inspired music. People clap, cheer, and celebrate. And why all the fuss? Why the grand acts of celebration? Heroes. Champions. Achievers of great feats. These are the people that you would hold a parade for. They have accomplished something—something that has not been done before, or rarely is, which has brought hope, joy, and excitement to a community.

That seems to be the case as we read this text. The multitudes are rejoicing, praising, and celebrating the "mighty works that they had seen" (Luke 19:37). Surely this is the limit of the great things this carpenter from Nazareth will do. We can place Him on His throne in Jerusalem and the world will be as it should!

But this is not your typical parade. Most parades come at the conclusion of the feat they intend to celebrate. Jesus certainly had done mighty works. Miracles, healings, even resurrections. Each of these has their purpose in the ministry of the promised Messiah, but they pale in comparison to the real purpose of this parade.

Jesus travels as a king on His way to coronation. But He travels knowing the crown He will receive is not the crown that the crowd expects. He also travels knowing that His greatest healing, His greatest miracle, is yet to come.

So it might seem odd that this is His championship parade. It might seem a little premature to allow celebration, when the season is not over yet.

And yet, the timing was more than appropriate. This truly is the "King who comes in the name of the Lord!" This King would be the atoning sacrifice for *all* people, through *all* time. Past. Present. Future. The Champion of our Salvation was entering into the fray. This was the beginning of the culmination of His mission here on earth. By His suffering, death, and resurrection, He would bring the reconciliation with the Father that would usher in the peace we so desperately need in our relationship with our Creator.

So we join with this multitude today. "Blessed is the King who comes in the name of the Lord! Peace in heaven and glory in the highest!" The Champion is in the arena, and His victory will be like nothing ever seen before.

Heavenly Father, as our devotions enter into the observance of Holy Week, may we focus on the works of our Savior, Jesus Christ, done on our behalf. May the assurance that Jesus has secured our victory through His suffering, death, and resurrection give us the confidence necessary to declare this truth to a world that so desperately needs to know it. We pray this in the name of our victorious Savior, Jesus Christ. Amen.

PROOF IN THE DETAILS

Go into the village in front of you, where on entering you will find a colt tied, on which no one has ever yet sat. (LUKE 19:30)

When our youngest child was five, she broke off a bone chip in her elbow from jumping off a playground swing. It required a minor surgical procedure to remove the chip and allow healing. As you would expect, there was great anxiety on her end while she was being prepped for the procedure. The machines, the tubes, the masks, the sterile rooms—all of these can be awfully intimidating for any patient, let alone a small child. Still, I marveled at the skill of the nurse. She calmly and patiently explained to our daughter what she would experience with each needle, thermometer, and blood pressure cuff. As each experience passed—exactly as her nurse had described—you could sense the anxiety and uncertainty begin to lift. Our daughter began to trust more fully that this nurse was here to care for her in her moment of need.

Jesus is fully aware that He is on the earth for the purpose of bringing healing to a world that so desperately needs it. Yet that world is cautious and pessimistic about His purpose and what might result. Jesus uses this opportunity to ease His followers' doubts and anxieties. He provides detailed instructions, describing what they would experience in securing His mode of transportation. In the details, Jesus provides the disciples assurance that if there is truth in His words regarding something as simple as a colt, how much more can they trust Him when He speaks and instructs them on even greater things.

Yet it goes much deeper than just locating a colt. This was not any livestock. Jesus gave specific instructions that this animal would be one "on which no one has ever yet sat." The use of such animals was typically reserved for holy purposes. The rider of this colt was not just any passenger, but the Holy One of Israel.

Perhaps more staggering in this reading is not the immediate fulfillment that takes place in His instructions to His disciples but the way Jesus prepares even His opponents to know who He is and why He is here. As the Pharisees rebuke Him, He replies, "the very stones would cry out" (Luke 19:40). Even creation recognized the Messiah, as the earth shook and cried out on the day of His crucifixion.

Like a doctor explaining what the patient would experience in the healing process after a procedure, the Savior of the whole world was providing detailed proof to build trust in the salvation that only He provides by His death and resurrection.

Gracious God, in Your mercy You provide us confidence in what You are doing for our salvation. You have given us the details from the messianic prophecies in the Old Testament to Jesus' teachings and His fulfillment as our Savior. You have comforted us by Your Word and Your Spirit. May that comfort encourage us to share the Good News of what Jesus has done with all those we come in contact with, by our words and our actions. We ask this in the strong name of Jesus. Amen.

ROCK TALK

I tell you, if these were silent, the very stones would cry out. (LUKE 19:40)

Have you ever heard a rock say something? Certainly if anyone claimed that a rock had talked to them, questions would instantly be raised about the person's grasp of reality. Yet here we have Jesus, in Luke's account, make a statement that seems somewhat nonsensical.

The wonder of Scripture is that to more fully understand it, we have to be willing to look at the whole and not just the part. When Jesus makes this assertion to His detractors, He makes reference to a concept that is not unfamiliar to the Word of God. When Habakkuk complains to the Lord about the oppressive rule of the king of Babylon, the Lord responds by stating that "the stone will cry out from the wall" (Habakkuk 2:11). This imagery was a promise that the supposedly secure structure of the Babylonian kingdom was still temporal, and the destruction of the king's dynasty would be like the loud crashing created by falling building materials of his "house."

Yet beyond nods to Old Testament prophecy, it is helpful that Luke is diligent in his geographical accuracy when reporting the Savior's ministry. He identifies Bethphage, Bethany, and the Mount of Olives as the beginning of this triumphal processional. The significance of this should not be understated. In the Gospel of John, chapter 8, Jesus stays on the Mount of Olives before heading to the temple where the crowd brings forward a woman caught in adultery. It is in that confrontation that Jesus challenges them: "Let him who is without sin among you be the first to cast a stone at her" (v. 7). One by one, the cry of the stones that certainly dropped to the ground, intended to condemn, now rang out to emphasize the forgiveness and new life that Jesus declared to the woman.

Later in John's Gospel we hear again from stones, this time in Bethany. Jesus stands at the foot of the tomb where his friend Lazarus has been placed upon his death. A simple directive to remove the stone from the tomb—and the "cry" of that stone as it precedes Jesus' command of "Lazarus, come out!" (John 11:43).

Justice. Forgiveness. Resurrection. While these might not be the direct words spoken by the stones in these Scriptures, they are the result of the salvation that even the natural world recognizes is needed. The cry is for a Savior who would restore the broken, bring peace to the hurting, and declare the victory of our God over sin, death, and the devil.

And in a week from this statement, one more stone will "cry out" to declare the significance of this teacher, riding into town on a colt, to such praise.

Creator of all things, we confess that too often we have left it to others to "cry out" about who You are and what You have done for us. We pray that as we hear Your Word, Your Spirit would strengthen us to declare Your wonderful works. We ask this in the name of our Rock, our Savior, Jesus Christ. Amen.

NOT YOUR EVERYDAY COLT

*You will find a colt tied, on which no
one has ever yet sat.* (LUKE 19:30)

When giving His disciples instructions, Jesus gets very specific about His mode of transportation. These instructions tend to leave us with more questions than answers. In the Greek, the word that is translated into English as "colt" serves to signify a young donkey.

Jesus is making a triumphal entry into Jerusalem. He's entering as the promised Messiah, who would be victorious over Israel's enemies. He's hailed as the King who comes in the name of the Lord. Certainly, royalty should be traveling on a majestic horse, a steed who is worthy of the rider.

While we may see the ironic necessity of the humility of a working-class animal, it should not be lost in the reading that Jesus does not call for the mature donkey, but rather the younger version. Jesus' directions give us further expectation when He says it should be one "on which no one has ever yet sat." This is not just any donkey. It's not just a young donkey. This animal is a first timer.

The significance of using an animal that has not been put to use before lends itself to the idea of purity, making such an animal ideally appropriate for holy purposes. If nothing else, that should signify to the crowd at hand that this is not the ruler so many of them anticipated but rather someone whose purpose was far more divine.

This is the pure, Chosen One of God. The promised Messiah who was born of a virgin—one who had been untouched. This was the Perfect One of God, who—like the unblemished lambs who were sacrificed on behalf of Israel's sins throughout the Old Testament—was without sin when He was placed on the cross, taking on the sins of all people for all time. This was the Lamb of God who would be placed in a tomb that had not been used, only to destroy the hold of death into eternity.

No, this was not the mode of transportation that seemed befitting of the Savior of the world. But this was the mode of transportation that signals the sinless, pure, and holy nature of its rider. A King who would come in the name of the Lord to bring the peace needed between a broken creation and its Creator.

Jesus, You are the perfect, pure, precious Lamb of God. By Your Word, help us to see You for who You are, the promised Messiah, the Savior of all mankind. Amen.

LET ME TELL YOU ABOUT *MY* JESUS

Blessed is the King who comes in the name of the Lord! (LUKE 19:38)

In the movie *Talladega Nights*, the main character, Ricky Bobby, a famous NASCAR driver, is gathered around the dinner table with his family. While offering grace, a discussion ensues about which Jesus they are praying to. Ricky Bobby claims baby Jesus as his prayer focus of choice, while Ricky's teammate, Cal, offers that he prefers his Jesus with a tuxedo T-shirt because it is a good mix of being formal and being able to party at the same time.

Thankfully, our theological understandings aren't guided by fictitious movie characters. But how far off is that scene from what we see in our reading? Even more concerning—how far off is this from the misperception of understandings we see in our world today?

The people along the route to Jerusalem were there because they had seen mighty works. When we as humans experience that which goes beyond our comprehension, we often explain it as something that is within our understanding. For those who had seen the healings, miracles, restoration, resurrections, and teachings of Jesus, they may have only been able to comprehend Him as a magician, as a fine orator or, at the very least, an earthly leader who could rule their people the way that *they* wanted to be ruled.

How often do we place Jesus in some of the same boxes? Simply a moral teacher with words of wisdom and perhaps some comforting thoughts in dealing with daily life. One who happened to be around when something unexplainable happened.

We see our Jesus as it is most convenient for our own desires and wants.

Praise God that this is not the Jesus on the road to Jerusalem, nor is it the Jesus we know today. This is the Jesus who was on a mission. Not to provide a happily ever after in this world, but to secure an everlasting after for you and me. This would not be the king that the Jewish people envisioned, but a King of kings. He would not do battle with soldiers of an earthly kingdom but would vanquish the spiritual forces of evil, sin, death, and the devil. That is a victory that will be ultimately realized when Jesus returns, and we enter into eternity with our victorious Savior in the new heaven and the new earth.

In the meantime, we still wrestle in the bounds of time, but we know where we can find Jesus. We can join with our brothers and sisters along that road shouting, "Hosanna! Blessed is He who comes in the name of the Lord!" (Mark 11:9). We can join with them as we receive His body and blood in, with, and under the bread and wine of the Lord's Supper. This is where we find Jesus. In His Word and Sacraments, as He brings us peace, forgiveness, and strengthening of faith. That is where you will find *the* Jesus!

Almighty God, we confess that, like the people along the path to Jerusalem, we make our Savior what we want Him to be. Help us by Your Word to see who Jesus really is. As we hear the Word and receive the Sacraments, guide and guard our hearts that we would know our salvation is secured by the King who comes in the name of the Lord! We pray all this in the name of our Lord, Jesus Christ, who lives and reigns with You and the Holy Spirit, one God, now and forever. Amen.

JESUS CLEANSES THE TEMPLE

And Jesus entered the temple and drove out all who sold and bought in the temple, and He overturned the tables of the money-changers and the seats of those who sold pigeons. He said to them, "It is written, 'My house shall be called a house of prayer,' but you make it a den of robbers."

And the blind and the lame came to Him in the temple, and He healed them. But when the chief priests and the scribes saw the wonderful things that He did, and the children crying out in the temple, "Hosanna to the Son of David!" they were indignant, and they said to Him, "Do You hear what these are saying?" And Jesus said to them, "Yes; have you never read,

'Out of the mouth of infants and nursing babies you have prepared praise'?"

And leaving them, He went out of the city to Bethany and lodged there.

CHALLENGING OUR EXPECTATIONS OF JESUS

And Jesus said to them, "Yes; have you never read, 'Out of the mouth of infants and nursing babies You have prepared praise'?" (MATTHEW 21:16)

W e often view Jesus as meek and mild. Of course, there is good reason for this—He welcomes little children, He is compassionate to the hurting, and He shows endless grace to sinners. But in this passage, we see another side of Jesus. He flips over tables. He drives out those who have turned God's temple into a den of robbers. This leads us to ask—what is going on here?

As Jesus' earthly ministry drew to a close, He came into the city of Jerusalem during the annual celebration of Passover. The city was teeming with pilgrims who came to make sacrifices to God in remembrance of His deliverance from their slavery in Egypt. Given the cumbersome nature of traveling with animals, it wasn't uncommon for pilgrims to buy an animal to sacrifice once they got into the city. But instead of purchasing animals in the marketplace, the transactions took place in the court of the Gentiles. The court of the Gentiles was a place where non-Jewish people might learn of the God of Israel. The temple was meant to be a place of worship and prayer. But instead, it was functioning as a marketplace for religious leaders to profit off of. Jesus was not okay with this.

After Jesus clears away those who are misusing the temple, we see people who are blind and physically disabled come for healing. Children begin to cry out in celebration over Jesus' healing and cleansing work. The religious leaders are "indignant" that Jesus, a man, is receiving such praise.

But Jesus quotes Psalm 8 to make clear to the chief priests and scribes that the children see who He is more clearly than they do and are responding appropriately.

This scene has the potential to break the mold of our expectations of Jesus as well. While we rightly take great comfort in Jesus' mercy toward us, we see here that He is relentless in His pursuit to make the dwelling place of God holy. Even now, Jesus sends the Spirit to make the church, God's temple, holy. Even now, He is at work in you, a temple of the Holy Spirit, to make you holy. Above all, we see Jesus' pursuit to make us holy through His blood shed for us on the cross. So now we, too, can cry out with the children in the temple, "Hosanna, to the Son of David," who makes us holy through His finished work on our behalf.

Lord Jesus, we thank You for Your sacrifice on our behalf that by the power of Your Spirit we, too, are made holy. Amen.

ABUSE OF AUTHORITY

*[Jesus] said to them, "It is writ-
ten, 'My house shall be called a
house of prayer,' but you make it a
den of robbers."* (MATTHEW 21:13)

Just a day before this scene in the temple, Jesus made His triumphal entry into Jerusalem. Matthew tells us this stirred up the whole city (see Matthew 21:10). Jesus is a public figure. He enters into the temple, a public place. And as He drives out the money-changers, He causes a public spectacle. The public nature of Jesus' action here is not an accident; He is publicly reprimanding the priests for failing to do their duty for the people. And then, as Jesus immediately begins to heal people following the cleansing of the temple, He is publicly demonstrating who He is, the Son of David who has come to save His people.

Throughout Scripture, we see that God establishes leaders for the well-being and flourishing of His people. And yet, again and again, we see those leaders fall short of this mandate: Jacob plays favorites. Aaron makes a golden calf. King Saul disobeys God's command. David abuses his power. Solomon allows idolatry to flourish. The books of 1 and 2 Kings show us failure after failure of those in authority to do right by the people God has called them to lead. Every time these leaders rebel, God's judgment falls on them for the sake of His people. In the same way, the religious leaders of Jesus' day fail to preserve the temple as a holy place for people to pray and worship the living God. So Jesus cleans house.

It is all too common in our day to see both civil and religious leaders fail in their roles. When we witness these abuses of authority, it is disheartening. When people we expect to lead us spiritually and civically abandon their duty, we see the devastation it can wreak on people's lives and faith. We see clearly in this text that Jesus is not okay with this misuse of authority. He doesn't just call it out—He cleans it out.

And yet, the reality remains that each of us fail to live into the vocations given to us by God. When we consider this reality, Jesus' cleansing of the temple seems terrifying. But we take hope that He is the true Son of David—He is the one leader who never fails, who doesn't misuse His authority but instead uses it that He might cleanse His people through His blood shed on the cross for us.

Lord Jesus, thank You for being a true leader who will never fail us. Teach us to trust in Your will for us. Amen.

JESUS' WORK OF RESTORATION

And the blind and the lame came to Him in the temple, and He healed them. (MATTHEW 21:14)

In cleansing the temple, Jesus turns a chaotic marketplace into a place of peace and prayer. He turns a place of monetary exchange into a place of divine encounter. As the temple is restored to its purpose, those who are blind and disabled approach Jesus and find healing as children shout His praises. Jesus is in the business of taking what's been misused and broken and restoring it for God's good purpose.

We see this work of restoration throughout Jesus' life and ministry. He restores sight to the blind and hearing to the deaf. He heals the sick and makes the lame to walk. He feeds the hungry and raises the dead to life. He pronounces forgiveness to sinners and restores them back to the people of God. Over and again, we see Jesus bringing about God's restoration. Jesus is in the business of taking what's been misused and broken and restoring it for God's good purpose. He continues this work even now.

See, Jesus' restoring work did not end with His cleansing of the temple. In fact, the restoration Jesus brought in the temple and throughout His ministry points us to His ultimate work of restoration where, on the cross, Jesus takes on our sin and guilt, our broken relationship with God, and restores us to a right relationship with the Father. As we come to Him broken by our sin and guilt, He cleanses us of all sin and restores us to live in God's good purpose for our lives. We now go through life assured that God is with us and working through us to accomplish His will in our lives.

This work of restoration is Jesus establishing and extending the healing rule and reign of God on earth as it is in heaven. In the temple, by calling Him the Son of David, the children clearly recognize Jesus for who He is, the King of kings. Jesus is our King. He reigns over this world and His church, and one day, He will return in glory to redeem and restore all things to Himself once and for all. As we look forward to that day of final restoration, we celebrate and take hope in the restoration our King won for us in His death and resurrection.

King Jesus, thank You for restoring me back to the Father. May I take hope in You as I anticipate the restoration of all things. Amen.

GOD'S PLANS FOR HIS TEMPLE

And Jesus entered the temple and drove out all who sold and bought in the temple, and He overturned the tables of the money-changers and the seats of those who sold pigeons. He said to them, "It is written, 'My house shall be called a house of prayer,' but you make it a den of robbers." And the blind and the lame came to Him in the temple, and He healed them. (MATTHEW 21:12–14)

The temple was central to the life and worship of the people of Israel. To more fully understand Jesus' actions in this passage, we will explore some Old Testament connections to this event.

Leviticus 1:14

"If his offering to the LORD is a burnt offering of birds, then he shall bring his offering of turtledoves or pigeons." All the people of Israel were to offer sacrifices to God, but the poor could not afford to offer something as expensive as a goat or a lamb. It was permitted, then, for the poor to offer a pigeon or a turtledove. Jesus' ministry often took place among the poor. When Jesus encounters the corruption in the temple, He cleanses it not only because they have disrupted a place of worship but because they have turned a place of worship into a place of exploitation of the poor whom Jesus loves.

Isaiah 56:7

"For My house shall be called a house of prayer for all peoples." After Jesus cleanses the temple, He quotes Isaiah. This is a passage where God makes clear the global scope of His mission. Knowledge and worship of Him as the true God is not reserved for the Israelites alone but for all people. Since the Gentile court had been turned into a marketplace, the Gentiles could not encounter God. Through cleansing the temple, Jesus returns the court of the Gentiles back to its original purpose, a place for the nations to learn of God's grace and mercy and to offer prayer and sacrifice to the only true God.

Isaiah 35:5–6

"Then the eyes of the blind shall be opened, and the ears of the deaf unstopped; then shall the lame man leap like a deer, and the tongue of the mute sing for joy." In this passage from Isaiah, the prophet speaks of what will happen when the kingdom of God is on earth as it is in heaven. As the people with blindness and physical disabilities are healed by Jesus in the temple, we see that He is the promised Messiah and that God's healing rule and reign is brought about through Him.

Lord Jesus, we praise You for coming for the poor, the outsider, and the hurting. Teach us to humbly receive Your grace. Amen.

WAS JESUS' ANGER A SIN?

*And Jesus entered the temple and drove
out all who sold and bought in the
temple, and He overturned the tables
of the money-changers and the seats of
those who sold pigeons.* (MATTHEW 21:12)

This Bible passage raises some questions:

Was Jesus' anger a sin?

Jesus was perfect. He never sinned. He perfectly fulfilled the Law. He was perfectly righteous.
Jesus' perfection comes through so clearly when
we read about Him helping those in need, speaking grace to those broken by sin, and walking in
lockstep with the will of the Father. And yet, as
we encounter Jesus' anger at the misuse of the
temple, people have often wondered if Jesus' anger
was a sin. The reality is that so often in our own
anger, we sin. We lash out at others. We cut people
down. We seek vengeance. But anger itself is not
sin—anger is an emotion. It is what we do when
we feel angry and what we are angry about that
determines whether our anger is sinful. Jesus is
angry that God's people are misusing a place for
worship, exploiting the poor, and failing to welcome
the Gentiles into an encounter with the true God.
It is out of His love for God and others that Jesus
cleanses the temple.

Why were the Pharisees more concerned about the children praising Jesus than about the tables He turned over in the courtyard?

This is a striking part of the passage. Jesus has
just flipped over tables, shouted, and used a whip
to drive the money-changers out of the temple. He
causes a huge disruption. And yet, Matthew tells
us it is when the chief priests and scribes "saw the
wonderful things He did" and heard the children
praising Him that they became "indignant." Why
were they mad about the "wonderful things"—that
is, Jesus' healing miracles—and seemingly not that
upset about Him cleansing the temple? Matthew is
setting up a contrast. He wants his readers to see
the blindness and hypocrisy of the religious leaders
of Jesus' day. Rather than be indignant over the
misuse and abuse occurring at the temple on their
watch, they are upset over the healing Jesus brings
and the praise He inspires. They are so consumed
with their own agendas that they miss the work of
the Messiah in their midst.

*Lord Jesus, in our anger, help us to not
sin. Open our eyes that we may not be blind to
Your healing presence in our lives. Amen.*

JESUS CLEANSES HIS TEMPLE STILL

And Jesus entered the temple and drove out all who sold and bought in the temple, and He overturned the tables of the money-changers and the seats of those who sold pigeons. (MATTHEW 21:12)

Jesus cleanses the temple of greed and distraction. He restores the temple to its purpose of being a place of worship and prayer. In 1 Corinthians 6:19, Paul tells us that our bodies are temples of the Holy Spirit. Just as Jesus cleansed the temple in Jerusalem, He has sent the Spirit into our lives to purify and sanctify us. The Holy Spirit works in us to cleanse us from our greed and distraction. He restores us to our purpose of living as God's children and shapes us to be people of worship and prayer. The sanctifying power of the Spirit does not happen in an instant, but He continues to shape our hearts and lives through the Word of God.

When we fall into the traps of greed, distraction, or even the spiritual blindness of the religious leaders in Matthew 21, God invites us to confess our sin to Him. As we do, He meets us with the grace Jesus gives to us through His death on the cross. This is why each Sunday in worship, we take time to confess our sin. We come honestly to God with our failures and shortcomings, and as we do God forgives us and cleanses us from all unrighteousness. On account of Christ's atoning death, He purifies us and makes us into His people, set apart for His purpose.

Throughout the New Testament, the apostles testify that the church is the temple of God. As Jesus insisted that the temple in Jerusalem be used for the purpose of worship, prayer, and mission.

Jesus is still at work today, ensuring that His church is a people who worship God in spirit and in truth, live lives of prayer, and are sent out on His mission that all may know the grace and love of God. The church can lose sight of her calling as the temple and we, too, need to be cleansed. Each week, as the church gathers around the Lord's Supper, we receive Christ's body and blood in the bread and wine. Jesus promises that in this Meal, He is offering us His forgiveness and strengthening our faith. We go out from the Table, forgiven, restored, and strengthened to live as His temple by the power of the Spirit, that others may encounter the presence of God through His indwelling presence in His people.

Lord Jesus, we pray You continue to cleanse and sanctify us by the power of the Spirit that we may be a living temple, proclaiming the Good News of Your victory. Amen.

JESUS' AUTHORITY IS CHALLENGED

Week 30—Mark 11:27–12:12

And they came again to Jerusalem. And as He was walking in the temple, the chief priests and the scribes and the elders came to Him, and they said to Him, "By what authority are You doing these things, or who gave You this authority to do them?" Jesus said to them, "I will ask you one question; answer Me, and I will tell you by what authority I do these things. Was the baptism of John from heaven or from man? Answer Me." And they discussed it with one another, saying, "If we say, 'From heaven,' He will say to us, 'Why then did you not believe him?' But shall we say, 'From man'?"—they were afraid of the people, for they all held that John really was a prophet. So they answered Jesus, "We do not know." And Jesus said to them, "Neither will I tell you by what authority I do these things."

And He began to speak to them in parables. "A man planted a vineyard and put a fence around it and dug a pit for the winepress and built a tower, and leased it to tenants and went into another country. When the season came, he sent a servant to the tenants to get from them some of the fruit of the vineyard. And they took him and beat him and sent him away empty-handed. Again he sent to them another servant, and they struck him on the head and treated him shamefully. And he sent another, and him they killed. And so with many others: some they beat, and some they killed. He had still one other, a beloved son. Finally he sent him to them, saying, 'They will respect my son.' But those tenants said to one another, 'This is the heir. Come, let us kill him, and the inheritance will be ours.' And they took him and killed him and threw him out of the vineyard. What will the owner of the vineyard do? He will come and destroy the tenants and give the vineyard to others. Have you not read this Scripture:

> 'The stone that the builders rejected
>   has become the cornerstone;
> this was the Lord's doing,
>   and it is marvelous in our eyes'?"

And they were seeking to arrest Him but feared the people, for they perceived that He had told the parable against them. So they left Him and went away.

WHAT GIVES YOU THE RIGHT?

By what authority are You doing these things, or who gave You this authority to do them? (MARK 11:28)

There was a man in His thirties acting in a way that was socially and religiously unacceptable. Taking teaching, rules, and customs into His own hands, this man infuriated those in charge, those who "knew the rules"—those who had lived with the rules for quite some time. But the people loved Him. He taught with authority, so they were forced to ask the question, "By what authority are You doing these things?"

For many today, this young man is the authority. Jesus has set the rules and standards by which we live. We run our churches, homes, and lives by what He has said. But Jesus came in such a way where His authority was earned, not inherited. Jesus was born into an unknown family. Jesus had no formal training. Jesus had no earthly authority handed to Him. Jesus won people over through His demonstration of selfless love, through His demonstration of power and authority over evil and darkness by the Word He spoke and His mighty acts. While many marveled at what they saw, others were deeply upset and disturbed.

We can understand both. Imagine some person with no credentials coming into your church or home and telling you that you've been doing things the wrong way. Imagine someone coming into your community and revitalizing people's relationships with God, but not using the leaders, pastors, and elders from the church. No, instead, He gathers together twelve young men, and He sends them on missions. While it might be awesome to witness, even today we could be confused or even agitated by such a person. We would want to know who gave Him the authority to act in such a way.

The chief priests, scribes, and elders had the authority in the Jewish Church. They were responsible for making sure Jesus' teaching and way of life was in accordance with the Scriptures. The problem was that *their* teaching and way of life was not in accordance with the Scriptures. They had betrayed and abused the authority God had given them. They tried to trap Jesus in a question, but the bigger problem was that they were trapped in hypocrisy. They were acting just like most of the leaders throughout the Old Testament: abusing their authority. Instead of trapping Jesus, they ended up trapped themselves.

This was the power of Jesus' authority. He did not need to justify Himself. His way of life was evidence. His message of hope and freedom was evidence. He was not worried about defending Himself because He was defending God's people "against the rulers, against the authorities, against the cosmic powers over this present darkness, against the spiritual forces of evil" (Ephesians 6:12). Jesus' message of freedom traps anyone seeking to enslave. Jesus' life was heading closer and closer to death on the cross, and the actions of this man demonstrated more and more the divine authority that was His alone.

Father in heaven, give us hearts that accept the authority of Jesus in our lives. Enable us to embrace His teaching and organize our lives and leadership by Him alone. In Jesus' name we pray. Amen.

JESUS' AUTHORITY

And Jesus said to them, "Neither will I tell you by what authority I do these things." (MARK 11:33)

We can't fit Jesus into any of our boxes. While He is kind, He is also harsh. While He takes questions, He gives out harder ones. While He reveals truth, He also hides His glory. While He shows love, He also talks about rejection. This passage of Scripture demonstrates how we cannot limit Jesus, no matter how hard we try.

The leaders of His day tried to define Jesus, tried to wrap their heads around everything He was saying and how different He was from anyone else they had ever encountered. After three years, they were no closer to understanding Him than they were when He restored a man's withered hand early in His ministry (see Mark 3:1–6). When they asked bluntly where He got His authority, Jesus made His answer contingent on their response to a question. The question about John's Baptism challenged the church leaders to clarify where power came from for other people too. When they refused, Jesus refused to answer them too.

But Jesus actually does answer their question. With a story. And the point of His parable is that the "vineyard" (in other words, the church) is God's, and not the workers'. Any authority in the church or world comes from God alone. And that authority comes *through* the Son, the "stone the builders rejected," the cornerstone that holds all things together and keeps all things standing.

Jesus is the owner, the builder, and the building material for the house of faith. Therefore, He gets to determine what is built and how it is accomplished. But those people who think they are the owners, the builders, or the raw materials of Jesus' church become angry when they find out things won't go their way.

And that is the message for us. Is God's church ours to build? protect? Do we have authority over God? Over how God is orchestrating things? Do we have any right to question God? Don't get me wrong: God invites our questions and challenges. But, like Job in the Old Testament, we had better be ready to be confronted with a whirlwind of difficult questions. We had better be ready to be silent in the powerful presence of our God. If we're willing to listen, however, we will hear the most wonderful news: the church is God's, and Jesus will protect it by His authority. I am part of God's church, and Jesus will protect me by His authority. I'm not in control, and that is a very good thing.

Father in heaven, You have given all authority to Jesus. We trust You. We listen to You. Help us to follow where You lead and accomplish what You've asked us to do. In Jesus' name. Amen.

GOD'S PLAN TO RESTORE HIS CREATION

He had still one other, a beloved son.
Finally he sent him to them, saying,
"They will respect my son." (MARK 12:6)

Is there a better picture of our world than a garden in rebellion against its owner? We are ready to accept the gift, even as we reject the gift-giver. An obvious question comes to mind: *Why would God give this kind of power and authority to people?* This question has plagued theologians, philosophers, and everyone else. How can a good, all-powerful God allow evil? To our puny minds, it looks like either God isn't good, or God isn't all powerful.

The real problem, however, is that *we* are the evil ones. To demand that God put an end to evil is to demand, at some level, that God puts an end to us. God desires more. Yes, the garden has been in rebellion ever since the thistles and thorns started to overtake the fertile fields in Genesis 3. Yes, humanity has been on a hunt to recapture what's been lost. But God promised to send a Son to destroy Satan, to redeem His lost people, to put an end to death, and to finally restore His perfect creation when He returns on the Last Day.

Jesus is the Son of God, born with a dragon ready to devour Him (see Revelation 12:4–5), cast into the wilderness to dwell with the beasts and battle the devil (see Mark 1:12), sent to the ravaged garden to collect God's possessions. Jesus is the one meant to subdue the garden, the true Adam, the proper Adam, the one who will stand up for His wife, who will stand against Satan, who will walk alongside God amid His creation.

Jesus crushed the rebellion by becoming the rebellion. Jesus put an end to God's wrath by drinking the cup of wrath Himself. Our good and all-powerful God planned from before creation to demonstrate that He destroys evil by destroying Himself, to reclaim all that is under the curse of evil.

This has been God's mission before He ever created Adam and Eve—to be the one to redeem Adam and Eve. No longer are we in rebellion. Jesus has won the battle—the battle against our own sin, the wicked serpent, and the penalty of death. Jesus has put an end to evil while saving those under its spell. God planted the tree of life, after all, that all humanity might eat of it in the garden and enjoy the presence of God forever. We just didn't know till Jesus came that the tree of life was a cross and the fruit was His body and blood.

Father in heaven, You have reclaimed us.
You are remaking us and all of Your creation.
In the face of evil, help us to trust You and
follow Jesus. Amen.

THE PERSECUTED MESSENGERS

Have you not read this Scripture:
"The stone that the builders rejected
has become the cornerstone; this was
the Lord's doing, and it is marvel-
ous in our eyes"? (MARK 12:10-11)

There is a distinction to be made between the message and the messenger—what is brought and who brings it. Ultimately, that is what the Pharisees were wondering about Jesus. Who had given Jesus this authority? Scripture says He was teaching them "as one who had authority, and not as their scribes" (Matthew 7:29).

Jesus' message and actions come with authority because the Father has granted that authority. Although Jesus faced near-constant criticism and judgment from religious leaders, He was always clear: "I can do nothing on My own . . . the Father has sent Me" (John 5:30-36); "I do nothing on My own authority, but speak just as the Father has taught Me" (John 8:28); "I am not alone, for the Father is with Me" (John 16:32). Jesus Himself also has the authority to do whatever He wants because He is the obedient Son.

But just as Jesus mentioned John the Baptist in John 5, Scripture reveals over and again how God's messengers have often been persecuted. Just look at Elijah, who was hunted like an enemy (see 1 Kings 19); Jeremiah, who was imprisoned for speaking God's Word (see Jeremiah 37:15); and John the Baptist himself, who was beheaded for standing on God's truth (see Matthew 14:1-12). Hebrews 11:36-37 shows how common it was that the faithful were beaten, stoned, imprisoned, and killed. God's messengers are not safe, even though their message is from God. God's messengers stand

between a holy God and unholy people, mediating like Moses for God's mercy to an undeserving people (Exodus 32:11).

The parable of the vineyard is a rich biblical metaphor that finds its roots in Psalm 80, running through Isaiah 5 and bearing fruit in Song of Solomon and all through the Gospels. Culminating in John 15, Jesus makes it explicit: "I am the vine; you are the branches" (v. 5). Instead of harvesting an abundant crop, however, life is stomped out in the Mark 12 vineyard parable. But "so shall He sprinkle many nations" (Isaiah 52:15)—the blood spilled, the cup offered, the fruit of the Son's life, given for you.

We know that the message and the Messenger are one in Jesus, the Word made flesh (see John 1:14). Jesus has appointed us to be His messengers, and He has blessed the "feet of those who preach the good news!" (Romans 10:15). He is the vine; we are the branches. Jesus has sent us, as 1 Peter 3:15-16 shares, with His authority, "to make a defense to anyone who asks you for a reason for the hope that is in you; yet do it with gentleness and respect, having a good conscience, so that, when you are slandered, those who revile your good behavior in Christ may be put to shame."

Dear Father, prepare us to speak Your
message of truth and love, hope and grace to a
world warring against the God they so desper-
ately need. In Jesus' name we pray. Amen.

JESUS' QUESTION AND OUR QUESTIONS

Jesus said to them, "I will ask you one question." (MARK 11:29)

Jesus is not afraid of our questions, but He often reframes them to provide us with the answers we are actually seeking. The same is true of this passage. Jesus was challenged with this question: Where do You get Your authority? Instead of answering, however, Jesus recentered the conversation on the real problem: What do you actually care about authority? The religious leaders didn't care about John the Baptist, and they didn't care about Jesus. They, like the people of God in the Old Testament, actually rejected the very authority God had put over them. As we read these passages and consider our own questions, we come to Jesus in humility and curiosity, seeking His wisdom and truth.

Why is it significant that these three groups of religious leaders are together?

Their question about authority flows from their very identity. These groups believe God has appointed them. The chief priests, elders, and scribes, essentially the entire religious establishment—experts in Jewish Law, in the Scriptures, and in religious practice—were bitter rivals and enemies, but here, they have banded together to take their stand against Jesus' challenge. Everything that gave meaning to their lives was being challenged by Jesus. When we are challenged by God, often we will cling to whatever power we can, hoping to retain control over our situation.

Why did Jesus bring up the ministry of John the Baptist?

John was also not part of the establishment. Since he was dead, he was no longer a threat to these leaders, but he was dearly beloved by the people. John had also shown his support for Jesus, baptizing and commissioning Him for ministry. If they said that John's authority was from God, then they had the answer to their question, "Where did you get your authority?" But if they said that John was merely some person out in the wilderness saying crazy things, they would expose their corrupt hearts and be judged by the masses. They refused to take a stand, for fear of judgment, and they gave up their authority to proclaim what was "from God."

Why did they not just arrest Jesus for cleansing the temple?

When the leaders asked, "Who gave You the authority to do these things?" they most likely had in mind Jesus turning over temple tables and driving out money-changers. They could only question Jesus, challenge His words and intentions, because they knew He was doing what was right: making the temple into the actual temple of God. Jesus cared more about God than money, and He proved it. Arresting Jesus would have proven that they cared more about money than God. Had the religious leaders moved against Jesus, they would have exposed their sinful and lawless practices.

Why did Jesus teach the parable of the vineyard and the owner?

Jesus was bringing much more than His judgment upon the leaders of His day. Jesus was bringing the judgment of the entire Old Testament. "What more was there to do for My vineyard, that I have not done in it?" God asks in Isaiah 5:4. How do we want God to answer His question today?

Dear Jesus, You are the vine, and we are the branches. Support and strengthen us as we find ourselves in Your grace. Amen.

WHO TENDS GOD'S VINEYARD?

What will the owner of the vineyard do? He will come and destroy the tenants and give the vineyard to others. (MARK 12:9).

Jesus was no stranger to the temple. In reality, it was His very presence that filled it from the start. Jesus was not opposed to the temple or the religious practices God had established through Moses. In fact, the religious leaders demonstrated that they were the ones opposed to the practices of their own God! This was the point of Jesus' parable: Don't mistake your will for God's will. Don't mistake your religious hopes for the actions and plans of God. Otherwise, we are in danger of not recognizing the presence of God in His own house and subjecting our Savior to suffering.

Christians gather to hear from God. Yes, it is important to be heard by God as well. But it is easy to become the type of people who are ready to ask, but unwilling to receive unless God gives us exactly what we asked for. Ready to seek, but unwilling to find anything but what we are seeking. Ready to knock, but unwilling to walk through the door unless it leads us to where we want to go. Ready to speak, but unwilling to listen unless it is what we want to hear. This is what Jesus found in His temple, presumably the last time He entered it before His crucifixion. He found a bunch of people with hearts so twisted that they couldn't even worship God in their midst. He found tenants ready to put their Lord to death. They were ready to let God know just how much they know, how much better they can steward His vineyard, how much greater everything would be if they were in charge. But Jesus told them how that will end: "He will come and destroy the tenants and give the vineyard to others."

God took the vineyard, His church, from the Jewish leaders in Jesus' day and gave it to Jesus' faithful disciples. Today, He has given the vineyard to us, to those ready to be faithful in their stewardship of God's temple. One of my favorite parts of the rite of Holy Baptism is the question and response:

> Do you renounce the devil . . . and all his works . . . [and] all his ways?
> *Yes, I renounce them.*
> Do you believe in God the Father . . . Jesus Christ, His only Son . . . [and] the Holy Spirit?
> *Yes, I believe.*
> (*LSB, p. 270*)

Parents, sponsors, and congregation speak alongside and on behalf of those being baptized. God has invited us into a conversation. It is not always a pleasant or fun experience, but God makes Himself known to His people. Let us be ready to hear from God. Let us welcome our God's presence, and with that, God's questions.

> Do you believe you are a sinner?
> *Yes.*
> Do you believe Jesus died for you?
> *Yes.*
> Do you believe the pastor's words are not his own, but God's?
> *Yes.*

Let us be convicted that our bodies and our congregations are temples of the Holy Spirit, and He is among us. Welcome to the vineyard; the Owner is coming, and He wants to talk. Are you ready to hear from Him?

Lord God, You have placed us into Your church. Sustain our faith and give us joy as we live in Your presence. In Jesus' name we pray. Amen.

JESUS IS TESTED

WEEK 31—LUKE 20:19–44

The scribes and the chief priests sought to lay hands on Him at that very hour, for they perceived that He had told this parable against them, but they feared the people. So they watched Him and sent spies, who pretended to be sincere, that they might catch Him in something He said, so as to deliver Him up to the authority and jurisdiction of the governor. So they asked Him, "Teacher, we know that You speak and teach rightly, and show no partiality, but truly teach the way of God. Is it lawful for us to give tribute to Caesar, or not?" But He perceived their craftiness, and said to them, "Show Me a denarius. Whose likeness and inscription does it have?" They said, "Caesar's." He said to them, "Then render to Caesar the things that are Caesar's, and to God the things that are God's." And they were not able in the presence of the people to catch Him in what He said, but marveling at His answer they became silent.

There came to Him some Sadducees, those who deny that there is a resurrection, and they asked Him a question, saying, "Teacher, Moses wrote for us that if a man's brother dies, having a wife but no children, the man must take the widow and raise up offspring for his brother. Now there were seven brothers. The first took a wife, and died without children. And the second and the third took her, and likewise all seven left no children and died. Afterward the woman also died. In the resurrection, therefore, whose wife will the woman be? For the seven had her as wife."

And Jesus said to them, "The sons of this age marry and are given in marriage, but those who are considered worthy to attain to that age and to the resurrection from the dead neither marry nor are given in marriage, for they cannot die anymore, because they are equal to angels and are sons of God, being sons of the resurrection. But that the dead are raised, even Moses showed, in the passage about the bush, where he calls the Lord the God of Abraham and the God of Isaac and the God of Jacob. Now He is not God of the dead, but of the living, for all live to Him." Then some of the scribes answered, "Teacher, You have spoken well." For they no longer dared to ask Him any question.

But He said to them, "How can they say that the Christ is David's son? For David himself says in the book of Psalms,

'The Lord said to my Lord,
 "Sit at My right hand,
    until I make Your enemies Your
    footstool."'

"David thus calls Him Lord, so how is He his son?"

RUFFLING FEATHERS

The scribes and the chief priests sought to lay hands on Him at that very hour, for they perceived that He had told this parable against them, but they feared the people. So they watched Him and sent spies, who pretended to be sincere, that they might catch Him in something He said, so as to deliver Him up to the authority and jurisdiction of the governor. (LUKE 20:19–20)

Pontius Pilate would have been on high alert. With the celebration of the Passover close at hand, people were streaming into Jerusalem from all over the Roman Empire. This high feast day would have brought with it the possibility of unrest for the Roman governor of Judea. There was always potential for not only more crime but for Jewish dissidents to rile up the crowds toward outright revolt.

Leaders of the temple knew that their colonial governor would be on edge. They cooked up a plan. Jesus of Nazareth was in the city; this would be their time to strike. Gathering a few men, they sent them as spies to catch Jesus in their web. The plan? Get Him to speak out against Rome. If they could do that, then Pilate would do the work of getting rid of this meddlesome, backwoods rabbi.

Jesus had gotten under their skin. These scribes and Pharisees saw a threat to their teachings, power, and way of life. He ate with sinners and the unclean. One of His disciples was a tax collector. Everywhere He went, crowds gathered to hear Him teach. They even suspected that His parable about the tenants of the vineyard, which we studied last week, was directed at them, calling them out for being wicked.

This was not a new story in the history of God's people. The prophets had encountered similar pushback from rulers and authorities who did not like the messages of repentance they delivered. God's people had a knack for losing sight of His ways. But Jesus was more than a prophet. He was the Messiah. His teachings were not redefining God's Law but instead returning them to what they were intended to be.

Even today, Jesus still is ruffling feathers. It would be easy enough to point fingers at others—even reading this story, it is more commonplace to identify with the scribes and Pharisees than with Jesus. Do we miss a greater teaching by missing this fact? Can we sit back and read the words of Jesus and see the places in our lives that need to change? Or have we prepared a cacophony of questions to try and drown out Jesus in hopes that we can justify our own prideful, self-centered actions?

Take a moment and think on the teachings of Jesus. Where are the places you are trying to hold onto your own ideals instead of following after Him?

Dear Jesus, too often I seek after my own ways instead of Yours. Today, I repent of putting myself first. Please help me to see Your ways. Thank You for the gift of salvation that frees me to live a life following after You. Amen.

WALKING UP TO THE LINE

Then some of the scribes answered,
"Teacher, You have spoken well."
For they no longer dared to ask
Him any question. (LUKE 20:39–40)

Taxes, coins, and Caesar. The resurrection and marriage. The Son of David. The religious elite of Jesus' day send spies to catch Him in either open rebellion to Rome or heresy. Their belief is viewed through a lens of power and authority, which they long to hold onto as long as they can.

Jesus had just told a parable of wicked tenants who had cast out the servants and then killed the son of the landowner. In a moment where Scripture not only tells the story but paints a picture this parable ends like this: "But He looked directly at them and said, 'What then is this that is written: "The stone that the builders rejected has become the cornerstone"? Everyone who falls on that stone will be broken to pieces, and when it falls on anyone, it will crush him'" (Luke 20:17–18).

Jesus had looked directly at them, His full attention on the scribes and Pharisees. It was a warning: *Do not be these tenants. Remember the prophets you rejected. Do not also reject the Son.*

Instead of heeding that warning, they took offense to it. Here, Jesus was giving them a way to escape the punishment that would come for them. Instead of being crushed by the cornerstone, it could have been their foundation. But, as people often do, they thought only of their own power. They sought to destroy Him by sending their spies.

Are you ever offended by the words of the Bible? There should be times that the Bible offends us. Our sin is contrary to the ways of God. We can be like the tenants, like the scribes and Pharisees,

ignoring the words of Scripture and of Jesus that seek to lead us to repentance.

Too often we think of Scripture and look for the line. How far is too far? We want to walk all the way up to the line of sin but make sure we don't cross it. This is the way of the religious leaders. They drew the lines. Rome wanted its taxes; they wanted their teaching validated. Jesus sees the ploy and deftly responds, countering their subterfuge.

Where are the areas you are looking for the line? You craft a question or thought process in such a way to excuse your own selfishness? It is the problem of sinful humanity. We want what we want.

In the process of sanctification, Jesus has all the answers. His saving work frees us from the need of finding the line and instead invites us to join in His new life, following in His ways. Our old selves will seek to trip Him up, to defend our sin, and justify it through some twisted means. Instead, see the Holy Spirit work. Take a hard look at your places of sin and seek repentance.

Lord, show me where I am self-centered, trying to justify my sinful ways. I repent of them. Help me to walk in Your ways. Amen.

THE KING AND HIS OPPOSITION

But He said to them, "How can they say that the Christ is David's son? For David himself says in the book of Psalms, 'The Lord said to my Lord, "Sit at my right hand, until I make Your enemies Your footstool."' David thus calls Him Lord, so how is He his son?" (LUKE 20:41–44)

Jesus is not messing around in these passages. In the Sermon on the Mount, He taught about the ways of the kingdom of God. It might be difficult to imagine anyone who would oppose that kingdom, but here, Jesus is seen to take a stand against men who would oppose His rule. He does not mince words. He claims the mantle of the cornerstone that will crush them. The enemies that God will make His footstool are standing in front of Him. Jesus' mission is too important for it to be pulled away by anyone.

What of Caesar? Surely the spies of the scribes and Pharisees have Jesus here. Everyone in Judea hates their occupiers. If Jesus says they should not pay taxes, Pilate will take Him. If Jesus says they should pay taxes, the crowds will turn against Him. Jesus deftly rebukes them with, "Then render to Caesar the things that are Caesar's, and to God the things that are God's" (Luke 20:25).

How about the resurrection and the ways of marriage? Surely Jesus will not know how to answer. Instead, He speaks of the ways of this world versus what is to come in the resurrection. While doing this, He takes the Sadducees to school on their own hypocrisy as they no longer believe in the bodily resurrection.

He tells them that He is the cornerstone. Referencing David, Isaiah, and Zechariah, Jesus takes upon Himself the prophecy of the stone that will cause stumbling.

Finally, He reminds them that David's son will be David's Lord. They look to a worldly lineage where the Christ would be a son of David as an heir to the throne. But Jesus is the Son of David and Lord of him. He is the Alpha and Omega. Here, He is pointing to His greater calling. He cannot be contained by their small view of the Christ. Instead of coming to reign over an earthly kingdom that is threatened by Rome or under the Law-based hypocrisy of its religious elite, He has come to usher in the kingdom of God.

Jesus is unafraid to push back against those who would try to wrest His kingdom away from Himself or those who follow Him. This world would try to threaten the King of kings, but He understands His mission. He knows why He has been sent. There is nothing that will stop Him from seeking and saving the lost.

Dear Jesus, thank You for defending Your kingdom. As Your child, I can rest in peace knowing that You will not let the kingdom of God belong to men or women who only seek to use it for selfish gain. Amen.

CHRIST IS OUR CORNERSTONE

But He looked directly at them and said, "What then is this that is written: 'The stone that the builders rejected has become the cornerstone'? Everyone who falls on that stone will be broken to pieces, and when it falls on anyone, it will crush him." (LUKE 20:17–18)

Jesus is often referred to as a cornerstone, a firm foundation. Both in the Old and New Testaments, Jesus is compared to a solid building block. Check out the following examples:

Psalm 118:21–22

"I thank You that You have answered me and have become my salvation. The stone that the builders rejected has become the cornerstone."

Isaiah 28:16

"Therefore thus says the Lord GOD, 'Behold, I am the one who has laid as a foundation in Zion, a stone, a tested stone, a precious cornerstone, of a sure foundation: "Whoever believes will not be in haste."'"

Zechariah 10:4

"From Him shall come the cornerstone, from Him the tent peg, from Him the battle bow, from Him every ruler—all of them together."

Acts 4:11

"This Jesus is the stone that was rejected by you, the builders, which has become the cornerstone."

Ephesians 2:19–22

"So then you are no longer strangers and aliens, but you are fellow citizens with the saints and members of the household of God, built on the foundation of the apostles and prophets, Christ Jesus Himself being the cornerstone, in whom the whole structure, being joined together, grows into a holy temple in the Lord. In Him you also are being built together into a dwelling place for God by the Spirit."

1 Peter 2:6–7

"For it stands in Scripture: 'Behold, I am laying in Zion a stone, a cornerstone chosen and precious, and whoever believes in Him will not be put to shame.' So the honor is for you who believe, but for those who do not believe, 'The stone that the builders rejected has become the cornerstone.'"

While the Cornerstone will crush those who come against Him, He is our hope. He was promised and provided. In Him is salvation and new life. He is the building block for the life of a follower of Jesus. Immovable and irreplaceable. The builders, these leaders of Israel, have rejected Him, but He is our cornerstone.

Heavenly Father, thank You for giving us Your Son as our cornerstone. Life in this world can feel shaky and uncertain but, in Jesus, we find a hope that does not let us down. Let us build our lives around Him. In Jesus' name. Amen.

WHY DID JESUS PROMOTE PAYING TRIBUTE TO UNGODLY CAESAR?

So they watched Him and sent spies, who pretended to be sincere, that they might catch Him in something He said, so as to deliver Him up to the authority and jurisdiction of the governor. So they asked Him, "Teacher, we know that You speak and teach rightly, and show no partiality, but truly teach the way of God. Is it lawful for us to give tribute to Caesar, or not?" But He perceived their craftiness, and said to them, "Show me a denarius. Whose likeness and inscription does it have?" They said, "Caesar's." He said to them, "Then render to Caesar the things that are Caesar's, and to God the things that are God's." And they were not able in the presence of the people to catch Him in what He said, but marveling at His answer they became silent. (LUKE 20:20–26)

Spies sent by the scribes and Pharisees were hard at work trying to get Jesus to trip up. Since Jesus was in Jerusalem, they knew that if the Romans felt any kind of rebellious ripples, they would come down hard on Him. These men knew that Pontius Pilate had the "authority and jurisdiction."

Pilate, as the local governor, had the authority to keep law and order in Judea. The religious rulers knew that Pilate and the Romans were brutal in their execution of the law—especially upon those who would speak out against the Roman Empire. Crucifixion was the main punishment for dissenters. Any rebellion that was put down would have its survivors crucified on a main highway as an example to any others who might think of opposing Roman rule.

Roman occupation was brutal and total. The taxes levied on local populations went to fund their occupiers. People paid for their own oppression. The scribes and Pharisees saw this as an opportunity—the people hated the Roman colonizers. If they could get Jesus to side with the Romans, then the people would push back against Him. Even better if He spoke against Rome—Pilate would make an example of Him.

Jesus deftly answers their question. Render to Caesar what is Caesar's and to God what is God's. A brilliant response, but also confusing. Does not all belong to God? Wouldn't even the money of Rome fall under His rule and reign?

Luther's two-kingdom theology helps us to understand what was happening here. God's kingdom of the right is concerned with the eternal matters of the life everlasting. It is a way that transcends the human government. However, this world still waits for its full realization. There exists, then, the kingdom of the left, the rule of government put before sinful mankind. This government is not perfect but instead works to keep peace as best as possible. While it can be conformed and reformed, God puts it in place to work as best it can for all the people under its purview. In this way, Pilate had jurisdiction and authority, even for a moment over Jesus. Not in the kingdom of God but in the earthly kingdom of Judea.

Holy Father, watch over my local, provisional, and national leaders. Grant them godly wisdom and let them rule for the good of all people. In Jesus' name. Amen.

REDIRECTED ON LIFE'S ROAD

Then some of the scribes answered, "Teacher, You have spoken well." (LUKE 20:39)

When I was a kid, we used to make a long drive each summer from Houston to Minnesota. Dad was born and raised on Galveston Island, Mom in the farmlands west of the Twin Cities. Packing five of us into a minivan, we would drive and camp our way up north. After several fun weeks spent picking raspberries, fishing, swimming in the lake, and climbing trees, we would pack back up and make the journey home.

Sometimes Mom and Dad would get lost. An exit would be missed, or a left turn would happen instead of a right, and a few minutes later, nothing looked familiar. Whoever was driving would pull over and something would happen that does not happen much anymore: they pulled out a paper map. It was a large, spiral-bound Rand-McNally map of the country. They'd find the closest crossroads and work their way back to where they needed to be.

Long gone are those days. Now if you miss an exit, your phone simply recalculates and redirects you the way you need to go. I remember some tense moments of trying to figure out where we were on a paper map, but now it is just a millisecond of recalculation on a smartphone.

When the spies of the scribes and Pharisees show up, they are trying to get Jesus lost. They are pushing for Him to make a wrong turn through which they can persecute Him. But instead, He redirects them. He takes their wrong turn and shows them the right way. Things of this earth become lessons for a life lived following Him.

As Christians, we can easily become distracted and lose sight of the kingdom of God. Getting lost in the things of this world gets us frustrated. How do we find our way? We let the King redirect us. He recalculates a route that brings us back in line with Him.

He gives us gifts to keep us focused. When the world would try to trick us with lies, He reminds us that we belong to Him. His church, Sacraments, Scripture, and the Body of Christ are everyday gifts that point us in the way to go. They deliver His good message time and again.

Sometimes, our sinful selves will try to trick God. Selfishly, we long to find loopholes to His good will and His calling on our lives. Other times, we are as weary travelers hearing the lies of the enemy who seeks to pull us from the path. These passages give us hope. In the earthly realms, we know that we are to live as good citizens of where we reside. In the kingdom of God, we are to live as people of the resurrection, knowing what is to come.

Jesus has spoken well.

Lord, may we walk as people who seek Your kingdom. In this earthly life, may we find purpose as citizens of our country, caring for our neighbors. Amen.

JESUS PRONOUNCES SEVEN WOES

WEEK 32—MATTHEW 23:13–39

But woe to you, scribes and Pharisees, hypocrites! For you shut the kingdom of heaven in people's faces. For you neither enter yourselves nor allow those who would enter to go in. Woe to you, scribes and Pharisees, hypocrites! For you travel across sea and land to make a single proselyte, and when he becomes a proselyte, you make him twice as much a child of hell as yourselves.

Woe to you, blind guides, who say, "If anyone swears by the temple, it is nothing, but if anyone swears by the gold of the temple, he is bound by his oath." You blind fools! For which is greater, the gold or the temple that has made the gold sacred? And you say, "If anyone swears by the altar, it is nothing, but if anyone swears by the gift that is on the altar, he is bound by his oath." You blind men! For which is greater, the gift or the altar that makes the gift sacred? So whoever swears by the altar swears by it and by everything on it. And whoever swears by the temple swears by it and by Him who dwells in it. And whoever swears by heaven swears by the throne of God and by Him who sits upon it.

Woe to you, scribes and Pharisees, hypocrites! For you tithe mint and dill and cumin, and have neglected the weightier matters of the law: justice and mercy and faithfulness. These you ought to have done, without neglecting the others. You blind guides, straining out a gnat and swallowing a camel!

Woe to you, scribes and Pharisees, hypocrites! For you clean the outside of the cup and the plate, but inside they are full of greed and self-indulgence. You blind Pharisee! First clean the inside of the cup and the plate, that the outside also may be clean.

Woe to you, scribes and Pharisees, hypocrites! For you are like whitewashed tombs, which outwardly appear beautiful, but within are full of dead people's bones and all uncleanness. So you also outwardly appear righteous to others, but within you are full of hypocrisy and lawlessness.

Woe to you, scribes and Pharisees, hypocrites! For you build the tombs of the prophets and decorate the monuments of the righteous, saying, "If we had lived in the days of our fathers, we would not have taken part with them in shedding the blood of the prophets." Thus you witness against yourselves that you are sons of those who murdered the prophets. Fill up, then, the measure of your fathers. You serpents, you brood of vipers, how are you to escape being sentenced to hell? Therefore I send you prophets and wise men and scribes, some of whom you will kill and crucify, and some you will flog in your synagogues and persecute from town to town, so that on you may come all the righteous blood shed on earth, from the blood of righteous Abel to the blood of Zechariah the son of Barachiah, whom you murdered between the sanctuary and the altar. Truly, I say to you, all these things will come upon this generation.

SOME OF JESUS' HARSHEST WORDS

The greatest among you shall be your servant. (MATTHEW 23:11)

n last week's reading, spies from the Jewish chief priests challenged Jesus with ingenious questions to turn the crowds against Him or make Him incriminate Himself in front of Pontius Pilate. Knowing their craftiness, Jesus easily eluded their traps. His closing question about the divine and human natures of the promised Christ left them unwilling to ask any more questions.

However, if they thought that their silence would keep Jesus quiet, they were badly mistaken. Jesus filled their silent void with some of the hardest words of His ministry. It is with these words that Jesus concluded His Holy Tuesday teachings. Having silenced His enemies, Jesus then warned the crowds against the Pharisees and scribes. Since these popular teachers refused to listen to His gentle rebukes and warnings, in tough love, He barraged His enemies with powerful rebukes, judgments, and warnings to lead them to repentance and faith.

We will hear Jesus saying over and over, "Woe to you, scribes and Pharisees" (see Matthew 23:13 for the first in the series). Overall, through chapter 23, Jesus used this phrase seven times. This is in keeping with other sevenfold series in the book of Matthew. Perhaps because of his background as a tax collector, Matthew often used groups of three, five, and seven. For example, there are seven parables in chapter 13. There are seven fulfillments of Old Testament prophecies in chapters 1–4 before Jesus begins His adult ministry of teaching and healing. These collections of seven related actions or words remind us of the foundational seven days

of creation and other important Old Testament occasions of seven. For example, the people of Israel walked around Jericho for seven days, circling the city seven times on the final day. Then, after a shout, the walls come down. So, just as God overcame the walls of Jericho through seven days, Jesus takes on the defenses of the Pharisees by these firm, repeated words: "Woe to you, scribes and Pharisees."

But it is not only the unbelieving Sadducees and hypocritical scribes and Pharisees that grieved Jesus—He looked at the vast majority of His Jewish people and He wept for Jerusalem. He desperately loved them and sought their salvation, but He felt the stinging pain of the endless doom they were bringing upon themselves—the wrath He would soon take upon Himself on the cross. They could have known peace between themselves and God, but so many refused to see Him as the Messiah. Yet, despite their rejection, Jesus went forward to the cross to pay for the sins of everyone, even those who rejected Him.

Heavenly Savior, remind us that true greatness comes through service and that You chose to humble Yourself to serve and save us. Amen.

FALSE RIGHTEOUSNESS AND TRUE REPENTANCE

Whoever exalts himself will be humbled, and whoever humbles himself will be exalted. (MATTHEW 23:12)

The Jewish people were impressed with the Pharisees—who passed themselves off as obedient Jews, satisfying God's will and doing even far more than His Law demanded—but Jesus publicly warned the Jewish people not to be taken in by their false righteousness. Righteousness with God does not come from our works, which are stained by selfish motives and arrogant pride. It is a gift God gives to us through His Word and Sacraments based on Jesus' perfect life of obedience in our place—and His suffering and death, which took away our sins.

The whole Old Testament system of sacrifices was meant to be God's gracious response to the guilt and contrition the Ten Commandments worked in God's people. Sacrificial animals bore the sin of the people and died in their place. But these countless animal sacrifices needed to be done over and again. Their true significance was in pointing ahead to the one-time sacrifice of the Lamb of God on the cross, which would forever satisfy God's wrath at our sins. He sacrificed Himself entirely for the sake of all people. Jesus, the perfect Son of God, needed no sacrifice for Himself. The complete value of His perfect life was given for the sake of the world. Then, in response to God's gracious forgiveness through that sacrifice, His people gratefully responded with works of love.

However, instead of seeking God's grace, the Jewish religious authorities felt the Commandments could be kept. Therefore, they convinced themselves that the traditions and man-made rules they diligently followed obliged God to welcome them into heaven. Jesus exposed this lie and warned the Pharisees to repent or be doomed to hell. It is a message to us as well to be wary of false pride and the thought that our works for the church somehow merit our eternal life with God.

Notice verses 34–35 of this week's reading. Jesus will not stop calling these Pharisees to repentance, faith, and salvation after His suffering, death, and resurrection. He will send apostles and other Christians to call them to repentance and faith, but they will persecute and kill those sent to them—like the Twelve and Stephen, thus bringing eternal punishment upon themselves. Thankfully, not all these rejected Jesus. Two Jewish leaders (Nicodemus and Joseph of Arimathea) believed in Jesus, and many more Pharisees and priests would believe the apostles' message and know salvation through Jesus Christ (see John 12:42; Acts 6:7).

Dear Lord, keep us from false pride, which only leads to disgrace. Instead, help us follow the path of Jesus, who gave His life as a ransom for all. In Jesus' name. Amen.

THE POWER OF CHRIST'S LOVE

How often would I have gathered
your children together as a hen gath-
ers her brood under her wings, and
you were not willing! (MATTHEW 23:37)

Jesus could not have been more direct in His words against the Pharisees and scribes. He described them with piercing words, calling them whitewashed tombs—beautiful on the outside, full of dead men's bones inside (see Matthew 23:27). We can imagine the initial shock this caused among the listening crowd. However, having lived under the domination of the Pharisees, many in the crowd likely agreed with Jesus. He said fearlessly what many had thought quietly to themselves.

Of course, Jesus' final words of condemnation of the Pharisees were not well received by them. Publicly disgraced and humiliated by Him, they stored up their wrath and unleashed it on Jesus at His Jewish trials. After condemning Him, they blindfolded Him and struck Him with their fists. This violence was the very result that Jesus sought. While the Pharisees and scribes wouldn't help men carry heavy spiritual burdens, they could condemn Jesus to die. By that death, the burden of sin was lifted from all people.

After Jesus confronted the Pharisees and scribes, He spoke to the people of Jerusalem. Jesus looked over the city upon which He had put His name for so many centuries and generations. Despite that boundless love and care by God, Jesus saw unbelief and rejection. Further showing His love, He wept for the devastation they were bringing upon themselves. Later, as He carried His cross through the streets of Jerusalem, women of Jerusalem wept for Him in pity. Jesus told them not to weep for Him, but for themselves and their children. His concern was for us and our salvation to the end.

The hypocritical show of the Pharisees' righteousness continued after Jesus' death and resurrection. When Stephen was witnessing to the Jewish high court, he condemned them, saying, "You stiff-necked people, uncircumcised in heart and ears, you always resist the Holy Spirit" (Acts 7:51). They boiled over in rage as they took him out of the city to kill him. It was a young Pharisee named Saul who held their coats as they stoned Stephen to death. Yet Christ converted Saul on the road to Damascus, and he became who we know as the powerful apostle Paul, missionary to the Gentiles. The hard-hearted Pharisee became the one who turned hearts and minds to Christ.

Dear Savior, You have borne the hatred of the world and yet You also carried the sins of all, even those who condemned You. Remind us of Your power and love shown on the cross. Amen.

FATAL PRIDE

[The scribes and Pharisees] do all their deeds to be seen by others. (MATTHEW 23:5)

Throughout Matthew, indeed all of the sacred Scriptures, God talks of true righteousness and the false righteousness practiced by the scribes and Pharisees.

Matthew 6:1

"Beware of practicing your righteousness before other people in order to be seen by them." In the Sermon on the Mount, Matthew 5–7, Jesus already had strong words against the Pharisees. They made a vain show of their street-corner prayers, their fasting, and their temple offerings. It was all done to be praised by others. But the Son of God saw through their vanity and knew the hardness of their hearts.

Matthew 20:27–28

"The Son of Man came not to be served but to serve, and to give His life as a ransom for many." If anyone could boast of true holiness and the knowledge of the Father, it would be Jesus. However, He is the greatest proof of the truth that the one who humbles himself will be exalted. He was obedient to death, even the death on the cross, but therefore God highly exalted Him above every name (see Philippians 2:8–9). By service even unto death, Jesus showed His true glory.

Matthew 5:20

"For I tell you, unless your righteousness exceeds that of the scribes and Pharisees, you will never enter the kingdom of heaven." After hearing Jesus attack the scribes and Pharisees, perhaps some in the crowd thought that Jesus was lowering the demands of the Kingdom. However, early in His ministry, Jesus had already pointed out that a greater righteousness was needed. How could anyone do more than the Pharisees? No one could, except for the absolutely holy Son of God who would give His life to bring righteousness to the world.

Zechariah 7:9

"Thus says the LORD of hosts, 'Render true judgments, show kindness and mercy to one another.'" The Pharisees perfected the smallest actions of spiritual devotion, giving a tenth of their spices. But they failed in the qualities that mattered: justice and mercy and faithfulness. God seeks kindness and mercy to the widow and orphan (see v. 10). These qualities benefit others unlike the empty show that the Pharisees were putting on.

Matthew 3:7

"When he saw many of the Pharisees and Sadducees coming to his baptism, [John] said to them, 'You brood of vipers! Who warned you to flee from the wrath to come?'" John the Baptist spoke of the Pharisees in almost the same words Jesus used in Matthew 23:33. Now in the last condemnation, Jesus dismisses the Pharisees to the coming judgment. They had no interest in repentance and forgiveness, so judgment would be their end.

Our Savior, You spoke hard words to the Pharisees who refused to see You as the Savior. Give us the faith to know You rightly so we might live forever. Amen.

THE TROUBLE WITH THE SCRIBES AND PHARISEES

So, do and observe whatever they tell you, but not the works they do. For they preach, but do not practice. (MATTHEW 23:3)

This passage raises some difficult questions:

Who are the scribes and Pharisees?

The scribes were recognized as the experts in the Torah of God (what we would consider the whole counsel of God, both Law and Gospel). The scribes were copyists, systematically copying the biblical scrolls by hand. While they were very familiar with the texts, they misinterpreted the Scriptures to be a collection of laws by which one could live a righteous life and earn heaven. The Pharisees were laypeople who committed themselves to live holy lives by carefully following these rules of the scribes.

Why does Jesus say to practice and observe what the Pharisees say but not what they do?

When the scribes and Pharisees were quoting the Word of God, that divine command still stood. Their hypocrisy and false teachings did not cancel the truth of God's Word when they read it. So today, we can still hear God's truth when the Bible's message is read and rightly preached, even when the preacher is a mere man and a sinner—as all people are.

What are the heavy burdens the scribes and Pharisees laid on people?

The scribes and rabbis had developed a whole set of man-made laws. They saw these laws as a hedge around the Commandments. If you obeyed their laws and traditions, you would be keeping God's Commandments. So they had rules about what chores could and could not be done on the Sabbath, for example. While it might be appealing to have someone tell you what to do, in the end, no one could keep all these extra rules. In pursuing their perfection, they watered down God's commands and failed to understand God's intent that we would be saved by His gracious promise of forgiveness through the coming Messiah, Jesus Christ.

What did Jesus mean by "clean the inside of the cup and the plate" in Matthew 23:26?

Jesus is speaking of the way the scribes and Pharisees were preoccupied with controlling their outward behavior to impress other people with their "holiness." They ignored their inner thoughts and desires, which were filled with sinful intentions. They carefully hid these desires from other people, forgetting that God judges the sins of our hearts and minds. When those interior desires are cleansed by God through repentance and absolution, then the whole life will be clean in God's eyes.

What did Jesus mean in verse 32, "Fill up, then, the measure of your fathers"?

Earlier generations of Israelites had persecuted and killed the prophets God sent them throughout the Old Testament. Now they were plotting to kill God's Son—a greater sin than even that of their fathers, which they claim they would not have done if they had lived in that time. Such blind hypocrisy!

Dear Jesus, keep us from the vanity of the Pharisees. Hold us firmly in the truth of Your teaching. Amen.

OUR ONLY TRUE TEACHER

And call no man your father on earth for you have one Father, who is in heaven. Neither be called instructors, for you have one instructor, the Christ. (MATTHEW 23:9-10)

Jesus gives seven warnings of woe in Matthew 23. In the Bible, seven is a number describing the completion of God's work. In these seven woes, Jesus exposes the true nature of the scribes and Pharisees, who live as hypocrites, pretending to be sincere worshipers of God when, deep in their hearts, they are unrepentant unbelievers. The scribes and Pharisees wanted the praise and position of being esteemed teachers. But Jesus makes it clear that we have only one Father in heaven and one true Teacher, the Son of God. We hear His words with faith brought by the Holy Spirit, who alone can turn hearts and minds to the truth.

In the service of Confession at the beginning of our worship, we are called to come before the Lord with honest and sincere hearts. We are to regret our sins of thought, word, and deed, seeking God's forgiveness and imploring Him to be merciful to us for Jesus' sake. Jesus' tears over Jerusalem reassure us that He is eager to save us and gather us under His wings for forgiveness, healing, and strength. And His Words of Absolution, given to His gathered disciples on the night after His resurrection, assure us of that forgiveness. His death was the single, lasting sacrifice that brought forgiveness to the world. This mercy is assured in His glorious resurrection.

Many hymns speak of God bringing us to faith and salvation. One that is especially well known is "Just as I Am, without One Plea" (*LSB* 570). Stanzas 4 and 5 describe our great need for God's welcome and restoration:

> Just as I am, poor, wretched, blind;
> Sight, riches, healing of the mind,
> Yea, all I need, in Thee to find,
> O Lamb of God, I come, I come.

> Just as I am, Thou wilt receive,
> Wilt welcome, pardon, cleanse, relieve;
> Because Thy promise I believe,
> O Lamb of God, I come, I come.

It is tempting to go through the motions when we gather in worship, distracted by the things we are eager to do that day or week. Jesus calls us to focus on the present moment. None of the earthly things that preoccupy us today will matter on the day He returns in glory. All that matters is how we stand in relation to Him by confession and faith. So let us draw near to God with true and contrite hearts, eager to receive the forgiveness and restoration God wishes to give to us for Jesus' sake.

Heavenly Father, draw us to You alone as our Father and make us listen to our only true, heavenly Teacher, Your Son. In Jesus' name. Amen.

THE PLOT TO KILL JESUS

WEEK 33—MATTHEW 26:1–16

When Jesus had finished all these sayings, He said to His disciples, "You know that after two days the Passover is coming, and the Son of Man will be delivered up to be crucified."

Then the chief priests and the elders of the people gathered in the palace of the high priest, whose name was Caiaphas, and plotted together in order to arrest Jesus by stealth and kill Him. But they said, "Not during the feast, lest there be an uproar among the people."

Now when Jesus was at Bethany in the house of Simon the leper, a woman came up to Him with an alabaster flask of very expensive ointment, and she poured it on His head as He reclined at table. And when the disciples saw it, they were indignant, saying, "Why this waste? For this could have been sold for a large sum and given to the poor." But Jesus, aware of this, said to them, "Why do you trouble the woman? For she has done a beautiful thing to Me. For you always have the poor with you, but you will not always have Me. In pouring this ointment on My body, she has done it to prepare Me for burial. Truly, I say to you, wherever this gospel is proclaimed in the whole world, what she has done will also be told in memory of her."

Then one of the twelve, whose name was Judas Iscariot, went to the chief priests and said, "What will you give me if I deliver Him over to you?" And they paid him thirty pieces of silver. And from that moment he sought an opportunity to betray Him.

PLOTTING AND BETRAYAL

Then the chief priests and the elders of the people gathered in the palace of the high priest, whose name was Caiaphas, and plotted together in order to arrest Jesus by stealth and kill Him. (MATTHEW 26:3–4)

This text comes at the end of Jesus' earthly ministry. During this time, Jesus continually spoke about what was to come and warned His disciples that His time on earth was drawing to an end. It begins with "After saying all these things" because before this, Jesus had been teaching them about events that would happen between His death, resurrection, ascension, and His return on the Last Day. He knows He will soon leave them and wants to prepare them for what is to come and teach them how they are to live their lives.

Jesus had been stirring up the chief priests, who were looking closely for a way to silence Him and protect their authority in the community. Before this was Palm Sunday, and huge crowds were in the city for the Passover festivities—so the chief priests wanted to keep their hands clean during this time. In John 11:47-51, it is clear that some of the ruling Jews were afraid Jesus would use the Passover to proclaim Himself the Messianic King and try to drive out the Roman government. To them, this was futile and only would result in a massacre of Jews. For the sake of the nation, one man must die, so they plotted to kill Him. But they all agreed this would have to wait until after the Passover feast. They could not see any way to get their hands on Jesus with the large crowds filling the city and hanging on His every word.

Seemingly, the solution comes to them in the form of Judas. Judas approaches them, after being rebuked when he criticized Jesus for allowing expensive oil to be poured on Him instead of selling it and using the profits for the poor. Judas tells the Jewish authorities that he will find the right time to capture Jesus. Judas had witnessed a beautiful act of love and, instead, saw it as a waste of money. Matthew 26:8 shows that Judas was not alone in criticizing the expensive anointing—other disciples also questioned Jesus about the seeming waste. But the Gospel of John shows us why Judas instigated this criticism. Judas—their bookkeeper—was a thief, stealing from the treasury of the disciples. Since a denarius was a day's wages, Judas knew nearly a whole year's worth of salary was slipping through his fingers. Or, more accurately, dripping off of Jesus' head.

While all of this plotting for Jesus' betrayal, arrest, and crucifixion is going on, however, there is also love. The Gospel of Matthew shares with us the devotion of the woman who breaks a jar of expensive perfume to pour on Jesus' head. It is a simple act, and it may even seem out of place with what is happening, but the act of taking this expensive jar and extending love to Jesus is wonderful. This act acknowledges her love for Jesus and her recognition of who Jesus is.

Heavenly Father, thank You for Jesus' ministry. May we read these words, meditate on them, and share Your love to the ends of the earth. In Jesus' name. Amen.

A WOMAN'S SILENT TESTIMONY

Jesus . . . said to them, "Why do you trouble the woman? For she has done a beautiful thing to Me. . . . In pouring this ointment on My body, she has done it to prepare Me for burial." (MATTHEW 26:10, 12)

This text in Matthew sets up the Passion of Jesus in the book of Matthew. We are given a glimpse into the end of Jesus' earthly ministry and the event that starts His journey to the cross. This event was the historical story that led Judas to betray Jesus and the price he was offered to do so. This was not something that happened overnight—at the beginning of chapter 26, it is clear that the chief priests and elders have been following Jesus in His ministry closely and that His popularity is growing. The crowds are getting bigger and bigger, and they see this as a threat. They now follow Jesus looking for a time to kill him.

Jesus continues to preach and teach His disciples and close followers. Simon the leper is one of those, and Jesus is there at his home resting. Jesus encounters a woman who pours oil on His head, and the disciples are perplexed by this act. Not only are they perplexed but they remark that this is a waste of money. Jesus is quick to defend her and corrects them, telling them that He will not be with them always, and she is honoring Him now. He also remarks that this kind gesture will be remembered whenever the Gospel is told (v. 13). Judas responds out of frustration and greed. Unable to get his hands on the precious oil, which was worth a year's wages, he seeks out the chief priests and settles for the price they set, thirty silver coins. With coins in hand, he agrees to work on finding the right time and place for them to arrest Jesus away from the crowds.

As Christians, we read this narrative with sadness and anger for the disciples' reaction, as well as Judas and the chief priests, but we also know the rest of the story. This leads us to Maundy Thursday and Good Friday. Through all of those events, the fragrance of that oil will linger, a silent witness of a woman's faith and devotion. She has prepared Jesus' body for the suffering and brutal treatment He will endure, as well as the brief, quiet rest in His tomb. On Easter Sunday, when Jesus will rise triumphant, the disciples will finally understand how His suffering and death saved the world. And as they tell the story of His loving sacrifice, they will recount hers as well.

Heavenly Father, we thank You for raising up faithful followers like this dear, unnamed woman who poured her expensive oil on our Savior. Thank You for His faithful journey to the cross. In Jesus' name. Amen.

DEMONSTRATIONS OF LOVE

Now when Jesus was at Bethany in the house of Simon the leper, a woman came up to Him with an alabaster flask of very expensive ointment, and she poured it on His head as He reclined at table. (MATTHEW 26:6–7)

These verses point us back to Jesus' mission in several ways. The greatest of these is love. As Jesus shared His love in words and deeds throughout His ministry, we see believers respond with great love for Him—very clearly in the case of this woman and the oil she lavishes on her Savior. She sacrifices a year's worth of wages, selflessly showing her love, care, and devotion for Jesus. She does this with loving kindness, and Jesus is quick to recognize this act, defend her costly sacrifice, and acknowledge that what she has done will be a part of the Gospel story forever. The simple act of waiting till Jesus was resting to pour the ointment in His hair also foreshadowed the sweet fragrance that would surround Jesus' sacrifice, a pleasing aroma to God, clear up to the hour when He would be buried in the tomb.

Her act of devotion is stirred by the unbounded love that Jesus has repeatedly shown throughout His ministry—and will show in an even greater way through the coming suffering, death, and resurrection that will win His great victory for us over sin, death, and Satan. Even though Judas will betray Him and the chief priests and soldiers plot to kill Him, Jesus is victorious. He has the last say, and there is nothing that can be done to change what God the Father has ordained.

Jesus also shows that ministry takes place in the home as He brings the Word to the home of Simon the leper. Matthew points out that Simon was a leper. Before Jesus came, he had been considered an outcast and driven from his home and society. Earlier, Jesus had cleansed Simon of his leprosy, allowing him to return to his home and family. Now we see Jesus enjoying Simon's hospitality as together they celebrate the restoration Jesus had accomplished. How wonderful that before the Passion and suffering that lies before Him, Jesus goes out of His way to spend one of His special, final evenings in Simon's home.

Throughout His earthly ministry, Jesus preaches, teaches, heals, and retreats to people's homes. He spent most of His time with the people, not in the temple courts. Jesus makes clear that His Gospel goes everywhere and is for all people. To this very day, He comes and stays in our homes with our families.

Jesus' final journey will not be easy, and the last few verses of our section point us to that. Although all the disciples are noted in Matthew 26:8, it is in Matthew 26:14 where Judas goes to see the chief priests. In the exchange between verses 14–16, we see that the value Judas and the chief priests place upon Jesus' life is thirty silver pieces. The price of thirty silver pieces also appears in Exodus 21:32; it was the price given to a master to repay him if one of his slaves had been killed. The cost of the slave's life is equated to the cost of Jesus' life. Quite a contrast to the woman who lavished a year's worth of wages on Jesus' head.

Lord Jesus, thank You for Your great love and ultimate sacrifice. Fill me with faith and gratitude that I may cherish You above all and love my neighbor more than myself. Amen.

JESUS' ANOINTING IN JOHN'S GOSPEL

Mary therefore took a pound of expensive ointment made from pure nard, and anointed the feet of Jesus and wiped His feet with her hair. (JOHN 12:3)

We have been looking at this passage from the Gospel of Matthew. When we look at similarities in the other Gospels as well as other Scripture references, we get a bigger picture of the life of Jesus. Matthew, Mark, and Luke give us the same time period for this event—two days before Passover, which we often refer to as Holy Tuesday. We also know that the chief priests and elders were gathered at the palace in preparation for the Passover as shared in John 6:4. This feast of the Jews was centered upon the deliverance of the Israelites from Egypt through the blood of the lamb. In Matthew, it indicates that they are in the palace, as shared in John 18:15 and Revelation 11:2, which was just outside of the temple that they would enter to celebrate Passover. Jesus knew what was to come, and He was preparing His disciples for His death and crucifixion. He says this in Matthew 26:1–2 but He foretells His death also in Matthew 20:18 and John 7:33 where He indicates that it is only a little longer that He will be with them.

In John 12:3, we see another woman anoint Jesus with expensive ointment. Six days before His death, He is anointed by Mary, the sister of Martha and Lazarus, whom Jesus raised from the dead. But unlike the woman in Simon's house, Mary anoints Jesus' feet, not His head. We may well be looking at two different anointings that both occurred in this final week of Jesus' life. But just as in the case with the woman in Simon's house, the disciples are quick to rebuke Mary and what she was doing. In verse 5, they say that it is a waste and could be used to help the poor. In the book of Matthew, this is spoken by the disciples, but John 13:29 indicates that Judas took advantage of his role as the treasurer to steal from the funds. Clearly seeing such a huge amount of money "wasted" on Jesus hit him hard, knowing he could have gotten his hands on it.

Already, we see the greed that led Judas to go to the chief priests to ask the cost of delivering Jesus to them. For Judas, Jesus was not worth a year's wages, but only the price of repayment for a dead slave. Acts 1:16 reveals that Judas's betrayal was to fulfill David's prophecy, and the cost of thirty silver coins was revealed in Zechariah. Ultimately, Jesus foretold of what was to happen earlier in Matthew 20:18–19 and all was fulfilled.

Heavenly Father, thank You for Your Word that reveals Your great salvation plan to us daily. Grant us open eyes and ears to read, mark, and inwardly digest it. In Jesus' name. Amen.

A LESSON IN GIVING

Why do you trouble the woman? For she has done a beautiful thing to Me. (MATTHEW 26:10)

This week's passage raises several challenges:

Why did Jesus' death take place during the Passover if the chief priests wanted to wait until after the feast?

Jesus' enemies wanted Him dead, but they could see no way to lay their hands on Him while the Passover crowds thronged Jerusalem. When Judas offered to betray Him, they were able to move up their deadly plot. But God scheduled Jesus' death for the Passover. The first Passover was in Exodus 12. Each Israelite family killed a Passover lamb and then painted its blood on the lintel and doorposts of their home. That night, the angel of death passed over their houses while it killed all the firstborn males of Egypt. Jesus is the Passover Lamb who came as our ultimate Sacrifice. His blood was painted on the cross, shed for the salvation of the world. Because He died for our sins, the angel of death will pass over us on Judgment Day. Through our Baptism, we are covered in Jesus' blood, marking us as children of God—our home is in heaven.

Why did the woman anoint Jesus' head with oil?

This woman was so filled with love and gratitude for her Savior that she wanted to honor Him in an opportunity that she knew may never happen again. She knew the cost of the oil that she was using, but it showed that no expense is enough to honor Jesus, our Lord and our Savior. She was humbled for the opportunity to bless Him after His travel and for what was to come—bearing the burden of the whole world. When the love in your heart is so overwhelming, you must share it, especially when it is Jesus.

What is the lesson here about money, expense, and giving?

We are to give to God with all our heart—and generously. The woman gave something that was not only expensive but showed how much she loved Jesus. This was not just a physical gift but represented a total surrender of body, heart, and mind. As Christians, we should reflect this and give wholeheartedly of our time, talent, and treasure from our heart, reflecting that all good and gracious gifts come from the Father. When we give like this, our Father in heaven recognizes this and, just as Jesus commended the woman for her gift, God commends us through His Son and the Holy Spirit, who guards and protects us.

Heavenly Father, may we show our love and gratitude to You in how we love and serve our neighbor. In Jesus' name. Amen.

REMEMBERED BY OUR LORD AND GOD

What she has done will also be told in memory of her. (MATTHEW 26:13)

The course for Jesus has been laid before Him since even before the fall of mankind in Genesis. As we read this account as Christians, we know the rest of the story. Jesus predicts His death, the woman pours the oil, and Judas betrays Jesus, handing Him over to the chief priests. We read this with sadness in our heart but also with thanksgiving. This course is difficult, but it is not done in vain. Jesus knew what His Father brought Him into the world to do, and He would finish it—dying and rising for the world. That truth allows us to read these verses with anticipated joy, knowing the Passover Lamb will give the ultimate sacrifice, shedding His blood for the world—including you.

Jesus is again showing His love for His Bride, the church, and at the same time, we see His human nature in the love He receives from the woman. The oil was not only expensive, but it was also very fragrant and left a sweet smell in the home even after Jesus left to go on His way, which would remind them of what had happened there. Jesus could have rebuked her but, instead, He commends her for what she has done for Him. These verses remind us that Jesus' earthly ministry was for His people. He continues this ministry through His people today—our pastors, teachers and those who are trained to share the Word and Sacraments with us. This woman is forever remembered for what she has done and has been written into the Gospel story. He says that this act is important to Him and for them because He will not always be there. Although we do not see Jesus today, we know He is present in His Word and Sacraments. And because we know He is present, we, too, should share the sweet fragrance of His love with all those we encounter, giving generously of ourselves and not being selfish with the gifts that were given to us.

When we furnish and decorate our churches, God is well pleased because we glorify Him with our gifts and set God's glory before all who will gather at His feet to hear His Word and receive His Sacraments throughout the generations to come.

Week after week, we remember the story of our Savior who humbled Himself, took our sins, suffered and died on the cross, and rose to life on the third day. And our Lord remembers and still proclaims the loving sacrifice of an unnamed woman who poured her ointment on His head while He sat at table in the home of a cleansed leper named Simon.

Heavenly Father, thank You for loving me, a poor, miserable sinner. In Jesus' name. Amen.

THE LAST SUPPER, PREPARATION, AND WASHING OF FEET

WEEK 34—JOHN 13:1–17

Now before the Feast of the Passover, when Jesus knew that His hour had come to depart out of this world to the Father, having loved His own who were in the world, He loved them to the end. During supper, when the devil had already put it into the heart of Judas Iscariot, Simon's son, to betray Him, Jesus, knowing that the Father had given all things into His hands, and that He had come from God and was going back to God, rose from supper. He laid aside His outer garments, and taking a towel, tied it around His waist. Then He poured water into a basin and began to wash the disciples' feet and to wipe them with the towel that was wrapped around Him. He came to Simon Peter, who said to Him, "Lord, do You wash my feet?" Jesus answered him, "What I am doing you do not understand now, but afterward you will understand." Peter said to Him, "You shall never wash my feet." Jesus answered him, "If I do not wash you, you have no share with Me." Simon Peter said to Him, "Lord, not my feet only but also my hands and my head!" Jesus said to him, "The one who has bathed does not need to wash, except for his feet, but is completely clean. And you are clean, but not every one of you." For He knew who was to betray Him; that was why He said, "Not all of you are clean."

When He had washed their feet and put on His outer garments and resumed His place, He said to them, "Do you understand what I have done to you? You call Me Teacher and Lord, and you are right, for so I am. If I then, your Lord and Teacher, have washed your feet, you also ought to wash one another's feet. For I have given you an example, that you also should do just as I have done to you. Truly, truly, I say to you, a servant is not greater than his master, nor is a messenger greater than the one who sent him. If you know these things, blessed are you if you do them."

CELEBRATING THE PASSOVER

And on the first day of Unleavened Bread, when they sacrificed the Passover lamb, His disciples said to Him, "Where will You have us go and prepare for You to eat the Passover?" (MARK 14:12)

The Passover was a time when the Jews celebrated God's deliverance of the people of Israel from slavery in Egypt. You can read more about it in Exodus 12. The Passover meal was a meal of several foods, including unleavened bread, lamb, and bitter herbs. In Egypt, after sacrificing the lamb, God directed the people of Israel to spread the lamb's blood on their doorposts. This marked their homes so that the angel of death passed over them (hence the name *Passover*) and did not harm anyone in the house. The blood of the lamb protected them. Those homes that did not have the blood of the lamb on their doorposts experienced tragedy. The firstborn son in every home without the protection of the blood of the lamb died. When the firstborn of the Egyptians died, Pharaoh, king of Egypt, freed the Israelites.

The people of Israel were instructed to celebrate the Passover every year. As Jesus prepares to celebrate the Passover in our texts, it is the Thursday of Holy Week. He has entered triumphantly into Jerusalem on Sunday, cleared the temple on Monday, taught in the temple on Tuesday, and here we are, ready for the Passover on Thursday.

As Jesus prepares to celebrate the Passover meal with His disciples, He will make all things new. He will usher in a new Meal from this ancient celebration, a Meal in which Jesus is present in unleavened bread. Jesus will institute a new Meal that we celebrate more than once a year: the Lord's Supper, where Jesus is present in, with, and under bread and wine to forgive our sins.

Then, on the following day, Good Friday, Jesus will be the Passover Lamb that dies once for all. By the blood of Jesus, our true Passover Lamb, we will not only be protected but forgiven. Jesus will take the punishment of the death of the firstborn, but Jesus will become the firstborn in a new and cosmically different way: Jesus becomes the firstborn from the dead. Jesus is risen from the dead, ascended, enthroned, and returning soon. When He returns, He will raise everyone from the dead, just as He is risen from the dead, never to die again.

Jesus, thank You for giving Yourself as our Passover Lamb that forgives sin once for all. As we celebrate the Lord's Supper, keep our hope fixed on You, the firstborn from the dead. Amen.

JESUS WASHES UNWORTHY FEET

[Jesus] laid aside His outer garments, and taking a towel, tied it around His waist. Then He poured water into a basin and began to wash the disciples' feet and to wipe them with the towel that was wrapped around Him. (JOHN 13:4–5)

As Jesus draws closer to the cross, the plot to betray Him takes shape. Judas has agreed with the chief priests to betray Jesus for thirty pieces of silver. Jesus, of course, knows this. He knows everything. Yet despite knowing that Judas will betray Him, Jesus still washes Judas's feet. Jesus still serves him. Despite knowing that Peter would deny Him, Jesus still washes Peter's feet. Despite knowing all of His disciples will abandon Him, Jesus still celebrates the Passover with them, institutes the Lord's Supper among them, teaches them, and prays for them in the hours before His death.

The reading for this week shows us the depth of Jesus' humility and service. As Jesus washes His disciples' feet, He is taking on a task only slaves could be forced to do. The feet of His disciples were all undoubtedly filthy, walking in sandals or bare feet in the sand and dust day after day. Yet Jesus grabs His basin of water and a towel and washes them one by one.

Peter misunderstands, as he so often does—Peter does not want to see his Lord humiliated like this and refuses to let Jesus wash his feet. Jesus corrects Peter. But then Peter misunderstands in the opposite direction, demanding Jesus wash his head and hands as well. Jesus then calls on His disciples to wash one another's feet, to follow His example of humble service.

How can we follow Jesus' example in our service to one another? Like Peter, how have we misunderstood, objected, or been reluctant when others have sought to serve us?

Jesus does not exclude anyone, not even Judas. Who have we excluded for whatever reason from our service? Whose feet are we being called to wash rather than send away?

We are told before Jesus washes His disciples' feet that Jesus knew "that the Father had given all things into His hands, and that He had come from God and was going back to God" (John 13:3). In this confidence, Jesus humbly serves.

We, too, know that Jesus has given us all we have. We also know that we have been born of God and will spend eternity with Jesus. In this confidence, we can humbly serve as well, following Jesus' example.

Jesus, thank You for the example You have set for us of loving, humble service. Help us to set aside our desire for power and control. Remove from us any unforgiveness or prejudice that would prevent us from serving others. Amen.

HUMBLE SERVICE

If I then, your Lord and Teacher, have washed your feet, you also ought to wash one another's feet. For I have given you an example, that you also should do just as I have done to you. (JOHN 13:14–15)

Jesus' mission to save the world from sin and death through His death and resurrection requires the sad and tragic reality that Jesus must die. His death is brought about by the plotting and scheming of religious leaders of whom John writes, "[Jesus] came to His own, but His own people did not receive Him" (John 1:11). The scheming religious leaders found aid from an unlikely source, one of Jesus' own hand-picked disciples: Judas Iscariot. Judas's betrayal of Jesus leads to the most important piece of Jesus' mission: His suffering, death, and resurrection.

Likewise, as Jesus washes His disciples' feet, He points us toward another important aspect of His mission: to set an example for us. Jesus, as the truly divine, truly human, sinless Son of God, is the only human being to ever live a life free from sin. If we follow the example of any other human being aside from Jesus, we will find ourselves following the example of a similarly sinful person.

But Jesus sets a perfect example for us to follow, a holy and innocent example beyond compare. In John 13, Jesus tells us outright that He is setting an example for us. As Jesus washes His disciples' feet, He shows us the kind of humble service and love we are called to emulate and imitate. We are called to be those who serve. We are not called to claim more power for ourselves. We are not called to demand that others serve us. We are called to follow Jesus and His example of humility and service.

Jesus takes this humility and service to its ultimate zenith in His sacrificial death for us. Paul encourages us to follow Jesus' example with these words:

Have this mind among yourselves, which is yours in Christ Jesus, who, though He was in the form of God, did not count equality with God a thing to be grasped, but emptied Himself, by taking the form of a servant, being born in the likeness of men. And being found in human form, He humbled Himself by becoming obedient to the point of death, even death on a cross. (Philippians 2:5–8)

May we likewise empty ourselves in humble service as we follow Jesus.

Jesus, You have washed away all of our sins and left us an example of service and humility. Strip us of our selfish pride and hunger for power, so that we might better serve the world and follow You. Amen.

A LARGE, UPPER ROOM

Wherever he enters, say to the master of the house, "The Teacher says, Where is My guest room, where I may eat the Passover with My disciples?" (MARK 14:14)

As Jesus prepares to celebrate the Passover with His disciples, one of the more interesting connections I see is to the location. The ESV translates the Greek word for the place where Jesus will celebrate the Passover as "guest room." This same Greek word is used in the Christmas narrative of Luke 2. After Jesus is born, we are told that the reason He is laid in a manger is "because there was no place for them in the inn" (Luke 2:7). The word that is translated as "inn" here is the same Greek word used for "guest room" in Mark 14.

It is interesting that when Jesus was born, there was no room for Him in the guest room, inn, or lodging place. He's laid in a bare manger, in the most unassuming of rooms. But now, as He is about to fulfill the prophetic words of the Scriptures by suffering, dying, and rising again for the sins of the world, the guest room is not only available and reserved for Jesus, but it comes fully furnished. It is a large upper room, likely in the home of a wealthy family.

After Jesus' death, resurrection, and ascension, 120 of His followers gather together in an upper room, praying and waiting for the gift of the Holy Spirit that will arrive on Pentecost. Could it be that the upper room of Acts 1 is the Upper Room from Mark 14? We cannot say for certain, but it would be logical that the same patron would continue to provide hospitality to Jesus' followers.

Another interesting connection I would like to point out is related to Jesus washing His disciples' feet. Jesus calls on His followers to wash each other's feet, to follow His example. Yet, there is only one other place I know of in the New Testament where we see foot washing. It is in 1 Timothy 5. Paul is giving instructions to Timothy regarding widows. Paul is hopeful that widows in Timothy's care will be those who have a reputation for good works, who have shown hospitality, and who have "washed the feet of the saints" (1 Timothy 5:10). It is not entirely clear how the ritual of foot washing was appropriated by the earliest Christians, but we see evidence that, at the very least, there were widows in Ephesus (where Timothy was stationed) who were washing the feet of their fellow Christians.

The hospitality of welcoming guests and washing feet may go overlooked in our day and age, but for Jesus and the culture He was born into, these were of high value.

Dear Jesus, thank You for making Your dwelling among us. Strengthen us to make room and show hospitality to others. Embolden us to follow Your example and wash the feet of our dear brothers and sisters in Christ. Amen.

JUDAS'S BETRAYAL

And as they were reclining at table and eating, Jesus said, "Truly, I say to you, one of you will betray Me, one who is eating with Me." (MARK 14:18)

One of the most challenging questions when reading these sections of Scripture is this: Why would Judas betray Jesus? Why would one of Jesus' closest followers and friends do this to Him? How could Judas, after spending three years learning from Jesus about how much God loves us, go and betray Jesus? It's not an easy question.

The Gospel accounts tell us several things about Judas. John tells us that Judas "was a thief, and having charge of the moneybag he used to help himself to what was put into it" (John 12:6). And our reading from John 13 this week also reveals this: "The devil had already put it into the heart of Judas Iscariot, Simon's son, to betray Him" (John 13:2). Satan had placed this betrayal on Judas's heart. And Judas obliged.

One of the saddest things about Judas's story is that after Jesus is condemned, he realizes the mistake he has made, the sin he has committed. Matthew tells us, "Then when Judas, His betrayer, saw that Jesus was condemned, he changed his mind and brought back the thirty pieces of silver to the chief priests and the elders, saying, 'I have sinned by betraying innocent blood'" (Matthew 27:3-4). The chief priests and elders' cold and unfeeling response to Judas is absolutely heartbreaking. They tell Judas, "What is that to us? See to it yourself" (Matthew 27:4).

Judas regrets and confesses his sin, but he has gone to the wrong place and the wrong people with his confession. The chief priests have no forgiveness. Only Jesus does.

It is fruitless to guess or speculate at what might have happened if Judas had not died by suicide, if Judas had waited and, like Peter, returned to Jesus after His resurrection. What might have been is hidden from us.

Yet we see how Jesus acts in mercy toward His other disciples who deny Him and abandon Him. He restores them. He forgives them. He appears to them and sends them out as witnesses of His resurrection. He sends the Holy Spirit upon them.

As we continue to follow Jesus, we bask in Jesus' promises. His promise to always be with us. His promise to hear our prayers. His promise to forgive us. His promise to seek and to save the lost.

Why does Judas betray Jesus? Satan spurs Judas's heart toward betrayal, and Judas was ready to accept Satan's proposal.

Lord Jesus, guard us from the presence of Satan. Protect us from the evil Satan would persuade us to participate in. Bring us to repentance and forgive us when we go astray. Amen.

ALL ABOUT PREPARATION

And the disciples set out and went to the city and found it just as He had told them, and they prepared the Passover. (MARK 14:16)

This week's readings are all about preparation—preparation for the Last Supper, preparation for Jesus' sacrificial death, and preparation of the disciples for all that is about to happen.

In our worship services, the Lord's Supper is one place where preparation is particularly evident. Before the service, a volunteer (perhaps an elder or a member of the altar guild) will make the altar ready, placing bread and wine into vessels that are then placed upon the altar and covered. During the service, the pastor will remove the covering and set out the elements, preparing them to be blessed. The congregation will sing and pray, giving thanks for all the wondrous gifts God has given us in Jesus.

Then the pastor will prepare the Lord's Supper by speaking the very words Jesus speaks. In so doing, we are reminded of the context, "Our Lord Jesus Christ, on the night when He was betrayed" (*LSB*, p. 162). After these words of our Lord, we are invited forward to receive Christ's body and blood for our forgiveness. We are invited to prepare our hearts to receive the Lord's Supper before coming forward. Many people sit quietly in contemplation and repentance. Some perhaps read the prayer from the first page of *Lutheran Service Book*. Some prepare by singing a hymn before they are invited forward to receive Christ's body and blood.

When the preparation is finished, we receive. For Jesus, when the preparation is finished, when the disciples' feet are all washed, when the Passover meal is complete, when Judas has left and gathered the troops, the time arrives for the sacrifice of the true Passover Lamb: Jesus.

In giving His very body and blood for us, Jesus sacrifices Himself. Countless Passover lambs had been sacrificed through the centuries up to that point. And they would have been sacrificed again and again year after year for the sins of the people. But in Jesus, the true and ultimate Passover Lamb, His sacrifice is done once for all. The sacrifice of Jesus forgives not just the sins of the past year but the sins of all time. The sacrifice of Jesus forgives not just the sins of the Jewish people but the sins of all people throughout time and space.

Lord Jesus, at Your gracious invitation, prepare our hearts to receive Your body and blood for our forgiveness. Thank You for preparing this mysterious Meal for us, and promising to be present there for our forgiveness, life, and salvation. Amen.

THE LAST SUPPER, HOLY COMMUNION

WEEK 35—MATTHEW 26:26–35

Now as they were eating, Jesus took bread, and after blessing it broke it and gave it to the disciples, and said, "Take, eat; this is My body." And He took a cup, and when He had given thanks He gave it to them, saying, "Drink of it, all of you, for this is My blood of the covenant, which is poured out for many for the forgiveness of sins. I tell you I will not drink again of this fruit of the vine until that day when I drink it new with you in My Father's kingdom."

And when they had sung a hymn, they went out to the Mount of Olives. Then Jesus said to them, "You will all fall away because of Me this night. For it is written, 'I will strike the shepherd, and the sheep of the flock will be scattered.' But after I am raised up, I will go before you to Galilee." Peter answered Him, "Though they all fall away because of You, I will never fall away." Jesus said to him, "Truly, I tell you, this very night, before the rooster crows, you will deny Me three times." Peter said to Him, "Even if I must die with You, I will not deny You!" And all the disciples said the same.

GOD IS WORKING IN THE WAITING

I tell you I will not drink again of this fruit of the vine until that day when I drink it new with you in My Father's kingdom. (MATTHEW 26:29)

Shoes on, ready to go. The Passover was a meal of anticipation. In Jesus' time, the Jewish people were no longer worried about the Egyptians, but they still felt enslaved to the Romans. They didn't have their freedom; their Promised Land was occupied. They were still longing for freedom, urgently waiting for God to act, earnestly praying it might just even be this night. Some of them were even wondering if Jesus might just be the One to do it.

Instead of celebrating with their families, Jesus' disciples gathered in the room He had chosen. They got everything ready, and they celebrated with a moment of quiet amid a hectic week. For hundreds of years, the same food was made: roast lamb, the sacrifice that died in place of Israel's firstborn (see Exodus 12:6); the bitter herbs of bitter slavery; the salt of generations of tears. Every element had significance, connecting the guests to their shared history as the people of Israel who had been set free.

But that's the thing about the Passover. The first Passover was celebrated *before* God's people were actually free. It was celebrated *in anticipation* of what God was going to do. The firstborn sons of Egypt had not yet been taken, and the people were still enslaved. The only thing that had changed was that the people of God *believed* He would do what He promised. The people of God ate in haste—and hope.

It could not have been easy to eat in the tension of that Maundy Thursday meal. Talks of betrayal, of arrest and trial, of death. Not only this, but Jesus revised the meal. He said that this was His body and His blood. Jesus promised forgiveness of sins. *Who can forgive sins but God alone?* Something was changing during this meal, where the Rabbi who doesn't even have a home of His own now became the host. Freedom was coming again—but a freedom far more expansive than that first Passover. There was no political overthrow, no reclaiming of the Promised Land. Just a man and His eleven disciples, going out to sing a hymn in the garden and wait.

And maybe that's exactly what this Meal is— eating in anticipation of a future you cannot see. Gazing upon the frailty of humanity, even as you witness the power of God. Even when you don't have evidence to believe, do you trust Jesus?

Father in heaven, we are waiting on You, hoping to receive all that You have promised us. We are hoping to receive You. Give us the patience to trust You and see You working in the waiting. In Jesus' name. Amen.

FILLING AND REFINING US

Now as they were eating, Jesus took bread, and after blessing it broke it and gave it to the disciples, and said, "Take, eat; this is My body." (MATTHEW 26:26)

God has been promising and providing for His people ever since He made Adam and Eve in His image. It started with the fruit and seeds (see Genesis 1:29), and it turned into grain and bread (see Genesis 3:18–19), and eventually, animals were given as food too (see Genesis 9:3). God rained down manna from heaven in the wilderness, and Jesus miraculously stretched five loaves for thousands of people. But this meal was the fulfillment of all. This bread, broken by the hands of Jesus, became the blessing of all time for all people.

Jesus was not celebrating a new meal, but an ancient one. The Passover was one of the most important holy days in the life of God's people. And the point Jesus made to His disciples was that He was bringing this meal to completion. "Today this Scripture has been fulfilled in your hearing" might as well have been changed to apply here: "Today, this Scripture has been fulfilled in your eating." Weren't the Israelites saved merely because they ate the meal as God planned? Because they spilled the blood of the lamb as God planned and painted it on their doorframes? That lamb and that meal were a prophecy of the true Lamb and the real Meal.

This was more than a fulfillment of the Passover; it was also a fulfillment of Zechariah 13. "Strike the shepherd . . . I will turn my hand against the little ones . . . and refine them as one refines silver" (Zechariah 13:7, 9). By striking the Shepherd, God was purifying the sheep. Just as God defied the gods of Egypt through the plagues, He was defying the idols of self-righteousness, political power, and religious bureaucracy by putting Jesus to death. All the disciples were about to flee from Jesus, as scared as the Israelites caught between Pharaoh and the Red Sea. God was working even in that. God was fulfilling what He had already spoken. God was fully turning the hearts of His people to Himself.

In just a few hours, Peter and the disciples would prove they needed the refining, that their hearts and wills weren't ready, that they would actually abandon their Messiah. They were trying to operate by their own strength and effort, but they needed to learn to rely on the strength that comes from Jesus alone. God's power would be fulfilled in their weakness. God's love would be clear as often as they come together to drink this cup.

Good Shepherd, thank You for taking upon Yourself the pain of suffering and rejection. Strengthen us through this Meal to confess that You are our God. In Your name we pray. Amen.

OUR GREAT DELIVERER

This is My blood of the covenant, which is poured out for many for the forgiveness of sins. (MATTHEW 26:28)

We need to be delivered from sin. This might seem obvious to some and controversial to others, but the reality is that we cannot pull ourselves out of our desperate situation. We must acknowledge that this is, in part, what God desired, that "all people [would] be saved and come to the knowledge of the truth" (1 Timothy 2:4). God wants to rescue His people. Look through the Old Testament—God is always saving. In fact, Jesus' very name comes from the Hebrew word *yeshua*, which means "salvation"!

A message that began with repentance and a kingdom coming is culminating in a life ending and blood being shed. Why? God could have had the people eat from a tree in Eden to receive life (see Genesis 3:22), but instead, God chose the bread of life. God could have relied on the blood of animals to deliver His people, but God chose the blood of His own Son. *Poured out for the forgiveness of sins.* This is the Kingdom coming, because a new rule is being established. This is repentance, because people are turning to a new source for salvation.

The Passover meal is the celebration of God's deliverance of the people of Israel, out of slavery and into the Promised Land. A lamb was sacrificed to pay for the life of Israel's firstborn, to cover over their own sin. The Old Testament demanded a sacrifice to redeem the firstborn son, a sacrifice to pay for the sins of God's people, a sacrifice to pay even for the sins of the high priest. As Hebrews 10:1 states, "Since the law has but a shadow of the good things to come instead of the true form of these realities, it can never, by the same sacrifices that are continually offered every year, make perfect those who draw near." This shadow was cast on Good Friday when the once-for-all sacrifice was made. And deliverance was given, as only God can do, on the night He was betrayed.

Sure, God could have made any sort of world He wanted. But He made this one. God could have written any sort of rules He wanted. But He designed life to function exactly the way it is. God will be fully God, and people will be fully people. God is both "just and the justifier of the one who has faith in Jesus" (Romans 3:26), and we are delivered from sin and death. All along, God has been the righteous, Holy One. But *God desires all people to be saved*. All along, God has been the one making things right, intimately involved in the little details, undoing what sin does. God is just and justifier.

Jesus gave His life only once for our salvation, but the Meal is as often as we eat and drink it. The celebration of deliverance happens every time Christians gather in worship. The new Passover meal, Holy Communion, points to a time when Jesus will take His place at the head of the Table once more—when heaven and earth meet in more than just body and bread, blood and wine. When we see Jesus face to face, raised to new life, finally and fully delivered from sin, death, and all evil. So get to the Table—what are you waiting for?

Great Deliverer, we celebrate You, Your work, Your love, Your salvation. Bring us to Your Table now in the Holy Meal and forever at the feast to come. Amen.

JESUS TAKES ON OUR SIN

For it is written, "I will strike the shepherd, and the sheep of the flock will be scattered." (MATTHEW 26:31)

Just as Communion connects with most everything in a worship service, so, too, does this scene have deep biblical significance. God eats with Abraham in Genesis 18, with Moses and the elders in Exodus 24, and provides bread from heaven for the wilderness journey. God sends miraculous food to Elijah and also provides miraculously for a widow. This isn't even getting into the New Testament where Jesus eats in homes wherever He is invited, where He provides unfathomable amounts of bread to feed the massive crowds, and where He tells parables about being invited to eat with others. A meal is a big deal to God. God has made it clear He is preparing a table—and we have been invited.

The Passover, as well, is a pillar of the Old Testament, starting with the first Passover in Exodus 12. It was to be a yearly celebration, a commemoration of God's faithfulness, even though the people forgot to celebrate it for almost four hundred years—until Josiah commanded it to take place again (see 2 Kings 23:21). It does not come as a surprise that the closer people come to slavery, the more they draw upon the power of this meal. We recognize our natural tendency toward sin, our slavery to it, and we celebrate our freedom regularly in this same Meal.

The Synoptic Gospels all contain this important moment in Jesus' ministry (see Mark 14:22–25; Luke 22:18–20), although John's Gospel puts the explicit teaching in John 6:53, "Unless you eat the flesh of the Son of Man and drink His blood, you have no life in you." Whatever John's reasoning, the effect is to elevate the as-often-as-we-do-this beyond the Passover meal for the Christian Church.

Jesus has earned many titles, including the Good Shepherd, but one of the most interesting is the title given Him by His forerunner John the Baptist: "Behold, the Lamb of God!" (John 1:36). This prophecy only makes sense in light of the Passover. Prophet, Messiah, Lord, Lamb. We must confess it does not fit with the rest, but we must confess this is who Jesus is. The submissive Lamb, who "opens not His mouth," but goes willingly to His death. The Prophet is willing to be muzzled, the Messiah is willing to lose, the Lord is willing to die for the sins of His accusers.

That is the second element of this passage: the betrayal of Christ. It comes from "a man, my equal, my companion, my familiar friend" (see Psalm 55:13). Jesus alone bore the punishment for our sin, and it is significant that He truly stood alone before the people of God, the government, and the world, "scorned by mankind and despised by the people" (Psalm 22:6). The righteous suffer at the hands of the unrighteous throughout Scripture. Abel's blood speaks (see Genesis 4:10), but Jesus' blood speaks "a better word" (Hebrews 12:24), a word of peace and forgiveness and hope, even in the face of betrayal. Because He stood alone, we can be certain that we never will.

Jesus, thank You for taking on our sin and the suffering we deserve and giving us the gift of Your body and blood in its place. Keep us faithful to You and feed us always with the Meal that gives us eternal life. Amen.

OUR FAITHFUL SAVIOR, TRUE TO HIS WORD

"Even if I must die with You, I will not deny You!" And all the disciples said the same. (MATTHEW 26:35)

Bread must be broken to be given and shared. Food must be divided to become a meal. The challenge of life and faith is leaning into the brokenness, the hardship, the suffering. We will be broken, and God will share our lives and suffering to give life to others. Peter was utterly destroyed by his betrayal of Christ, broken at the core of his being. God was preparing to give Peter to the church as the servant leader. This scene in Jesus' life helps us see two things at work, side by side: (1) Jesus will be denied in His brokenness, and (2) Jesus will not deny His own in their brokenness. This helps to frame the challenges we encounter in this passage.

What is a covenant?

A covenant is like a contract, except it is one-sided in God's case. God makes promises to His people, and "all of the promises of God find their Yes" in Jesus (2 Corinthians 1:20). Throughout the Scriptures, God promises children, blessings, freedom, love—and God's people constantly broke the Law or fell away. God refuses to go back on His Word, so we can be certain that if God said it, God will do it. And Jesus sealed it all with the blood of the covenant. All promises were fulfilled between God and His people. The work of redemption is complete. Martin Luther divided Scripture between Law and Promises. No matter how broken or terrible things get, God will not change His mind about what He promised. Therefore, we can cling to God's faithfulness in Jesus no matter what.

Why does Jesus say they will scatter like sheep?

Jesus knows His disciples—how vulnerable they are. Sheep are not courageous animals; they do not put up a fight. And that is the kind of creature the disciples will imitate. In John 10, we learn Jesus is the Good Shepherd, and combining that with Zechariah 13 and Psalm 23, we can see that Jesus is the one who lays down His life for His sheep—who will be with us through the valley of the shadow of death, even if He is abandoned in His own valley.

Why does Jesus say He will meet them in Galilee?

Jesus plainly tells them that He can see the other side of this. There will be another table; there will be an overflowing cup, there will be a dwelling place forever. His resurrection is coming. But I believe there is another reason. The disciples needed to know that Jesus was aware of their sin but would not leave them in it. John's Gospel relayed this same message from that night: "I will not leave you as orphans; I will come to you" (John 14:18). Jesus was coming back. Jesus made a promise. And God never breaks His promises.

Holy Father, we praise You for Your faithfulness, for always following through on Your Word. Help us believe what You have spoken and to be faithful with our own promises too. In Jesus' name. Amen.

THE JOY OF THE MEAL

When they had sung a hymn,
they went out to the Mount of
Olives. (MATTHEW 26:30)

We all have our mealtime routines. They are like a well-rehearsed play we have done so often that we forget our peculiarities until we sit at someone else's table. *Wait—salad frst, and then the main course? Who needs two forks? Where's dessert? Why is this meal being delivered?* The same is true of Communion: common cup or individual, kneel or stand, walk away or wait. But what's important is not the differences—it's what we share: community, food, connection. True fellowship.

What Jesus did on the first Maundy Thursday became formative for all Christians, so much so that Paul repeats verbatim in 1 Corinthians 11 what it says in the Gospels. Lutheran pastors still speak those same words at Communion today. It is what we have in common with our brothers and sisters in Christ—even those eleven apostles who walked away from the first table to sing a song, get worried, and run away. The Meal is where we share in the most fundamental Christian community: one Body, one loaf, one cup, one Christ, one church, one Lord and Father of us all (see Ephesians 4:6).

What is more important to our spiritual journey than being formed in that oneness, in that unity? What is more important than gathering with other Christians around Word and Sacrament? What is more fundamental than sharing a meal and walking together by its strength? What is more refreshing in our seasons of weariness or more humbling in our seasons of happiness than to be shoulder-to-shoulder with people going through all sorts of trials and temptations and blessings and bounty—and

receive the same body and blood of our Lord and Savior Jesus Christ?

In this Meal, we don't only join with those in the room with us. There is only one body, which means this is the Body of Christ, broken for you and every other Christian on this planet and in the heavens above. This Meal joins us with Jesus. This Meal joins us with all of His table guests: parents, children, dear friends, enemies, relatives, and all who have gone before us.

One of my favorite celebrations is Maundy Thursday where the whole focus is on the Lord's Supper. Before we deal with the pain of the cross, we deal with the joy of the Meal. We hold these two opposing forces together, and we celebrate the God who holds all of us together. And almost every Sunday, we hear these same Words of Institution during Communion. No matter how far removed we are from the day Jesus was crucified, we are formed into broken, forgiven, expectant disciples, following our Savior now into forever. And that's a routine we can all get used to.

Holy Father, thank You for loving and leading us. You bless us with the celebration of Your Son's body and blood in Communion; please keep us steadfast in You as we follow Jesus. In His name we pray. Amen.

JESUS PRAYS IN THE GARDEN OF GETHSEMANE

WEEK 36—LUKE 22:39–46

And He came out and went, as was His custom, to the Mount of Olives, and the disciples followed Him. And when He came to the place, He said to them, "Pray that you may not enter into temptation." And He withdrew from them about a stone's throw, and knelt down and prayed, saying, "Father, if You are willing, remove this cup from Me. Nevertheless, not My will, but Yours, be done." And there appeared to Him an angel from heaven, strengthening Him. And being in agony He prayed more earnestly; and His sweat became like great drops of blood falling down to the ground. And when He rose from prayer, He came to the disciples and found them sleeping for sorrow, and He said to them, "Why are you sleeping? Rise and pray that you may not enter into temptation."

THE GARDEN OF RESOLVE

And He came out and went, as was His custom, to the Mount of Olives, and the disciples followed Him. And when He came to the place, He said to them, "Pray that you may not enter into temptation." And He withdrew from them about a stone's throw, and knelt down and prayed. (LUKE 22:39–41)

After the Passover meal and song, Jesus and His disciples leave to go and pray. The pathways to the Garden of Gethsemane would have taken them out of the city walls of Jerusalem and onto the Mount of Olives. As it was Passover there would have been a full moon.

Gethsemane takes on a dual meaning. In a direct translation, it means "olive press" but, on this night, the meaning also includes the burden of crushing emotional weight. Judas had already left the company to betray Jesus to the high priest. At Gethsemane, the weight of that betrayal, along with the knowledge of what was to come, would press down on the Savior.

Jesus would pray. He would ask in verse 42, "Remove this cup from Me." The magnitude of the sacrifice to come caused Him great distress. His sweat would be mixed with blood. Yet also, He would find the resolve with the help of His Father. Here in the garden, He would not turn away. He would follow the will of the Father. While the cross would be the greatest action of love ever taken for humanity, the resolve in the garden was another step in a long line of God's steadfast love for His creation.

You can still walk the paths of this garden today. Just east of Jerusalem, you will find a grove of olive trees. You can walk among the trees as Jesus did and ponder what it might have been like on that Thursday night all those years ago. It is not some supernatural plane of existence where gods play and humans cannot roam. It is a simple olive grove. A place to find quiet outside a city full of pilgrims for the Passover.

On that night, Jesus not only displayed His love for us but He also taught us how to pray. The task before Him was daunting. He asked His Father for another way. He knew what needed to happen, yet still He prayed for the cup to be taken. He was unafraid to pray. But He also trusted His Father: "Not My will, but Yours, be done" (v. 42). Even as He approached death, He modeled for us an attitude of prayer that is unafraid to share the deepest places of the heart while at the same time trusting that God's will is good.

Lord, thank You that Your Son showed resolve in the garden. May we, too, be bold enough to pray as He did, knowing You will answer and strengthen us in our times of suffering and temptation. In Jesus' name. Amen.

REALIGNING OUR HEARTS THROUGH PRAYER

And He withdrew from them about a stone's throw, and knelt down and prayed, saying, "Father, if You are willing, remove this cup from Me. Nevertheless, not My will, but Yours, be done." (LUKE 22:41-42)

Growing up, my dad had a funny phrase that continues to have impact into my adulthood: "Prayer ain't doin' nothin'." Prayer can be a funny thing and feel silly at times. Please excuse me while I go and mutter, seemingly to myself, to an unseen God. But prayer does work.

Prayer impacts our lives as Christians in two major ways. First, it brings to God the things that are impacting our lives. Good or bad, we take it to the Lord in prayer. Throughout Scripture, there are incredible instances of the power of prayer—it is a way to bring the things of your world to the Lord. Not just *the* world but specifically *your* world. It is a conversation between you—the creation—and your Creator. We bring before God our petitions, the things of our heart for our neighbors and ourselves, asking for Him to work.

Second, prayer transforms our hearts. Often, there is emphasis placed on what God can do for us through prayer. God still is working on us as we pray. When we come to Him, the Spirit is there. In prayer, we find the Spirit realigning our hearts to the way we were created to be. God works through these times of conversation to change who we are. He makes us more devoted disciples.

Jesus models this for us in the Garden of Gethsemane. He prays for what is weighing Him down. He has been focused on the goal of salvation and, in this moment, He asks that there might be a way other than His death. But He also trusts the will of the Father. An angel is sent to strengthen Him. Why would the Messiah, the Son of God, member of the Trinity, need to pray? One of the great reasons is this: He was modeling for us what we are to do in our darkest hour. He was showing us that God wants to hear our deepest desires and fears. He also shows that trusting God is the greatest gift that prayer can give.

When you run into trouble, hardship, or anxiety, take it to the Lord in prayer. These passages in the garden prove to us once again: prayer ain't doin' nothin'.

Lord, teach me to pray as Jesus prayed in the garden. In Jesus' name. Amen.

JESUS' UNWAVERING LOVE

And there appeared to Him an angel from heaven, strength-ening Him. (LUKE 22:43)

Could Jesus have changed His mind? It seems as though His time in the Garden of Gethsemane opens up that possibility. Would Jesus have turned away from His mission at the last moment because it would have been too hard? He had been tempted, scorned, and persecuted throughout His ministry. He could have made the garden the beachhead for an invasion of the armies of heaven.

Yet He would not. These passages in the garden reveal to us not the indecision of the Savior, but instead His unwavering love, even as the great sacrifice stood right in front of Him. Earlier in the book of Luke we read, "When the days drew near for Him to be taken up, He set His face to go to Jerusalem" (Luke 9:51). That phrase "He set His face" is one of the most encouraging in the New Testament. It was here that Jesus began the transition of His ministry. He goes from a traveling Messiah—teaching, healing, and performing signs—and puts His feet on the road to the cross. It was always His intention. But that turn of phrase signifies His intention. He is going. There is no doubt. That is where His face is set.

This was the purpose of His ministry, of the whole plan of salvation. As Jesus prays at Gethsemane, it not only teaches us how to pray, as we've already talked about this week, but it also shows us the depth of His love. He was feeling the weight of what was to come but He would not change the will of the Father. He knew the sorrow and suffering He was about to endure. But instead of calling on heaven for reinforcements to change the plan, He asks to do the will of the Father. An angel is sent not to save Him from the coming sacrifice but to strengthen Him for it.

Nothing would pull Him away from His mission. Not betrayal, the weight of sorrow He experienced, or even His sleeping friends. He knew what He must do.

All this is a testament to the steadfast love the Creator has for His creation. In spite of all that was to come, Jesus sees the salvation of humanity as the most important task at hand—proving once again the deep love He has for us.

Heavenly Father, let me rejoice that Jesus would not abandon me. In Jesus' name. Amen.

THE LORD'S PRAYER

Father, if You are willing, remove this cup from Me. Nevertheless, not My will, but Yours, be done. (LUKE 22:42)

How do we pray for God's will? Jesus teaches us in the book of Matthew:

And when you pray, you must not be like the hypocrites. For they love to stand and pray in the synagogues and at the street corners, that they may be seen by others. Truly, I say to you, they have received their reward. But when you pray, go into your room and shut the door and pray to your Father who is in secret. And your Father who sees in secret will reward you. And when you pray, do not heap up empty phrases as the Gentiles do, for they think that they will be heard for their many words. Do not be like them, for your Father knows what you need before you ask Him. Pray then like this: "Our Father in heaven, hallowed be Your name. Your kingdom come, Your will be done, on earth as it is in heaven. Give us this day our daily bread, and forgive us our debts, as we also have forgiven our debtors. And lead us not into temptation, but deliver us from evil." (Matthew 6:5–13)

Jesus retreats to pray. He does not stand on the temple mount declaring what He is planning to do but instead follows His teaching to go to a secluded place to pray. His prayers are not as the Gentiles, full of empty phrases, but instead right to the point. He prays for God's will to be done.

The Lord's Prayer may seem rote. We pray it weekly. But if we slow down, we see throughout the Gospels that it is reflected in how Jesus prays. In the garden, He does the same thing. He may not use the same words, but He prays in the same style. We know that these prayers were heard: "In the days of His flesh, Jesus offered up prayers and supplications, with loud cries and tears, to Him who was able to save Him from death, and He was heard because of His reverence" (Hebrews 5:7).

This whole scene in the garden is both story and teaching. Jesus knew it would be part of His path to the cross, written down by the apostles, conveyed in the first three Gospels. But He also knew the benefit it would have as Scripture for the saints who would believe without seeing. It is a gift to the church. A glimpse into the implementation of His teachings in His own life.

Our Father who art in heaven, hallowed be Thy name, Thy kingdom come, Thy will be done on earth as it is in heaven; give us this day our daily bread; and forgive us our trespasses as we forgive those who trespass against us; and lead us not into temptation, but deliver us from evil. For Thine is the kingdom and the power and the glory forever and ever. Amen. (LSB, p. 162)

TWO GARDENS

And He came out and went, as was His custom, to the Mount of Olives, and the disciples followed Him. (LUKE 22:39)

The Garden of Gethsemane is mirrored by another garden in Scripture: Eden. In that first garden, humanity was created and lived in paradise. In the fall, it all went away. Paradise had become a wasteland.

But there was the promise of the Son of Man, the one who was to come. Here, He is found once again in a garden. Among the olive groves was the One who had been promised to redeem the created beings for their Creator.

In Eden, humanity followed its own will. Adam and Eve broke the commandment of God and found that the knowledge of good and evil would break them. They were ejected from paradise and found only toil, hardship, and disease. Their son invented murder. Their grandchildren and great-grandchildren continued the trend, propagating a species that turned in on themselves.

In Gethsemane, Jesus follows the Father's will. Where Adam and Eve did not resist temptation, Jesus does. Instead of selfishly saving Himself, He is strengthened for the sacrifice to come. From His act would flow a blood that would transform sinners into saints.

In Eden, there was a fall. It broke the world. Every sorrow and heartache came from that one moment. And humanity wasn't the only thing that was broken—the whole world fell at that point. Like a piece of glass slowly shattering, the fall impacted everything around it. In that garden, everything was broken.

In Gethsemane, we find the One who would conquer. Jesus is the Savior, and He is unashamed to share His trepidation of the cross. But it does not stop Him from that path. In and through Him, all things will be made new. The lion will lie down with the lamb. There will be no more tears. Upon His return, there will be a new heaven and a new earth. It will be the Garden of Eden as it was meant to be. At that Passover evening all those years ago, our Savior remained steadfast in His mission, His journey, His love. He would not walk away. He would conquer the enemy that had destroyed creation.

Lord, help me recognize the work of the two gardens. May I be aware of my own failings, which were born in Eden, and my nature that would seek to lead me from You. May I rest assured in the knowledge that You, the Champion of Gethsemane, have claimed me. I no longer am a fallen member of Eden. I am a child of God. In Jesus' name. Amen.

GOD'S WONDERFUL GIFT

And when He rose from prayer, He came to the disciples and found them sleeping for sorrow, and He said to them, "Why are you sleeping? Rise and pray that you may not enter into temptation." (LUKE 22:45–46)

We teach children to say their prayers before bed. This is not a terrible practice, but sometimes as adults, it becomes a dangerous one. You have spent all day working. It is finally time to crawl into the sheets. Well, let's add prayer time. You are barely through praying for your sick friend when your closed eyes become more than a reverent sign of prayer. Next thing you know, you are popping up, realizing that you fell asleep mid-prayer.

It is hard to blame the disciples as they sleep under the olive trees. They have spent all day in the Passover festivities. Not only that, but it has been a busy week since they entered Jerusalem. Now combine with it their fear after Jesus has told them He will be betrayed and crucified. The temptation to sleep instead of pray is evident. And they do. Jesus returns and finds them asleep. He tells them to stand so they can avoid the temptation of slumber.

How often do we put prayer on the back burner? It becomes the thing we do at church and before meals. We fall asleep at night when our pillows seemingly hold more peace than God. Prayer is an invitation to be in relationship with the Creator. But it is also a gift given to His people. Christians don't pray to somehow make God feel better. It's not as if His "God battery" needs a recharge and our prayers bring the energy He needs.

No. Prayer is God's gift for His people.

James would write this: "Every good gift and every perfect gift is from above, coming down from the Father of lights, with whom there is no variation or shadow due to change" (James 1:17). Prayer is a gift, not an obligation. It does not get a Christian more merit badges. Instead, it is the way in which we make our hearts known to God and He transforms our hearts to His will.

As Jesus walks into the Passion, He prays. Think on that. The worst week of His life, and He gets away to pray. How often do we ignore prayer? It is a gift for us that we might grow and find peace. God gives so many gifts: salvation, the Bible, the Sacraments, and on and on. In prayer, He gifts us with an open line to communicate with Him.

If Jesus walks into the beginning of His suffering in prayer, should we not constantly encounter the broken world in which we live with prayer? This is why prayer has a big role in worship each service. May it have a big role in our daily lives as well.

Gracious Father, You invite and command us to pray. Help me see the precious gift and claim it always. In Jesus' name. Amen.

JESUS' ARREST AND ARRAIGNMENT

WEEK 37—JOHN 18:1–14, 19–24

When Jesus had spoken these words, He went out with His disciples across the brook Kidron, where there was a garden, which He and His disciples entered. Now Judas, who betrayed Him, also knew the place, for Jesus often met there with His disciples. So Judas, having procured a band of soldiers and some officers from the chief priests and the Pharisees, went there with lanterns and torches and weapons. Then Jesus, knowing all that would happen to Him, came forward and said to them, "Whom do you seek?" They answered Him, "Jesus of Nazareth." Jesus said to them, "I am He." Judas, who betrayed Him, was standing with them. When Jesus said to them, "I am He," they drew back and fell to the ground. So He asked them again, "Whom do you seek?" And they said, "Jesus of Nazareth." Jesus answered, "I told you that I am He. So, if you seek Me, let these men go." This was to fulfill the word that He had spoken: "Of those whom You gave Me I have lost not one." Then Simon Peter, having a sword, drew it and struck the high priest's servant and cut off his right ear. (The servant's name was Malchus.) So Jesus said to Peter, "Put your sword into its sheath; shall I not drink the cup that the Father has given Me?"

So the band of soldiers and their captain and the officers of the Jews arrested Jesus and bound Him. First they led Him to Annas, for he was the father-in-law of Caiaphas, who was high priest that year. It was Caiaphas who had advised the Jews that it would be expedient that one man should die for the people.

The high priest then questioned Jesus about His disciples and His teaching. Jesus answered him, "I have spoken openly to the world. I have always taught in synagogues and in the temple, where all Jews come together. I have said nothing in secret. Why do you ask Me? Ask those who have heard Me what I said to them; they know what I said." When He had said these things, one of the officers standing by struck Jesus with his hand, saying, "Is that how You answer the high priest?" Jesus answered him, "If what I said is wrong, bear witness about the wrong; but if what I said is right, why do you strike Me?" Annas then sent Him bound to Caiaphas the high priest.

BETRAYAL, ARREST, AND PRELIMINARY HEARING

So the band of soldiers and their captain and the officers of the Jews arrested Jesus and bound Him. First they led Him to Annas, for he was the father-in-law of Caiaphas, who was high priest that year. (JOHN 18:12–13)

The journey to the cross has begun. Jesus is in the garden. We know from the other Gospels that this is the Garden of Gethsemane, a place that Jesus had been to before. The disciples did not know what was going to come, but Jesus did. John names Judas, the one who betrayed Him, as he enters the garden leading a mob that included soldiers, officers of the chief priests, and the Pharisees. Jesus faces them head-on and asks who they are looking for—not just one time but twice—to clearly identify who they were looking for, even though Judas is there to help identify Him. When Jesus says the words "I am He" (John 18:5), they all fall to the ground. These words would be familiar to them from Moses' encounter with God in the Torah and the burning bush: "I AM WHO I AM" (Exodus 3:14). Jesus claims to be the Son of God, and by the sheer power of His divine voice, His enemies fall to the ground before Him.

As this unfolds, the disciples awaken from their slumber, not knowing what is going on but wanting to protect Jesus. Peter draws his sword and strikes a soldier, cutting off his ear. Jesus immediately steps up to stop him and heals the severed ear (see Luke 22:51). Taking charge of the situation, Jesus commands the soldiers to let His disciples go, and they comply.

Only the Gospel of John tells us about Jesus being brought in front of Annas, who is the father-in-law of Caiaphas and a former high priest whom the Romans had deposed. Since high priests served for life, many Jews, perhaps even John, saw Annas as the rightful high priest. Clearly, he still has a strong influence in the land, so Jesus is sent there as a first examination of the potential charges to help Caiaphas build a case against Jesus. Jesus was given the opportunity to explain Himself, but He instead gave Annas the question back. Jesus' ministry was in public, preaching and teaching in areas that were accessible to all the Jews, and it was never hidden from Annas, Caiaphas, the Pharisees, or chief priests. They were never able to capture Him in any false teaching, but yet they challenge Him on who He is. Jesus' response is met with the physical response of a slap by one of the officers—and there will be more physical mistreatment to come for Jesus as He is questioned by the leaders. Jesus simply asks them to point out what He did wrong to be slapped like that. And if they couldn't point anything out, He asks why the officer slapped Him. The officer is unable to respond. The Jewish authorities feel threatened, and Annas knows he has nothing on Jesus. He sends Jesus on to Caiaphas and the Jewish ruling council.

Lord Jesus, thank You for suffering mistreatment and going to the cross to save us. Help us to not question You but rely on Your grace. Amen.

JESUS REMAINED CALM

Jesus said to Peter, "Put your sword into its sheath; shall I not drink the cup that the Father has given Me?" (JOHN 18:11)

Jesus has begun His journey to the cross. He knew what was going to happen from the beginning and yet He continues willingly—and even reminds Peter that this is a cup that His Father has given Him. Jesus had warned His disciples of what was going to happen to Him. Three times He had predicted His betrayal, arrest, crucifixion, death, burial, and resurrection. There are many other references that Jesus made during His earthly ministry where He told them that He would leave this earth as well.

These verses also show us the larger narrative of those who were plotting against Jesus. We know that Judas approached the chief priests about betraying Jesus. When they enter the Garden of Gethsemane, they are concerned about an uprising; there are more than just the chief priests in the crowd that are with Judas. Once Jesus is bound, He is led to Annas, the former high priest. Annas asks about His disciples and His teaching. He is looking for a response that he can use against Jesus to help his son-in-law Caiaphas build a case against Him, but Jesus protects His disciples by remaining silent about them. Instead, He affirms His teachings are a matter of public record. He leaves it in their hands and hearts to think and examine themselves and their actions again Him.

The cost to Jesus was great, but the reward was even greater. The love of God the Father is expressed to us through His Son, whom He sent to suffer and die for our sins. This text gives us more insight into the ultimate betrayal that was sealed with a kiss. We see the world's reaction to Jesus through those that were there. The soldiers, who were fearful at the power of God but also intent on arresting Jesus. Peter, whose fear and recklessness drove him to protect his Lord and risk an escalation of harm and chaos. Annas, who tried to exert his perceived power against Jesus. The officer, who struck Jesus' face when he had absolutely no reason to do so.

All of these feelings and reactions are ones that we, as Christians, struggle with in our lives. Despite all of that, in these verses, we see Jesus remaining calm and willingly accepting what is to come—trusting His Father and knowing the ultimate victory. That is the example we should follow at all times and in all circumstances.

Lord Jesus, our Savior, thank You for being an example in my life. More importantly, thank You for suffering such disgrace to save us all from our sins. Teach me to trust in You always and follow Your example, willing to accept the trials of life, knowing You have won the ultimate victory for me. Amen.

JESUS' GREAT BOLDNESS

The high priest then questioned Jesus about His disciples and His teaching. (JOHN 18:19)

Jesus came to save us. His ministry on earth points us to the promise that God the Father made in the Garden of Eden to Adam and Eve. These verses were foretold in the Old Testament. This was the journey of the promise given to us so many years ago. During Jesus' ministry, He told His disciples what was going to happen in many and various ways. They may not have understood or, more likely, did not want to believe that it would happen, but God always keeps His promises, and Jesus lived that in His daily life.

In the garden, upon seeing the crowd approach, Jesus does not cower back. He boldly steps forward to address them and shield His disciples. He is the first to speak and asks the throng who they are looking for. Again, He knows exactly who they are looking for, but He asks this question to fulfill Scripture. Peter swings his sword with lethal force at the head of a servant named Malchus, cutting off his ear. Peter was focused on protecting Jesus. That is not what Jesus wanted, though—He came to save Peter. To save us. Peter's job was to flee with the other disciples. When God the Father made the promise to Adam and Eve in the Garden of Eden, Old Testament Scripture continued to reveal the One who was coming to save us. Jesus lived His life fulfilling the Scripture and giving thanks to the Father for the life He led, always pointing us back to the promise.

In fact, we know that Jesus lived out His mission daily. When He was questioned by Annas, Annas didn't ask about who He was but rather about His ministry, wanting to catch Jesus in falsehood or inconsistency and to expose His disciples. Annas was not even the acting high priest—he was looking for a way to help his son-in-law, Caiaphas, charge Jesus with crimes against the government. Yet Jesus' response is to say how openly He has spoken and taught in the synagogue (see v. 20) where everyone, including Annas, would have heard or known others who had heard Him speak. Jesus is struck in the face for His response, but He again asks them what He has said wrong, and there is no response. In this question, Jesus takes the moment and shows it back to them—a moment of looking in the mirror to examine their response to Jesus. Jesus was bold in His teaching, and He never hid who sent Him or the love, grace, and forgiveness that is found in God.

Heavenly Father, give us the boldness to speak Your truth of love, grace, and forgiveness to all we meet. In Jesus' name. Amen.

JOHN'S UNIQUE PERSPECTIVE

When Jesus had spoken these words, He went out with His disciples across the brook Kidron, where there was a garden, which He and His disciples entered. (JOHN 18:1)

Since these verses are part of Jesus' journey to the cross, His betrayal and arrest is reflected in each of the four Gospels—Matthew, Mark, Luke, and the passage we are looking at in John this week. We will take a look at a few items that are unique to this Gospel.

In verse 1, John tells us that the Garden of Gethsemane is across the brook of Kidron, which is referred to in 2 Samuel 15:23 where David and his faithful followers passed when he fled from his son Absalom, who tried to steal his throne. This is a place of escape, which aligns with Jesus' intentions for going to that garden for quiet time and a place to pray. Judas knew the place because Jesus had often taken His disciples there before.

We are given more of the conversation in verses 4–8 of John's Gospel when Judas enters the garden. Jesus identifies who He is to the crowd after asking them, "Whom are you seeking?" Jesus first asked this question when He began His ministry and called the first disciples. Jesus would ask this question again on Easter to Mary Magdalene at the tomb in John 20:15. He asks and answers this question to protect His disciples and fulfill the Word He had spoken in John 17:12. Simon Peter reacts and cuts off the servant's ear, but in the Gospel of John, we learn the servant's name—Malchus. In verse 11, Jesus rebukes Peter for his action and speaks of the cup He must drink. This is the cup of suffering that Jesus speaks about in Matthew 20:22; it is also mentioned in Isaiah 51:22 where it is called the cup of staggering, the vessel of God's wrath at sinners. This was our cup to drink, but Jesus took it instead for us to drink it no more. Instead, Jesus gives us the cup of salvation.

In verses 12–14, John alone shows us Jesus being taken to Annas. In the Gospel of John, we are told that Annas is the father-in-law of Caiaphas. This was no mere coincidence. We are told in Luke 3:2 that Jesus, the Word, came during the time of Annas and Caiaphas. And in Acts 4:6, we are told of the relationship of Annas, Caiaphas, John, and Alexander, which illustrates the longtime power of this family and their position in society. Finally, in verses 19-24, we see that the Gospel of John is similar to the other accounts of Jesus' betrayal and arrest with only slight variation.

Heavenly Father, thank You for giving us Your Word, which speaks to us daily. May we continue to dig into Your Word, knowing You will meet us there and show us Your glory. Amen.

"I AM HE"

When Jesus said to them, "I am He," they drew back and fell to the ground. (JOHN 18:6)

This week's passage brings up many questions:

What is the role Judas plays in John's account?

John certainly makes sure to show and share all of Judas's flaws and his ultimate betrayal. In John 12, Judas criticizes the woman for pouring oil on Jesus' feet and is even identified as a thief for the money he was taking. Leading up to Jesus' arrest in the Garden of Gethsemane, Jesus identifies him as the one who would betray Him, and He says this in front of all the disciples (John 13:26). Judas then becomes the leader of the mob that goes out to find and arrest Jesus. Judas knew they might find Jesus in the Garden of Gethsemane since Jesus had taken His disciples there before. Even though Jesus and Judas knew what was going to happen, the mob brought weapons, anticipating that they would face resistance. In John's account, Jesus identifies Judas in the mob and calls him out. In the other Gospels, Judas gives a signal, a kiss, to identify Jesus. Since John points out that Judas was standing there with the soldiers, he also felt the power of Jesus' words and was driven to the ground when Jesus said, "I am He." This posture of recognition would soon strike Judas with deep remorse for betraying his Lord and Savior.

What is the significance of Jesus' words "I am"?

This was touched upon on the first day of this week. In Exodus 3:14, God reveals himself as I Am to Moses at the burning bush. This is His name, and this name reveals the power of His identity. As God speaks to Moses at the burning bush, Moses falls to the ground and keeps his head bowed in respect at the might of our God. Jesus often uses "I am" throughout the Gospels, tying God the Father to Himself. He says He is the Good Shepherd; the Bread of Life; the Way, the Truth, and the Life; the True Vine. All of these statements point to the divine nature of Jesus. Finally, in Revelation 1:8, Christ tells John, "I am the Alpha and Omega," the beginning and the end. In His final words of Scripture, God the Father identifies that Jesus is all things, from the beginning and end, which is why we believe in Him.

Why does Jesus heal Malchus?

Jesus has just identified Himself to the mob that He was who they were looking for. Jesus was surrendering to the law without hesitation, resistance, or fight. Jesus knew what was to happen, and He participated willingly. He did not want anything to stop what the Father had sent Him to do, nor did He want Peter or the other disciples to endanger themselves. Jesus' final miracle on earth is to heal His enemy—at the same time undoing the crime Peter had committed. What a beautiful way to show love and forgiveness to us. He did not want any chaos or violence during this time. Instead, He accepted it and lovingly helped those who needed Him all the way to the end of His earthly ministry.

Lord Jesus, my Savior, thank You for willingly going to the cross and dying for my sins. May I live my life as a resurrected person, living Your example and sharing Your story of love with all I meet. Amen.

WILLING OBEDIENCE

Annas then sent Him bound to Caiaphas the high priest. (JOHN 18:24)

As we read the Gospel of John, he writes as a disciple who followed Jesus' earthly ministry and he makes sure to give us a lot of details. Jesus knew what was to come, and we see His human nature as He goes to a place to retreat and pray. The weight of the world on His shoulders, knowing the cup He would bear. Yet it weighs heavy on Him. In the Gospel of Luke, Jesus is praying, and blood is mingled with the sweat pouring out of Him. The stage is being set, and we read with anticipation, using the word *kyrie*—Lord, have mercy. These details paint the picture of Jesus' journey to the cross. We are grateful for this journey, knowing that His sacrifice saves us today and we live our life as Easter people.

These verses continue to take us on Jesus' journey to the cross, and we read this so often not thinking about how we would react in place of those in this account. Are we like Simon Peter, who retaliates and strikes someone down? Are we like the mob carrying our weapons, ready to attack? Are we the mob as they fall to the ground in fear? Maybe it is a little of all three. As Christians, we can often struggle with our responses to others. Reading through these verses, we are struck by this scene and maybe even more frustrated as Jesus went willingly. He willingly lets Annas question Him, lets a soldier strike Him, and lets Himself be bound and handed over to Caiaphas. This is not the image of Jesus that we dwell on—instead, we tend to focus on the people's action and reaction. But let us focus on Jesus, who willingly went with the mob, healed the soldier's ear, and remained silent to Annas, knowing that the Father had this already planned out for Him and His willing acceptance of this.

As we gather at the altar to receive His body and blood given and shed for us, Jesus' words echo in our ears, "Do this, in remembrance of Me." In remembrance of His obedience, His humility, His steadfastness, and His burning love, which led Him to lay down His life to protect and save us.

May we also take a posture of humility and willingness as the world hurls its sin and conflict all around us. Our victory has been won.

Heavenly Father, we thank You for Your Son's loving obedience. May we live our lives reflecting Your love. In Jesus' name. Amen.

JESUS' JEWISH TRIALS

WEEK 38—MATTHEW 26:57–68

Then those who had seized Jesus led Him to Caiaphas the high priest, where the scribes and the elders had gathered. And Peter was following Him at a distance, as far as the courtyard of the high priest, and going inside he sat with the guards to see the end. Now the chief priests and the whole council were seeking false testimony against Jesus that they might put Him to death, but they found none, though many false witnesses came forward. At last two came forward and said, "This man said, 'I am able to destroy the temple of God, and to rebuild it in three days.'" And the high priest stood up and said, "Have You no answer to make? What is it that these men testify against You?" But Jesus remained silent. And the high priest said to Him, "I adjure You by the living God, tell us if You are the Christ, the Son of God." Jesus said to him, "You have said so. But I tell you, from now on you will see the Son of Man seated at the right hand of Power and coming on the clouds of heaven." Then the high priest tore his robes and said, "He has uttered blasphemy. What further witnesses do we need? You have now heard His blasphemy. What is your judgment?" They answered, "He deserves death." Then they spit in His face and struck Him. And some slapped Him, saying, "Prophesy to us, You Christ! Who is it that struck You?"

SIX TRIALS

Then those who seized Jesus led Him to Caiaphas the high priest, where the scribes and elders had gathered. (MATTHEW 26:57)

Jesus lived in an awkward time.

The Romans conquered the Jews and ruled the Holy Land as occupiers. To maintain peaceful relations, the Romans permitted the Jews to retain many of their cultural and religious customs. This was a messy proposition because for the Jews, politics and religion were intertwined. Separation of church and state was an alien concept.

Exhibit A of political-religious interconnectedness: Caiaphas and the Sanhedrin. Caiaphas was the high priest, an office he held for eighteen years, including Pontius Pilate's entire tenure as Judean governor. Caiaphas presided over the Sanhedrin, a ruling council that decided contested matters related to worship, doctrine, and the proper functioning of Jewish society.

Sanhedrin comes from a Greek word meaning "sitting together." Many times in the New Testament, the Sanhedrin is named "the council." In Acts, several believers stood before the Sanhedrin: Peter and John (Acts 4), all of the apostles (Acts 5), Stephen (Acts 6), and Paul (Acts 22 and 23).

The most famous biblical account of the Sanhedrin was Jesus' trial before them, recorded in the Gospels. Because of the delicate dance of Jewish-Roman authority, Jesus ended up being passed back and forth between various leaders for a total of six trials. During the first three, He faced religious charges before Jewish leaders; during the latter three, He faced secular criminal charges before Roman leaders.

His Jewish trials were before (1) Annas, the former high priest; (2) Caiaphas, the current high priest, as well as the Sanhedrin; and (3) an early morning trial again before "the whole council" (Mark 15:1). The religious authorities then handed Jesus over to (4) Pilate, who shuffled Him over to (5) Herod, who passed Him back to (6) Pilate for final judgment.

As Jesus stood trial before the Sanhedrin, many of the council's actions toward Jesus were shady and almost certainly illegal.

- Night meetings of the Sanhedrin were not permitted.
- Passover was underway, and capital trials were not to be held before a festival day.
- There was no evidence against Jesus, only the testimony of false witnesses.
- Jesus was given no defense counsel.
- Jesus wasn't even tried in a formal court of law but at the high priest's house (see Luke 22:54).

In their pride and self-importance, Caiaphas and the Sanhedrin were not concerned about due process. Their motive was to eliminate Jesus, a perceived threat to their power and prominence among the people. So they declared Him guilty of blasphemy and threatening to destroy the temple (false charges), beat Him, and turned Him over to Pilate.

Jesus willingly endured the injustice and mistreatment for our sakes.

Lord Jesus, You were condemned unjustly. By Your grace, we are pardoned. We praise You for Your sacrifice for us. Amen.

SUPREME INJUSTICE

Now the chief priests and the whole council were seeking false testimony against Jesus that they might put Him to death, but they found none, though many false witnesses came forward. (MATTHEW 26:59–60)

To say that Jesus' treatment by the Sanhedrin was unfair is a colossal understatement. Yet in spite of it all, God accomplished His purpose: the salvation of the world.

Let's be perfectly clear—no one took Jesus' life from Him. He willingly gave His life as the sacrifice for the world's sins. He said in John's Gospel, "For this reason the Father loves Me, because I lay down My life that I may take it up again. No one takes it from Me, but I lay it down of My own accord. I have authority to lay it down, and I have authority to take it up again. This charge I have received from My Father" (John 10:17–18).

Notice what Jesus is saying. As He spoke about laying down His life, His did so in the context of His Father's mission. In everything He did, Jesus acted in accord with His Father's will. Before the creation of the world, the Father appointed His only-begotten Son to redeem the world. By submitting Himself to crucifixion, Jesus submitted to His Father's plan.

Under the delusion of self-righteousness, Caiaphas and the Sanhedrin were certain that *they* were carrying out God's will. They thought that by killing Jesus, they were protecting their society from a menace. After Jesus raised Lazarus from the dead, the Jewish leaders assembled to plot His assassination. A respected voice spoke up: "But one of them, Caiaphas, who was high priest that year, said to them, 'You know nothing at all. Nor do you understand that it is better for you that one man should die for the people, not that the whole nation should perish'" (John 11:49–50). Caiaphas thought he was being a good leader and imparting practical wisdom: better for one man to die than for that one man to incite the masses and incur the wrath of Rome.

But Caiaphas was clueless that he and his cohorts were bad guys in a divine drama that would culminate in their nemesis achieving victory over sin and the grave. Through their wicked actions, God achieved a holy objective: one man died that He might give salvation for humankind.

Perhaps you've faced injustice, maybe even at the hands of people who thought they were doing the right thing but were, in fact, very wrong. You've probably experienced the unfairness of life—evil is often called good, wrong is considered right, and immorality is deemed acceptable.

Take heart. Jesus suffered the most severe injustice of all, and through His sacrifice, God accomplished the greatest good of all. Surely God works all things together for the good of those who love Him (see Romans 8:28).

Lord Jesus, You suffered the worst injustice of all. When I'm discouraged by unfairness, give me solace in knowing that You understand. Help me remember Your example and emulate it. Amen.

THE SUPREME JUDGE

Jesus said to him, "You have said so. But I tell you, from now on you will see the Son of Man seated at the right hand of Power and coming on the clouds of heaven." (MATTHEW 26:64)

As He stood before Caiaphas and the Sanhedrin with His immediate future in the balance, Jesus made an astounding statement about the distant future. The silent treatment had exasperated Caiaphas. He wanted an answer—now. He barked at Jesus, "I adjure You by the living God, tell us if You are the Christ, the Son of God" (Matthew 26:63). Under oath, Jesus answered, "You have said so. But I tell you, from now on you will see the Son of Man seated at the right hand of Power and coming on the clouds of heaven."

What an incredible reversal! Caiaphas was acting as a judge, presiding over Jesus' trial. But Jesus promised a day when He, the Son of Man, will return as Judge.

Jesus' favorite term for Himself is Son of Man. In Matthew's Gospel, Jesus calls Himself the Son of Man thirty times. The title reminds us that Jesus was fully God and fully human, Son of God and Son of Man. Jesus' favorite title also points back to an Old Testament prophecy depicting the coming Messiah as the Son of Man.

In Daniel 7, Daniel describes an awesome scene. God, called the Ancient of Days, takes His seat in the heavenly throne room. Then someone approaches God.

And behold, with the clouds of heaven there came one like a son of man, and He came to the Ancient of Days and was presented before Him. And to Him was given dominion and glory and a kingdom, that all peoples, nations, and languages should serve Him; His dominion is an everlasting dominion, which shall not pass away, and His kingdom one that shall not be destroyed. (Daniel 7:13–14)

We've seen these words! On the clouds. One like a son of man. Jesus' words match this prophetic language. Caiaphas knew Jesus was making a spectacular claim, and so the high priest tore his robes and declared Jesus' words blasphemous.

Blasphemy is language that dishonors God. Jesus was not the one dishonoring God, Caiaphas was. The high priest had set himself against God by opposing God's Son, who stood before him. In a complete reversal, the man Caiaphas judged will one day return to judge all of the living and the dead, including Caiaphas raised from the dead. God "has fixed a day on which He will judge the world in righteousness by a man whom He has appointed; and of this He has given assurance to all by raising Him from the dead" (Acts 17:31).

The judged will be the Judge. And all who are covered in His blood will be declared innocent by grace through faith!

Lord Jesus, You sit at the Father's right hand and will one day return in judgment. Until that great day, keep my heart fixed on You. Amen.

STANDING FIRM
UNDER PRESSURE

And Peter was following Him at a distance, as far as the courtyard of the high priest, and going inside he sat down with the guards to see the end. (MATTHEW 26:58)

An important detail is easy to miss in this text. The action centers on Jesus, Caiaphas, and the Sanhedrin, but another notable person in the passage is Peter.

Apparently, the guards were either unaware or didn't feel threatened by the presence of the man who just hours (or minutes) earlier had chopped off the ear of the high priest's servant when Jesus was arrested in the garden (see John 18:10). In addition to being the only Gospel to identify Peter as the knife-wielding disciple, John also informs us that another disciple (most likely John himself) knew the high priest and vouched for Peter to gain admission into the courtyard of the high priest.

Peter's appearance in the narrative right before Jesus' trial before the Sanhedrin prepares the reader for what comes after the trial: Peter's triple denial of Jesus. To use a literary term, Peter is a foil for Jesus at this point in the narrative. The courage and faithfulness of Jesus stands in sharp contrast to Peter's cowardice and failure under pressure.

We'd expect more from Peter. Previously in the Gospel account, he's a man of courage and faith. In addition to defending Jesus in the garden, on an earlier occasion, Peter boldly declared Jesus' divinity. When Jesus asked the disciples, "But who do you say that I am?" (Matthew 16:15), Peter spoke up: "You are the Christ, the Son of the living God" (Matthew 16:16).

Peter also promised unwavering loyalty to Jesus. After the Last Supper, when Jesus predicted that His followers would scatter under duress, Peter declared, "Though they all fall away because of You, I will never fall away" (Matthew 26:33) and "Even if I must die with You, I will not deny You" (Matthew 26:35).

So as Peter sits with the guards to see the end of Jesus' trial, the scene is set for a heroic intervention, a display of solidarity with his master and friend. But that's not what happened.

As Peter watched, Jesus set the bar high. Under pressure, Jesus held to His testimony. After hearing false witnesses, Jesus stood by the truth. With everything hanging in the balance, Jesus gave a strong confession.

Peter crumbled. Jesus did not.

If you've ever folded under pressure, you're not alone. Peter did too. But Jesus did not. He is always present to forgive you, strengthen you, and set you on your feet again.

Lord Jesus, You stood firm while under intense pressure. Forgive me for the times when I have been weak under pressure and strengthen me to withstand temptations and trials gracefully. Amen.

SOMETIMES SILENCE IS THE BEST RESPONSE

But Jesus remained silent.
(MATTHEW 26:63)

This week's reading raises one big question:

Why did Jesus remain silent?

Jesus could have defended Himself against false witnesses, but He allowed their testimony to go unanswered. No rebuttal. No defense. Silence.

The religious leaders were grasping at straws. They were desperate for anything that could incriminate Jesus. Their opinion of Jesus was based on emotion, not fact. Instead of following the evidence where it led, Jesus' opponents had already made up their minds about Him and were searching for something incriminating. "Now the chief priests and the whole council were seeking false testimony against Jesus that they might put Him to death, but they found none, though many false witnesses came forward" (Matthew 26:59–60).

Finally, two witnesses came forward with an accusation almost connected to the facts—but not exactly. They misquoted Jesus as saying, "I am able to destroy the temple of God, and to rebuild it in three days" (Matthew 26:61). The quote from Jesus closest to those words is John 2:19: "Destroy this temple, and in three days I will raise it up."

Notice the discrepancies. Jesus did not say He would destroy the temple—He implied that they would. And He said He would raise it up, not rebuild it. The evangelist makes clear that Jesus was referring to His body, the true temple of God, not a building (see John 2:21). False witnesses twisted Jesus' words. He could have objected. He could

have set the record straight. But He remained silent. Why?

First, His silence was, in itself, a response—a way of saying that the charges were so ridiculous that they didn't merit an answer. He did not dignify their lies with a verbal reply. Silence is a legitimate reply. It communicates. It sends a message. We don't have to be baited into an argument. Sometimes, you have to speak up to set the record straight, so that rumors and lies don't persist. Other times, it's best to remain silent, to allow your accusers' words to fall to the ground and die there.

Second, Jesus is the Lamb of God, a role He fulfilled to perfection. As the prophet Isaiah predicted, "He was oppressed, and He was afflicted, yet He opened not His mouth; like a lamb that is led to the slaughter, and like a sheep that before its shearers is silent, so He opened not His mouth" (Isaiah 53:7). Jesus was the complete fulfillment of Old Testament prophecy.

Sometimes silence is the best response.

Lord Jesus, Lamb of God, You remained silent in the face of false accusations. Thank You for Your restraint and commitment to endure whatever was necessary for my salvation. Through the power of Your Holy Spirit, enable me to follow Your example of restraint and commitment. Amen.

JESUS' BODY AND BLOOD—FOR YOU

Then they spit in His face and struck Him. And some slapped Him, saying, "Prophesy to us, You Christ! Who is it that struck You?" (MATTHEW 26:67–68)

Just hours before Jesus' trial before the Sanhedrin, He ate the Last Supper with His disciples. In instituting the Holy Meal, He said some amazing things that have deep significance for us as His followers:

"Take, eat; this is My body" (Matthew 26:26). In the Lord's Supper, we eat the body of Jesus. This is the same body that stood before Caiaphas and the Sanhedrin. This is the same body that was spit upon, struck, and slapped. Like a lamb that is led to the slaughter, Christ sacrificed this body for you and me. And in His endless grace, He gives us this body every time we eat the bread of Holy Communion.

"Drink of it, all of you, for this is My blood of the covenant, which is poured out for many for the forgiveness of sins" (Matthew 26:27–28). In the Lord's Supper, we drink the blood of Jesus. This is the same blood that leaked from broken vessels under His skin as He was beaten and bruised at His trial. This is the same blood that poured from His body on the cross as He died for our sins.

In Holy Communion, the Lamb of God who died for the sins of the world comes to us. He comes to us to forgive our sins. No, you and I were not in the company of the Sanhedrin as they interrogated Jesus and declared Him deserving of death. But we are responsible for His death in another way. Christ died for the sins of the world, and that includes our sins. When we are mean-spirited to others, we sin against Jesus. When we treat others unjustly, we are acting in opposition to the God of justice. Jesus willingly went to the cross for our sins.

And by His sacrifice, we are redeemed. Your sins are not counted against you. In His trial, sins that Jesus did not commit were counted against Him. These sins were fabrications, concocted offenses with no basis in fact.

On the cross, too, sins that Jesus did not commit are counted against Him. These sins are real—your sins and my sins. In exchange, we receive pardon! "For our sake He made Him to be sin who knew no sin, so that in Him we might become the righteousness of God" (2 Corinthians 5:21).

As you eat His body and drink His blood, this gift of complete forgiveness is yours!

Lord Jesus, You gave Your body and blood for all people on the cross, and You give Your body and blood to me in Your Holy Supper. Nourish me with Your grace so that I may serve You with a free conscience and a heart overflowing with joy. Amen.

PETER'S DENIALS, JUDAS'S DEATH

WEEK 39—MATTHEW 26:69–27:10

Now Peter was sitting outside in the courtyard. And a servant girl came up to him and said, "You also were with Jesus the Galilean." But he denied it before them all, saying, "I do not know what you mean." And when he went out to the entrance, another servant girl saw him, and she said to the bystanders, "This man was with Jesus of Nazareth." And again he denied it with an oath: "I do not know the man." After a little while the bystanders came up and said to Peter, "Certainly you too are one of them, for your accent betrays you." Then he began to invoke a curse on himself and to swear, "I do not know the man." And immediately the rooster crowed. And Peter remembered the saying of Jesus, "Before the rooster crows, you will deny Me three times." And he went out and wept bitterly.

When morning came, all the chief priests and the elders of the people took counsel against Jesus to put Him to death. And they bound Him and led Him away and delivered Him over to Pilate the governor.

Then when Judas, His betrayer, saw that Jesus was condemned, he changed his mind and brought back the thirty pieces of silver to the chief priests and the elders, saying, "I have sinned by betraying innocent blood." They said, "What is that to us? See to it yourself." And throwing down the pieces of silver into the temple, he departed, and he went and hanged himself. But the chief priests, taking the pieces of silver, said, "It is not lawful to put them into the treasury, since it is blood money." So they took counsel and bought with them the potter's field as a burial place for strangers. Therefore that field has been called the Field of Blood to this day. Then was fulfilled what had been spoken by the prophet Jeremiah, saying, "And they took the thirty pieces of silver, the price of Him on whom a price had been set by some of the sons of Israel, and they gave them for the potter's field, as the Lord directed me."

TWO BROKEN SINNERS

And immediately the rooster crowed. (MATTHEW 26:74)

Peter had been so close to Jesus and had seen so much of Jesus' power and love. During those final, peaceful hours, Peter vowed to be the last man standing, faithful no matter what. But when things fell apart, he proved to be just like everyone else.

Peter and John had followed as Jesus was led to the grounds of the high priest's residence. John, being known to the high priest's family, entered the courtyard, and brought Peter in also.

In the courtyard, a woman recognized Peter. Taken aback, Peter denied being with Jesus. To avoid further attention, Peter headed to the gate of the courtyard. Once again, a servant girl confronted him. This time, Peter expressed his denial with an oath to add credibility to his response.

Boastful, brash Peter stood in the darkness until joining some soldiers near a fire. But he was recognized and questioned a third time. He tried to deny it, swearing that he didn't know Jesus. He was doomed, until the rooster crowed. Suddenly the guards turned away from him because the doors of the high priest's palace opened, and Jesus was led out to be taken to Pilate.

Peter turned with them and saw the swollen, bloody face of Jesus, who stared back at him (see Luke 22:61). Jesus' condemnation was Peter's release. Those who a moment ago had surrounded him now joined the escort to Pilate's quarters, and Peter found himself alone.

Here Matthew transitions to Judas, the disciple who betrayed the Lord. Matthew tells us that when Judas saw the consequence of his betrayal, he changed his mind. Judas approached the religious leaders again, this time to confess and return the money. But they cared nothing for Judas's change of heart. Judas goes to the temple and hurls the bag of coins into the entrance of the Holy Place. The leaders can't put the dirty money back in their accounts, so they buy a field to be used as a cemetery for "strangers." This fulfills Old Testament prophecy (see Jeremiah 6; also Zechariah 11:12–13, where the money is used to remove Israel's shepherd).

Judas was overcome by guilt but was convinced Jesus could never accept him back. He forgot that Jesus could have betrayed him to the other disciples but chose instead to let him leave the Supper unharmed. He also forgot that Jesus was willingly laying down His life and no one could take it from Him—not Annas, Caiaphas, or Judas.

Judas's sin was no less forgivable than Peter's sin. Had he waited until Sunday morning, he would have seen Jesus' victory over death, and could have been restored to the Lord and the other disciples the same way Peter would be. But Judas took matters into his own hands. He hanged himself and is damned to hell (see John 17:12).

Dear Jesus, give us the courage to always confess that we know You, Savior and Son of God. Amen.

EVEN THE MOST DEVOTED CHRISTIANS SIN

A servant girl came up to him and said, "You also were with Jesus the Galilean." (MATTHEW 26:69)

There is nothing worse for us than to be separated from God. God is our life, the vine that supports the very life we as branches have. Who would cut off that life-giving connection? While it seems unthinkable, our texts give us two instances where a man steps away from Jesus but soon regrets it deeply.

These acts of betrayal came just a few hours after Jesus said to His disciples that one among them would betray Him. This was in the context of the Supper and His washing of their feet. This was a high point of their three years of following Jesus—how could they be closer than having Jesus wash their feet and sharing His body and blood through the bread and wine of the Supper? But this gift of life and this closeness would soon be broken.

Both Peter and Judas were near Jesus on this dark night, and they might have done so much more. But Judas, for the love of money, led the soldiers to Jesus. And Peter, fearing for himself, denied that he knew Jesus at all. As with Judas and Peter, Satan strikes at our weakest point and causes us to turn from God too. Peter's sin was no greater than that of the disciples who ran away. Judas's sin was no greater than the chief priests who carried out their evil plan. These men's stories are recorded so we will see that even Jesus' closest friends were weak. We all sin, just as these two men did. None of us can stand on our own power.

Yet the Gospels record that Peter repented and later received Jesus' forgiveness. Here is the primary message for us: even the most devoted Christians sin, but when we repent, Jesus forgives us. He carried our sins to the cross and suffered for them in our place. His sacrifice atoned for our sins. Therefore, because of His love for us, we will never be separated from God.

Lord Jesus, hold us firmly in the faith so we can always confess that You are our Savior. Help us remain faithful to death so that we receive the crown of life. Amen.

STEPPING FORWARD INTO TRIAL AND CRUCIFIXION

When morning came, all the chief priests and the elders of the people took counsel against Jesus to put Him to death. (MATTHEW 27:1)

What good Jesus had done in these three years of His ministry. He healed countless people of every illness imaginable. He cast out demons numbering even into the thousands. He raised the dead, to the astonishment of the crowds. He taught the Word of God as only the Son of God could speak. He taught with authority, giving firm hope of forgiveness for those who sought that forgiveness. He confounded His enemies when they tried to stop His gift of forgiveness. All this good could have continued. There would be more who were ill, more demons to be silenced, more storms to calm, and more crowds to feed.

But from an earthly point of view—from the disciples' point of view—all that would never happen if Jesus were to die. They could not understand what good His death would do. But Jesus knew the whole picture. He insisted on pursuing His death as the next necessary step. More physical healing and more teaching would not save the world. Without His suffering and death for the sins of the world, every single soul would be lost, including the Twelve and all those who received His healing. And so Jesus set His face firmly toward the cross.

Jesus' last hours show that even His closest followers still did not completely understand Him—why it was necessary that He should die and then rise again. They clung to the hope that He would choose the path of simple life, not death.

The religious leaders did not acknowledge Jesus as the Messiah, so they saw His death as no loss at all. By His death, they would remove an unstoppable rival. Once again, they could be the authorities on faith and life. This bothersome carpenter from Nazareth would finally be silenced.

But with His divine knowledge, Jesus knew precisely what was to happen. The betrayal had to happen so that He could step freely into the hands of the soldiers. But He knew that this step would be frightening to His disciples. So He encouraged His friends to pray against temptation, and He prayed for them too. Along with His example of prayer to the Father, Jesus had previously given them the gift of the Lord's Supper, the new covenant by which to sustain their faith. With a heart for those He loves, Jesus provides a means by which we receive Him and His blessed grace and mercy.

Lord Jesus, we are in awe of Your courage and determination as You step forward into the trial and crucifixion. Keep us bold to confess You as the one who saves us from death through Your death. Amen.

MURDEROUS CROWDS AND FAITHFUL WITNESSES

And Peter remembered the saying of Jesus, "Before the rooster crows, you will deny Me three times." (MATTHEW 26:75)

And all spoke well of Him and marveled at the gracious words that were coming from His mouth. And they said, 'Is not this Joseph's son?'" (Luke 4:22).

Jesus grew up in the small town of Nazareth and was known as the carpenter, the son of Joseph. When He was thirty years old, Jesus began His public ministry—He was baptized by John the Baptist and then tempted for forty days in the desert. He then began to teach publicly, praised by those who heard Him.

He then returned to Nazareth and spoke in the synagogue on the Sabbath. Initially, the townspeople were impressed by what He said. But they turned on Him quickly. Jesus said that He was the fulfillment of the Old Testament, but the crowd of people who thought they knew Him was enraged. How could this son of Joseph be so boastful? They brought Him to the brow of a hill outside town, intending to kill Him. But Jesus walked through the crowd and went away.

They were sure they knew Him and, on the basis of what they knew, they sought to kill Him. He would not die at the hands of that Nazareth crowd nor die on that hill outside of town. But now He chose to die through another denial and betrayal, surrounded by a murderous crowd, on another hill outside of town.

Acts 3:14–15

"But you denied the Holy and Righteous One, and asked for a murderer to be granted to you, and you killed the Author of life, whom God raised from the dead. To this we are witnesses." What a change in Peter! Three times he denied knowing Jesus on that Maundy Thursday night. But following Pentecost, Peter fearlessly preaches Christ in Jerusalem, confronting many of those who had a hand in the crucifixion of Jesus.

How striking that the one who denied Jesus now reminds the crowd in Jerusalem that they had rejected the Savior, the very Messiah for whom they were waiting. Instead of saving the Lord of Life, they gave freedom to the murderer Barabbas. But this was the plan of God that through His Son, the guilty would be released and the innocent One would die. Now Peter is glad to be the witness of God's plan. He traces the entire journey from Jesus' ministry to His death and then victorious resurrection. Let us listen to Peter's witness and find the words that lead to the Author of Life.

Heavenly Father, give us the courage to be faithful witnesses of Jesus, pointing the world to hope in the power of His death and resurrection. Amen.

JUDAS'S BETRAYAL AND PETER'S DENIAL

And they took the thirty pieces of silver, the price of Him on whom a price had been set. (MATTHEW 27:9)

This passage raises several questions:

Why did Peter have to deny Jesus three times?

Jesus predicted that Peter would deny Him three times, but He did not cause Peter to deny Him. Peter's fear led him to progressively stronger denials of Jesus—first he disowned Jesus, then he swore an oath, and finally called curses upon himself. Panicking, he was more afraid in that moment of being arrested by the Jewish authorities than he feared God's punishment on Judgment Day.

These public denials contrasted sharply with Peter's earlier actions. Peter was the first of the disciples to express his belief in Jesus as the Son of God and had been the one to step out of the boat and walk to Jesus. But Peter's courage failed him this dark Maundy Thursday night.

Why would Jesus have chosen Judas as a disciple in the first place?

Judas, who betrayed Jesus, was also the money handler for the disciples. John records that Judas helped himself to the apostles' funds. Matthew's Gospel was written to a wide readership who knew Old Testament prophecy and history. He draws on Jeremiah and Zechariah to show the bigger picture of how Jesus was the fulfillment of God's covenant with His people, that Jesus was the true King of Israel. Judas was a key actor in the plan of salvation. Judas was not predestined to betray Jesus to fulfill prophecies uttered hundreds of years before his birth. Old Testament prophecies of human sin never caused humans to sin against God, otherwise God would be guilty of making people sin (see James 1:13, "Let no one say when he is tempted, 'I am being tempted by God,' for God cannot be tempted with evil, and He Himself tempts no one"). Though He knew Judas would betray Him, Jesus genuinely loved Judas and sought to turn him from his sin over and again with the Last Supper and in the Garden of Gethsemane.

What is the difference between Judas's betrayal and Peter's denial?

In one sense, there is no difference. Both men sinned. Both did just as Jesus said they would. What happened after their sin is the primary lesson for us. Judas felt remorse but did not repent. Peter felt remorse and did repent. Peter was forgiven and went on to serve the Lord with the whole of his life. Judas served only himself, even to the last moment of his life. The Holy Spirit guarded Peter in the saving faith of Christ Jesus, and he received the greatest gift any believer can hope for—forgiveness and redemption that only the Son of God can give.

Lord Jesus, help us to know our sins but, even more, to know Your forgiveness won through Your suffering on the cross. By that suffering and death, forgive us! Amen.

THE RICHNESS OF JESUS' FORGIVENESS

And again he denied it with an oath: "I do not know the man." (MATTHEW 26:72)

Peter's denial and Judas's betrayal remind us of our own weakness, selfishness, greed, and cowardice. In Confession, we bring these sins before our Father in heaven and ask for forgiveness for Jesus' sake. As with David in Psalm 51, we ask for a clean heart and a new spirit. Our desire is fulfilled in so many parts of the Divine Service. Through Absolution, the Word of God, the sermon, and Holy Communion, God forgives our sins, strengthens our faith, and fills us with His Holy Spirit. By the Spirit, we are empowered to boldly confess our faith in Jesus Christ to the world.

As we might expect, these important verses about Peter's denial and the despair of Judas are found in all the lectionaries as part of the reading for Holy Week. Central to our verses is the failure of Peter to give a full confession of Jesus. A hymn that speaks to that, along with the coming cross, is "Stricken, Smitten, and Afflicted" (*LSB* 451), especially stanza 2.

> Tell me, ye who hear Him groaning,
> Was there ever grief like His?
> Friends through fear His cause
> disowning,
> Foes insulting His distress;
> Many hands were raised to wound Him,
> None would intervene to save;
> But the deepest stroke that pierced Him
> Was the stroke that justice gave.

Also important is the theme of witness to the truth of God, which is the center of many hymns. Stanzas 2 and 3 of "Hark the Voice of Jesus Crying" (*LSB* 826) remind us that we need not be a famous apostle to give a witness to Jesus.

> If you cannot speak like angels,
> If you cannot preach like Paul,
> You can tell the love of Jesus,
> You can say He died for all.
> If you cannot rouse the wicked
> With the judgment's dread alarms
> You can lead the little children
> To the Savior's waiting arms.

> If you cannot be a watch-man,
> Standing high on Zion's wall,
> Pointing out the path to heaven,
> Off'ring life and peace to all,
> With your prayers and with your bounties
> You can do what God commands;
> You can be like faithful Aaron,
> Holding up the prophet's hands.

We may not be well known, and we might not have exclusive insights into Jesus, but we can answer the world, "Yes, yes, indeed, I do know Him and, better than that, He has known me for all time."

Lord Jesus, help us to see the depth of Your suffering and the richness of the forgiveness that You bought through the cross. Amen.

JESUS' TRIALS BEFORE PILATE AND HEROD

WEEK 40—LUKE 23:1–25

Then the whole company of them arose and brought Him before Pilate. And they began to accuse Him, saying, "We found this man misleading our nation and forbidding us to give tribute to Caesar, and saying that He Himself is Christ, a king." And Pilate asked Him, "Are You the King of the Jews?" And He answered him, "You have said so." Then Pilate said to the chief priests and the crowds, "I find no guilt in this man." But they were urgent, saying, "He stirs up the people, teaching throughout all Judea, from Galilee even to this place."

When Pilate heard this, he asked whether the man was a Galilean. And when he learned that He belonged to Herod's jurisdiction, he sent Him over to Herod, who was himself in Jerusalem at that time. When Herod saw Jesus, he was very glad, for he had long desired to see Him, because he had heard about Him, and he was hoping to see some sign done by Him. So he questioned Him at some length, but He made no answer. The chief priests and the scribes stood by, vehemently accusing Him. And Herod with his soldiers treated Him with contempt and mocked Him. Then, arraying Him in splendid clothing, he sent Him back to Pilate. And Herod and Pilate became friends with each other that very day, for before this they had been at enmity with each other.

Pilate then called together the chief priests and the rulers and the people, and said to them, "You brought me this man as one who was misleading the people. And after examining Him before you, behold, I did not find this man guilty of any of your charges against Him. Neither did Herod, for he sent Him back to us. Look, nothing deserving death has been done by Him. I will therefore punish and release Him."

But they all cried out together, "Away with this man, and release to us Barabbas"—a man who had been thrown into prison for an insurrection started in the city and for murder. Pilate addressed them once more, desiring to release Jesus, but they kept shouting, "Crucify, crucify Him!" A third time he said to them, "Why? What evil has He done? I have found in Him no guilt deserving death. I will therefore punish and release Him." But they were urgent, demanding with loud cries that He should be crucified. And their voices prevailed. So Pilate decided that their demand should be granted. He released the man who had been thrown into prison for insurrection and murder, for whom they asked, but he delivered Jesus over to their will.

KING OF THE JEWS AND MUCH MORE

And Pilate asked Him, "Are you the King of the Jews?" And He answered him, "You have said so." (LUKE 23:3)

Appointed by emperor Tiberius to be governor of Judea, Pontius Pilate was responsible for keeping the peace, collecting taxes, minting coins, managing construction projects, presiding over civil court, and pronouncing sentences. Pilate also had the right to appoint the Jewish high priest (he had kept Caiaphas on as high priest well after Rome's customary four-year term). Pilate did not live in Jerusalem; he lived in Caesarea. But during the Jewish festivals, he stayed in Jerusalem to oversee the city, especially during the biggest festival of the year—Passover.

Pilate rose through the Roman military to reach his governor position. The province of Judea was subject to insurrection and unrest, so a military governor was appointed. Even by Roman standards, Pilate was a brutal governor. He did not hesitate to resort to military force, even killing Galileans in the temple courts who were plotting an insurrection rather than arresting them and bringing them to trial (see Luke 13:1).

Ordinarily, Pilate would not have been intimidated by Jewish crowds, but Pilate was in competition with Herod. Luke 23:12 notes that up to Good Friday, Pilate and Herod had been enemies. Herod sought rule over Judea and Jerusalem and sent bad reports to Caesar, accusing Pilate of being incompetent in governing the Jews. When Jesus was brought before him that morning, Pilate knew his political future was in jeopardy. At all costs, he had to show he could prevent a riot and control the Jewish leaders. That would be a difficult task with as many as two million Jewish pilgrims in Jerusalem.

Pilate questioned Jesus about what He had done. What an opportunity to sum up Jesus' three years of ministry. This could have been a time for the witness of so many to testify about Jesus' healing and teaching. Let those who were healed and even raised from the dead speak! Peter, in particular, could have given witness to all Jesus had done, but Peter denies knowing Jesus three times (see Luke 22:54–62). While Jesus could have spoken at great length Himself, He says very little. When Pilate asks if He is the King of the Jews, Jesus affirms that Pilate has said so, thereby deepening Pilate's worry. What is Pilate to do with a man who says He is the King of the Jews and who may be much more than that? What to do with a man who could raise the dead? Pilate and the crowd answered, "Crucify Him."

Lord Jesus, You stood on trial with silent nobility. Preserve us in the certainty that You are the King of the Jews and the Son of God, Savior of the world. Amen.

PILATE'S DESPERATE
SEARCH FOR A WAY OUT

*A third time [Pilate] said to them,
"Why? What evil has He done?
I have found in Him no guilt
deserving death."* (LUKE 23:22)

During the night, the religious leaders had tried to convict Jesus. Now, in the light of day, they meet with Pilate and bring three new charges against Jesus: they accuse Him of stirring up an insurrection, encouraging people not to pay their taxes, and claiming to be the King of the Jews.

The only charge that concerns Pilate is Jesus' kingship. Jesus' answer that His kingdom is not of this world is enough to satisfy Pilate—he tells the Jewish leaders that he has found Jesus innocent of the charges they made against Him.

That is where Pilate should end this trial. He should use his soldiers to give Jesus safe passage. But to avoid a riot or losing control of the crowds, he wants the Jewish leaders to make that choice. So he turns to a custom whereby he offers the Jews the choice of two harmless political prisoners he can release. This time he takes the most dangerous prisoner he has—Barabbas—and offers him alongside Jesus. But he underestimates these leaders' fear and hatred of Jesus. They demand that Pilate release Barabbas and crucify Jesus.

Having failed, Pilate desperately searches for another way out. That's when he realizes that Jesus is from Galilee—the district ruled by Herod—so he refers the matter to his enemy. For a long time, Herod had been curious about Jesus, the Galilean prophet who was performing miracles. Herod thinks Jesus might be John the Baptist brought back to life, so Herod wants to see Jesus either to witness the miracle of resurrection or, at least, to be entertained with a new miracle. He questions Jesus, but Jesus has absolutely nothing to say to Herod.

That silence is broken when the religious leaders raise their accusations again. When they demand that Herod condemn Jesus to death, Herod hands the case back to Pilate. Pilate tries one more desperate gamble—he has Jesus viciously scourged and then presents Jesus to the Jewish leaders and the crowd, saying, "Behold the man!" (John 19:5). He implies that this crippled, beaten figure is no threat. But seeing Jesus in this condition, they again demand crucifixion, threatening to report to Caesar that Pilate is sheltering a rival king.

In complete desperation, Pilate goes in and asks if Jesus understands that he has the authority to crucify Jesus or to release Him. Jesus responds that Pilate would have no authority over Him except that it had been given to him from above. Pilate is defeated. Seeing that a riot is beginning to break out, in futility, he tries to wash his hands of the responsibility for Jesus' death and hands Jesus over to their will.

*Dear Jesus, we can never thank You
enough for enduring the trial, the beatings,
and the cross, all to save us. Thank You for
bearing all this evil to rescue us. Amen.*

JESUS' CLEAR PURPOSE

For this purpose, I was born and for this purpose I have come into the world—to bear witness to the truth. Everyone who is of the truth listens to My voice. (JOHN 18:37)

Although they served in high places in the Roman government and had reputations as cruel men, Pilate and Herod were weak leaders who chose to give in to a vocal crowd rather than uphold the law and the authority of their position. They were concerned about the size of the crowd and of the threat of an uprising. Yet both had authority over the religious leaders, and either of them could have refused to cooperate with them. Both had taken Jesus into their custody and could have protected Him. Moreover, after their interrogations, both Pilate and Herod found Jesus to be innocent, so they could have called out the religious leaders as liars.

When Jesus told His followers that these events would take place, they did not accept it. Jesus choosing to die was incomprehensible to them. They had seen Jesus preach to thousands and perform miracles. He calmed raging storms, cast out screaming demons, and raised the dead. How could He possibly choose to die? He was life itself. They knew Him to be the Chosen One, the Messiah, the very Son of God. They believed Him to be the King who would release them from Roman rule and restore the kingdom to Israel. How could it be, then, that Jesus would be defeated?

Furthermore, the followers of Jesus had to ask what good would His death do. There were so many yet to be healed, fed, and sheltered. If Jesus were to die, it would be more than the loss of one holy man. It would be the end of the hopes of so many. Darkness and evil would have won if Jesus were to die.

But Jesus was not defeated. He was in full control. While Herod and Pilate struggled to escape the angry demands of the crowd, Jesus was silently fulfilling His purpose. The divine plan was being carried out, even through the anger of the crowd and the cowardice of Pilate. Jesus was fulfilling all the prophecies of the Old Testament as only the Lamb of God could do. Condemned for our sins and sentenced to death in our place, Jesus carried our sins and our hope of salvation.

Lord Jesus, You came to the world with a clear purpose—to speak the truth that would bring eternal life to the world. Keep us clearly hearing Your message of truth. Amen.

THE REJECTED SAVIOR AND KING

Everyone who is of the truth listens to My voice. (JOHN 18:37)

Many passages from the Bible illuminate this week's readings:

Matthew 20:18

"And the Son of Man will be delivered over to the chief priests and scribes, and they will condemn Him to death." The Jewish leaders will be satisfied with only one outcome: crucifixion. There is no hint of hearing witnesses or the discovery of truth. They are set on only one end—the cross. And Jesus has this same goal. He saw this day from eternity and knew He must be condemned by His own people. John had summed it up already at the start of his Gospel: "He came to His own, and His own people did not receive Him" (John 1:11). But He endured to bring grace and mercy to all, even those who rejected Him.

John 1:14

"We have seen His glory, glory as of the only Son from the Father, full of grace and truth." When Jesus says that "everyone who is of the truth listens to My voice" Pilate then asks, "What is truth?" (John 18:37–38). Pilate had given up hope of knowing any sure truth. But Jesus was the incarnation of truth, and His words continue to bring life through the work of the Holy Spirit. Through the Spirit, we recognize the truth of Jesus and the grace and life He brings the world.

John 18:14

"It was Caiaphas who had advised the Jews that it would be expedient that one man should die for the people." Caiaphas, the high priest, had no problem seeing one man die so that the whole nation should be saved. The ruling Jewish council worried that the Romans would see Jesus as a threat and destroy all Jews because of Him. But Caiaphas argued that it was better for one man to die to save the nation. With this, Caiaphas announced the very principle that Jesus was following. He was the one willing sacrifice who would save all people through His voluntary death.

Matthew 2:2

"[The Wise Men asked], 'Where is He who has been born king of the Jews? For we saw His star when it rose and have come to worship Him.'" Wise Gentile scholars sought the newborn Jesus and recognized Him as the King of the Jews. This was Jesus' birthright, not won by the power of Roman swords. At Jesus' trial, Pilate presents Jesus as the King of the Jews. The crown of thorns and purple robe were intended as mockery. But they have become lasting marks of His kingship. He came not only to be found and loved but also to be rejected by the very ones He was saving.

Lord Jesus, thank You for being the truth of God and the Eternal King of all people. Preserve us in Your kingdom. Amen.

JESUS' SILENT SUFFERING

[Pilate said,] "Your own nation and the chief priests have delivered You over to me. What have You done?" Jesus answered, "My kingdom is not of this world." (JOHN 18:35–36)

This week's readings bring up several challenging questions:

Why was Barabbas chosen instead of a different criminal?

The Gospel writers tell us two robbers were already scheduled for crucifixion that very day. It is likely that three men were condemned to be crucified that day, and the man in the center was mostly likely to be Barabbas, the ringleader of an insurrection that had resulted in murder. Pilate set Barabbas alongside Jesus, confident that the Jewish leaders did not consider Jesus to be as great a threat to law and order and to their own rule as Jewish authorities.

But Pilate failed to understand how great a threat the Jewish leaders considered Jesus to be for their positions as spiritual leaders. Their hatred of Jesus was so great that they let a murderous criminal go free. But that shows us what Jesus' death was all about. Our Savior took Barabbas's place—your place and mine. Because He took our place upon the cross, we can go free and live with Him forever.

Why was there so much back-and-forth between Pilate and the people and between Pilate and Herod?

On the surface, at least, Pilate was following customary court proceedings. He tried to get to the crux of the accusation and, when he recognized that Jesus had committed no crime against the government, he told this to the religious leaders. He was reluctant to condemn a man he saw as innocent. However, Pilate was faced with a very large and vocal crowd, and this frightened him even more than his own conscience. Giving in seemed safer than standing up to them. A cruel and unconscionable man, Pilate ordered scourging and brutality at the hands of the Roman soldiers against a man he knew was absolutely innocent.

Why does Jesus stay silent during the trials?

Jesus knew the hearts and minds of the religious leaders—and the Roman leaders as well. He knew that nothing He could say would change their minds or the situation, so He did not cast pearls before swine. By staying silent, Jesus remains in control. He confounds the Roman leaders and frustrates the Sanhedrin. However, Jesus speaks to Pilate—not to secure His own safety and release but to give Pilate a chance to hear the truth that might have led to repentance and faith. Throughout these trials, Jesus takes on abuse and mockery, and ultimately crucifixion and death, for our sake. He delivers us from these evils by His willing submission.

Heavenly Savior, You saved us by silently suffering the insults and ignorance of men. Keep us always in the truth that You are the King and Savior of all. Amen.

THE MAN WHO BORE THE SINS OF THE WORLD

So Jesus came out, wearing the crown of thorns and the purple robe. Pilate said to them, "Behold the man!" (JOHN 19:5)

In our texts this week, we've heard accusations in abundance shouted between Herod, Pilate, and the Jewish leaders. While many were quick to accuse others, Jesus stood quietly. Pilate presented Him to the crowd, saying, "Behold the man!" Behold the One who is taking the guilt of the world onto Himself. Jesus, the Son of God, was absolutely innocent and did not deserve the suffering, punishment, and death that He suffered. But Jesus suffered as our substitute, bearing the sins of the world. In that great exchange, announced in the Absolution, our sins are taken from us, and we are clothed with Jesus' perfect righteousness.

In worship, we confess our sins and guilt, acknowledging that we deserve punishment for all we have done. If we had to suffer that punishment, it couldn't be contained in one day, however dark it might be. Our sins should be punished here on earth and throughout eternity for all we have done. Like Barabbas, we deserve to suffer earthly punishment and eternal separation from God in heaven. Barabbas might not have known much about Jesus or the reason he was set free that morning. We, however, know exactly who saved us by His sacrifice, purely out of His mercy and love.

Given the important events of Good Friday, many themes from our texts are found in Lutheran hymnody. The crown of thorns is movingly described in stanza 1 of "O Sacred Head, Now Wounded" (*LSB* 449):

O sacred Head, now wounded,
With grief and shame weighed down,
Now scornfully surrounded
With thorns, Thine only crown.
O sacred Head, what glory,
What bliss, till now was Thine!
Yet, though despised and gory,
I joy to call Thee mine.

Another hymn that captures a key part of our text is "Stricken, Smitten, and Afflicted" (*LSB* 451). Stanza 2 describes Jesus' trial, the many accusations He faced, and the lack of support from His disciples.

Confessing our sins, believing His words of forgiveness, and responding in song and prayer, we praise God for His great loving sacrifice and the life He gives us for the sake of His Son, Jesus.

Our Savior, help us always to see You as the man who bore the sins of the world and the beloved Son of God, given to save the world. Amen.

JESUS SUFFERS AND IS LED TO THE CROSS

WEEK 41—MARK 15:16–32

And the soldiers led Him away inside the palace (that is, the governor's headquarters), and they called together the whole battalion. And they clothed Him in a purple cloak, and twisting together a crown of thorns, they put it on Him. And they began to salute Him, "Hail, King of the Jews!" And they were striking His head with a reed and spitting on Him and kneeling down in homage to Him. And when they had mocked Him, they stripped Him of the purple cloak and put His own clothes on Him. And they led Him out to crucify Him.

And they compelled a passerby, Simon of Cyrene, who was coming in from the country, the father of Alexander and Rufus, to carry His cross. And they brought Him to the place called Golgotha (which means Place of a Skull). And they offered Him wine mixed with myrrh, but He did not take it. And they crucified Him and divided His garments among them, casting lots for them, to decide what each should take. And it was the third hour when they crucified Him. And the inscription of the charge against Him read, "The King of the Jews." And with Him they crucified two robbers, one on His right and one on His left. And those who passed by derided Him, wagging their heads and saying, "Aha! You who would destroy the temple and rebuild it in three days, save Yourself, and come down from the cross!" So also the chief priests with the scribes mocked Him to one another, saying, "He saved others; He cannot save Himself. Let the Christ, the King of Israel, come down now from the cross that we may see and believe." Those who were crucified with Him also reviled Him.

HE WOULD NOT LET HIS PAIN BE DULLED

And the soldiers led Him away inside the palace (that is, the governor's headquarters), and they called together the whole battalion. And they clothed Him in a purple cloak, and twisting together a crown of thorns, they put it on Him. And they began to salute Him, "Hail, King of the Jews!" (MARK 15:16–18)

The Jewish religious leaders had tried to do away with Jesus quietly because they feared the Passover crowds who were all in on Jesus. Then it became a spectacle that they were able to turn to their advantage. Freedom for Barabbas, crucifixion for Jesus. Pilate decided not to go against the crowd, now turned against Jesus, and gave Him over to his battalion for crucifixion. Roman occupying troops were accustomed to doling out punishment. Since He was King of the Jews, they added some extras: they gave Jesus thorns for a crown and a purple cloak. Blood would have flowed from Jesus' head onto His garments. Once they were done mocking Him, the Romans whipped and beat Him.

It was Roman custom that prisoners facing crucifixion would carry their own cross to the site of their execution. But Jesus had been so badly whipped and beaten that after a short while, He could no longer carry the heavy lumber that made up the device of His death. A man from what would now be the north African country of Libya, Simon of Cyrene, was pulled from the crowd and forced to carry Jesus' cross.

Once Golgotha had been reached, the execution was carried out. Jesus was offered wine mixed with myrrh. This mixture would have dulled His pain, yet still He refused. Jesus was nailed to the cross, which is strangely omitted from every Gospel account. It is not until Thomas speaks in John 20:25 that the use of nails is confirmed: "Unless I see in His hands the mark of the nails, and place my finger into the mark of the nails, and place my hand into His side, I will never believe."

Pilate followed Roman custom and placed a sign above Jesus that publicized His crimes: "Jesus of Nazareth, King of the Jews." It is not known why Pilate chose this as the epitaph. It is possible that he was calling out the Sanhedrin who did not agree with it. Or was it for the purpose of demoralizing the Jewish people under Roman rule? They had welcomed Jesus on Sunday as their King, yet here He hung to die.

Jesus suffered. From His beatings and whippings, His skin would have been flayed as He was hung upon the rough cross, exacerbating His torture. Yet He would not let His pain be dulled. There have been many arguments of who killed Jesus. The Jewish leadership? Roman occupiers? No. All that happens here, no matter how horrific, is because our sin was that much worse. Jesus endured it all for us. May we remember the importance of this in our time of need: Jesus did not turn away.

Lord, prepare my heart as I remember the suffering of Your Son for me. In Jesus' name. Amen.

THE CONSEQUENCE OF EVERY SINFUL ACTION

And the soldiers led Him away inside the palace (that is, the governor's headquarters), and they called together the whole battalion. And they clothed Him in a purple cloak, and twisting together a crown of thorns, they put it on Him. And they began to salute Him, "Hail, King of the Jews!" And they were striking His head with a reed and spitting on Him and kneeling down in homage to Him. And when they had mocked Him, they stripped Him of the purple cloak and put His own clothes on Him. And they led Him out to crucify Him. (MARK 15:16–20)

Jesus suffered. There is no way around it. It was not only something He had to do; it was the purpose of God become Man. While they are disturbing, these events must happen.

Sin can easily be glossed over, forgotten, or explained away. Humans justify sinful nature and actions on a consistent basis. But when confronted by these passages, Christians realize that every sinful action has consequences. Every falsehood, lustful glance, prideful moment, selfish desire—every one was laid upon Jesus.

Jesus' lot to suffer was necessary for the rescue of the ones He loved.

In the 1990s, there was little access to the internet. Back then, to get a new book on spirituality or Christian living, a magazine was necessary. These magazines would not only carry books but other items for Christian people. One such item was an off-white T-shirt featuring the picture of a bloodied Jesus—His face turned away, His back clearly visible with bloody gashes from being whipped. The text on top and bottom of the picture read: "Want to know what true love is? Read between the lines." This shirt was over the top and bordered on bad taste—but it was also true.

Jesus chose to suffer and die for us. The lines on His back, the blood that poured from a thorny crown, and the piercings in His hands and feet declared His love. In the Old Testament, there is a word applied to God and His affinity for humanity: *chesed.* Often translated as "steadfast love," it is what Jesus displays in these passages. It is the point. No pain, no suffering, will turn Him away. He has a steadfast love that He will display to save those who are far off. Want to know how unbreakable that love is? Read between the lines.

Jesus, thank You for suffering for me. Amen.

WHY DOES JESUS GO TO THE CROSS?

And the soldiers led Him away inside the palace (that is, the governor's headquarters), and they called together the whole battalion. And they clothed Him in a purple cloak, and twisting together a crown of thorns, they put it on Him. And they began to salute Him, "Hail, King of the Jews!" And they were striking His head with a reed and spitting on Him and kneeling down in homage to Him. And when they had mocked Him, they stripped Him of the purple cloak and put His own clothes on Him. And they led Him out to crucify Him. And they compelled a passerby, Simon of Cyrene, who was coming in from the country, the father of Alexander and Rufus, to carry His cross. And they brought Him to the place called Golgotha (which means Place of a Skull). (MARK 15:16–22)

I f you want to know the mission of Jesus look no further. Or maybe pull up similar verses in Matthew 27:27–33, Luke 23:26, and John 19:1–17. It all leads to this. When the promise of a Messiah is made by God in the Garden of Eden, He knew that this was the path to salvation.

What would you have done? Imagine knowing your whole life, truly God and truly human, that this was the road you were walking toward. Suffering a death that was gruesome, torturous, and drawn out. Yet Jesus willingly goes, like a sheep led to slaughter.

And why? Why would He go? Because we are incredible people? Because of some amazing thing we will do? No. "For while we were still weak, at the right time Christ died for the ungodly. For one will scarcely die for a righteous person—though perhaps for a good person one would dare even to die—but God shows His love for us in that while we were still sinners, Christ died for us" (Romans 5:6–8).

Jesus takes on the brutal suffering of Holy Week for you—not some better version of you. Not you once you get your act together. For. You. While you were still weak. You did not have to earn His suffering and death, yet He still freely gives it. A gift beyond compare. Not because you are better but to make you better. This bloody journey turns sinners into saints. And Jesus chooses it for you.

Jesus, thank You for choosing to suffer for me. Thank You for taking on the cross for me. May I live in gratitude for what You did. Amen.

THE ATONING SACRIFICE

And they brought Him to the place called Golgotha (which means Place of a Skull). And they offered Him wine mixed with myrrh, but He did not take it. And they crucified Him and divided His garments among them, casting lots for them, to decide what each should take. And it was the third hour when they crucified Him. (MARK 15:22–25)

These scenes are the crescendo of the Gospel narrative. Take time to read through these following verses to see the plan of salvation arriving in Mark 15.

Leviticus 17:11

"For the life of the flesh is in the blood, and I have given it for you on the altar to make atonement for your souls, for it is the blood that makes atonement by the life."

Psalm 22:14–16, 18

"I am poured out like water, and all My bones are out of joint; My heart is like wax; it is melted within My breast; My strength is dried up like a potsherd, and My tongue sticks to My jaws; you lay Me in the dust of death. For dogs encompass Me; a company of evildoers encircles Me; they have pierced My hands and feet . . . they divide My garments among them, and for My clothing they cast lots."

Psalm 69:21

"They gave me poison for food, and for my thirst they gave me sour wine to drink."

Isaiah 25:7–8

"And He will swallow up on this mountain the covering that is cast over all peoples, the veil that is spread over all nations. He will swallow up death forever; and the Lord GOD will wipe away tears from all faces, and the reproach of His people He will take away from all the earth, for the LORD has spoken."

Isaiah 53:5–7

"But He was pierced for our transgressions; He was crushed for our iniquities; upon Him was the chastisement that brought us peace, and with His wounds we are healed. All we like sheep have gone astray; we have turned—every one—to his own way; and the LORD has laid on Him the iniquity of us all. He was oppressed, and He was afflicted, yet He opened not His mouth; like a lamb that is led to the slaughter, and like a sheep that before its shearers is silent, so He opened not His mouth."

God has been telling the story throughout Scripture of His Son who would be the atoning sacrifice. May we rejoice that our sin was put on His shoulders.

Lord, thank You for providing a sacrifice when my sin separated me from You. In Jesus' name. Amen.

THE TRUEST TITLE THAT COULD HAVE BEEN GIVEN

And the soldiers led Him away inside the palace (that is, the governor's headquarters), and they called together the whole battalion. And they clothed Him in a purple cloak, and twisting together a crown of thorns, they put it on Him. And they began to salute Him, "Hail, King of the Jews!" And they were striking His head with a reed and spitting on Him and kneeling down in homage to Him. And when they had mocked Him, they stripped Him of the purple cloak and put His own clothes on Him. And they led Him out to crucify Him. And they compelled a passerby, Simon of Cyrene, who was coming in from the country, the father of Alexander and Rufus, to carry His cross. And they brought Him to the place called Golgotha (which means Place of a Skull). And they offered Him wine mixed with myrrh, but He did not take it. And they crucified Him and divided His garments among them, casting lots for them, to decide what each should take. And it was the third hour when they crucified Him. And the inscription of the charge against Him read, "The King of the Jews." And with Him they crucified two robbers, one on His right and one on His left. (MARK 15:16–27)

Amid all of this suffering, there is an insult that hangs above Jesus' head. It is placed there by Pontius Pilate, and it reads, "King of the Jews." This was His crime—He claimed to be the King of the Jews.

It is strange that this is the crime Pilate uses to identify the reason for Jesus' crucifixion. John 19:20 tells us it was written in three languages: Greek, the common tongue of the Empire; Aramaic, the local dialect; and finally in Latin, the official, legal language of Rome. Every person passing the cross would be able to read this charge. It infuriated the ruling religious leaders. The Jewish high priests, Pharisees, and scribes did not claim Jesus as their king. Pilate mocked them. He knew of their belief in a Messiah who would come and rescue them. This sign derides that idea. This was the dream of their Messiah, their king. The best they could offer was hanging here, crucified by Rome. They protested vigorously, but this time Pilate stood firm—"What I have written I have written" (John 19:22).

Little did Pilate know that this was not a written conviction of a crime but, in fact, the truest title that could have been received. Jesus was the King of the Jews, Israel reduced to one. His people, the Promised Land, all of it, was for the purpose of His coming. He was the man come to free many. Not from the tyranny of Rome but from the tyranny of sin. He would remove it as He hung on that cross. King of the Jews, yes. But truly the King of kings.

Dear Jesus, on the cross, You declare victory over death. You are King of kings and Lord of lords, and You have called me friend. I rejoice in this Good News. Amen.

FINDING JOY IN JESUS' SUFFERING

And those who passed by derided Him, wagging their heads and saying, "Aha! You who would destroy the temple and rebuild it in three days, save Yourself, and come down from the cross!" So also the chief priests with the scribes mocked Him to one another, saying, "He saved others; He cannot save Himself. Let the Christ, the King of Israel, come down now from the cross that we may see and believe." Those who were crucified with Him also reviled Him. (MARK 15:29–32)

Every year, the church calendar leads the Body of Christ through the season of Lent. When you hear "Lent" you might think of giving up chocolate or pizza, fasting, or fish fries. But the purpose of Lent is to remind the church that it is in need of a Savior.

Take a moment. Read the full passage assigned for this week. Jesus allows Himself to be subjected to torture and hung upon a cross. He does this out of the love He has for you. You need a Savior. You have a debt you cannot pay. Jesus took that burden with every strike of the whip and hammer of the nail. It is all for you.

Upon many churchly vestments, the letters *INRI* are written. These stand for Pilate's declaration of Jesus' crime in Latin, which was fastened to the cross above His head: *Iesus Nazarenus Rex Iudaeorum,* translated as "Jesus of Nazareth, King of the Jews." What Pilate meant to mock Him has become the banners of His church. The people of God have taken up that which was intended to insult and turned it into a rallying cry.

There is joy in the suffering of Jesus. It does not make sense, yet there it is. Jesus takes on scorn, torture, and death for His people. He has come to seek and save the lost. In what should be gruesome, we find hope. In His blood poured out for us, we find a way back to God. In His flesh torn for us, we find a home in the kingdom of heaven. Every week, we partake of flesh and blood to be renewed over and again. His suffering delivers to us the gifts of the family of God.

It does not make sense that so much suffering would be a blessing, yet it is.

It does not make sense that an insult would become a promise for all people emblazoned across time and space.

Yet, through Jesus' suffering and death, we find the perfect sacrifice. The price we could not pay, He did. He went willingly.

Because of this, we find hope in suffering. God did not leave His creation behind. He has redeemed us through the blood of His Son.

Read through the passages for this week again. Rejoice—your King has come. He has paid the price you could not pay. Endured the suffering that you could not. Died the death that was meant for you. You needed a Savior, and God provided His Son.

Rejoice. Jesus calls you friend. Go in peace, saint of heaven, to love and serve the Lord.

Heavenly Father, let me find hope in the suffering and death of Jesus. In Jesus' name. Amen.

JESUS IS CRUCIFIED

Week 42—Luke 23:32–43; John 19:25–27

Two others, who were criminals, were led away to be put to death with Him. And when they came to the place that is called The Skull, there they crucified Him, and the criminals, one on His right and one on His left. And Jesus said, "Father, forgive them, for they know not what they do." And they cast lots to divide His garments. And the people stood by, watching, but the rulers scoffed at Him, saying, "He saved others; let Him save Himself, if He is the Christ of God, His Chosen One!" The soldiers also mocked Him, coming up and offering Him sour wine and saying, "If You are the King of the Jews, save Yourself!" There was also an inscription over Him, "This is the King of the Jews."

One of the criminals who were hanged railed at Him, saying, "Are You not the Christ? Save Yourself and us!" But the other rebuked him, saying, "Do you not fear God, since you are under the same sentence of condemnation? And we indeed justly, for we are receiving the due reward of our deeds; but this man has done nothing wrong." And he said, "Jesus, remember me when You come into Your kingdom." And He said to him, "Truly, I say to you, today you will be with Me in paradise." . . .

But standing by the cross of Jesus were His mother and His mother's sister, Mary the wife of Clopas, and Mary Magdalene. When Jesus saw His mother and the disciple whom He loved standing nearby, He said to His mother, "Woman, behold, your son!" Then He said to the disciple, "Behold, your mother!" And from that hour the disciple took her to his own home.

ISN'T IT IRONIC?

Two others, who were criminals, were led away to be put to death with Him. And when they came to the place that is called The Skull, there they crucified Him, and the criminals, one on His right and one on His left. (LUKE 23:32–33)

Golgotha.
Calvary.
The Skull.

Across history, you are hard-pressed to find a form of punishment carried out by a legitimate government as gruesome and grotesque as crucifixion. It was not a coincidence that the location outside Jerusalem where the Romans carried this out was given a moniker so universally associated with death. And the fact of the matter was that the punishment was carried out so publicly, in such humiliating fashion, that it was intended not only to punish the guilty but to scare citizens into compliance as they passed by the horrific scene.

In this environment, it was not uncommon for mourners to witness a loved one suffer or for leaders of the community to stand and watch in contempt of the Roman officials carrying out their atrocious discipline. Scoffing and mocking was reserved for the oppressors who had brought this suffering to their community. There were clear lines separating "them" from "us" in this climate, and crucifixion was one of the boldest of those lines.

Yet, as we stand at the foot of the cross, there are no cries for justice. There is no disgust that an innocent man was suffering through this appalling punishment. Instead, we hear scoffing, insults, and jeers hurled at the crucified. Suddenly, a faction of the people who were so opposed to the ruling power are now standing with them, side by side.

A people who were so opposed to anyone who was not like "them" that they would observe strict laws regarding such contact are now publicly celebrating the carrying out of this oppression.

There is great irony that these sworn enemies who struggle to get along day in and day out are united around an experience taking place in relation to one of their most destructive chasms. Two entities, united in death.

The greater irony would be in the words spoken by Jesus from that cross. The instrument intended to punish the wrong-doer would now be the instrument that God uses to unite mankind to Himself. When Jesus says, "Father, forgive them, for they know not what they do" (Luke 23:34), He includes the Romans, the religious leaders, and all those who are blinded to their sin by their own agenda, arrogance, and struggle. Jesus prays from His moment of suffering not for Himself—not for only one people or another—but instead unites all of mankind in our need for forgiveness. And that forgiveness would be satisfied on a hill that recalls a skull—where death would find its end.

Isn't *that* ironic?

Gracious heavenly Father, through Your Son, Jesus Christ, You have united us to You by His death and resurrection. Even as an undeserving people, help us to see past ourselves and find peace in the sure forgiveness and salvation won by the Lamb of God on the cross. In Jesus' name. Amen.

EVERYONE BUT HIMSELF

[Jesus] said to him, "Truly, I say
to you, today you will be with
Me in paradise." (LUKE 23:43)

While in college, a close friend surmised about ministry that "it's all about people, man!" That premise is one that has been emphasized in various areas of the world as it considers what leadership is. One speaker on leadership suggested that good leaders recognize that when they walk in a room, they now have a relationship with every person in that shared experience. Cultivating those relationships then becomes the primary focus of the leader to provide the best possible environment for all those involved. In social terms, this would be known as "reading the room."

As Jesus hangs on that cross, He has every reason to cry in agony, to lament His situation, and to condemn those who are carrying out this injustice. Yet Jesus takes moments throughout these hours to care for others, beginning with His prayer for those who had put Him on the cross, that they would be forgiven for the sin they did not even realize they were committing. Then to the criminal who hung on the cross next to Him—a man who recognized the wrong he had done, the just nature of his punishment, and who acknowledged the truth of who Jesus was. Jesus spoke into this man's last moments of desperation with the promise of hope that exists for all who have Spirit-given faith in Christ. Finally, to His mother, knowing that in the social circumstances she was in, she would be in need of someone to care for her. Knowing this, Jesus follows God's Commandment and honors His mother in the provision of John's household.

In each of these encounters, Jesus establishes that these individuals have value and worth, no matter their circumstances. The ignorant, the broken, and the grieving. In a moment when Jesus easily could have made it about Himself, He instead sets aside His own circumstances and cares for those around Him. There is no question about His purpose on that cross. As Jesus displays the greatest act of unconditional love, laying one's life down for another, He has not Himself in mind but those for whom He lays that life down. And that includes you and me.

Jesus Christ, our Lord and Savior, You had others in mind, even amid Your worst suffering. Help us, by Your Holy Spirit, to see the needs of others around us and care for them regardless of our own circumstances. Amen.

BETCHA WON'T DO IT

The rulers scoffed at Him, saying, "He saved others; let Him save Himself, if He is the Christ of God, His Chosen One!" (LUKE 23:35)

B etcha won't do it!"
These are often famous last words before a sibling, cousin, or some other companion from your youth attempts a feat that is either too extreme to consider attempting or too ridiculous to consider attainable. And often those are the pretext to a story that is shared for years—maybe even generations—to come.

The challenge of those words is often too great a temptation for anyone to refuse. Understandably so; we don't want to appear like someone who lacks the intestinal fortitude to step up to the plate. Yet, as we step into the challenge, we often get the perspective needed to realize it's not worth it.

As Jesus hangs on the cross, the religious leaders hurl insults and scoff at the supposed Messiah. They question His legitimacy as God's "Chosen One." They challenge that if He really is who He says He is, then He would save Himself. "Betcha can't get off of that cross!" Yet this challenge really is shortsighted. In fact, in their own words, the rulers actively admit that this same man hanging on the cross *has* saved others! They freely own up to the truth that He has done some amazing things. And yet, like a distrusting sibling, they prod Him to "do it again."

Here shines the real mission that Jesus had. There is no question that He could have gotten down off of that cross. He once said about His life, "For this reason the Father loves Me, because I lay down My life that I may take it up again. No one takes it from Me, but I lay it down of My own accord" (John 10:17–18). Yet Jesus knew that His purpose was not to prove Himself in the challenges of the spiritually blind. Instead, He proves His resolve and strength by remaining on the cross. Knowing that this suffering and death would satisfy the punishment for all sins, of all people, for all time, He remained on the cross. He knew full well that His mission was not to appease the doubtful, but to provide salvation to the broken, redeem the lost, and restore peace between man and God. And even in all of that, His greatest feat was yet to come in His resurrection just a few days later, giving us a certain hope for our eternity.

Here in the humiliation, suffering, pain, and torture, we see the fullness of the character of God. Where you and I would have used such divine power to remove ourselves from the situation, Jesus uses His unlimited power to remain—something that none of us could have accomplished no matter how much you bet us. Something that could only be accomplished by the Son of the Living God, the Christ of God, His Chosen One!

Almighty Son of God, we give You thanks that in Your grace and mercy, You remained on that cross, taking on the punishment of God's wrath that we ourselves deserved but most certainly could not have tolerated. May we proclaim the truth to those who doubt Your power as our Messiah, that they might see by Your Word and Spirit who You really are. All this we ask in the powerful name of our Savior, Jesus Christ. Amen.

HOW IT FEELS TO BE ME

My God, My God, why have You forsaken Me? Why are You so far from saving Me, from the words of My groaning? (PSALM 22:1)

The circumstances that we come up against in our lives are such that it causes us to feel alone, singular in our experience, and hopeless for a resolution. In those moments, we can't imagine that anyone can fully comprehend what we must be going through. Least of all God Himself. How can He know what it feels like to be me?

Perhaps if we, and Mr. Petty, spent some time in the Psalms, we would find that we are not entirely alone in our suffering. Psalm 22 paints quite the picture, especially if we focus on verses 6–18. King David, facing great opposition in his life, seems to be overwhelmed by the sense that he is all alone, forsaken and ignored by his God. Mocked by his enemies, surrounded by those who would do him harm, weakened, pierced, out of joint, his defeat a mere formality as his garments are divided among his oppressors.

Written nearly 2,600 years before you, me, or Tom would come on the scene, this hymn of lament is balanced with a chorus of hope. David knew that God had delivered His people in the past—that He would be the hope for the present and would be their help in all that was yet to come. What David did not know at the time was that God would deliver His people in the same way that they were suffering. Mocked by enemies, surrounded by those who would do Him harm, beaten, pierced, out of joint, stricken, smitten, and afflicted.

This psalm, given our benefit of hindsight looking back at the empty tomb of Jesus, comforts us with the confidence that Jesus has been in our position. He knows what it feels like to be forsaken, alone, ridiculed, and to face the wrath of God. He took on our sin, which included our suffering, and drowned it in the pouring out of His blood for the forgiveness of our sins. We never have to doubt if He knows what it's like to be me.

Gracious God, in the suffering and death of Jesus, He placed Himself amid our human experience. He took on the punishment we deserved so that we no longer have to fear our enemies of sin, death, and the devil—because we are Your redeemed people. May we live lives that proclaim the sure comfort of that truth. In the name of Jesus. Amen.

IT'S NEVER TOO LATE

And He said to him, "Truly, I say to you, today you will be with Me in paradise." (LUKE 23:43)

In teaching high school theology classes for two decades, I have heard just about every hypothetical question imaginable from students. In particular, a popular pressing question is "If I swear or cuss at the moment I die, would I go to heaven?" The premise of that question is one that I love to unpack with them. I begin by asking, "What sins did Jesus die for on the cross?" Often with one eyebrow raised, wondering where this is going, they typically respond correctly: "All of them."

"For your whole lifetime?"

"Sure."

"So if Jesus died for all of your sins, including the one you committed as you died, what would keep you out of heaven?"

More often than not, this response leaves the student stumped, confusion evident on their face. So it provides an opportunity to uncover the Gospel to counter the Law that they are living under.

This common question that my students so often ask places the responsibility for saving ourselves on us instead of recognizing the only source of salvation—Jesus, through His death and His resurrection. Our confidence in our salvation finds its foundation based in our trust that Jesus fully paid it all. His innocent suffering and death covers all of our sins, even to the point of death.

This was the sure salvation that Jesus proclaimed to the criminal on the cross in our reading. Amid the punishment for his own crime, this individual recognized that the man on the cross next to him was blameless, innocent. The Holy Spirit led his repentant heart to recognize the Christ and to seek mercy. Knowing that he was receiving the punishment deserved, he asked that Jesus simply remember him when He entered His kingdom. In doing so, he acknowledged that Jesus, and only Jesus, was the sole source of salvation. This trust is the faith that God creates in us in our Baptism, through the Word, and by the Holy Spirit. It is a faith that grants us access to the Father through Jesus Christ. It was the faith in the Savior that allowed Jesus to comfort him with the certainty of paradise that would be realized by the criminal that very day.

The salvation of the criminal was not dependent on the timestamp of his sin but rather on the cleansing blood of Jesus that was being poured out on that same day. Blood that cleanses us from all of our sins, for all time, until that day when, by the work of Jesus, we, too, will be with Him in paradise.

Jesus, You are our only source of salvation. We confess that we weigh our sin to gauge our worthiness when You are the only one who is worthy. Create in us the repentant faith of the criminal, by Your Spirit, so that we might humbly come to the cross and receive the salvation that comes only by Your death and resurrection. Amen.

WHAT WE HAVE LEFT UNDONE

Jesus said, "Father, forgive them, for they know not what they do." (LUKE 23:34)

As a freshman in my first week of high school, after moving from another state two days before school started, I sat alone at an empty table during lunch. A senior decided to take that opportunity to make an example of me, and in front of the whole lunchroom, moved my tray away from that table while declaring it a "senior table." In my embarrassment, I spent the rest of the lunch in the bathroom.

By God's grace, the rest of my high school experience was much more enjoyable, and I moved on to college with limited trauma. Then God decided to show His sense of humor. That same senior happened to be attending the college I had chosen to go to, happened to find out that I went to the same high school he went to, and decided to introduce himself to me.

To my surprise, this senior was oblivious to our interaction those short four years before. We ended up becoming good friends, and when I felt comfortable enough, I brought that experience to his attention. When confronted with his wrong, the friend nearly went pale. He was horrified that he had done that, not realizing the hurt he had inflicted.

As God's children, we come into the presence of the Lord in worship and often enter with an attitude of humility. We begin our Divine Service with the admission of our guilt in the Confession. We acknowledge, like the thief on the cross, that "we have sinned . . . in thought, word, and deed, by what we have done" (*LSB*, p. 151). Not only that, though, we confess that like the Romans, the religious leaders, and that senior student, we have committed acts that we aren't even aware of too.

On the cross, the Savior of the world, suffering torturous death, could have been excused from thinking of others in that moment. Yet here He is, speaking words of forgiveness, restoration, and comfort to those who need it most. Those who know it—and those who are not as aware.

In the Absolution of the Divine Service liturgy, that same Jesus, through the ordained servant of the Word, speaks those same restorative words to us. For the things we know we have done and the things we don't even realize. But what's more, He calls us to come to Him on behalf of those who sin against us. To lift in prayer those who "trespass against us" (p. 162). Not for swift punishment but for the salve of the redemption of sins provided by the blood of the Savior.

Jesus sets the example for us—from the cross to our ears—to share with a world that desperately needs to know the salvation that comes from Him.

Merciful Father, as we reflect on the mountain of our sins that Jesus bore on the cross, help us to come to You on behalf of those who sin against us, that they might know of Your forgiveness just as we do through our Savior, Jesus Christ. In Jesus' name. Amen.

JESUS DIES

WEEK 43—MATTHEW 27:45–54; LUKE 23:44–49; JOHN 19:28–30

Now from the sixth hour there was darkness over all the land until the ninth hour. And about the ninth hour Jesus cried out with a loud voice, saying, "Eli, Eli, lema sabachthani?" that is, "My God, My God, why have You forsaken Me?" And some of the bystanders, hearing it, said, "This man is calling Elijah." And one of them at once ran and took a sponge, filled it with sour wine, and put it on a reed and gave it to Him to drink. But the others said, "Wait, let us see whether Elijah will come to save Him." And Jesus cried out again with a loud voice and yielded up His spirit.

And behold, the curtain of the temple was torn in two, from top to bottom. And the earth shook, and the rocks were split. The tombs also were opened. And many bodies of the saints who had fallen asleep were raised, and coming out of the tombs after His resurrection they went into the holy city and appeared to many. When the centurion and those who were with him, keeping watch over Jesus, saw the earthquake and what took place, they were filled with awe and said, "Truly this was the Son of God!" . . .

It was now about the sixth hour, and there was darkness over the whole land until the ninth hour, while the sun's light failed. And the curtain of the temple was torn in two. Then Jesus, calling out with a loud voice, said, "Father, into Your hands I commit My spirit!" And having said this He breathed his last. Now when the centurion saw what had taken place, he praised God, saying, "Certainly this man was innocent!" And all the crowds that had assembled for this spectacle, when they saw what had taken place, returned home beating their breasts. And all His acquaintances and the women who had followed Him from Galilee stood at a distance watching these things. . . .

After this, Jesus, knowing that all was now finished, said (to fulfill the Scripture), "I thirst." A jar full of sour wine stood there, so they put a sponge full of the sour wine on a hyssop branch and held it to His mouth. When Jesus had received the sour wine, He said, "It is finished," and He bowed His head and gave up His spirit.

JESUS' LAST WORDS

Now from the sixth hour there was darkness over all the land until the ninth hour. And about the ninth hour Jesus cried out with a loud voice, saying, "Eli, Eli, lema sabachthani?" that is, "My God, My God, why have You forsaken Me?" (MATTHEW 27:45–46)

I pulled off a couple of all-nighters in college. I was able to get my schoolwork done throughout the night, but the next day was pretty rough. This pales in comparison to the all-nighter Jesus went through. After grueling hours wrestling with God in prayer, He was arrested at midnight and then put through a bogus trial all night where He was mocked, spit on, and beaten. He was then brought to Pilate at 6:00 a.m. and Herod at 7:00 a.m. Despite His innocence, He was condemned to crucifixion by the religious and political authorities of His day. He was flogged, crowned with thorns, and struck on His head.

At 9:00 a.m., He was crucified. Now, in our text for this week, Jesus has been hanging on the cross for three hours. As the Son of God suffers on the cross, Matthew tells us there was darkness over the whole land. This is no brief solar eclipse, but darkness reigned as the Light of the World was dying on the cross. But, just as God used the plague of three days of darkness to help deliver His people from slavery in Egypt, these three hours of darkness would lead to the delivery of all people from sin, death, and the devil.

As Jesus suffered over the course of these next three hours, the Gospel writers take note of His final words from the cross, all spoken shortly before His death. Matthew tells us that even in the experience of being forsaken by the Father as He bears the sins of the world, Jesus cries out in faith as He quotes Psalm 22:1 and says, "My God, My God, why have You forsaken Me?" John points to the humanity of Jesus and His faithfulness to God's plan even to the very end when Jesus makes reference to Psalm 69:21 and says, "I thirst." Now that all had been accomplished, Jesus declares that "it is finished." His work of salvation is completed. Finally, Luke gives us Jesus' final words from the cross. With His last breath Jesus commends Himself to the Father. He was faithful to the end.

Over the course of twelve hours, Jesus was mocked, stripped, beaten, spit upon, betrayed, abandoned, falsely accused, falsely condemned, crucified, bore the sin of the world and the wrath of God, and finally died. This all happened. And it all happened because of Jesus' love for you. He endured the worst this world has to offer that you might be forgiven of your sin and restored to the Father. There is no greater love.

Lord Jesus, You went to the cross for us. You endured so much for us. We thank and praise You that, on account of Your death, we have forgiveness and new life. Amen.

GOD IS MOST FULLY REVEALED IN SUFFERING

And behold, the curtain of the temple was torn in two, from top to bottom. And the earth shook, and the rocks were split. (MATTHEW 27:51)

The nineteenth-century German philosopher Friedrich Nietzsche famously wrote, "God is dead. And we have killed him." Nietzsche meant that in modern society, we so often live as if there is no God—but in our text for this week, his words find a fuller expression. The Son of God has died. Jesus is coeternal with the Father and the Holy Spirit. He is the one by whom all things were created and by whom all things receive life. Jesus is the light of the world. He is the one who made light come from darkness and enlightens our hearts with the truth of God's Word. He came into this world. He took on our humanity. He proclaimed the Gospel and healed the hurting—and He was killed for it. The source of all life experienced death. The source of all light died in darkness.

Considering the cosmic significance of His death, it is no surprise that as Jesus breathes His last, a lot happens. Matthew tells us the earth shook and the curtain of the temple was torn in two. The curtain in the temple that separated sinful humanity from the holiness of God was ripped apart. Even as darkness hovered over this whole scene, as the light of the world was extinguished, a ray of light emerges—in Jesus' death, what separated God and humanity has been rent asunder and true communion with God is made possible.

We see a picture of this communion with God occur just moments after Jesus' death and the tearing of the temple curtain. The Roman centurion, who no doubt took part in the crucifixion and was standing near the cross as Jesus died, began to praise God and profess that Jesus was the Son of God. Jesus' death on the cross was so moving that a Gentile who helped execute Jesus suddenly found himself praising God and proclaiming Jesus as the Son of God.

We rightly praise God when He blesses us with good things in life. And yet we see in Jesus' death and the centurion's profession that God is most fully revealed in suffering. Because it is in Jesus' Passion and death that the curtain was torn in two and we are now invited into a reconciled relationship with God. May we, like the centurion, praise God for Christ's atoning death and proclaim Him as the eternal Son of God, our Lord and Savior.

Lord Jesus, You died that I might live. You gave of Yourself that I might receive the love of the Father. Teach me to live in this truth always. Amen.

RECONCILED WITH GOD THROUGH JESUS

And . . . the curtain of the temple was torn in two. (LUKE 23:45)

Since Genesis 3, humanity has lived with the reality that sin separates. When Adam and Eve disobeyed God, they realized they were naked and immediately tried to cover themselves up. When we speak a cruel word to someone, it creates a separation in our relationship with that person. When we lie, it creates distrust between people. When there is a threat of violence, barriers have to be erected. Sin separates. Above all, sin separates us from God. We were created to know God and walk with Him. But in our sin, we have cut ourselves off from His loving presence. Jesus came into this world to atone for our sins, to make us right with God. In His death on the cross, Jesus joins together God and humanity once and for all.

Jesus brings about this reconciliation between God and humanity through experiencing separation from the Father. As Jesus cries out, "My God, My God, why have You forsaken Me" (Matthew 27:46), He goes through hell and takes our sin with Him. No longer will our sin separate us from God. It has been removed from us, and Christ has taken it upon Himself. As Jesus declares, "I thirst" (John 19:28), we see He is fully human and has the same bodily needs that we do—yet He was perfect on our behalf. He drank the bitter wine, that we might one day enjoy the marriage feast of the Lamb. When Jesus proclaims, "It is finished" (John 19:30), He completes the work of salvation on our behalf. And as Jesus commits His spirit to the Father, we take hope that, on account of Jesus' death, when we die, our souls will be with God in paradise even as we anticipate the resurrection of our bodies from the dead. Jesus' unending faithfulness moves us to faith in Him.

Every word Jesus spoke from the cross, every pain He endured, was done in fulfillment of His mission to reconcile lost sinners to their loving heavenly Father. Because Jesus is fully human, He suffered and died the death we deserve. Because Jesus is fully God, He perfectly fulfilled God's will and gave of Himself for us out of divine love. In His person, Jesus is fully God and fully human. And on account of His death, He fully unites God and humanity once and for all. It is finished. Mission accomplished. May we have faith to receive this Good News.

Lord Jesus, thank You for being faithful to Your mission of reconciling us to the Father through Your death on the cross. Amen.

THE PSALMS AND THE CROSS

Then Jesus, calling out with a loud voice, said, "Father, into Your hands I commit My spirit!" (LUKE 23:46)

Many of Jesus' words from the cross are either direct quotations or, at the very least, references to various psalms. For this devotion, we will look at the psalms Jesus makes reference to while He is on the cross.

Psalm 22:1

"My God, My God, why have You forsaken Me? Why are You so far from saving Me, from the words of My groaning?" Amid the anguish of the cross, Jesus cries out these memorable words. We see here that Jesus was quoting Psalm 22. This is a psalm of King David. Though David did not experience the same level of suffering as Jesus, he clearly felt as though God had forsaken him. He felt as if God was deaf to his cries of pain. This is a very human experience. Whether it's through difficult life circumstances or seasons of spiritual dryness, we've all had moments where God seems far off and deaf to our cries. But the promise of the cross is that because Jesus was forsaken, we never will be. So even when God seems far off, we can look to the cross and see that He meets us in our pain.

Psalm 69:3

"I am weary with my crying out; my throat is parched. My eyes grow dim with waiting for my God." The Gospel of John tells us that Jesus said "I thirst" as He hung from the cross. This is a simple statement and makes sense of Jesus' physical state. He had not eaten or drunk anything for twelve hours and had suffered much blood loss. He had to be dehydrated. And yet, beyond the physiology of needing a drink, Jesus was pointing to the words of Psalm 69. In this psalm, David begins by crying out to God that he is drowning and needs God to rescue him. By the end of the psalm, David praises God for His deliverance. On the cross, Jesus was drowning under the waters of our sin. And yet, it is through the cross that He brings about God's deliverance, that we might be saved from the guilt and shame that seeks to drown us. Through this simple statement of thirst, Jesus points us to our hope of deliverance.

Psalm 31:5

"Into your hand I commit my spirit; you have redeemed me, O LORD, faithful God." Jesus' very last words are words of trust in the Father and an allusion to this psalm. As David commits his spirit to God in life, Jesus commits His spirit to God at the moment of His death. Just as Jesus walked with the Father in life, He continues that walk with the Father in death. We, too, are invited to commit our spirits to God throughout our earthly journey and, when the time comes for our death, we take hope that our walk with God continues into eternity.

Lord Jesus, we praise You because You meet us in our humanity to redeem us for eternity. Amen.

OPEN TOMBS AND CALLING ELIJAH

Some of the bystanders . . . said, "This man is calling Elijah." (MATTHEW 27:47)

This week's passages raise some difficult challenges:

Why did bystanders believe Jesus was calling out for Elijah?

After Jesus cried out in the previous verse, "Eli, Eli, lema sabachthani," some of the bystanders thought He was calling out to Elijah. There are two reasons why they thought so. The first reason is simply phonetic. As you can see in the text, Jesus cried out "My God" in Aramaic, and the word for that is *Eli*, which sounds pretty similar to the first two syllables in the name *Elijah*. But there's a deeper reason they thought He was calling for Elijah. The last book of the Old Testament, Malachi, prophesies that Elijah will come before the Messiah. This prophecy was fulfilled in the ministry of John the Baptist, who came in the spirit and power of Elijah. The people standing near Jesus at the cross did not understand this and thought that Jesus was asking Elijah why he had not come to rescue Him on the cross. But Jesus knew what He was doing. He didn't need Elijah to rescue Him, He was rescuing the world.

What does it mean that the tombs were opened, and dead people came back to life?

After Jesus dies, we see just a few verses later in Matthew's Gospel that the bodies of many saints "who had fallen asleep" (v. 52) were raised. This is a strange occurrence. What is going on here? On the cross, when Jesus declares it is finished, we know that His work of salvation is complete. He has trampled over death by death. Sin, death, and the devil no longer have any claim over us. As an initial celebration of this victory, God raised these saints by His power to demonstrate a foretaste of the feast to come. Just as these saints were raised at the time of Jesus' death, one day, we will all be raised to new life when He returns in glory.

Even in these challenging portions of our text, we see that God is working all things for our good and our salvation. The confusion over Jesus calling out to God helps us see that God is fulfilling salvation history through the coming of our Messiah. The strange incident of the dead saints rising to life after Jesus' death tells us that Jesus' victory is now our victory—and one day, we, too, will rise to new life.

Lord Jesus, we thank You that You didn't step down from the cross but endured the pain that we might have eternal victory in You. Amen.

THE CROSS IS THE ABSOLUTE CENTER

And [Jesus] bowed His head and gave up His spirit. (JOHN 19:30)

The cross is the absolute center of the Christian faith. The last three of Jesus' six hours on the cross that we've looked at in these passages show us a Savior who gave everything to redeem and save us. His physical pain was literally excruciating (*ex*, meaning "out of," and *cruciatus*, meaning "the cross"). He suffered emotionally as He was mocked and many of His followers abandoned Him. He suffered socially as He was falsely accused and condemned. Above all, He suffered separation from the Father. Jesus went through the full depths of hell on the cross, that we might never face eternal separation from God. The cross gives us a picture of the depth of love that God has for us. That is why our churches are decorated with crosses and why we are marked with the sign of the cross in Baptism and in worship.

When Jesus dies, the curtain of the temple is torn in two. This is often shown in our churches by an opening in the altar rail. No longer do we need a priest to mediate our relationship with God—Jesus is our great High Priest. As Jesus dies, the earth shakes. This points us to the truth that one day, all of creation will be redeemed fully from the fall. As Jesus dies, the dead rise from their grave. This shows us that Jesus is our conquering King. Our enemies of sin, death, and the devil have no claim on us—we have victory in King Jesus. This list can go on and on. As Jesus cries out that it is finished, we have confidence that He has done it. He has done all that is necessary for our salvation. There is nothing we can add to the salvation won for us through His death. We now simply trust in His finished work on our behalf and rest in the goodness and mercy of our God.

The cross is the center of the Christian faith, and it is the center of the Christian life. It is the place to which Holy Communion returns us every time we receive it, feeding us with the very body given and the blood shed by Jesus for our forgiveness. We live from the cross, forgiven and free. We live for the cross, proclaiming the forgiveness found in the cross to a lost and sin-soaked world. We live embracing the cross—amid our suffering and pain, we have a God who is not removed from us but meets us in our darkness and trouble. We live carrying our crosses, seeking to follow Jesus with our whole lives, no matter what resistance comes our way. May we never lose sight of the cross. May we lift high the cross and proclaim His love and victory.

Lord Jesus, thank You for the cross. Teach us to live from the cross and for the cross all of our days. Amen.

JESUS' BODY IS BURIED, HIS TOMB IS GUARDED

WEEK 44—MATTHEW 27:55–66

There were also many women there, looking on from a distance, who had followed Jesus from Galilee, ministering to Him, among whom were Mary Magdalene and Mary the mother of James and Joseph and the mother of the sons of Zebedee.

When it was evening, there came a rich man from Arimathea, named Joseph, who also was a disciple of Jesus. He went to Pilate and asked for the body of Jesus. Then Pilate ordered it to be given to him. And Joseph took the body and wrapped it in a clean linen shroud and laid it in his own new tomb, which he had cut in the rock. And he rolled a great stone to the entrance of the tomb and went away. Mary Magdalene and the other Mary were there, sitting opposite the tomb.

The next day, that is, after the day of Preparation, the chief priests and the Pharisees gathered before Pilate and said, "Sir, we remember how that impostor said, while He was still alive, 'After three days I will rise.' Therefore order the tomb to be made secure until the third day, lest His disciples go and steal Him away and tell the people, 'He has risen from the dead,' and the last fraud will be worse than the first." Pilate said to them, "You have a guard of soldiers. Go, make it as secure as you can." So they went and made the tomb secure by sealing the stone and setting a guard.

JESUS' BURIAL

And Joseph took the body and wrapped it in a clean linen shroud and laid it in his own new tomb. (MATTHEW 27:59-60)

In this passage, we see the faithful women who had followed and supported Jesus throughout His ministry standing at a distance, watching as their Lord was crucified. Three women are named specifically: Mary, the mother of James and Joseph; Mary Magdalene, who was previously possessed by seven demons; and Salome, the mother of apostles James and John. Mary, the mother of Jesus, was also present at the cross, as was John, the only disciple present at the time of Jesus' death.

Crucifixion was a brutal and inhumane execution, and often lasted a number of days. In the rest of the Roman Empire, it was not uncommon for the bodies of dead crucifixion victims to remain on their crosses for some time. However, according to Jewish law, bodies could not be left on crosses overnight. Since the next day was a Sabbath day, the Roman soldiers hastened their death by breaking the legs of the thieves crucified with Jesus. But since Jesus was already dead, they thrust a spear into His side to be certain of this.

With the hour already being late, it was necessary to attend to Jesus' body as soon as possible on that Friday afternoon. To avoid Jesus being buried in a common grave with the two criminals, Joseph of Arimathea and Nicodemus, prominent members of the Sanhedrin who believed in Jesus, boldly stepped forward and received permission from Pilate to take His body down and bury it.

The fact that members of the Sanhedrin were involved in Jesus' burial would have caused quite a stir because touching a dead body would have made them unclean. But their faith in Jesus was so strong that they were willing to take the risk. Moreover, the fact that Joseph had secured enough linen for a shroud and Nicodemus had brought spices showed that they had planned and coordinated their task in advance.

The unbelieving religious leaders were initially alarmed at the natural events that occurred at the cross, but by the next day, the Sabbath, they remembered that Jesus had said He would rise after three days. Fearful that His disciples might steal the body and claim that He had risen from the dead, they asked Pilate to send guards to protect the tomb. The sealing of the burial place was to show evidence of any tampering with the grave, and the positioning of armed guards was intended to keep Jesus inside—and thieving disciples out.

But the resurrection of Jesus, which we celebrate each year at Easter, proved the religious leaders' efforts were in vain. Even more than that, their efforts gave strong evidence that Jesus truly rose from the dead. Disciples too frightened to stand by Jesus in His arrest or stand by at His crucifixion would never try to sneak past guards to steal His body. Stone, guards, or seals could not contain the power of the Lord. Through His death and resurrection, Jesus redeemed the world and defeated death.

Dear Lord, we thank You for the incredible love and sacrifice You showed us through Your death on the cross. We are humbled by the faith of the women who stood at a distance, watching as You suffered and died, and of Joseph of Arimathea and Nicodemus, who risked their well-being to bury Your body. Please help us to have the same unwavering faith and hope, even in the face of hardship and persecution. Amen.

THE DEVOTION OF JESUS' FOLLOWERS

When it was evening, there came a rich man from Arimathea, named Joseph, who also was a disciple of Jesus. He went to Pilate and asked for the body of Jesus. (MATTHEW 27:57-58)

In Matthew 27:55-66, we see the last moments of Jesus' earthly life and His subsequent burial. As we read, we are reminded of the contrast between the love and devotion shown to Jesus by His followers and the hatred and dishonor shown by His enemies.

Jesus' death was a cruel and painful one, yet He remained faithful to His mission until His last breath. In His final moments, He cried out to God, showing His trust and reliance on His Father even in the face of great suffering. On the other hand, Jesus' enemies continued to oppose Him even in death, dishonoring Him by lying about Him and seeking to contain His body.

Despite the cruelty of Jesus' death, He was given a respectful burial by those who loved Him. Joseph of Arimathea and Nicodemus, members of the Sanhedrin, obtained permission from Pilate to take Jesus' body and bury Him. They prepared His body with expensive spices and fine linen, a sign of love and respect for their Lord. This shows us that even in death, Jesus was treated with dignity and honor by those who followed Him.

The actions of Jesus' enemies further strengthen the reliability of the Gospel accounts of His resurrection. The fact that they had a guard set and, after the resurrection happened anyway, bribed the guards to not only say they fell asleep but that the disciples stole the body, further proves that Jesus had risen. If no guard had been in place, they could have easily argued that Jesus' disciples had come and stolen His body while no one was watching.

The main overall message of this passage is that Jesus' death and burial were not the end. Despite the cruelty and dishonor He faced in death, He rose again, conquering sin and death. This passage serves as a reminder of the ultimate triumph of love and grace over hate and sin, as well as the importance of honoring and showing love to those who have passed on.

This passage also shows the devotion of Jesus' followers and the hatred of His enemies. It serves as a reminder that even in the darkest of circumstances, the love and devotion of those who believe in Jesus will always endure. The love shown to Jesus in His death and burial is a testament to the faith and trust that His followers held for Him. And the fact that God the Father provided one Joseph to be Jesus' earthly father and another Joseph to bury His dead body proves Jesus was right to commend Himself into His Father's loving hands.

Dear Lord, we thank You for the gift of Your Son, Jesus Christ, and for the sacrifice He made for us on the cross. Help us to always show love and respect to those who have passed on and to honor their memory. We ask for Your strength and guidance as we navigate this world and for Your continued grace and mercy in our lives. In Jesus' name we pray. Amen.

JESUS RESTED ON
THE SEVENTH DAY

And Joseph took the body and wrapped it in a clean linen shroud and laid it in his own new tomb, which he had cut in the rock. And he rolled a great stone to the entrance of the tomb and went away. (MATTHEW 27:59–60)

Despite the cruel and brutal death He endured, Jesus' devoted followers showed their love and respect for Him by preparing His body with spices and fine linen, laying Him in an unused tomb, and treating Him with dignity. Yet His enemies sought to dishonor Him further, lying about Him and trying to prevent any claims of resurrection by setting a guard at the tomb and sealing it.

But this passage points to the heart of Jesus' mission and the truth of His resurrection. The reality of Jesus' death and the evidence of His beaten, lifeless body leaves no doubt that He was fully man and fully God. He did not simply appear to die but suffered an actual death in the flesh. And it was not just any death but a death on a cross, the most severe and humiliating form of execution.

Jesus' death was not the end of the story but the ultimate sacrifice for the forgiveness of our sins. He died for us, taking upon Himself the punishment we deserved so that we may have eternal life with Him. All this took place on the sixth day of the week, the same day in Genesis 1 when God created man and woman in His image. On the seventh day of creation, God the Father rested—and now, on the seventh day, Jesus rests in the tomb, awaiting His glorious resurrection from the dead on the eighth day: the beginning of a new week for all humanity. He would rise on that day, just as He had predicted, proving once and for all that He is, indeed, the Son of God.

Matthew 27:55–66 is a powerful passage that points to Jesus and His mission in a profound way. Through His death and resurrection, Jesus conquered death and sin, making it possible for us to have eternal life. As we reflect on this passage, let us give thanks for the truth of the resurrection and the hope that it brings to our lives.

Dear Lord, we give You thanks for the powerful witness of the empty tomb and the truth of Jesus' resurrection. We ask that You help us understand the significance of this event and the impact it has on our lives. Give us the strength to live as witnesses to the truth of the resurrection and to share the hope that it brings to all who believe. We ask for Your continued guidance and support as we seek to live out our faith in the world. Help us always remember the love and sacrifice of Jesus and never forget the power of His resurrection. In Jesus' name we pray. Amen.

THE FAITHFUL WOMEN

There were also many women there, looking on from a distance, who had followed Jesus from Galilee, ministering to Him. (MATTHEW 27:55)

As we reflect on the events of the crucifixion of our Lord and Savior, Jesus Christ, let us turn our attention to the women at the foot of the cross. The account in Matthew 27:55–66 tells us that among the spectators at Jesus' crucifixion were many women who had followed Jesus from Galilee, ministering to Him. These women were not just any women but were faithful disciples of our Lord who had seen and experienced the power of His teachings and miracles.

Similarly, in John 19:25, we see that among these women at the cross were Mary, the mother of Jesus; His aunt, the wife of Clopas; and Mary Magdalene. These women were not just bystanders but deeply committed to Jesus and His mission. They had traveled with Him, supported Him, and now they stood at the foot of the cross, witnessing the most terrible event of all time.

However, as we know from Psalm 38:11, even friends and companions can stand at a distance when we are suffering. Yet these women did not abandon Jesus in His hour of need. Instead, they were there, showing their unwavering love and devotion to Him, even in the face of such great adversity.

The same can be said of the women in Luke 8:2–3, who were healed by Jesus and continued to follow Him and support Him. These women were not just recipients of His miracles but also witnesses to His love and compassion. And, as we see in Matthew 20:20, even the mother of the sons of Zebedee came to Jesus to ask something of Him, showing her faith in Him and the power of His teachings.

Finally, Mark 15:40 tells us that among the women at the cross were Mary Magdalene, Salome, and Mary, the mother of James and Joses. These women, who had been with Jesus from the beginning, now stood at the foot of the cross, showing their love and devotion to Him even in the face of His suffering and death.

Let us take a moment to pray and reflect on the example set by these faithful women. Let us ask for the grace to have such an unwavering devotion to our Lord, even in the face of suffering and adversity.

Heavenly Father, we come to You today, reflecting on the events of the crucifixion of our Lord and Savior, Jesus Christ. We thank You for the examples set by the women at the foot of the cross, showing us the depth of their love and devotion to Jesus, even in the face of His suffering and death. Grant us the grace to have such unwavering faith in You, Lord. May we constantly be reminded of the example set by these women, and may we strive to live a life of faithful devotion to You, our Lord and Savior, now and forever. Amen.

STEPPING OUT OF THE SHADOWS

After these things Joseph of Arimathea, who was a disciple of Jesus, but secretly for fear of the Jews, asked Pilate that he might take away the body of Jesus, and Pilate gave him permission. So he came and took away His body. (JOHN 19:38)

This week's passage raises some difficulty:

Why did Joseph of Arimathea not come forward in support of Jesus sooner?

As we read the account of Matthew 27:55-66, we are struck by the courage and faith of Joseph of Arimathea. We may wonder why he didn't speak up at Jesus' trial. He was a prominent member of the Sanhedrin. Although he was a disciple of Jesus, he kept his faith hidden out of fear of persecution from the other religious leaders. Perhaps he remained silent during the trial or abstained from the guilty vote—or perhaps Caiaphas knew of his sympathy toward Jesus and made sure he and Nicodemus were not summoned to the illegal night trials. Whatever the case may have been, when the opportunity presented itself, Joseph boldly stepped forward to give Jesus a proper burial.

We can learn much from Joseph's actions. Like him, we may sometimes feel the need to keep our faith hidden, especially in the face of opposition or persecution. However, we can remember that our faith in Jesus should be a source of strength and courage, not something we need to hide or be ashamed of.

When Jesus was dead, Joseph took courage and used his authority as a member of the Sanhedrin to convince Pilate to release Jesus' body to him to give Him a proper burial. This act of love and devotion was a service to Jesus and a declaration of his faith.

As Christians, we have the opportunity to follow in Joseph's footsteps and be public about our faith, even in the face of opposition. The cross reminds us of Jesus' sacrifice and His love for us. We can take comfort in knowing that we have a Savior who died for us and rose again to give us eternal life.

However, we may sometimes find ourselves in situations where we feel afraid to confess our faith openly. It can be challenging to stand up for what we believe in when faced with persecution or the threat of losing our reputation and security. But like Joseph, we have the power of the Holy Spirit within us to give us strength and courage to stand firm in our beliefs.

Let us always remember the love that Jesus has for us and the sacrifice He made for our salvation. Let us follow in the footsteps of Joseph of Arimathea and be public about our faith, standing firm in our beliefs and confessing our love for Jesus, no matter the consequences.

Dear Lord, we thank You for sending Your Son, Jesus, to die for our sins. We are grateful for the sacrifice He made for us and the love He has shown us. Please give us the strength and courage to openly confess our faith, even in opposition. Please help us to remember that You are always with us and will never leave us. Please give us the power of the Holy Spirit to provide us with strength and comfort as we navigate through life. We ask this in Jesus' name. Amen.

JESUS' BURIAL AND OURS

And [Joseph] rolled a great stone to the entrance of the tomb and went away. Mary Magdalene and the other Mary were there, sitting opposite the tomb. (MATTHEW 27:60–61)

As we reflect on the events of Matthew 27:55–66, we see the incredible sacrifice that Jesus made for us on the cross. This passage tells us about the women who followed Jesus to the cross, witnessed His death, and then watched as Joseph of Arimathea took His body and laid it in a tomb. This was a somber moment as Jesus, the Son of God, lay dead in a grave.

However, this moment was not the end of the story. Just as surely as Jesus died on the cross, He rose again on the third day, defeating death and the power of sin. This powerful truth profoundly impacts us, both then and now.

As we read in Psalm 116:15, "Precious in the sight of the LORD is the death of His saints." Jesus' death and resurrection sanctifies our own deaths and graves. Whenever we visit the grave of a loved one or think about our death someday, we can find comfort in the knowledge that Jesus has already conquered death and that He will raise us too, when He returns to judge the living and the dead.

This passage also connects directly to our Baptism, as Paul writes in Romans 6:3–4: "Do you not know that all of us who have been baptized into Christ Jesus were baptized into His death? We were buried therefore with Him by Baptism into death, in order that, just as Christ was raised from the dead by the glory of the Father, we too might walk in newness of life." In our Baptism, we are united with Christ in His death and resurrection and receive the promise of eternal life.

As we celebrate the death and resurrection of our Lord in our liturgical worship, we are reminded of the powerful message of this passage. Our service at the graveside committal includes this prayer:

Almighty God, by the death of Your Son Jesus Christ You destroyed death, by His rest in the tomb You sanctified the graves of Your saints, and by His bodily resurrection You brought life and immortality to light so that all who die in Him abide in peace and hope. Receive our thanks for the victory over death and the grave that He won for us. Keep us in everlasting communion with all who wait for Him on earth and with all in heaven who are with Him, for He is the resurrection and the life, even Jesus Christ, our Lord. Amen. (LSB *Pastoral Care Companion*, p. 135)

Whether at the graveside of a loved one or gathered in church for worship, we can find comfort and peace in the knowledge that Jesus has already defeated death and that surely we, too, will one day rise again.

Dear Lord, we thank You for the incredible sacrifice that You made for us on the cross. We are grateful for Your love and mercy and the promise of eternal life through Your death and resurrection. Please help us remember the power of this truth, even in the face of death, and to find comfort in the knowledge that You have already defeated death. Amen.

JESUS' RESURRECTION AND MARY MAGDALENE

WEEK 45—JOHN 20:1–18

Now on the first day of the week Mary Magdalene came to the tomb early, while it was still dark, and saw that the stone had been taken away from the tomb. So she ran and went to Simon Peter and the other disciple, the one whom Jesus loved, and said to them, "They have taken the Lord out of the tomb, and we do not know where they have laid Him." So Peter went out with the other disciple, and they were going toward the tomb. Both of them were running together, but the other disciple outran Peter and reached the tomb first. And stooping to look in, he saw the linen cloths lying there, but he did not go in. Then Simon Peter came, following him, and went into the tomb. He saw the linen cloths lying there, and the face cloth, which had been on Jesus' head, not lying with the linen cloths but folded up in a place by itself. Then the other disciple, who had reached the tomb first, also went in, and he saw and believed; for as yet they did not understand the Scripture, that He must rise from the dead. Then the disciples went back to their homes.

But Mary stood weeping outside the tomb, and as she wept she stooped to look into the tomb. And she saw two angels in white, sitting where the body of Jesus had lain, one at the head and one at the feet. They said to her, "Woman, why are you weeping?" She said to them, "They have taken away my Lord, and I do not know where they have laid Him." Having said this, she turned around and saw Jesus standing, but she did not know that it was Jesus. Jesus said to her, "Woman, why are you weeping? Whom are you seeking?" Supposing Him to be the gardener, she said to him, "Sir, if you have carried Him away, tell me where you have laid Him, and I will take Him away." Jesus said to her, "Mary." She turned and said to Him in Aramaic, "Rabboni!" (which means Teacher). Jesus said to her, "Do not cling to Me, for I have not yet ascended to the Father; but go to My brothers and say to them, 'I am ascending to My Father and your Father, to My God and your God.'" Mary Magdalene went and announced to the disciples, "I have seen the Lord"—and that He had said these things to her.

FROM THE DEEPEST GRIEF TO THE HIGHEST JOY

Jesus said to her, "Woman, why are you weeping? Whom are you seeking?" (JOHN 20:15)

Because Jesus had been hastily buried by Joseph of Arimathea and Nicodemus late Friday afternoon, as soon as possible the day after the Sabbath, Mary Magdalene went to Jesus' tomb to prepare Jesus' body for proper Jewish burial. Upon arrival, she saw that the stone had been rolled away. What a shock—that large a stone would not be easily dislodged.

Since the tomb was open, Mary looked in and saw Jesus' body was missing. Deeply upset, she ran back to alert Peter and John, who both rushed to the tomb. What a race of alarm and confusion! John, arriving first, stood at the entrance and peered inside. Moments later, Peter arrived and went right in, and John followed him. They noted that the linen that had been wrapped around Jesus' body was still in place with the spices, but Jesus' body was no longer inside it. The cloth that had been around His head was neatly folded off to the side.

This was a curious sight that eloquently testified to Jesus' resurrection. Grave robbers would most likely have taken the body with the cloths to get their hands on the precious spices in it. They would not likely have unwrapped the body, but even if they had unwrapped it, they would never have taken the time to rewrap the cloths.

But within the tomb, the cloths looked as though Jesus' body had simply vanished from within them. In His resurrection power, there was no barrier to Jesus. Later, the disciples would see this power again when Jesus suddenly appeared to them through locked doors and then later vanished from their sight.

When the disciples returned to their hiding place in the city, wondering what had happened, Mary was once again at the tomb. She stood weeping over the loss of her Lord. Suddenly, she looked into the tomb and saw two angels at the foot and head of where Jesus had been laid. The angels asked why she was crying. Mary answered that Jesus' body had been taken and she didn't know where He was.

When she turned, she saw another figure standing outside the tomb. He also asked why she was crying. She assumed this was the gardener. Thinking he might have removed Jesus' body, she asked where he had taken Jesus. Mary did not recognize this figure was the risen Jesus until He spoke her name. When He said "Mary," she immediately knew who He was.

From the deepest grief to the highest joy, Mary reached out to take hold of Him and never let Him go. However, John records that Jesus told her not to cling onto Him but to go and tell His brothers that He had risen and was returning to the Father.

Dear Jesus, risen with power and love, let us each day come to the Easter morning tomb, knowing that You are alive and with us forever. Amen.

GOD'S QUIET WAYS

They said to her, "Woman, why are you weeping?" She said to them, "They have taken away my Lord, and I do not know where they have laid Him." (JOHN 20:13)

We might have expected Jesus' resurrection to be a glorious spectacle that no one could miss. Shouldn't this great event have had an audience of disciples and other followers and even some of His enemies? But God often works in quiet ways. Easter morning began in the simple darkness. Breaking that silence, an earthquake signaled that something extraordinary was happening. Many must have felt the earthquake that morning, but only the guards saw the angels roll the stone away. For Mary, the discovery of Jesus' resurrection was a quiet surprise. She saw nothing at the tomb but the stone already rolled away and the body missing.

The excitement of the morning grew as Peter and John ran to the tomb. The two disciples served as the best kind of witnesses. They did not know what to expect when they reached the tomb. They had last known the tomb to be sealed, but it was now open and empty! Also, the state of the undisturbed grave cloth made a huge impression. It had not been unwrapped, simply vacated.

Then we see Mary Magdalene again. Mary was the woman whom Jesus had lovingly freed of her demons. While Jesus had not yet appeared to the disciples, He met Mary to her great surprise by the tomb. And His directive to her—that she was to go and tell—was the first commission. What a change from her expected work. She had asked Jesus, supposing that He was the gardener, where the body was so that she could carry it away to safety. But now she did not have to carry His dead body—she carried the joyous news that He was alive.

What a story she had to tell! She had seen Him, and He had said her name with all His familiar knowledge and love. She tried to hold Him tightly, never to let go. Once He was lost in death, but now He was here with her. But He assured her she did not need to cling to Him.

His body lay in the grave long enough that there was no question about His physical death, but His body had not yielded to decomposition. In addition, Jesus' body lay in the grave on the Sabbath. Jesus had accomplished His work of salvation in the six days beginning with His Palm Sunday entrance into Jerusalem, completed on Friday afternoon when with a loud voice He proclaimed, "It is finished" (John 19:30). On the Sabbath day, His body rested in the tomb, awaiting the beginning of a new week—and a new age for believers.

Our risen Savior, reassure us each day that the greatest miracle was true and is still true—You have risen from the dead and live forever with us. Amen.

FINALLY, DEATH IS DEFEATED

[Jesus said,] "Go to My brothers and say to them, 'I am ascending to My Father and your Father, to My God and your God.'" (JOHN 20:17)

When God completed His creation of the heavens and the earth on the sixth day, He said that it was very good. Death was not part of that creation. But when Adam and Eve ate the forbidden fruit, sin and death came and shattered creation. It could have been the end of Adam and Eve so that their family tree would be one, sad, broken branch.

However, death and brokenness were not the end of God's story. God promised to raise up one of Eve's descendants, His own Son, to crush the head of the serpent who had tempted and deceived her. It would be a balance of God's power and His willingness to take death onto Himself. He would crush the ancient enemy, but also, He would choose to let the sting of death pierce Him.

Yet death was not the final page of God's message to the world. His Son took on death, but He reclaimed His life on the third day. His resurrection gave proof that He had conquered Satan, sin, death, and hell. Now life has been restored to His creation—and to all people who believe in Him. By His resurrection, we have life now as His justified and forgiven children. We also wait for a greater life to come in our resurrected bodies.

Jesus' resurrection is the central event of the Bible. The essential news is not just the empty tomb but seeing and hearing Jesus in bodily form after He rose from that tomb. He was not a ghost or a hopeful vision—He raised His own body, once on the cross and now alive. His resurrection appearances complete the promises He made that He would step out of death. While even the disciples doubted this, Jesus brought the proof that He had kept this most amazing promise. If He can rise from the dead, then there is no enemy or power that can overcome Him. Therefore, just as Jesus sent Mary to tell the others that she had seen the Lord, so He sends us to tell the world that Jesus lives. Now and finally, death is defeated. Nothing can tear us away from His care since God is at peace with us for Jesus' sake.

Dear Jesus, You could not come only to live and die but You came to live, die, and rise again, showing a complete victory over death. Keep us in that power here and into eternity. Amen.

DO NOT BE AFRAID

Then the other disciple, who had reached the tomb first, also went in, and he saw and believed. (JOHN 20:8)

Jesus' resurrection is recorded in other places in the Bible:

Matthew 28:2

"And behold, there was a great earthquake, for an angel of the Lord descended from heaven and came and rolled back the stone and sat on it." How should the story of the greatest event in the world's history be told? Should it slowly unfold in silence? Or should it be told with stunning power and crashing sound? The announcement of the resurrection of Jesus is the most important news we can imagine. His resurrection and the announcement of His renewed life balance that which is hidden and that which is plainly seen. We don't see the moment of His resurrection or His passing through the stone. But, lest this event be missed, the angel and the earthquake make it clear that something momentous has happened. Yes, let the earth shake—its Creator has come back from the dead and will never die again. Let the angel move the stone and then sit on it in triumph. The Savior has risen, and the news now can spread.

Matthew 28:5–6

"But the angel said to the women, 'Do not be afraid, for I know that you seek Jesus who was crucified. He is not here, for He has risen, as He said.'" The women come to the tomb, filled with sorrow but moved by love and faithfulness to Jesus. But for all their devotion, they needed the compassion of the angels. As occurs so often in Scripture, the first words from the angels are, "Do not be afraid."

The essential message of Easter is not terror or loss, nor is it an accusation against those who fled from Him on Good Friday. The words of the tomb are this: "Do not be afraid." The tomb is empty and the One who was dead is alive among them—and also with us today. Remember the angel's words. Do not be afraid.

Ephesians 1:13

"In Him you also, when you heard the word of truth, the gospel of your salvation, and believed in Him, were sealed with the promised Holy Spirit." Mary had the wonderful experience of seeing Jesus and talking with Him. This was her certainty. Ask her, "Did Jesus actually rise?" We can imagine her saying with absolute conviction, "Yes! I saw Him, I spoke with Him, and He knew me. Yes, Jesus is alive!" We can have the same certainty when we hear the truth, the Gospel, because it is the means by which the Holy Spirit brings faith to us. We are sealed in this truth, now and unto eternal life.

Dear Jesus, keep ever before our eyes the words of Scripture, the eyewitness testimony that Mary Magdalene and others gave of Your resurrected body. Be with us always, and reassure us of Your victory over sin, death, and the grave. Amen.

EVIDENCE OF JESUS' RESURRECTION

Jesus said . . . "Do not cling to Me, for I have not yet ascended to the Father; but go to My brothers and say to them, 'I am ascending to My Father and your Father, to My God and your God.'" (JOHN 20:17)

A few questions arise from this week's passage:

Why were the burial cloths important?

They give eloquent testimony of Jesus' resurrection. The way they were lying there indicated that Jesus' body had vanished from them. If the disciples had wanted to stage the resurrection, they would have had to sneak past the guards and would not have risked staying to unwrap the body and then wrap the linen cloth back the way it had been. Grave robbers would have wanted to take the body with the linen cloth and the expensive spices. The burial cloths went from being a sad testimony of Jesus' death to a witness of His powerful resurrection.

What does it mean that the disciple believed but did not understand the Scripture?

There has been some debate among theologians on this verse. Many think it means John remembered Jesus' prophecy and believed He had risen. Others think it simply means Peter and John believed what Mary had told them, that someone had come and stolen Jesus' body. The full understanding of Jesus' death and resurrection likely became clear when Jesus appeared to the disciples on Easter evening. Then Jesus explained His fulfillment of the Old Testament, as He had done on the road to Emmaus with two disciples earlier. With Jesus' appearance and His clear explanation of the Old Testament prophecies, then the disciples could have the wonderful combination of faith and understanding. Jesus had to die and rise again to fulfill God's promises and, on Easter, they could both believe and know this was done.

Why did Jesus tell Mary not to cling to Him?

Jesus was not telling her that He could not be touched but was telling her not to keep holding on to Him. Perhaps she thought she had lost Jesus once and she was never going to let Him go now that He was alive again. We can understand Mary's desire to hold Jesus. Like the woman in the parable of the lost coin in Luke 15:8–10, once Mary found the object of her search, she intended to keep hold of Him. But Jesus assured her that He was not going to disappear from the world. She would have other opportunities to see Him before He returned to the Father in heaven. For now, He had an important task for her to accomplish—that of spreading the news of His resurrection.

Holy Spirit, strengthen our faith in Jesus' resurrection and increase our understanding of all that was accomplished by His death and resurrection. In Jesus' name. Amen.

JOY AND CONFIDENCE FROM JESUS' RESURRECTION

Supposing Him to be the gardener, she said to Him, "Sir, if you have carried Him away, tell me where you have laid Him, and I will take Him away." Jesus said to her, "Mary." (JOHN 20:15–16)

Jesus' resurrection gives us the greatest joy and confidence, no matter what difficulties we face in life, whatever sadness strikes us. In our text, Mary went from sorrow to overwhelming joy in a moment. Jesus said her name as only He could to cut through her sorrow. So also, for us, joy comes through Easter's message. Even the death of a loved one or our own impending death can't hold us in terror because just as Jesus rose from the dead, He will raise us and our loved ones from the dead on the Last Day. When He returns to earth, He will lift us up in our resurrected bodies so that we will live with Him in the restored creation forever. Our worship each week repeats this hope. Worship is a joyful return to the resurrection of Easter and the certainty that Jesus is with us.

This important text is used as the Gospel for Easter Sunrise. Of course, there are many Easter hymns that express the truth of our text too. One that is very familiar is "I Know That My Redeemer Lives" (*LSB* 461). Stanza 5 captures the sorrow and fear of Mary, which are comforted by Jesus:

He lives to silence all my fears;
He lives to wipe away my tears;
He lives to calm my troubled heart;
He lives all blessings to impart.

Another hymn that is likely less known but that expresses Mary's Easter experience is "Christians,

to the Pascal Victim" (*LSB* 460). Stanza 2 speaks to Mary:

"Speak, Mary, declaring
What you saw when wayfaring."
"The tomb of Christ, who is living,
The glory of Jesus' resurrection;
Bright angels attesting,
The shroud and napkin resting.
My Lord, my hope, is arisen;
To Galilee He goes before you."

One final hymn speaks very well to a part of our text. Stanza 4 of "Jesus Lives! The Victory's Won" (*LSB* 490) gives us the assurance that we will never be separated from the risen Jesus. When Mary wanted to cling to Jesus so that she would never lose Him, Jesus gave her reassurance. We all have that comfort as this hymn expresses it:

Jesus lives! I know full well
Nothing me from Him shall sever.
Neither death nor pow'rs of hell
Part me now from Christ forever.
God will be my sure defense;
This shall be my confidence.

Our Risen Savior, thank You for using Your divine power to break open Your grave and to bring eternal life to all who believe in the joyful Easter message. Amen.

THE REPORT OF THE GUARDS

WEEK 46—MATTHEW 28:11–15

While they were going, behold, some of the guard went into the city and told the chief priests all that had taken place. And when they had assembled with the elders and taken counsel, they gave a sufficient sum of money to the soldiers and said, "Tell people, 'His disciples came by night and stole Him away while we were asleep.' And if this comes to the governor's ears, we will satisfy him and keep you out of trouble." So they took the money and did as they were directed. And this story has been spread among the Jews to this day.

A FALSE REPORT

While [the women] were going, be-
hold, some of the guard went into the
city and told the chief priests all that
had taken place. (MATTHEW 28:11)

The book of Matthew was written for a Jewish audience. Keeping that in mind, Matthew writes this week's passage to address the rumors that were being spread to discredit Jesus' resurrection during the time he wrote the book. In the verses before this, the guards were guarding the tomb when the angel of the Lord appeared, and they "became like dead men" (v. 4). When they came out of this state, they rushed to the chief priests to report what had happened. This passage begins with acknowledging that the women were already on their way to tell the disciples all they had seen and so some of the guards had to also go on their way. They were in fear of what this would mean for their lives—how could they explain what had happened and what they saw or did not see? The tomb was sealed by them and yet the stone had been rolled away to show Jesus' body was no longer there. Under Roman law, they had to be executed for failing to guard the tomb as ordered.

The guards knew they had to confess what had happened. As guards, reporting to their commander would be the expectation. However, instead of going to Pilate, these guards go directly to the chief priests. In Matthew 27:65, Pilate tells the chief priests, "You have a guard of soldiers. Go, make it as secure as you can"—which can either mean to send their own temple guards or that Pilate gave them some Roman soldiers to act as guards. The fact that the chief priests promise to protect them if word gets back to Pilate indicates these are most likely Roman soldiers.

In Rome, the penalty for "sleeping on the job," letting a guarded body be stolen, was death, which means these soldiers should have been executed. The passage says that they told the chief priests all that had taken place. Instead of washing their hands of the guards as they had done with Judas, we see the chief priests work again with the elders to hide the truth and control the narrative. Instead of the shouts of "Crucify Him," they tell the guards to tell the story that they fell asleep and the body was stolen by the disciples. They count on the guards to spread this rumor, giving them "a sufficient sum of money" (Matthew 28:12) and then promising to deal with the governor if news got to his ears. Not only do the soldiers go and tell this falsehood, but the reading also indicates that this is spread among Jews even to the day Matthew wrote his Gospel.

The cost was steep for the chief priests and elders to bribe the soldiers and Pilate—far more than they had paid Judas—but the news of Jesus' resurrection still spread, and the church grew. Thanks be to God.

Heavenly Father, thank You for sending
Your Son to be the ultimate sacrifice. May we
live our lives in that freedom—not in fear or in
hiding but boldly in our lives. In Jesus' name.
Amen.

THE BRIBE

And when they had assembled with the elders and taken counsel, they gave a sufficient sum of money to the soldiers and said, "Tell people, 'His disciples came by night and stole Him away while we were asleep.'" (MATTHEW 28:12–13)

This week's passage is only included in the book of Matthew. He wrote it to debunk the lie of the chief priests and elders that the disciples had stolen Jesus' body. These Jewish leaders worked very hard to discredit and defeat Jesus, telling the people that this man was just a false prophet. We see that, at every corner, the Jews were trying to shut out the name of Christ. Verse 15 reminds us of the false narrative that is still being spread today in many and various ways. In spite of all the lies of the soldiers, chief priests, and elders, Jesus is victorious. The women ran from the tomb and told the truth that would spread to the disciples and to the ends of the earth, starting at Pentecost.

These verses remind us how deceitful Satan is. Even with his head mortally wounded under Jesus' foot, he still does all he can to make God out to be a liar. The chief priests and elders, as well as the high priest and all those involved in the crucifixion, should have investigated if Jesus had, indeed, risen on the third day as He said He would. They should have been quick to repent of their sins and proclaim Him as the Christ. Instead, under Satan's influence, they continue to plot to silence Jesus. They had known it was risky to seek His death so close to the Passover, and yet they proceeded. This "incident" of Jesus' earthly body disappearing from the tomb they were guarding threatened to destroy everything they had been doing and the influence they had on people.

These verses remind us of the victory that is in Christ's resurrection. The soldiers did not know how to explain what had happened, but they knew that Jesus' body was no longer in the tomb that they were guarding. They knew the answer; the priests and elders knew the answer as well. It is this answer that led them to lie and create their own narrative. The guards were told to go out and spread lies to everyone they could—and the chief priests and elders were preparing to lie to the governor and bribe him to look the other way once the news had reached his ears. This is why they were willing to pay the sum of money to the soldiers. They had done this before, as we read in week 37: they were willing to pay the small price of thirty silver coins to Judas to betray Jesus, and now they are paying the guards dearly to continue this betrayal. The price was steep, but in their eyes, the cost of their status in the community was even more steep. They were willing to do whatever it took to quiet all rumors of Jesus' resurrection—and also ruin the name and reputation of His disciples.

Heavenly Father, we pray for those who would deny You and speak lies against Your name. Give us the grace to forgive and share the Good News with them, that you may lead them to repentance and faith. In Jesus' name. Amen.

MISSION ACCOMPLISHED, DESPITE HIS FOES

This story has been spread among the Jews to this day. (MATTHEW 28:15)

Jesus did what He said He would do—He was crucified on the cross, died and was buried, and, on the third day, rose again. This is what the Father sent Him to do. This is what had been promised since the fall in the Garden of Eden to Adam and Eve. This is the anticipated Savior creation had been waiting for. We see that this has happened. The guards who were there knew it, although they were in a sleeplike state of fear. When they awoke, they knew exactly what had happened. They were unable to comprehend what had happened, but they realized their lives were on the line and how important it was to quickly go and tell the chief priests and elders what had happened. Jesus predicted His death and resurrection in the later months of His earthly ministry, and many heard Him, including His enemies. His resurrection was a culmination of His ministry and the ultimate act of revealing both His earthly and divine nature. His resurrection was also the ultimate defeat over death and the devil, making Satan's accusations void because He was the Paschal Lamb who fulfilled all that was spoken about Him.

The soldiers never denied what had happened or what happened to them. They ran to the chief priests to find out what they should do about it. The chief priests and the elders they gathered also knew what had happened. This is a testimony to Christ and the acknowledgement of His identity as I Am. This points us to Jesus and the power in His death and resurrection. Their response was to deny Jesus' resurrection and spread a lie to counter that narrative—and, in the process, also try to hurt Jesus' disciples. The sum of money (see v. 12) and the lie (see v. 13) were only meant to hurt and undo what Jesus had done. The chief priests and elders were ready to feed that lie to the governor and willing to protect the soldiers as well.

We know that the content of their lie is not that case—Jesus lives, and He always will. There is no denying His Word and what He came on this earth to do. His mission was to come into this world and, through His earthly ministry, preach and teach God's Word, glorifying Him and bringing people to the knowledge of the love of God through Himself, Christ Jesus, our Lord. And He came to die for the sins of the world, rising to life again on the third day to defeat death and promising eternal life to all who believe. No matter what lies and what money was exchanged—mission accomplished.

Lord Jesus, thank You for dying on the cross and rising again. Defeat the railing of Your enemies, keep Your church safe, and empower us to boldly proclaim and defend the truth. Amen.

INVENTING A LIE

Tell people, "His disciples came by night and stole Him away while we were asleep." (MATTHEW 28:13)

I n this week's section of Scripture we learn more about the hierarchy of politics during this time. Since this part of the reading is only contained in this book, we look in the book of Matthew to learn more insight to the who, what, when, where, why, and how.

Who are these guards?

They are either the temple guards from the chief priests or Roman soldiers from Pontius Pilate. But if they were temple guards, why would the chief priests need to satisfy the governor if word came to him that they had fallen asleep at the tomb? What was that to a Roman governor? It is far more likely these were Roman guards—Roman soldiers.

Why these guards?

They are Roman guards stationed to maintain peace throughout the city during this high festival. In Matthew 27:64-66, we learn that the chief priests requested Pilate to send his men to guard the tomb for fear that the body would be stolen by Jesus' disciples, and Pilate agreed.

When does this all happen?

The chief priests send the guards to guard the tomb on Saturday, the Sabbath day after the Friday "day of Preparation" (Matthew 27:62) since they remembered Jesus said that He would be buried and rise again on the third day. On Sunday morning, some of the soldiers run back to the chief priests after the angel comes down and rolls the stone away. While the soldiers are running to the chief priests, the women who have seen Jesus have hurried off to tell the disciples.

Where does this take place?

The soldiers encounter the angel at the tomb, and they hurry to the chief priests and council who are at the temple. A similar scene would have occurred when Judas returned to the chief priests after changing his mind and regretting his betrayal. In Matthew 27:3-8, Judas brought the silver coins to the chief priests and council, wanting to wash himself of the trial and condemnation of Jesus. They would have also been in the temple as part of the Passover festivities.

Why do this?

The soldiers knew the punishment for losing what they were put in charge of guarding, but they knew they had to report what had happened. The chief priests and council had been looking for ways to kill Jesus, and now they had done it. Judas, Peter, Pilate, Barabbas—all these people were part of the story, and the chief priests worked hard to make sure the narrative of a stolen body was spread to all.

How is this all done?

The chief priests and elders gave the guards money to spread the lie that the disciples had stolen the body, and they were ready to bribe the governor. As this passage clearly tells us, this lie kept spreading. All four Gospels—Matthew, Mark, Luke, and John—give us a full picture of Jesus' journey to the cross, tomb, and resurrection.

Heavenly Father, we thank You for Your word to meditate on. Open our ears to listen and our mouths to speak and proclaim Your Word to the ends of the earth. In Jesus' name. Amen.

WHY DO LIES SPREAD LIKE WILDFIRE?

And if this comes to the governor's ears, we will satisfy him and keep you out of trouble. (MATTHEW 28:14)

This week's passage raises some potentially difficult questions:

Why did the lie about grave-robbing successfully spread among the Jews?

Satan knew the Jewish people would more likely believe Jesus' body had been stolen than He had risen from the dead. The people also feared excommunication and persecution from the Jewish leadership. Going along was easier than resisting and holding to the disciples' witness. Also, the testimony of the soldiers carried some weight. But perhaps the biggest reason is because the people had a glorious view of the mission of the Messiah, and dying on a cross was not a part of that vision. Witnessing Jesus being whipped, mocked, spit on, carrying His cross, nailed to that cross, and speared was not what they envisioned at all. When this all took place, doubt grew, which allowed fear to grow and the lie to spread even more quickly.

Why did the guards go to the chief priests instead of to their commander in the army?

The guards knew that if they had gone to the commander, they would have received a death sentence right away. That was the Roman law, and they were condemned under that law. Instead, they went to the chief priests for whom they were working. Therefore, they went to the chief priests and elders and not only told them what had happened but made themselves available to be given a new order, to go and spread the word that the disciples had stolen His body. In addition, they were paid for coming to them and spreading this lie.

How could the chief priests have been able to "satisfy" the governor, Pontius Pilate?

As we can clearly see from Jesus' trials before Pilate, there was no love lost between Pilate and the chief priests. Even when they pressured him to rewrite the notice that hung above Jesus on the cross, Pilate refused to give in to them, saying, "What I have written I have written" (John 19:22). It likely would have taken a sizeable bribe for the priests to convince Pilate not to investigate more closely. Or it is possible that Pilate just wanted to move on from this miserable and humiliating incident and put it all behind him. Either way, if news did reach Pilate, he decided his political future was more important than the truth.

Heavenly Father, may our hearts not give in to fear or doubt but instead rely on You, knowing You are stronger than anything that we could face. In Jesus' name. Amen.

CONFESSION AND ABSOLUTION

While [the women] were going, behold, some of the guard went into the city and told the chief priests all that had taken place. (MATTHEW 28:11)

As we read this passage, we can see a reflection of ourselves in each of the people in the text. The women in verse 11, for example, who hurried off quickly to tell the disciples what had happened. When do you joyfully go out to spread the Good News to those in your life? Maybe the guards in verses 11 and 12, who go to tell the chief priests and elders, knowing that their jobs and their lives are on the line, taking money and spreading lies about Jesus. When have you had an opportunity to share the Gospel but were afraid to speak up? Maybe even in your workplace? As Christians, we live in a world where we are constantly persecuted. Are there times when we have compromised our identity as baptized children of God to go with the crowd? Or have we been the chief priests and elders, willing to do whatever it takes to cover up our own sinful nature, even if at the cost of others and spreading lies? No matter who we sometimes reflect, we know that we should reflect Jesus.

This passage gives us the opportunity to reflect on who we are and how we behave. This is the same self-examination that we get to do weekly in divine worship during Confession and Absolution. As we partake in Confession, we have the opportunity for silent reflection and then hear the Words of Absolution—Jesus' own forgiveness. We know that these words have been spoken from ancient times. We receive the same grace and forgiveness that was offered and given to the women, guards, chief priests and elders, connecting us through time to one another.

The challenges that the people faced during that time are still applicable to us today. Allowing our fear to grow and turn into anger, doubt, or a host of other emotions is not what God calls us to do. Instead, we look to His Word, confessing our sins and asking for repentance. The strength and power in the act of Confession and Absolution connects us to the Father, reassuring us of His love, grace, and forgiveness. Instead of being the soldiers who spread lies, may we be like the women who ran joyfully away to tell the disciples the good news of great joy for all people. Amen.

Heavenly Father, move my heart to sincere repentance and confession through Your holy Law, and assure me of Your gracious forgiveness for Jesus' sake through the Gospel's absolution. In Jesus' name. Amen.

JESUS APPEARS ON THE ROAD TO EMMAUS

Week 47—Luke 24:13–35

That very day two of them were going to a village named Emmaus, about seven miles from Jerusalem, and they were talking with each other about all these things that had happened. While they were talking and discussing together, Jesus Himself drew near and went with them. But their eyes were kept from recognizing Him. And He said to them, "What is this conversation that you are holding with each other as you walk?" And they stood still, looking sad. Then one of them, named Cleopas, answered Him, "Are You the only visitor to Jerusalem who does not know the things that have happened there in these days?" And He said to them, "What things?" And they said to Him, "Concerning Jesus of Nazareth, a man who was a prophet mighty in deed and word before God and all the people, and how our chief priests and rulers delivered Him up to be condemned to death, and crucified Him. But we had hoped that He was the one to redeem Israel. Yes, and besides all this, it is now the third day since these things happened. Moreover, some women of our company amazed us. They were at the tomb early in the morning, and when they did not find His body, they came back saying that they had even seen a vision of angels, who said that He was alive. Some of those who were with us went to the tomb and found it just as the women had said, but Him they did not see." And He said to them, "O foolish ones, and slow of heart to believe all that the prophets have spoken! Was it not necessary that the Christ should suffer these things and enter into His glory?" And beginning with Moses and all the Prophets, He interpreted to them in all the Scriptures the things concerning Himself.

So they drew near to the village to which they were going. He acted as if He were going farther, but they urged Him strongly, saying, "Stay with us, for it is toward evening and the day is now far spent." So He went in to stay with them. When He was at table with them, He took the bread and blessed and broke it and gave it to them. And their eyes were opened, and they recognized Him. And He vanished from their sight. They said to each other, "Did not our hearts burn within us while He talked to us on the road, while He opened to us the Scriptures?" And they rose that same hour and returned to Jerusalem. And they found the eleven and those who were with them gathered together, saying, "The Lord has risen indeed, and has appeared to Simon!" Then they told what had happened on the road, and how He was known to them in the breaking of the bread.

CHRIST'S MISSION AND OURS

That very day two of them were going to a village named Emmaus, about seven miles from Jerusalem, and they were talking with each other about all these things that had happened. (LUKE 24:13–14)

Passover had ended. Those who had come into Jerusalem for the holy feast would be returning to the places from which they came. It wouldn't be surprising that the topic on many lips would have been the crucifixion of Jesus. To some, He would have been simply a rabbi who had moved past His station and been punished for it. But, for those who followed Him, there would have been deep sorrow. They thought He was the Messiah—then He was arrested and executed. What now?

There had been reports from some of His closest followers that the tomb was now empty. But could that truly be trusted? Two disciples walked the road from Jerusalem toward Emmaus, captivated in their conversation about that week's events. They were joined by a stranger who engaged with them on the topic and opened up the Scriptures to them in amazing ways. They asked this stranger to stay with them, and when the blessing was spoken, they fully realized who it was—Jesus, their Savior, alive before them. Jesus immediately disappeared, and they ran to tell their friends.

Could you imagine the wonder and awe these disciples experienced? They knew Jesus was dead. They were unsure of the tales of the women at the tomb and the apostles who agreed with them. As they walked, Jesus joined them, and they did not realize who He was. Jesus taught them, broke bread with them, and then left. But here they had seen it with their own eyes. He was alive.

What would you give to have that experience on that dusty road? Their mourning turned to incredible joy! The best surprise. Jesus was alive. The day's journey they had just walked was then reversed, and they ran back to their friends in Jerusalem. They believed. They had seen Jesus. He was everything they believed.

In these moments, Jesus was preparing the early church for its mission. He would appear and encourage many of His disciples, with these two on the road to Emmaus included in that number. His revelations to the men and women of the church during His forty days with them would give them a zeal for His work that would lead them from Jerusalem to Judea and to the ends of the earth.

Lord, may I find the joy that the disciples on the road to Emmaus experienced in their discovery that You were alive. May Your Word, Supper, Baptism, and Holy Spirit be revelations to me time and again to encourage me in the mission to which Your church is called. Amen.

JESUS WALKS WITH US

While they were talking and discussing together, Jesus Himself drew near and went with them. But their eyes were kept from recognizing Him. And He said to them, "What is this conversation that you are holding with each other as you walk?" And they stood still, looking sad. Then one of them, named Cleopas, answered Him, "Are You the only visitor to Jerusalem who does not know the things that have happened there in these days?" And He said to them, "What things?" And they said to Him, "Concerning Jesus of Nazareth, a man who was a prophet mighty in deed and word before God and all the people, and how our chief priests and rulers delivered Him up to be condemned to death, and crucified Him. But we had hoped that He was the one to redeem Israel. Yes, and besides all this, it is now the third day since these things happened." (LUKE 24:15–21)

Jesus walked and listened. Cleopas and an unnamed disciple told Him all the events of that week. They poured out their hearts and hopes of Jesus being the Messiah, the one to redeem Israel. Jesus let them share. All their confusion and pain pouring out as they walked.

Then, once they were done, Jesus opened the Scriptures to them. From Moses to all the Old Testament prophets, Jesus explained how He had fulfilled every prophecy, all the while not revealing who He was. These two disciples were amazed to the point that they asked Him to stay with them.

Over dinner, Jesus revealed Himself, then immediately disappeared. But He had accomplished what He wanted—He taught these two the depth of Scripture and then revealed the truth of His resurrection. Not only would Cleopas and his friend be amazed by the physically present Jesus but they had His in-depth teaching on who He was as the Messiah.

As Christians, we look forward to Jesus' second coming. It will be a glorious day full of joy and resurrection as Jesus builds the new heaven and earth. It is unlikely that we will see Jesus physically before that return, as these two did over dinner, but Jesus still works in this way. Through prayer, we can come before Him as the disciples did on the road to Emmaus. He calls us to share the confusion, pain, and hurt we experience in this life. He reveals Himself through physical ways to us in His Word, His Supper, and Baptism. He surrounds us with the Body of Christ to be His messengers. The Holy Spirit comes to comfort us.

Even when we don't recognize His presence, Jesus has promised to be with us. May we rejoice as the disciples on the road to Emmaus did when we recognize the Savior among us.

Dear Jesus, thank You for being with us. May we find joy in the ways You have revealed Yourself to us. Amen.

WHAT KIND OF MESSIAH ARE WE SEEKING?

"But we had hoped that He was the one to redeem Israel. Yes, and besides all this, it is now the third day since these things happened. . . ." And He said to them, "O foolish ones, and slow of heart to believe all that the prophets have spoken! Was it not necessary that the Christ should suffer these things and enter into His glory?" And beginning with Moses and all the Prophets, He interpreted to them in all the Scriptures the things concerning Himself. (LUKE 24:21, 25–27)

Even after the week that had transpired, there were still misconceptions about the Messiah. These disciples on the road to Emmaus shared that they had hoped Jesus would redeem Israel. They were still shortsighted on who He was and what He had come to do. Their hope was for the earthly kingdom of Israel and its people.

Jesus takes them to school. He walks them through the Old Testament prophets. He shows them who the Messiah is meant to be—He has come not to conquer the enemies of Israel but instead the villains of all humanity: sin, death, and the devil.

Even disciples of Jesus were still confused about His purpose. But He lays it out for them here. Using the whole narrative of Scripture, He lays out the plan and purpose of the Messiah. Salvation is and always has been the goal. Jesus uses this technique to make sure His disciples get the point. His death and resurrection are to redeem the world, not just grant power back to Israel as an earthly kingdom. It reflects the words from John: "For God did not send His Son into the world to condemn the world, but in order that the world might be saved through Him" (John 3:17).

How often do we want Jesus to be that kind of Messiah in our lives? We confuse His actual mission with our own, wanting the Son of God to come and take care of the enemies of our choosing, real or imagined. Jesus is treated as a genie to be commanded instead of the Word made flesh come for us. It is good to read that even those who walked with Him were confused by His true mission. Thanks be to God that the Scriptures record these interactions for our benefit. May we rejoice in the work that God is doing in and among His people. He came to defeat the true enemies of all humanity, not just earthly powers. It has been revealed to us just as it was all those years ago to two disciples along the road to Emmaus.

Heavenly Father, I repent of the times I worked to make Your plan for salvation obey me. May I slow down today to see the work of Jesus as it truly is and not as I may wish it to be for selfish gain. In Jesus' name. Amen.

JESUS HIDES AND REVEALS HIMSELF

While they were talking and discussing together, Jesus Himself drew near and went with them. But their eyes were kept from recognizing Him. (LUKE 24:15–16)

The road to Emmaus has become a cornerstone of biblical accounts, yet it starts so strangely. Two disciples walk a dusty road, and Jesus joins them, but "their eyes were kept from recognizing Him." Jesus was walking and talking with them, but neither noticed who He was. What an odd thing! But it is not the first time this has happened for Jesus. There are times throughout Jesus' ministry where He has either been hidden from people who do not recognize Him or His teaching has been kept out of grasp of recognition, including John 20:14: "Having said this, she turned around and saw Jesus standing, but she did not know that it was Jesus" and Luke 18:34: "But they understood none of these things. This saying was hidden from them, and they did not grasp what was said."

For those that would come after His earthly ministry, Jesus actually promises something along these lines: "For where two or three are gathered in My name, there am I among them" (Matthew 18:20). It is incredible to see that those who were physically with Him and hearing Him did not always recognize Him or His ways. But we who have come after His incarnation can rejoice that though we may not see Him, He promises to be with us wherever we gather in His name.

Look, though, what happens when Jesus appears: "When He was at table with them, He took the bread and blessed and broke it and gave it to them. And their eyes were opened, and they recognized Him. And He vanished from their sight" (Luke 24:30–31).

Jesus reveals Himself to them! He is not always hidden. He had been doing this throughout His ministry.

> Immediately He made His disciples get into the boat and go before Him to the other side, to Bethsaida, while He dismissed the crowd. And after He had taken leave of them, He went up on the mountain to pray. And when evening came, the boat was out on the sea, and He was alone on the land. And He saw that they were making headway painfully, for the wind was against them. And about the fourth watch of the night He came to them, walking on the sea. He meant to pass by them, but when they saw Him walking on the sea they thought it was a ghost, and cried out, for they all saw Him and were terrified. But immediately He spoke to them and said, "Take heart; it is I. Do not be afraid." (Mark 6:45–50)

He still reveals Himself today through His Word. May we rejoice that we have a Savior who, though sometimes we do not recognize Him, reveals Himself to us.

Dear Jesus, reveal Yourself to me today through Your Word, Your Sacraments, and Your church. Amen.

UNKNOWN DISCIPLES

That very day two of them were going to a village named Emmaus, about seven miles from Jerusalem, and they were talking with each other about all these things that had happened. . . . Then one of them, named Cleopas, answered Him, "Are You the only visitor to Jerusalem who does not know the things that have happened there in these days?" (LUKE 24:13–14, 18)

Who were these two disciples? Here we only find mention of Cleopas. Some traditions of the early church claimed that he was actually Clopas, brother of Joseph and uncle of Jesus. We find a clue to this from John 19:25: "But standing by the cross of Jesus were His mother and His mother's sister, Mary the wife of Clopas, and Mary Magdalene." *Clopas* is the Hebrew form of the Greek name *Cleopas*.

There is no way to know for certain if this is the true identity of this man. It is held loosely as a possibility for who he was, but the naming of two of these people as disciples means they were within the orbit of Jesus as He went about His ministry. The twelve apostles were the closest to Jesus during this time, but there were those who still followed closely and were not numbered among the Twelve. Just look at Luke 10. Jesus sends out seventy-two of His disciples. This means, conservatively, there were at least sixty other people besides the Twelve who were following Jesus closely enough to be sent out by Him.

It is reassuring that we do not know exactly who these two people were. A student of Scripture can quickly rattle off the twelve names of the apostles. But it is a blessing that here, we find two unknown people to whom Jesus appears physically. He is not here to set up a religion that only benefits the religious elite. No—He is for all people, even the unknown ones.

Right after His resurrection, Jesus spends the day with these two on the road, walking, talking, and teaching. Even though they are not of the Twelve, they are worthy of His time. Nowhere do we find a history of the disciples on the road to Emmaus outside of this account. Instead, they rejoice and run to share the news with the disciples back in Jerusalem. They are an example to Christians everywhere—not seeking glory or fame but there instead to bask in the light of the Savior and share their experiences with Him.

What a joy! We, too, are the unknown disciples, experiencing Jesus as we journey through life. May we follow the lead of these two who celebrated what Jesus had taught and done for them.

Lord, may I rejoice in what You have done! Set aside my own needs for recognition to live a life instead that declares Your love to all those around me. Amen.

PROPELLED TO TELL THE GOOD NEWS

And He said to them, "O foolish ones, and slow of heart to believe all that the prophets have spoken! Was it not necessary that the Christ should suffer these things and enter into His glory?" And beginning with Moses and all the Prophets, He interpreted to them in all the Scriptures the things concerning Himself. . . . And their eyes were opened, and they recognized Him. And He vanished from their sight. They said to each other, "Did not our hearts burn within us while He talked to us on the road, while He opened to us the Scriptures?" And they rose that same hour and returned to Jerusalem. And they found the eleven and those who were with them gathered together, saying, "The Lord has risen indeed, and has appeared to Simon!" Then they told what had happened on the road, and how He was known to them in the breaking of the bread. (LUKE 24:25–27, 31–35)

Every week, believers in Christ gather together. Traditionally, this takes place on Sunday mornings, though some may meet in the evening or throughout the week. During this time, Scripture is taught through songs, readings, and preaching. In our verses this week, we see a model of Jesus taking these two disciples on the road to Emmaus to church.

He takes their preconceived notions and realigns them to His mission. He teaches through the prophets to help them see the actual mission of the Christ. When their eyes are opened, they rejoice and run to tell their friends.

When we join in the worship service, we should walk in with similar hearts: ready to be taken on a journey. We come as people in need of growth and correction, repentance and forgiveness. We receive all these things and more through the gift of the gathered people of God.

This knowledge of Jesus should propel us into action. The two disciples in this story have walked the dusty road from Jerusalem to Emmaus. Estimated to be between six and seven miles, they run back to find their friends after walking all day. Their joy in the Savior propels them forward—the news is too good to keep to themselves.

What is our reaction to coming together in worship? During the Divine Service, can we slow ourselves down to recognize that the same Jesus who walked that road to Emmaus has joined us where we have joined in worship? He is present with us through His promises, His Word, and the Sacraments. Can we stop trying to seek to experience Him through some overly contrived, miraculous need and instead realize that He is already there?

May we be propelled into the world. The disciples on the road experienced the beginning of the movement of the early church, which would explode outward from Jerusalem to take the Gospel across the known world. May we, too, be propelled from our places of worship into the world to connect disconnected people to the Savior—He who walks the road with us.

Lord, slow me down to see You at work each week. Propel me out in joy to love You and love my neighbor. May I take the message of the Savior to those who are disconnected from You. In Jesus' name. Amen.

JESUS APPEARS TO THOMAS

Week 48—John 20:19–31

On the evening of that day, the first day of the week, the doors being locked where the disciples were for fear of the Jews, Jesus came and stood among them and said to them, "Peace be with you." When He had said this, He showed them His hands and His side. Then the disciples were glad when they saw the Lord. Jesus said to them again, "Peace be with you. As the Father has sent Me, even so I am sending you." And when He had said this, He breathed on them and said to them, "Receive the Holy Spirit. If you forgive the sins of any, they are forgiven them; if you withhold forgiveness from any, it is withheld."

Now Thomas, one of the twelve, called the Twin, was not with them when Jesus came. So the other disciples told him, "We have seen the Lord." But he said to them, "Unless I see in His hands the mark of the nails, and place my finger into the mark of the nails, and place my hand into His side, I will never believe."

Eight days later, His disciples were inside again, and Thomas was with them. Although the doors were locked, Jesus came and stood among them and said, "Peace be with you." Then He said to Thomas, "Put your finger here, and see My hands; and put out your hand, and place it in My side. Do not disbelieve, but believe." Thomas answered Him, "My Lord and my God!" Jesus said to him, "Have you believed because you have seen Me? Blessed are those who have not seen and yet have believed."

Now Jesus did many other signs in the presence of the disciples, which are not written in this book; but these are written so that you may believe that Jesus is the Christ, the Son of God, and that by believing you may have life in His name.

SHEER DISBELIEF

Jesus came and stood among them and said to them, "Peace be with you." (JOHN 20:19)

Our text for this week begins on Easter evening with the followers of Jesus locked in a room together for fear of the Jews. This fear had been building for quite a while—for three years, Jesus had been preaching, teaching, healing, and casting out demons. As He went about His ministry, He encountered numerous religious leaders who opposed Him. These religious leaders even began to plot how to kill Jesus.

A couple of weeks before our text, Jesus' friend Lazarus had died. Jesus told His disciples they were headed back to Judea, and they protested, reminding Jesus that the Jews were seeking to stone Him to death (see John 8:48–59). Jesus informed them they were going back because Lazarus had died. Thomas replied, "Let us also go, that we may die with Him." But Jesus was not intending only to mourn Lazarus—Jesus raised Lazarus from the dead.

Then, a week before Easter, Jesus rode into Jerusalem on a donkey to shouts of *hosanna*, which means "save us now." The Jewish leaders got upset with Jesus then as well, telling Him to rebuke His followers for calling Him the "King who comes in the name of the Lord" (Luke 19:38).

A few days before our text, Judas went to the Jewish leaders and agreed to betray Jesus to the Jewish leaders for thirty pieces of silver. Jesus was arrested, put on trial before the Jewish religious leaders, and condemned to death. These religious officials used their influence over the Roman governor, Pontius Pilate, to pressure him to sentence Jesus to death.

Jesus was crucified, executed, assassinated.

But on Easter morning, Jesus rose from the dead. He had predicted this would happen on several occasions, but somehow, this went unremembered by the grieving, fearful disciples.

Despite reports from Easter morning of Jesus being raised, in our text on Easter evening, the disciples find themselves still filled with fear, locked in a room together.

Even though the doors are locked that Easter evening, Jesus appears among them, proclaims peace to them, breathes the Holy Spirit on them, and sends them out into the world.

But one of Jesus' disciples is missing: Thomas. The other ten apostles tell Thomas the news later, but Thomas refuses to believe. He even goes so far as to state that unless he sees and touches Jesus' wounds, Thomas will never believe that Jesus is risen.

After an entire week of hearing the witness of the other ten disciples, as well as the witness of Mary Magdalene, whom Jesus had appeared to first, Thomas still refuses to believe. But Jesus graciously appears again, this time with Thomas present, and invites Thomas to cease his disbelief.

Jesus, thank You for appearing to so many people who became witnesses of Your resurrection. Strengthen us to cease our disbelief and cling to Your blessing of us who have not seen and yet believe. Amen.

WITNESSES OF JESUS' RESURRECTION

Now Jesus did many other signs in the presence of the disciples, which are not written in this book; but these are written so that you may believe that Jesus is the Christ, the Son of God, and that by believing you may have life in His name. (JOHN 20:30–31)

After John's Gospel records Jesus' appearance on Easter evening with Thomas absent, and then again with Thomas present eight days later, John tells those reading and listening to his Gospel the reason he has recorded all these words and actions of Jesus: "So that you may believe that Jesus is the Christ, the Son of God, and that by believing you may have life in His name."

After Jesus rises from the dead, He does not ascend into heaven without appearing to people. We are told in 1 Corinthians 15 that the resurrected Jesus appeared to more than five hundred people at one time. These witnesses of Jesus' resurrection proclaim that Good News throughout the world, Thomas included. Jesus sends them to be His witnesses here in John 20, as well as in Matthew 28 and Acts 1.

Jesus calls on Thomas to stop disbelieving but rather to believe. Jesus rebukes Thomas for his refusal to believe but blesses those who have not seen Him risen from the dead yet still believe the Good News proclaimed by those who have witnessed Jesus risen from the dead. You and I, who have not seen Jesus risen from the dead but still believe in His death and resurrection for our forgiveness, are among those Jesus blesses in this passage.

This episode with Thomas is a great reminder to us that our faith is not about seeing. Faith comes through the Word of Christ. Faith comes through the Holy Spirit, working where and when He wills. Faith comes through receiving the Good News of Jesus' death and resurrection for our forgiveness, given to us freely.

In our lives of faith, we need not demand more proof from Jesus. We can trust the words written and the actions recorded. We can trust those who witnessed Jesus risen from the dead. And we can confess alongside Thomas, proclaiming, "My Lord and my God" (John 20:28).

And, as John tells us, by believing in Jesus as the Christ, the Son of God, we are given life in His name. We are given new life as new creations, baptized in Jesus' name. More than that, we are given eternal life with Jesus. In that new creation of eternal life, we will, indeed, see the resurrected Jesus face to face, just as Thomas did.

Jesus, thank You for the words of the Scriptures and the testimony of all those who proclaim Your Good News. Strengthen us to continue to be witnesses of Your resurrection so that more people would have life in Your name. Amen.

SEEKING AND SAVING THE LOST

On the evening of that day, the first day of the week, the doors being locked where the disciples were for fear of the Jews, Jesus came and stood among them and said to them, "Peace be to you." (JOHN 20:19)

One of my favorite lines from Jesus is, "For the Son of Man came to seek and to save the lost" (Luke 19:10). In His mission to restore fallen creation, Jesus seeks out those who are lost. Jesus saves those who are lost. Jesus does this by His death on the cross, which saves us from sin, and by His resurrection from the dead, which saves us from death and gifts us with eternal life.

We see the fruit of Jesus' mission more than once in this week's reading from John 20. The ten are lost. When Jesus appears to them, they are lost. Even though they have heard the incredible news Mary Magdalene brought them of Jesus' resurrection, they are still in a locked room in fear. Even though John and Peter race to the tomb of Jesus and find it empty, they still go back to that locked room. Jesus seeks them out. He finds them. He stands among them. He speaks peace to them. He breathes the Holy Spirit on them. He fills their hearts with joy.

Thomas was lost. Even though he heard from the other ten apostles—and Mary and several others regarding Jesus' resurrection—Thomas refused to believe. Thomas was so lost that he began making demands of Jesus. Touching Jesus' very wounds was the only way Thomas was going to leave his prison of unbelief.

Jesus seeks out Thomas. Jesus does not leave Thomas lost in his disbelief. Jesus appears to Thomas and speaks peace to him. Jesus saves Thomas from the despair of unbelief.

This reading concludes with John reminding us of the purpose of his Gospel: to bring us to faith in Jesus, the Messiah, the Son of God. Moreover, by faith in Jesus, we would have life in Jesus' name.

Jesus sends His disciples out into the world with the Holy Spirit to forgive sins. Jesus sends His disciples to continue the mission to seek and save the lost and to be witnesses of His resurrection.

Jesus' mission comes to fruition among us every time our sins are confessed and forgiven—every time those who are lost in unbelief are sought and saved in the waters of Baptism where they receive the Holy Spirit and life in Jesus' name.

Jesus, thank You for Your dedication to seeking and saving the lost. Thank You for seeking and saving us. Strengthen us as we encounter those who are lost to point them toward You and Your forgiveness. Amen.

THOMAS AND NATHANAEL

Then [Jesus] said to Thomas, "Put your finger here, and see My hands; and put out your hand, and place it in My side. Do not disbelieve, but believe." Thomas answered Him, "My Lord and my God!" (JOHN 20:27–28)

This reading from John 20 may bring to mind many different Bible passages. As Jesus breathes onto His disciples, we may be reminded of God breathing life into Adam in Genesis 2. As He breathes on them, Jesus says, "Receive the Holy Spirit" (v. 22). Jesus had promised they would receive the Holy Spirit in John 7. And we see on numerous occasions how God's people are filled with the Holy Spirit—Jesus' followers are filled with the Holy Spirit on Pentecost in Acts 2, and Luke notes numerous occasions throughout the book of Acts where Jesus' followers are filled with the Holy Spirit too.

But the story I am most reminded of is from the beginning of John's Gospel. Jesus' interaction with Thomas reminds me of Jesus' interaction with Nathanael in John 1. Jesus had already called Philip to follow Him. Philip went and told Nathanael the news, saying, "We have found Him of whom Moses in the Law and also the prophets wrote, Jesus of Nazareth, the son of Joseph" (John 1:45). Nathanael responds with skepticism, sarcasm, and disbelief: "Can anything good come out of Nazareth?" (John 1:46). Likewise with Thomas, Jesus had appeared to the ten other disciples, who then told Thomas the news. But Thomas responds with disbelief.

When Jesus appears to Nathanael, the briefest of conversations has Nathanael confessing, "Rabbi, You are the Son of God! You are the King of Israel!"

(John 1:49). When Jesus appears to Thomas, the briefest interaction has Thomas confessing, "My Lord and my God" (John 20:28).

To both Nathanael and Thomas, Jesus asks a poignant question about their belief. To Nathanael, "Because I said to you, 'I saw you under the fig tree,' do you believe? You will see greater things than these" (John 1:50). To Thomas, "Have you believed because you have seen Me? Blessed are those who have not seen and yet have believed" (John 20:29).

These parallels remind us that none of the disciples were perfect. Each made mistakes. Each had forgotten or failed to believe Jesus' promise that after His suffering and death, He would, indeed, rise from the dead. As Jesus' followers and disciples, we make mistakes too. We may become stubborn and obstinate, demanding more of our Lord. Yet in His mercy, He comes to us, draws a confession of faith from us as well, and points us back in the right direction to follow Him.

Jesus, thank You for loving us despite our foolish stubbornness that too often refuses to believe Your promises. Thank You for drawing near to us and revealing Yourself to us. Amen.

JESUS IS ONLY REVEALED AND RECOGNIZED WHEN HE CHOOSES

Eight days later, His disciples were inside again, and Thomas was with them. Although the doors were locked, Jesus came and stood among them and said, "Peace be with you." (JOHN 20:26)

This week's reading prompts no shortage of challenging questions:

Why wasn't Thomas with the other disciples on Easter evening?

Where was he? We could speculate on his being with family for the Passover or on some preference to be alone in the grief, but ultimately, we do not know. But more importantly, we should not be too concerned about Thomas's absence. There were several men and women gathered together in the same place in the days between Jesus' death and ascension. And we see several occasions where they leave the group and go off by themselves. Mary Magdalene was at the tomb of Jesus on Easter morning by herself. Peter and John raced to see the empty tomb on Easter morning too. Cleopas and his traveling partner were headed to Emmaus before Jesus appeared to them. The doors were locked, but people were clearly coming and going as they wished.

But the doors being locked brings up another question:

Why does John point out the locked doors both times Jesus appears to the group?

I think this is for several reasons. First, to note their fearfulness of the Jewish religious leaders that had brought about Jesus' death. Second, though, I believe John points this out to reveal the miraculous powers of the resurrected Jesus. Jesus doesn't come through the door. He doesn't climb through a window when nobody is looking. He appears. One minute He is not visible, the next minute He is. Likewise, in other resurrection appearances, Jesus is only recognized when He chooses to be recognized. Mary Magdalene does not recognize Jesus until He says her name. The Emmaus disciples do not recognize Jesus until the breaking of the bread. In the appearance after our text, the seven disciples don't recognize Jesus on the shore until He provides the miraculous catch of 153 fish. And on the road to Damascus, Jesus appears to Saul (also known as Paul).

Likewise, on these two occasions, Jesus is only revealed and recognized when He chooses to be. He can appear where and when He wishes and always appears where He promises to appear. Since this is the case, we can trust Jesus is present among us as He promised to be. We can trust that Jesus is present in the Lord's Supper as He promised, saying, "This is My body" and "This is My blood." We can trust that Jesus is present among us as we gather together for worship in His name. And we can trust that Jesus hears our prayers as He promised.

Jesus, thank You for promising to be among us. Thank You for keeping Your promises. Amen.

JESUS' GIFTS OF PEACE AND FORGIVENESS

And when [Jesus] had said ["Peace be with you"], He breathed on them and said to them, "Receive the Holy Spirit. If you forgive the sins of any, they are forgiven them; if you withhold forgiveness from any, it is withheld." (JOHN 20:22–23)

As Jesus appears to the ten disciples, He breathes out the Holy Spirit on them and tells them, "Peace be with you. As the Father has sent Me, even so I am sending you" (John 20:21). Likewise, Jesus tells them, "If you forgive the sins of any, they are forgiven them; if you withhold forgiveness from any, it is withheld" (v. 23).

As we gather for worship, we see this action and these words of Jesus bearing fruit. Here Jesus institutes a particular vocation with the express duty of forgiving sins. In our congregations, these words of Jesus bear fruit each time Absolution is pronounced on God's people: "I therefore forgive you all your sins in the name of the Father and of the Son and of the Holy Spirit" (*LSB*, p. 151). As those words are proclaimed to us, whether in private confession and absolution or in corporate Confession and Absolution, Jesus' words are fulfilled.

If your congregation ever uses Divine Service, Setting Four from *Lutheran Service Book*, you will find John's words at the conclusion of this reading sung as part of the Alleluia and Verse: "These are written so that you may believe that Jesus is the Christ, the Son of God" (John 20:31).

It is also worth noting Jesus' first words when He appears, both to the disciples in Thomas's absence and in Thomas's presence. Jesus proclaims, "Peace be with you" (John 20:19, 26).

In our worship services, we likewise share and receive peace. In some congregations, we "pass the peace" either at the beginning of the service or before the Lord's Supper. In some liturgies, after the Words of Institution, the pastor will say or sing, "The peace of the Lord be with you always" (*LSB*, p. 163, for example).

After we receive Christ's body and blood for our forgiveness, we are dismissed with a blessing that includes these words: "Depart in peace" (*LSB*, p. 164).

And the final words placed upon us in the Benediction, the same words placed upon God's people for generations from Moses and Aaron onward, are these words of peace: "The LORD bless you and keep you; the LORD make His face smile upon you and be gracious to you; the LORD lift up His countenance upon you and give you peace" (Numbers 6:24–26).

Jesus brings peace to the uneasy minds and fearful hearts of the disciples that Easter evening. Jesus brings peace eight days later to a stubborn, demanding, unbelieving Thomas as well. Jesus brings peace to our uneasy minds and our fearful hearts each time we are gathered for worship.

Dear Jesus, thank You for Your forgiveness. Thank You for the peace that passes all understanding, which only comes through Your forgiveness. Amen.

JESUS REINSTATES PETER

Week 49—John 21:1–19

After this Jesus revealed Himself again to the disciples by the Sea of Tiberias, and He revealed Himself in this way. Simon Peter, Thomas (called the Twin), Nathanael of Cana in Galilee, the sons of Zebedee, and two others of His disciples were together. Simon Peter said to them, "I am going fishing." They said to him, "We will go with you." They went out and got into the boat, but that night they caught nothing.

Just as day was breaking, Jesus stood on the shore; yet the disciples did not know that it was Jesus. Jesus said to them, "Children, do you have any fish?" They answered Him, "No." He said to them, "Cast the net on the right side of the boat, and you will find some." So they cast it, and now they were not able to haul it in, because of the quantity of fish. That disciple whom Jesus loved therefore said to Peter, "It is the Lord!" When Simon Peter heard that it was the Lord, he put on his outer garment, for he was stripped for work, and threw himself into the sea. The other disciples came in the boat, dragging the net full of fish, for they were not far from the land, but about a hundred yards off.

When they got out on land, they saw a charcoal fire in place, with fish laid out on it, and bread. Jesus said to them, "Bring some of the fish that you have just caught." So Simon Peter went aboard and hauled the net ashore, full of large fish, 153 of them. And although there were so many, the net was not torn. Jesus said to them, "Come and have breakfast." Now none of the disciples dared ask Him, "Who are you?" They knew it was the Lord. Jesus came and took the bread and gave it to them, and so with the fish. This was now the third time that Jesus was revealed to the disciples after He was raised from the dead.

When they had finished breakfast, Jesus said to Simon Peter, "Simon, son of John, do you love Me more than these?" He said to Him, "Yes, Lord; You know that I love You." He said to him, "Feed My lambs." He said to him a second time, "Simon, son of John, do you love Me?" He said to Him, "Yes, Lord; You know that I love You." He said to him, "Tend My sheep." He said to him the third time, "Simon, son of John, do you love Me?" Peter was grieved because He said to him the third time, "Do you love Me?" and he said to Him, "Lord, You know everything; You know that I love You." Jesus said to him, "Feed My sheep. Truly, truly, I say to you, when you were young, you used to dress yourself and walk wherever you wanted, but when you are old, you will stretch out your hands, and another will dress you and carry you where you do not want to go." (This He said to show by what kind of death he was to glorify God.) And after saying this He said to him, "Follow Me."

BABY, WE'VE GOT HISTORY

When they had finished breakfast, Jesus said to Simon Peter, "Simon, son of John, do you love Me more than these?" (JOHN 21:15)

When we reflect on our personal histories, we see relationships that went through their highs and lows, sometimes shaping us for the better and sometimes shaping us for the worse. We may have had a moment where a relationship hit such a low and circumstances dictated that it would remain there for some time.

Peter's relationship with Jesus, his Teacher, looked more like a roller coaster as we read through the Gospels. From the humbling moment they met (when Peter recognizes the Messiah in Luke 5:8–10 after following His directions results in a miraculous catch of fish) and Peter asks Jesus to depart from him because he is an unworthy sinner, to the powerful confession of Jesus as the Christ (see Matthew 16:16–20), there were many highs. Yet, just like a roller coaster, the immediate drops of being rebuked for trying to dissuade Jesus as He predicts His suffering (see Matthew 16:21–23), to Peter's denial of Jesus when His Teacher was on trial, show how quickly we, in our human frailty, can rise and fall.

Imagine the devastation and guilt that must have washed over Peter as he contemplated the last words he spoke to the man he had claimed to be the Christ just before that same man was put to death. Peter is clearly a flawed individual. Is this really who Jesus wants to feed His sheep?

Like Peter, our history with Jesus is equally as flawed. Like Peter, we proclaim Jesus to be the Christ with the same mouth that, in turn, denies Him by our words and actions. Thankfully, mercifully, those histories also lead to the restoration of our relationships with God through the death and resurrection of Jesus. God is not looking for the perfect history to declare His grace but rather His grace is declared in the histories of imperfect persons redeemed by the blood of the Lamb.

Almighty God, we confess that our relationship with You has not always been the picture of perfection. We thank and praise You that, in Your mercy and grace, You have restored us through the suffering, death, and resurrection of Jesus Christ. By Your Holy Spirit, give us the strength to feed Your sheep by sharing the Good News of Jesus with everyone You have entrusted to us. We ask this all in the name of our Savior, Your Son, Jesus Christ. Amen.

ROCK SOLID

*Simon, son of John, do you
love Me?* (JOHN 21:16)

I f you take a close look at our reading, you will find a very interesting omission. It won't stand out like it should because it is blurred between the narrative description of this encounter and the specific words recorded as spoken between the parties involved.

John accounts for two individuals being involved in this conversation, Jesus and Simon Peter.

But Jesus never addresses him as Simon "Peter" in this scenario.

This seems odd, especially if we recall that Jesus Himself was the one who tabbed Simon as Peter earlier in His ministry because Simon's confession of Jesus as the Christ was the "rock" on which the church would be built.

That seemingly solid "rock" was even bolder when Jesus predicted that His disciples would abandon Him in His time of need, and Simon declared that he would never fall away, even if everyone else did. A strong statement from what we have come to understand through the Gospels as a strong personality. A personality that was not as strong when the pressure was really on. A personality that relied on his own strength in the time he most needed a firm foundation. A personality that abandoned the "Rock" that he had, at one time, declared to be the Christ.

So Jesus addresses the "rock"-less Simon. The son of John.

We would be remiss to take this omission as only a word of rebuke, but instead, it established an important truth for the disciple and for us. Without Christ, the Rock of our Salvation, we are weak and powerless. We are unable to live up to the brash claims we boast. Yet Jesus does not want Peter, or us, to think that we are without hope.

No. Instead, Jesus ties Peter's greatest hope to his greatest failure. Just as Peter denied the same person he claimed he would not—three times in that courtyard—Jesus provides the same number of opportunities for Peter to declare his love for the Savior. Only this is not by the strength of the denier—rather, it is by the "Rock" that had been denied.

In His death and resurrection, Jesus had covered every denial, every broken promise, every failure that Simon, son of John—or you or I—would ever commit. Peter was a witness to that truth. The strength of that redemption, the certainty of that Rock, and the complete work of the Holy Spirit is what will strengthen Peter, and us, to confess that we love Him.

Christ, our Rock, too often in our lives we have denied You by our thoughts, our words, and our actions. We ask Your forgiveness. May we be reminded by the Word that we have been completely redeemed. In our moments of weakness, remind us that we are strengthened when we stand firmly on You, our Rock. Amen.

A SPECIAL TASK

Jesus said to Simon Peter, "Simon, son of John, do you love Me more than these?" He said to Him, "Yes, Lord; You know that I love You." He said to him, "Feed My lambs." (JOHN 21:15)

When I was growing up, my dad would often spend what free time he had doing a variety of woodworking projects. I loved to be in the garage or basement as he would repair furniture or create new items. The smell of sawdust and the hum of saws cutting through raw materials are core memories. But more than anything, I loved when he would afford me the opportunity to take a turn in any step of the project. Often, this would require that he guide me through the skill needed to accomplish the task. How to safely push a piece of wood through the table saw. How to measure an angle for a cut. How to guide a nail into the proper spot. Yet even when he would allow me to do something "on my own," he was never far away, watching over my effort, at the ready to guide as needed.

It meant so much for me to be able to participate in the project that my dad was working on. No matter what it was, I knew it must be important, especially if it was something that was worth his time.

When Jesus reinstates Peter, He calls him to take part in a task of great importance. He actually lays the foundation for this in Luke 22:31–32. At the Last Supper, Jesus prefaces His prediction of Peter's denial with the encouragement that Jesus was praying for Peter's faith not to fail. Knowing that he would fail, though, Jesus instructs Peter to "strengthen your brothers" (v. 32) when he has turned again.

If I had made a mistake when helping my dad, he would have certainly been justified to complete the task on his own. In fact, he may have been better off not asking me at all. He was more than qualified to complete the project on his own. And still, even after I failed, he would come alongside me and give me another opportunity to be a part of making it better.

On His own, God is more than capable to strengthen believers by His Spirit. He does not need our help to feed His sheep. And still He asks Peter to take up this task—to join the heavenly Father in the care of His people. Jesus assures Peter that he is still loved and still desired to participate in the tending of God's sheep. For each misstep Peter has made, Jesus reminds him that the full and free forgiveness Christ has won renews and strengthens him for the task ahead. A task to which He calls you and me as well.

Gracious heavenly Father, we confess that like Peter, we have failed You in so many ways. And yet, by Your grace and mercy, You call us to new life through Jesus. You invite us to share that Good News with others. By Your Holy Spirit, give us the strength and courage to do just that in our daily walk. We ask this in the name of Jesus. Amen.

FOLLOW ME

And after saying this [Jesus] said to [Simon Peter], "Follow Me." (JOHN 21:19)

In college, I was afforded the opportunity to be on the baseball team. While I managed to set the school record for innings warmed up in the bullpen without actually getting in the game, I did manage to stay in the program for four years and was tabbed a captain during my senior year. In our fall workouts, a younger teammate became problematic, missing a number of practices and scrimmages. This caused waves among many of the other players and, thinking we were well within our responsibilities, the other captains and I called a players-only meeting. That meeting led to a gross airing of grievances and a vote to dismiss the player from the team. Certain we had taken admirable initiative, we brought our decision to our coach, who promptly chided us for wildly overstepping our bounds.

It took several years for me to fully understand how we had erred. We just didn't know what we didn't know. Our teammate had been wrestling with a family health crisis that had led to his questionable behavior. Only our coach knew that—and knew that what that player needed more than anything was a team whom he could escape to and lean on in that valley of life. Years later, having been head coach of my own baseball program, I better understand my coach's perspective and actions. In more than one situation, I have had to look deeper into the situation than the surface results to determine what is best for each player and team.

From the outside, we may look at the reinstatement of Peter with similar questioning. "Feed Your sheep? This guy? The one who talked a big game and then *completely* abandoned You when things

got tough?" One has to wonder if somewhere in the back of Peter's mind, his Jewish upbringing rang out with the words of Isaiah 40:11: "He will tend His flock like a shepherd, He will gather the lambs in His arms; He will carry them in His bosom, and gently lead those that are with young." In front of Peter was the Good Shepherd. The Promised One, who was sent to seek out the lost and return them to the flock. This Good Shepherd who knew that the lamb standing in front of Him had turned away and really did not deserve to return. There was Jesus gathering Peter back into His arms. There was Jesus directing him to feed His sheep, to tend to His lambs. And really, who better?

Peter had lived as the lost sheep. Blinded by his own arrogance, pride, and stubbornness, he had lost his way. Who better to seek out the lost, arrogant, and stubborn so that they might know the redemptive love that they can escape to and be embraced by in their valley of the shadow of death? Jesus instructs Peter to "follow Me." Given his experience, and ours, who better to serve the Kingdom this way?

Jesus, our Good Shepherd, You sought us out and brought us back to the Father when You stretched out Your arms on the cross to redeem us. Help us by Your Word and Holy Spirit to follow You. Give us the confidence and courage to feed Your sheep and tend to Your lambs, so that they might know who their Good Shepherd is. We ask this in Your holy and precious name. Amen.

WHAT'S IN A NAME?

Feed My lambs. . . . Tend My sheep. . . . Feed My sheep. (JOHN 21:15–17)

In the spring of 2021, Milwaukee Brewers fans walked into the same stadium venue they had for the last twenty seasons—with one major difference. No longer did the PA announcer welcome fans to beautiful Miller Park. Now, they were entering American Family Field. Several seasons removed from the change, you can still find many fans refusing to acknowledge the new name and calling the home of their beloved team by its original title. It is almost as if the fans are concerned the successes through past seasons will disappear with the signage on and around the stadium as it changes.

It should not be lost on the reader that some unfamiliar names end up being assigned to several aspects of our text. Names that might bring concern that the ultimate results are affected. Jew and Gentile. Young and old. The bold and the weak. The names might change, but the redemptive work of Jesus does not. His death and resurrection is for all.

We addressed the fact that the disciple whom Jesus had named *Peter* for boldly declaring Jesus as the Christ was addressed without that same title after denying the Savior. It did not remove the truth that Jesus was the Christ, but it did reflect a change in the relationship—Simon's need for redemption because of his sin.

And if we look just a little more deeply, we could ask why Jesus needed to use the term *lambs* when He had previously called Peter to feed His *sheep*. Aren't those really the same thing? But from our youth, we know that when the term *lamb* is mentioned, we are talking of a sheep, but in its own youth. Jesus expects Peter to not just feed those who are "worthy" but also the least of these.

Similarly, if one were to share John's account, the longtime followers of Yahweh likely bristled at the use of the name "Sea of Tiberias," which Herod Antipas had bestowed on the lake to honor the current Caesar. "It will always be the Sea of Galilee to me!" Yet no matter the name of the body of water, this was still the same place that many of the highlights of Jesus' ministry took place—from walking on water to calming the storm to calling the disciples to be fishers of men. Even with a name that honors the secular ruler, it didn't change the reality that events took place here where Jesus showed Himself to be the Messiah.

Teacher. Rabbi. Promised One. Christ. Messiah. Lamb of God. No matter what name is attributed to Him, His name is the name above all names because of what He accomplished on the cross and in His resurrection. That is the one thing we can be confident will never change.

Name above all names, in Your grace and mercy, You have called us by name to walk in Your marvelous light. May we proclaim Your name, the name of Jesus, to all the world—that they might know of Your wonderful deeds, of Your sacrificial love, and Your power over sin, death, and the devil. We ask all this in the powerful name of our Risen Savior, Jesus Christ. Amen.

RUNNING TO EMBARRASSMENT

When Simon Peter heard that it was the Lord, he put on his outer garment, for he was stripped for work, and threw himself into the sea. (JOHN 21:7)

The child hides in the treehouse, knowing that it will be difficult for the parent to get up there and confront her about the damage done to an item in the house. The coworker ducks into another hallway as they see their supervisor approaching, having recently lost an important account because of a clerical error they made. The student skips a class, knowing that the portion of the group assignment they were responsible for never got done.

When we have fallen on our face, disappointed those who are important to us, or committed some act that brings a fullness of shame to our lives, we do not run toward those we have offended. We feel helpless because the weight of what we have done eats at our conscience, causing us to raise our levels of self-doubt, perceived ineffectiveness, and self-contempt.

Peter was no different. It is hard to think that after denying Jesus multiple times, in such a seminal moment, that this proud, brash man wasn't devastated or looking for the closest hole to crawl into.

Yet here is Peter. Jumping into the water, fully clothed. Rushing to land to be near the same Jesus he had abandoned. The same Jesus who would welcome him to the shore to be fed. The same Jesus who would ask him over and over and over if he loved Him. The same Jesus who would call him to the most meaningful and important task he would take up for the remainder of his life.

When we come to worship, we have the opportunity to join Peter. When we jump into the renewing waters of Baptism with our shame and sin and the Savior claims us as His own. When that same Savior welcomes us to the Table to partake in the Lord's Supper. That same Savior feeds us with His body and blood through the bread and the wine so that we know the restoring forgiveness of Christ. That same Savior does this time and again—even as we sin, time and again. Through this same Meal, the Savior strengthens us to not trust in ourselves but in His strength, by the Holy Spirit, to participate in the feeding of His sheep.

So let us join Peter—running to our embarrassment, forgiven by our Redeemer, Jesus. Restored to relationship with Him, empowered to serve Him by serving those He has set before us.

Almighty God, we confess that we, like Peter, have a multitude of embarrassments and sins that would cause us to turn from Your presence. We ask Your mercy, for the sake of Your Son, Jesus. May we, like Peter, run to You, the only source of redemption, renewal, and restoration. By Your Word and Sacrament, strengthen us in that forgiveness, that Your Holy Spirit would embolden us to lift high the cross of Jesus and point the world to the empty tomb so that they would know that He is risen! We ask all of these things in the name of Your Son, our Savior, the Risen Jesus Christ. Amen.

THE GREAT COMMISSION

Now the eleven disciples went to Galilee, to the mountain to which Jesus had directed them. And when they saw Him they worshiped Him, but some doubted. And Jesus came and said to them, "All authority in heaven and on earth has been given to Me. Go therefore and make disciples of all nations, baptizing them in the name of the Father and of the Son and of the Holy Spirit, teaching them to observe all that I have commanded you. And behold, I am with you always, to the end of the age."

NO MORE TIME FOR DOUBT

When they saw Him they worshiped Him, but some doubted. (MATTHEW 28:17)

The disciples were not ready for this. They weren't ready for their leader to be crucified as a criminal. They weren't ready to be alone. But now, here they are, certainly not ready to be in the presence of a dead man who has come back to life. If Jesus' death was a lot to deal with, His resurrection was even more so. Everyone dies, so that can be grasped. But no one can pull himself out of a grave, right? Wrong.

What were they to make of this? Certainly, Jesus told them all this ahead of time, but they dismissed it. Now, kneeling before their Rabbi, they took a leap of faith: they worshiped Jesus. They followed Jesus for three years, yes. They took notes on His sermons and learned everything they could. They cast out demons in His name and had supernatural experiences. But for a Jew, this step would have been one of the hardest to make. Jews believed in a spiritual realm, but they did not believe that a human could ever be God.

If there was anyone that knew Jesus was a man, it would have been these eleven men. They went everywhere with Him for three years. They saw everything. That's what John leads with in his first Epistle: "That which was from the beginning, which we have heard, which we have seen with our eyes, which we looked upon and have touched with our hands, concerning the Word of life" (1 John 1:1). Their Rabbi was not merely a man; Jesus was God. This is what they realized after He was risen. Everything they thought they knew about Him, about their Scriptures, about the God of their fathers, shifted and transformed.

The Magi knew right away. They came to Jerusalem when Jesus was a toddler "to worship Him" (Matthew 2:2). They didn't have the same issues of faith and doubt that a Jew would have. Today, we might not either. Our doubt might be more about doing what He said. For most of us, our doubt is not really about Jesus—it's about us.

To doubt is to waver between two options, to come to a crossroads, to know there is no way of going back from this. Like Peter trying to walk on water, the disciples were grappling with something beyond comprehension. Peter almost drowned because he stood in doubt. "O you of little faith, why did you doubt?" (Matthew 14:31). But not this time. He had doubted enough. It was time to worship. Will we watch the water, will we waver, or will we fix our eyes on Jesus?

Jesus, Messiah, You are worthy of our worship and praise. We bring our hearts to You, forsaking our fear and doubt. Amen.

OUR TURN TO MAKE DISCIPLES

*Go therefore and make disciples
of all nations.* (MATTHEW 28:19)

Jesus appeared to His followers a number of times after He rose from the dead, but in Matthew, Jesus shows up only twice—once to the women and once to the eleven apostles. And Matthew doesn't give us much of what He said. Even this tells us much about Jesus. First of all, Matthew prioritizes the fact that He was raised from the dead over what He said and did in Jerusalem after He was raised from the dead. Secondly, Jesus wanted to meet them in Galilee. He told them that on the night He was betrayed (see Matthew 26:32), and He told the women to remind them (see Matthew 28:7). Why Galilee? He was crucified in Jerusalem, they were all still there, and there were a lot of other people too. Why would Matthew skip over Jesus' Jerusalem appearances?

For Matthew, Jesus' Great Commission is most important. In context, Jesus has a clear point for His disciples: "You've got work to do. I've got a plan for you." Jesus didn't appear to the whole world after rising from the dead, but instead only to His followers. Jesus said everything we the readers needed to hear before He died, and that is the message the apostles are sent with—"all that I have commanded" (Matthew 28:20). Third, Jesus sent them with His authority to make disciples wherever they went. Jesus was passing along the role of rabbi to them, except none of them were ever called rabbis. They were called apostles, people sent out on a mission. There is only one Rabbi, but the whole world is capable of being His disciples.

Jesus proved His power over life and death. Jesus was worthy of worship. And Jesus intentionally included His disciples in the plan moving forward. Make disciples. Although the sentence begins with "Go," the real imperative is to "make disciples." The disciples have become experts in this; it's a long, intentional walk of humbly following and submitting to the Savior. It's baptizing in the name of the true God—Father, Son, and Holy Spirit—and bringing other people into His family. It's sharing the Word and living it out. It's a mission that Jesus could have done all by Himself, but instead He empowers His disciples and sends them with His authority.

The disciples-turned-apostles did what Jesus called them to do. We are a demonstration of their faithful discipleship. Why? Because they passed along not only the teaching but the mission. There is still only one Rabbi. But there is an apostolic church built on this foundation; millions upon millions have been turned into disciple-makers. They have taken their life-changing experience with the risen Jesus everywhere. Matthew preserved this message for the church so that we can be certain it is our turn. The authority to go and make disciples, to baptize and to teach, has been given to us. While we could hope for Jesus Himself to do this, He instead has found us, claimed us, and sent us— we, the church, with the authority and presence of Jesus, making disciples. Are you ready to go?

Father in heaven, we are humbled that You have appointed us to carry the Gospel message everywhere we go. Strengthen us with Your Spirit to keep Your word in our hearts and in our mouths. In Jesus' name. Amen.

SPREADING JESUS' AUTHORITY

Jesus came and said to them, "All authority in heaven and on earth has been given to Me." (MATTHEW 28:18)

Sinful humans don't care much for authority. Actually, we sinners don't care much for God's authority. We don't mind taking the authority for ourselves or setting up our own authorities. Not only is it an innate idea in our own sinful minds but Satan has worked it in there as well. "You won't die!" the serpent said in Genesis 3. "You don't need God and His silly rules. You can be like God!" Thinking we are becoming our own rulers, we actually set Satan upon his throne over the kingdoms of this world (see Matthew 4:8). We are God's creatures, and by our created nature, we will always be under authority; the question is whose?

Jesus came to break the powers and authorities of this world in the most outrageous way. Jesus proved His power by forsaking His power. Jesus demonstrated His divinity through becoming a human. Jesus showed His authority over life by giving up His life. And Jesus declared here, before He ascended into heaven, that He has received all authority. Everywhere. Over everything. Sin, death, and the devil: nothing has power over Him, and nothing can rule other than Him. This was the mission all along. Jesus has undone everything that holds fallen humanity captive.

Only Jesus could bring heaven and earth together. Only Jesus could overcome death by going through death. Only Jesus could carry out the plan laid by the Father. This is the culmination of Jesus' purpose, the kind of God we've been expecting to see all along: "All authority . . . has been given to Me." Immanuel, God with us, has united again the Creator and His creation.

But why would He be leaving earth and going to heaven if, in fact, He is bringing the two together? Why, instead of taking all things to Himself, does He share that authority with His disciples? Jesus has not only brought heaven and earth back together; He has decided to restore us to the work we had from the beginning. The command in Genesis 1:28, "Be fruitful and multiply and fill the earth and subdue it," comes to fruition in Matthew 28. In light of Jesus, then, being fruitful and multiplying is first about making disciples. Filling the earth and subduing it is about making sure God's kingdom reaches every corner.

Peace between God and people. Purpose and presence between God and people. All because of Jesus. That is why His final words are this: "I am with You always" (Matthew 28:20)—Jesus is not leaving us alone, but He is taking His throne. And we get to work. Where are you taking Jesus' authority today?

Dear Jesus, we submit to You because You are Lord of all. Give us fruitful lives and empower us to multiply Your grace in our homes and communities. And as You promised, be with us always. Amen.

SENDING HIS CHURCH INTO THE WORLD

Now the eleven disciples went to Galilee, to the mountain to which Jesus had directed them. (MATTHEW 28:16)

Just as Jesus directed His disciples to a mountain in Galilee, so He directs all of His people where to go. This mountain was not Sinai, where the Law was given (see Exodus 20), nor Jerusalem, where the temple was, nor the Mount of Olives, where the disciples fled from Jesus. No, Jesus brings them home. They are "men of Galilee" (Acts 1:11), and Jesus brings them to a place of safety and comfort—a place they had probably been with Him many times. It all came together for them here, like the disciples on the road to Emmaus. The prophecies and parables all clicked into place, just as Luke 24:45 said, "He opened their minds to understand the Scriptures." Jesus prepared them to take bold steps by bringing them to a place where they could hear it.

The Scriptures testify of God's ultimate authority, from Abraham referring to God as Judge over all the earth (see Genesis 18:25) to the angels singing "Worthy are You, our Lord and God, to receive glory and honor and power, for You created all things, and by Your will they existed and were created" (Revelation 4:11). In other words, "Our God is in the heavens; He does all that He pleases" (Psalm 115:3). But it is clear that God shares His power, that there is One coming to sit on the throne alongside Him. In Psalm 110:1, David prophesies, "The LORD says to my Lord: 'Sit at My right hand, until I make Your enemies Your footstool.'" Daniel 7:13–14 foresees the coming of "one like a son of man, and He came to the Ancient of Days and was presented before Him. And to Him was given dominion and glory and a kingdom."

Jesus is clear that this refers to Him, first by referring to Himself as the Son of Man. And He explicitly says, "All things have been handed over to Me by My Father" (Matthew 11:27) and "You have given [Me] authority over all flesh, to give eternal life" (John 17:2). The apostles pick up on this theme, and although they do not regularly refer to Jesus as God, they ascribe to Jesus all the qualities and attributes of God. Peter concluded his very first sermon with this: "Let all the house of Israel therefore know for certain that God has made Him both Lord and Christ, this Jesus whom you crucified" (Acts 2:36). Paul testifies to this too: "God has put all things in subjection under His feet" (1 Corinthians 15:27).

The sending of the church into the world is not a hope nor a wish—it is reality. "This gospel of the kingdom will be proclaimed throughout the whole world" (Matthew 24:14) became the prayer of the church. "You will be My witnesses," Jesus promised the disciples in Acts 1:8, and the rest of the book shows how they did just that. Jesus prayed for us, for "those who will believe in Me through their word . . . I in them and You in Me, that they may become perfectly one, so that the world may know that You sent Me and loved them even as You loved Me" (John 17:20, 23). Jesus is with us; will we go where He tells us?

God, You have revealed Your will and Your ways to us. Give us a love for Your Word and a willingness to do what You say. In Jesus' name we pray. Amen.

DOUBTS AND CONFUSION

Baptizing them in the name of the Father and of the Son and of the Holy Spirit, teaching them to observe all that I have commanded you. (MATTHEW 28:19–20)

Jesus commanded His disciples to teach others. Since Jesus often received questions—and asked a fair amount of His own—we can be sure that God desires to hear our questions too.

What is the significance of the phrase "the eleven" in Matthew 28:16?

After becoming so used to hearing about the Twelve, this number change is jarring. All of them ran away, but only one betrayed. The simple phrase "the eleven" reminds us of Judas's fall from the Twelve and his suicide. No one is worthy to be with Jesus, but Jesus restores and commissions the Eleven, who all repent by faith and come to Him in Galilee.

If He has this authority over the nations, why doesn't Jesus use that authority to stop criminals and national leaders from committing atrocities?

We must start the answer to this question by remembering that Jesus will stop all evildoers when He returns to judge the world. Jesus wills for all people to live in peace, but He still limits the sins and crimes of others, and makes their sins work to our advantage. When this type of question comes to mind, make it specific, make it a prayer, and take it to Jesus. We know He can do whatever He wants, and maybe Jesus will reveal to us what His great purpose is (see Romans 8:28) when people intend evil.

What is the significance of Jesus sending His disciples to "all nations"?

God's promise to Abram was that "in you all the families of the earth shall be blessed" (Genesis 12:3), and God always fulfills His promises. While in His public ministry, Jesus focused on the lost sheep of Israel. He still demonstrated the scope of His mission in how He treated foreigners and Samaritans. The church wrestled with this until Acts 15, when the Holy Spirit finally led them to declare that the church was sent not just to Jews, or to make people Christ-following Jews, but rather to be a blessing to and in all nations.

What does it mean to be baptized in the name of the Father, and of the Son, and of the Holy Spirit?

We are named by our parents because they brought us into the world. We are named by God because He has brought us into the Kingdom. The family name is the name into which we are baptized: Father, Son, Holy Spirit. Notice that Jesus said this is the *name*, not plural *names*. Being baptized in this way is to be brought into God's eternal family. Welcome home!

What does it mean that we are taught to keep the Lord's commands or sayings?

The apostles were tasked with teaching other disciples and guarding against the lies and false teachings that were working their way into God's people. Protecting Jesus' commands is clearly teaching the truth and warding off the false teachings Satan tries to sow among us. We truly care for ourselves and future Christians when we keep, guard, and observe God's Word.

Jesus, thank You for hearing us, for listening even when we don't know what to say. Speak Your truth and love into our souls. Amen.

OUR COMMISSION

And behold, I am with you always, to the end of the age. (MATTHEW 28:20)

One of the greatest joys as a pastor is welcoming people into the kingdom of God, celebrating a beautiful moment in others' lives, fulfilling Matthew 28:16–20 in the words of the baptismal liturgy: "I baptize you in the name of the Father and of the Son and of the Holy Spirit" (*LSB*, p. 270). Declaring someone to be a son or daughter of the King is fulfilling the Great Commission. The church carries this blessing to each generation.

But there is also a burden to share during a Baptism. "The wages of sin is death, but the free gift of God is eternal life in Christ" (Romans 6:23). All of us—even babies—are subject to the curse of death. That is why Baptism is for everyone—because we are all in need. None of us, even adults, can work or do anything to receive this gift of life God freely offers. The pastor asks the parents, sponsors, friends, family, and the whole congregation to be part of the spiritual journey of each baptized member. This is a blessed burden because it means that we are invested in each person baptized in our church and responsible for them learning to observe all that Jesus commanded too. What a weighty honor that Jesus has entrusted to His church.

Matthew 28 is used for pastors' ordinations, building dedications, and a whole host of church blessings. But the Great Commission is not only about what happens in the church building on a Sunday morning. These words are for every person, every day, as you go. Jesus starts less with a command and more a description. Wherever you go, be about the business of discipling. Jesus knew exactly where each of His apostles would go, but they had no clue. The same is true for us. We don't know exactly where life will lead us, but we know for certain Jesus will be with us.

Every person, every day. The Great Commission applies that far and further. God desires all people to be saved, and our lives take us to them. Our callings bring us into contact with people who don't know that God loves them and desires them. They don't know that they are children of the King and have a new name waiting for them in the waters of Baptism. Whether or not we are pastors, we have the presence of Jesus. We keep God's Word. And we are responsible for making disciples. We do it by being the church and investing in every person in our pews. We do it by raising our children faithfully (as we promise in the rite of Baptism), by treating our spouses with honor, by entering our jobs with prayer and discernment, by sharing the Good News of a loving God with all who will listen. This is the blessed burden, the love of Christ for us and through us—to be the church, together and apart, because no matter what, Jesus is always with us.

Father, Son, and Holy Spirit, we rejoice because You love us and send us with Your love. Give us eyes to see, hands to help, and words to speak to those who need You. In Jesus' name we pray. Amen.

JESUS' ASCENSION

WEEK 51—LUKE 24:50–53

And He led them out as far as Bethany, and lifting up His hands He blessed them. While He blessed them, He parted from them and was carried up into heaven. And they worshiped Him and returned to Jerusalem with great joy, and were continually in the temple blessing God.

ESTABLISHING AND RULING HIS CHURCH

And He led them out as far as Bethany, and lifting up His hands He blessed them. While He blessed them, He parted from them and was carried up into heaven. (LUKE 24:50–51)

Jesus' ascension is a major turning point in the overall narrative of the Gospel. Here, Jesus leaves behind His earthly ministry. This is the beginning of the work of the church in His stead. Jesus will not be visible but will still be ruling and reigning from the right hand of the Father.

The ascension of Jesus is an incredible gift He gives to His people. From this point in history, the followers of Jesus will take seriously His commission to take the Gospel out from where they are into the whole world. Persecution in Jerusalem will drive them out into the surrounding countryside and across borders to take the Good News of Jesus to the ends of the earth. These were people who trusted the promise that Jesus would always be with them.

Christianity would flourish during this time. Unafraid of death, men and women declared salvation found in Jesus wherever they went. Because of Jesus' ascension, they would receive the Holy Spirit on Pentecost. Their greatest enemy, Saul, would become the apostle we know as Paul, planting churches and sending letters that became many of the books of the New Testament, permanently blessing the church.

It is amazing to think that Jesus would leave. Having conquered death, shouldn't He stay here on earth, establishing and ruling His church? But that is exactly what Jesus was doing by ascending into heaven. As He told His disciples, "It is to your advantage that I go away, for if I do not go away, the Helper will not come to you. But if I go, I will send Him to you" (John 16:7). Jesus will establish and rule His church through the Holy Spirit and the Word of God. The Spirit would come on Pentecost and empower the apostles and the church to make disciples of all nations. He would inspire the apostles to write and oversee the writing of the New Testament, just as He inspired the prophets to write the Old Testament.

The church would not stop. No. These people had met the Savior, and their lives were changed. With the power of the Holy Spirit, they went out and sought to change the lives of others. Meeting in the temple courts, in synagogues, by rivers, in homes, and on hills, they shared the story of how God became man to redeem His people.

Acts 2 tells us this about these people: "And they devoted themselves to the apostles' teaching and the fellowship, to the breaking of bread and the prayers. And awe came upon every soul, and many wonders and signs were being done through the apostles" (Acts 2:42–43).

What the church did in following Jesus, even after He ascended, has changed the history of the world. And it is because the Savior entrusted His people with His mission.

Lord, may I remember that You are always with us, ruling Your church and working through us. Even as You have ascended, may I see Your mission as one that You invite me to join. As I have been saved, may I take Your message of salvation to the world. Amen.

THE JOY OF JESUS' ASCENSION

And they worshiped Him and returned to Jerusalem with great joy, and were continually in the temple blessing God. (LUKE 24:52–53)

The disciples were astonished. How do you think you would feel if, all of a sudden, your friend started rising up into heaven? There is a great scene in Acts 1 that explains a little further:

> And while they were gazing into heaven as He went, behold, two men stood by them in white robes, and said, "Men of Galilee, why do you stand looking into heaven? This Jesus, who was taken up from you into heaven, will come in the same way as you saw Him go into heaven." (Acts 1:10–11)

After they watched Jesus ascend, they stood and waited. Just staring at the sky, wondering when He'd come back. God had to send some angels to encourage them on their way. The communication is clear: "Jesus was here with you but now He has ascended. Keep going about His business." Remember back to the crucifixion. The temple curtain was torn in two. This signified the fact that each of us has access to the throne of God through Jesus Christ. Jesus' ascension is another affirmation of that fact.

These ascension verses are incredibly short for a miraculous thing that has happened. But what a powerful message to the disciples. Jesus is saying to them, "I've given you everything you need. I can go back to the Father. Go about My work."

Why, when baptized, do people not immediately ascend to heaven as Jesus did here? Because there is purpose for them on earth. It is covered in the two greatest commandments: love God and love your neighbors. Jesus' ascension shows how deeply He has invested in His people. Even as His visible, physical presence is removed, there is no need to fear.

Many could see Jesus' ascension as a sad event. Instead, it is a joyful one. He is now present at all times in all places with His people. There is nothing holding Him back. He has truly defeated sin, death, and the devil. By ascending, He is enabling His people to go forth in power to deliver that message to the world.

Lord, may I see Jesus' ascension as a joyful event. May I continue to find the places where He is at work in my life. In Jesus' name. Amen.

FINDING PURPOSE AS WE FOLLOW HIM

While He blessed them, He parted from them and was carried up into heaven. (LUKE 24:51)

The work of the incarnation was done. Jesus was the promised Messiah. He had come into the world both fully God and fully man. Now, His time of physical manifestation was over. Even this was how the mission was supposed to go.

When we consider other man-made gods of the vast pantheons in human history, mankind is viewed in subservience to the immortals. God, all knowing and all powerful, sees things differently. Events in the Garden of Eden had separated humanity from their Creator. But our God's plan was always to send Jesus, God and man wrapped into one. In this way, sin could be defeated by the perfect sacrifice. God did not view humanity as a servile culture to be subjugated. Instead, He looked at humanity and loved what He had created. Despite every flaw and inconsistency, He cared deeply for His creation. Out of that love, He would send His Son. Out of that love, He would give His creation purpose.

Imagine if salvation were the end. Jesus saves us, and that's the end of the story. It would be an incredible blessing for sure, but God keeps the journey going. He gifts His people with purpose. Jesus' return to heaven lets them know that He will always be with them. His return from incarnation to sit at the right hand of God means that He is at all times and in all places with His people. It may be hard to see Him at times, but He is there. Paul would write, "Now we see in a mirror dimly" (1 Corinthians 13:12).

Salvation is not the end of our journey but, instead, it is a beginning. Jesus ascends but still calls us forward. He gives us purpose in this life that otherwise can be monotonous and laborious. It is a gift on top of salvation that we should be called to join Him in His mission. To live out our vocations in such a way that we show our love to God and to our neighbors in all that we do. Christians do not sit idly by and wait for Jesus to return. No, we are called out into the world to point into a dim mirror and tell people what we see: a Savior who is for them and His kingdom that is to come.

Dear Jesus, call me into Your service. Help me to find purpose as I follow You. You bless me with salvation and continue to bless me as I learn more about Your ways. Amen.

JESUS ASCENDED SO THE SPIRIT COULD COME

And He led them out as far as Bethany, and lifting up His hands He blessed them. (LUKE 24:50)

As we have discussed this week, the ascension was a gift. Jesus goes to heaven, but He doesn't leave His people. Look at the good news that is to come in the book of Acts, chapter 2:

> When the day of Pentecost arrived, they were all together in one place. And suddenly there came from heaven a sound like a mighty rushing wind, and it filled the entire house where they were sitting. And divided tongues as of fire appeared to them and rested on each one of them. And they were all filled with the Holy Spirit and began to speak in other tongues as the Spirit gave them utterance.
>
> Now there were dwelling in Jerusalem Jews, devout men from every nation under heaven. And at this sound the multitude came together, and they were bewildered, because each one was hearing them speak in his own language. And they were amazed and astonished, saying, "Are not all these who are speaking Galileans? And how is it that we hear, each of us in his own native language? Parthians and Medes and Elamites and residents of Mesopotamia, Judea and Cappadocia, Pontus and Asia, Phrygia and Pamphylia, Egypt and the parts of Libya belonging to Cyrene, and visitors from Rome, both Jews and proselytes,

> Cretans and Arabians—we hear them telling in our own tongues the mighty works of God." . . . So those who received [Peter's] word were baptized, and there were added that day about three thousand souls. (Acts 2:1–11, 41)

It was all part of the plan. The explosion of the early church happens because Jesus leaves. He gives the reins of preaching and teaching over to the apostles and disciples. Even though He is not physically present, He still is working miracles! Languages spoken so that all at Pentecost could hear the Gospel in their native language. Three thousand baptized! Jesus is reigning!

Jesus even told His followers He would have to leave for them to receive the Holy Spirit. "Nevertheless, I tell you the truth: it is to your advantage that I go away, for if I do not go away, the Helper will not come to you. But if I go, I will send Him to you" (John 16:7). Jesus' departure was a blessing for His people. The Holy Spirit had arrived.

Heavenly Father, may the Holy Spirit be at work in my life. May I be convicted in my sin and encouraged in my sanctification. I give thanks that Jesus ascended so that the Helper could come. In Jesus' name. Amen.

HE WENT OUT BEFORE THEM AND ALONGSIDE THEM

And they worshiped Him and returned to Jerusalem with great joy, and were continually in the temple blessing God. (LUKE 24:52-53)

Jesus was their rock and foundation. How could the disciples return to Jerusalem with great joy? When a good friend moves far away or family from out of town leaves after a good visit, do you feel joy?

These followers of Jesus knew what this meant for them. At this time, they had a greater grasp on who Jesus was and, as Messiah, what He had done. They could rejoice because His leaving didn't mean abandonment. In fact, He had just promised that He would be with them always.

As a Christian, there are many times that joy is felt when it seems like there should be sorrow. It is the benefit of a salvation that allows us to focus on the Kingdom. We know that one day, all who are in Jesus will be resurrected. There will be a new heaven and a new earth, and all tears will be wiped away. The disciples rejoiced because while they were with Jesus, they had experienced this kingdom to come.

In the beginning of the book of Mark, Jesus declares, "The kingdom of God is at hand" (1:15). How could the Kingdom be at hand? Well, where is the Kingdom? Wherever the King goes. Jesus was saying, "Literally reach out your hand! Touch the King, and you can feel the kingdom of God." He walked among His people. The woman who struggled with a flow of blood believed this so deeply that she reached out to touch Jesus' garments to be healed—and she was. Jesus looked at her and said, "Daughter, your faith has made you well; go in peace, and be healed of your disease" (Mark 5:34). She believed the King had come and brought the Kingdom with Him.

Why did the disciples rejoice even though Jesus had ascended?

They began to understand that the Kingdom now went with them. The power and authority of Jesus was with them at all times. Before they followed Him through the countryside. Now He went out before them and alongside them. They were empowered by Him to go and do the work of the Kingdom. No longer did they need to return to the temple for sacrifice. The forgiveness of sins, the sacrificial Lamb, had covered them, and in their journey, He walked with them.

Dear Jesus, help me to see where You are working in the world around me. Though I have yet to touch You with my hands, anchor my hope in Your promises. You have gone before me and beside me. May I go boldly as a child of Your kingdom. Amen.

HE INVITES YOU INTO HIS WONDERFUL MISSION

And He led them out as far as Bethany, and lifting up His hands He blessed them. While He blessed them, He parted from them and was carried up into heaven. And they worshiped Him and returned to Jerusalem with great joy, and were continually in the temple blessing God. (LUKE 24:50–53)

Regularly, through both the Apostles' and Nicene Creeds, Christians confess that Jesus ascended into heaven. This week, we have talked about the reasons why: He entrusted those He had saved with His mission through the gift of the Holy Spirit. He had to leave. By leaving, He gave a great gift to the church—a purpose to go and declare His Gospel to the world.

It is a gift of purpose. He starts at salvation but continues to work on His creation. This is our theology of sanctification and vocation. He is continually re-creating us back to what we were supposed to be before sin entered the picture. Not only that, but He wants the world to know the message.

What is stopping you? The ascension is a declaration that wherever you go, Jesus goes with you. He has given you purpose to love God as you go. He has given you a mission to love your neighbors as you go. The ascension is the confirmation that you have everything you need to be about the work of the Kingdom.

Salvation? You have it. Cling tight to the waters of your Baptism, for Jesus chose you in them.

The Holy Spirit? A gift for all those who believe.

The right words? You have the Holy Spirit!

The permission and authority? Go read Matthew 28:19–20.

The push over the edge? The ascension.

God's plan of salvation was His plan of creation. Humanity always labored at the purposes of the Creator. In the garden, Adam and Eve were called to care for what God had made. Again, He is inviting His creation to share in the deep love He has for the world. For all nations, tribes, and tongues.

He invites you into this wonderful mission. To encourage His saints and to connect the disconnected back to Him. Even better—it is not on your shoulders! You get to be a part of the plan, but He is doing the work! In freedom, He invites you to come and be a worker in His harvest fields.

He left because He wants you to be a part of it all, from beginning to end, sharing His creation and walking alongside Him as in the garden. One day, you will see Him face to face, but until that day, go in joy, knowing you are part of His kingdom work in the world.

Lord, challenge me to be about Your work in this world. Open my eyes that I may see the blessing it is to be a part of the plan You have for Your kingdom. I give You thanks that You invite me along for this journey. In Your Son, Jesus' name, I pray. Amen.

JESUS FORETELLS HIS RETURN

WEEK 52—MARK 13:3–13, 24–27

And as [Jesus] sat on the Mount of Olives opposite the temple, Peter and James and John and Andrew asked Him privately, "Tell us, when will these things be, and what will be the sign when all these things are about to be accomplished?" And Jesus began to say to them, "See that no one leads you astray. Many will come in My name, saying, 'I am He!' and they will lead many astray. And when you hear of wars and rumors of wars, do not be alarmed. This must take place, but the end is not yet. For nation will rise against nation, and kingdom against kingdom. There will be earthquakes in various places; there will be famines. These are but the beginning of the birth pains.

"But be on your guard. For they will deliver you over to councils, and you will be beaten in synagogues, and you will stand before governors and kings for My sake, to bear witness before them. And the gospel must first be proclaimed to all nations. And when they bring you to trial and deliver you over, do not be anxious beforehand what you are to say, but say whatever is given you in that hour, for it is not you who speak, but the Holy Spirit. And brother will deliver brother over to death, and the father his child, and children will rise against parents and have them put to death. And you will be hated by all for My name's sake. But the one who endures to the end will be saved. . . .

"But in those days, after that tribulation, the sun will be darkened, and the moon will not give its light, and the stars will be falling from heaven, and the powers in the heavens will be shaken. And then they will see the Son of Man coming in clouds with great power and glory. And then He will send out the angels and gather His elect from the four winds, from the ends of the earth to the ends of heaven."

OUR RETURNING JUDGE

Peter and James and John and Andrew asked Him privately, "Tell us, when will these things be, and what will be the sign when all these things are about to be accomplished?" (MARK 13:3–4)

We close this year with Jesus with the one event in Jesus' life that has not yet occurred—His promised return. Last week, we looked at Jesus' ascension into heaven. In His discussion of end-times events before His death in Holy Week, Jesus prepared His disciples, and us, for the time between His ascension and His return. The great future event of Christ's return is often overlooked or forgotten by Christians and is scorned by unbelievers.

It is easy to focus on the present and to be thankful that Jesus is with us each moment. We are glad to hear that His power still surrounds us in daily dangers. His guidance is still with us, and we can ask for even more wisdom and leading by the Spirit. When we look at our past, we see our failures and sins, but then we cry out for the forgiveness that comes faithfully every day. We are thankful for Jesus' daily presence in His familiar Word and also through the Sacraments.

While we are reassured by Jesus' strength each day, the enemies of Jesus see no evidence of His presence. They point out that He can't be seen, and the world continues to limp along with every sin we've ever known. Unbelievers say, "He left, and He hasn't come back. It's some two thousand years now since He left. How can you still be waiting?"

But we do wait because of His promises. We still look heavenward, knowing that He is both here with us and will also come back in undeniable glory. It is important for us to be mindful of that day. All earthly activities will stop, and each person will be judged by the God-man, Jesus Christ. At that point, the preoccupations of our brief, earthly lives will shrink away to complete insignificance, and each person will face eternity either with God in the restored creation, or apart from God in the endless torment of hell. Living ever mindful of that moment will rightly order our priorities in life and help us see the urgency to make disciples of all nations before it is too late. We invite the world to share our confidence. Our Savior rose from the dead not to escape the world but to return to raise us also from the dead. Then He will bring us to the new heaven and the new earth He has prepared for us.

Returning Lord, come with Your power to judge the world and to raise us as Your people. Rescue us for all eternity! Amen.

ALL PEOPLE WILL SEE JESUS RETURNING

And then they will see the Son of Man coming in clouds with great power and glory. (MARK 13:26)

The temple of Solomon was a spectacular building, perhaps the most spectacular building in the world at that time. It was destroyed by the Babylonians, but then, after seventy years of captivity, it was rebuilt by the returned exiles. But the rebuilt temple was only a shadow of Solomon's glorious building.

In about 20 BC, Herod the Great started a construction project that expanded the temple grounds with courtyards, walls, and buildings. This new construction included massive stones, some greater than forty feet long, ten feet thick, and eight feet high (according to the Jewish historian Josephus). When Jesus' disciples commented about its beauty, Jesus told them the almost incomprehensible prophecy that it would be totally destroyed without a single stone remaining upon another.

On the Tuesday before His crucifixion, as He was leaving the temple for the last time, Jesus predicted the destruction of the temple. As they sat on the Mount of Olives, within view of the magnificent temple, four of the disciples asked Him what His words meant and when such an incredible event would occur. Peter, James, John, and Andrew, the first of the Twelve that Jesus called into ministry, were in on this private conversation. It must have seemed impossible that God would allow such a beautiful place of prayer and worship to be destroyed.

However, before Jesus returns, there will be danger not only for buildings but for Christians who stand firm in the faith. Jesus teaches us about the persecution the Christians will endure, as well as the false teachers who will arise among us. Just as the prophecies about the Messiah were fulfilled in Christ Jesus, the prophecies of the end times (that is, the entire New Testament era) will be fulfilled exactly as Jesus said. These have been, are, and will be terrible times. Relationships among families and in the church will be ripped apart in bitter arguments. The world will turn against Christians and will hate them.

Until that time, though, we are to continue to preach the Gospel of Jesus Christ to all nations. Jesus sent us the Holy Spirit to guide and strengthen us in this ministry. We do not work in vain, and we do not work alone. God is with us, now and unto eternity.

When Jesus describes His return, there will be no mistaking when it is happening. The world as we know it—all of the natural world, all civilizations—will come to a halt. All people will see Jesus returning through the heavens in great glory with His angel hosts. Those who believe in Jesus as Savior and Lord can be confident that He will "gather His elect" (Mark 13:27) to take them into eternity with Him.

Heavenly Savior, come with Your power to rescue Your people. Complete Your promises to return, restore Your creation, raise the dead, and renew Your people with eternal life. Amen.

THE DAY IS DRAWING NEAR

And you will be hated by all for My name's sake. But the one who endures to the end will be saved. (MARK 13:13)

Jesus' mission was basically to undo the damage to God's creation that Adam and Eve brought when they fell into sin and plunged the entirety of creation into destruction and death. First, in His first coming, Jesus restored the relationship between God and humans by becoming one of us. His perfect life has been given to us so that the demands of the Law might be satisfied. His taking the sins of all people upon Himself and being punished on the cross in our place means we will never suffer as He did. His glorious resurrection has restored humanity to God so that all those who believe in Jesus as the Son of God and Savior will be with Him forever in paradise.

When Jesus returns in His second coming, He will restore the heavens and the earth to their original perfection. There will no longer be any curse within all of creation. No longer will there be sickness, suffering, or death. Those terrible consequences of sin will be banished from our eternal lives with God. For those who trust in Jesus, there will be eternal glory and joy, living with God and the holy angels in the new heaven and the new earth for all eternity.

For those who reject Jesus Christ, there will be eternal suffering and torment. God does not desire this for any of His human creatures, and Jesus died for the sins of all. But those who reject Jesus will be rejected by God and spend eternity being punished with Satan and all his fallen angels. Jesus came to warn those who refused Him as Savior that their rejection would have eternal consequences.

Jesus does not tell His disciples—or us—when that Last Day will come. That is for God alone to know. But as often as we see the signs He predicted, we are reminded that the day is drawing near so that we may always be watchful for His return. We need not fear the end of the world. Instead, we can pray that it comes and comes quickly. We are not fearfully waiting for the end of the world—but we are waiting for the return of our Savior and King.

Heavenly Father, give us strength to stand firm in the faith. Send the Spirit to all who face persecution, even death, that they might speak Your word boldly and clearly. In Jesus' name. Amen.

HE COMES WITH POWER TO RAISE AND RESCUE HIS PEOPLE

And then He will send out the angels and gather His elect from the four winds, from the ends of the earth to the ends of heaven. (MARK 13:27)

What can we expect to be in store before Christ's return? Several Bible passages throughout the Bible give us information.

Acts 1:6–7

"So when they had come together, they asked Him, 'Lord, will You at this time restore the kingdom to Israel?' He said to them, 'It is not for you to know times or seasons that the Father has fixed by His own authority.'" It is natural that the disciples wanted to know the exact time when Jesus would return. It only made sense that now, having conquered death, Jesus would conquer the oppressive Romans. He could then show Himself to be the all-powerful King of the Jews. However, Jesus' power would be shown through the coming of the Spirit on Pentecost and the spread of the Gospel message to thousands. His kingdom is now a kingdom of grace and the enduring faith of Christians.

2 Thessalonians 2:8

"And then the lawless one will be revealed, whom the Lord Jesus will kill with the breath of His mouth and bring to nothing by the appearance of His coming." Jesus' predictions of the time between His ascension and His return on Judgment Day are so frightening that mere wars are only the beginning. The real concern will be with the many who will claim to be Jesus and thereby gather a following. But do not follow and do not fear! Though it will appear that the false christs have power to condemn Christians, there will be a final judgment. As 2 Thessalonians 2 describes, when Jesus returns, He will destroy those imitation christs. Just as God gave life to Adam by the breath of His mouth, so in contrast, Jesus will destroy these deceivers through the breath of His mouth. Those who will appear so strong will be exhausted and destroyed by God's breath alone.

Matthew 26:64

"Jesus said to him, 'You have said so. But I tell you, from now on you will see the Son of Man seated at the right hand of Power and coming on the clouds of heaven.'" Jesus comes despite the futile power of His enemies who imagined that, by His death, they had ended His reign as king. But Jesus was always the eternal Son of God, and even stepping into the tomb could not rob Him of His divine nature. He is now seated at the right hand of God the Father, ruling the world already. Furthermore, He will come with such power that every enemy will have to agree that He is Lord. He comes with power to raise and rescue His people, to the eternal shock of His enemies.

Gracious heavenly Father, thank You for sending Your Son to save us. We look forward to the day when You will send Him to judge the living and the dead, restore Your creation, and raise us to eternal glory. Bless us as we await that day that we may joyfully share the story of Your love and Jesus' salvation. In Jesus' name. Amen.

HE WILL HOLD US FIRMLY IN THE FAITH

But in those days, after that tribulation, the sun will be darkened, and the moon will not give its light. (MARK 13:24)

Jesus' prediction of the time before His return raises some questions for us:

What is the significance of Jesus' first words about judgment being "See that no one leads you astray" (Mark 13:5)?

In light of that Day of Judgment, nothing is more important for us than to be in faith, trusting Jesus Christ alone as our Lord and Savior. More important for each of us than watching the events around us or trying to decipher how close that day may be, is to be sure that we aren't deceived into putting our faith in something or someone besides Jesus Christ. We must also be aware that false spiritual leaders will claim to be Christ—and, sadly, they will mislead some.

Why would Jesus permit such horrible persecution against His Christians, His Bride?

His divine love for lost sinners is so great that He did not shrink back from sharing the Good News of God's love, even though it meant suffering, flogging, crucifixion, and death for Him. And though Christ loves us dearly, He cares deeply for those who oppose and persecute us, too, so He sends His own disciples and brothers and sisters to them, even if their response is bitter rejection and persecution.

How does the Holy Spirit give us the words to say in times of opposition and persecution?

Jesus is not saying we need not make any preparations or we should skip studying the Scriptures.

The more we mature in our faith through worship, Bible study, prayer, and receiving the Sacraments, the more confident we will be in the face of opposition and persecution. But Jesus promises that even in times of great stress where we want to be sure we don't misrepresent Jesus, we need have no fear. The Holy Spirit will give us the right words to say at the moment we need them.

What does it mean that the sun will be darkened, and the moon will not give its light?

This is speaking either of a profound darkness that will strike (like the three days of utter darkness in Egypt with the ninth plague), or the glorious light of Jesus Christ in comparison to which the sun will appear dark and the moon will not be visible. Clearly, when the natural order of day and night ceases and Christ shines out in His creation, the end will have come for this world and all who are in it.

Lord, we cannot endure by our own power. Hold us firm in the faith until we die and then gather us to the eternal life You have prepared. Amen.

COME QUICKLY, LORD JESUS!

And the gospel must first be proclaimed to all nations. (MARK 13:10)

We live in that in-between time, the end times, as we await the return of our Lord Jesus Christ. Sometimes we get lulled into a false sense of security by the long passage of time, the two thousand years that have come since Jesus ascended into heaven. But we are reminded in the Divine Service every week that the Final Day will, indeed, come. Both the Apostles' and Nicene Creeds speak of Jesus' return at the end of the Second Article. The last three Sundays of the Church Year focus on that day and prepare us for it. The season of Advent reminds us that Jesus is coming again.

One other wonderful connection is the table prayer many Christians use, which begins "Come, Lord Jesus." These are the next-to-last words of the Bible, found in Revelation 22:20: "He who testifies to these things says, 'Surely I am coming soon.'" John, the author, responds: "Amen. Come, Lord Jesus!" We all look eagerly for His final return and are reminded of His presence at every meal.

Many hymns, of course, focus on the return of Jesus and the time of waiting now. A favorite for many is "Stand Up, Stand Up for Jesus" (*LSB* 660). The call to firm faith and bold witness is clear in stanza 2:

Stand up, stand up for Jesus;
The trumpet call obey;
Stand forth in mighty conflict
In this His glorious day.
Let all His faithful serve Him
Against unnumbered foes
Let courage rise with danger
And strength to strength oppose.

With all the church, the saints in heaven, and those yet waiting, let us sing with confidence. Let the world rage against God and His people. Christ will come at the time He knows best and will gather us to Himself. Our life together will be without end. May He come, yes, quickly, and may we live together evermore.

Come quickly, Lord Jesus, and gather Your people who wait in faith. Preserve us here in the faith and rescue us at the time You know best. Amen.

AUTHORS' PAGE

Amy Bird is a World Vision senior editor and CPH author (read more from Amy in *Lutheran Life* magazine). She studied communication and theology at Concordia University Wisconsin and holds an MA in systematic theology from Concordia Seminary, St. Louis. Previously, she served as communication specialist for LCMS Youth Ministry and media director for the LCMS Youth Gathering. Amy lives in Illinois with her husband, Aaron, who serves as a pastor. They have one daughter, Lydia.

Rev. Ted Doering received his undergraduate degree from Concordia University Texas (2009) and a master of divinity from Concordia Seminary, St. Louis (2014). He was called to be a church planter in Round Rock, Texas, and Narrative Lutheran Church launched in 2015, where he remains the pastor to the present day. Over the years, he has authored Bible studies, blog posts, evangelism helps, and two books: *Myth of the Millennial* and *Walking Together*. He and his wife, Chelsey, live in Central Texas.

Rev. Alfonso (A. J.) Espinosa is a graduate of Concordia University Irvine (BA) and Concordia Theological Seminary, Fort Wayne, Indiana (MDiv). He received an MA in Christian apologetics from Biola University and a PhD in theology from the University of Birmingham (England) in 2009. Dr. Espinosa is the senior pastor at St. Paul's Lutheran Church of Irvine, California, and a member of the Board for National Mission of The Lutheran Church—Missouri Synod. In addition to writing the faith-and-culture trilogy, he has served as an author for *The Lutheran Difference*, a study notes team member for *The Lutheran Study Bible*, and a contributor to the Biblical Response series.

Deaconess Noemí E. Guerra was born and raised in Panama. She graduated from Concordia Seminary, St. Louis, in 2013. Noemí serves with the LCMS, Texas District as the district-wide evangelist development leader and with Lutheran Hour Ministries as writer and cohost of the *Sentido Latino* podcast, as well as the writer of the Spanish daily devotions. She married Rev. Lincon Guerra in 2001, and they have three children: Joash, Lincon Aaron, and Lizzie.

Hannah Hansen is a freelance writer, brand strategist, and web designer who is passionate about helping churches effectively present themselves online. After earning her BA in English, Hannah worked as a copywriter at Concordia Publishing House and as a content specialist at an advertising agency before becoming self-employed. She currently lives in sunny Oceanside, California, where her husband serves as pastor.

Chad Janetzke is head of the theology department at Martin Luther High School in Greendale, Wisconsin. He has served as a commissioned minister at Lutheran grade schools and high schools in Minnesota, Texas, and Wisconsin for the last two decades, as well as a morning session Bible study leader at the 2019 and 2022 LCMS Youth Gatherings. He is blessed to be husband to Erin and father to Maddie, Emma, and Lilly.

Rev. Andrew R. Jones lives in the Bay Area of California where he enjoys writing, hiking, and adventures with his wife, Stephanie. He has served the church on three continents in varying roles, including campus ministry, international mission work, professor of preaching, and parish pastor. He is the author of *Ten Questions to Ask Every Time You Read the Bible*, and his writings speak to the importance of spiritual formation amid a hectic world.

Rev. Gabe Kasper is the lead pastor at University Lutheran Chapel at the University of Michigan. Before his current role, he spent five years as a church planter in Austin, Texas. His passion for preaching and teaching has led him to speak across the country on a variety of theological, philosophical, and cultural topics. He is a graduate of Concordia Seminary, St. Louis, and has an MPhil from Eastern Michigan University. In his spare time, Gabe enjoys soccer, reading books, and listening to punk rock. He and his wife, Melissa, have three great kids.

Rehema Kavugha serves at Lutheran Church Extension Fund as the director of Synod relations and has been serving at LCEF since May of 2019. A graduate of Concordia University, Nebraska, she received a bachelor's degree in K–12 music with her LTD, a bachelor of fine arts in vocal music and, in 2019, received her MBA. She was a Lutheran school music teacher for six years (2007–2013) and served as director of student development at Concordia University, Nebraska (2013–2019). Rehema was born in Houston, Texas, and her family is originally from Tanzania, East Africa. She now lives in St. Louis, Missouri.

Rev. Dr. Christopher M. Kennedy is the senior pastor of Shepherd of the Hills Lutheran Church, School, and Child Care in San Antonio, Texas, where he has served since 2008. He is the author of *Equipped: The Armor of God for Everyday Struggles*, *Grace under Pressure: Responding Faithfully to Stress*, *Jesus Said What?*, and *Unfailing: God's Assurance for Times of Change*. He has earned a bachelor's degree in communication, a master's of divinity, and a doctorate in ministry. He and his wife, Ashley, are parents of four children: Caleb, Ethan, Emma, and Zachary.

Rev. Ethan Luhman graduated from Concordia Seminary, St. Louis, in 2015. He served as associate pastor of St. Paul's Lutheran Church in Saratoga Springs, New York (2015–2018), associate pastor/campus pastor at First Immanuel Lutheran Ministries/River of Life in Cedarburg and Saukville, Wisconsin (2018–2022), and creator of digital ministry, firstmin.church (2020–2022). He is currently serving as associate pastor at Concordia Lutheran Church in San Antonio, Texas (2022–present). He lives in San Antonio with his wife, Sherry, and four children, Abram, Owain, Roman, and Leighton.

Rev. Daniel E. Paavola grew up on a dairy farm outside New York Mills, Minnesota. Dan and Holly were married in 1979 and have three children: Christy, Steve, and Nicole. Dan graduated from Concordia Theological Seminary, Fort Wayne, in 1983, and then went on to earn a master's of theology degree from Princeton Theological Seminary in 1984. He was a pastor for twelve years at St. Paul's Lutheran Church in Butternut, Wisconsin, a small town in the North Woods. He then moved to teach theology at Concordia University Wisconsin in 1996 and earned his PhD in theology from Concordia Seminary, St. Louis. Dan is the author of several books published by Concordia Publishing House, including *Our Way Home*; *Patience and Perfection*; *Grace, Faith, Scripture: Portrait of a Lutheran*; and *Flowing from the Cross*. His hobbies include motorcycling, woodworking, and driving their 1917 Model T Ford car.

Rev. Wayne Palmer graduated from Concordia Theological Seminary, Fort Wayne, in 1992. He served as sole pastor of Trinity Lutheran Church in Friedheim, Missouri (1992–1999), and Concordia Lutheran Church in Frohna, Missouri (1999–2007). He was writer and theological editor at Lutheran Hour Ministries (2007–2016) and is senior editor of Bible resources at Concordia Publishing House (2016–present). He lives in St. Louis with his wife, Pamela, and son, Jacob.